I0797084

LIVE TO SEE THE DAY

LIVE TO SEE THE DAY

Impossible Goals, Unimaginable Futures,
and the Pursuit of Things That May Never Be

MARK MEDLEY

McCLELLAND & STEWART

Hardcover edition published 2026

LIBRARY AND ARCHIVES CANADA CATALOGUING IN PUBLICATION

Title: Live to see the day : impossible goals, unimaginable futures, and the pursuit of things that may never be / Mark Medley.
Names: Medley, Mark, author.
Identifiers: Canadiana (print) 20250285118 | Canadiana (ebook) 20250285126 | ISBN 9780771062261 (hardcover) | ISBN 9780771062278 (EPUB)
Subjects: LCSH: Goal (Psychology) | LCSH: Motivation (Psychology) | LCSH: Persistence. | LCGFT: Biographies.
Classification: LCC BF505.G6 M43 2026 | DDC 153.8092/2—dc23

Grateful acknowledgement is made for permission to reprint the following: p. vii: Excerpt from *In the Country of Last Things* by Paul Auster, copyright © 1987 by Paul Auster. Used by permission of Viking Books, an imprint of Penguin Publishing Group, a division of Penguin Random House LLC. All rights reserved; Excerpt from "Bigfoot!" by The Weakerthans, from the album *Reunion Tour*, courtesy of John K. Samson; p. 146: Excerpt from Garth Brooks's "The River," words and music by Garth Brooks and Victoria Shaw. Copyright © 1989 by Universal Music - MGB Songs and Major Bob Music Co., Inc. International Copyright Secured. All Rights Reserved. *Reprinted by permission of Hal Leonard LLC.* Additional permission from Alfred Music.

Cover design by Kate Sinclair
Cover art: Parachuting from balloons (1900), Courier Litho. Co. / Artvee
Typeset in Dante MT Pro by Erin Cooper
Printed in Canada

McClelland & Stewart
A division of Penguin Random House Canada
320 Front Street West, Suite 1400
Toronto, Ontario, M5V 3B6, Canada
penguinrandomhouse.ca

1 2 3 4 5 30 29 28 27 26

For T, of course

The end is only imaginary, a destination you invent to keep yourself going, but a point comes when you realize you will never get there. You might have to stop, but that is only because you have run out of time. You stop, but that does not mean you have come to the end.

PAUL AUSTER, *In the Country of Last Things*

I'll go through it all again
Watch their doubtful smiles begin
But the visions that I see believe in me.

THE WEAKERTHANS, "Bigfoot!"

CONTENTS

LIVE TO SEE THE DAY

PROLOGUE

THE FINISH LINE

She knew she wasn't going to win. In fact, she often introduced herself this way: *I'm Liz White, I'm running for office, and I know I'm not going to win*. This would be delivered with an apologetic smile, maybe a gentle laugh, as if she were letting you in on a joke. As if to underscore the foolishness of what she was saying. The person she was addressing, standing on their porch or leaning against a scuffed door frame, might tilt their head, like a puppy hearing an unfamiliar command, unsure if what they heard was, in fact, what Liz had said. But, yes, it was true. Liz was under no illusions when it came to success; the riding in which she was campaigning, composed of mostly well-to-do neighbourhoods on the eastern edge of downtown Toronto, would go to the incumbent Liberal—maybe the New Democratic candidate if things broke just the right way. But the Animal Protection Party of Canada, of which Liz White was the long-time leader? It was not going to happen. It had never happened. It would never happen.

Onward. One house, then the next. Up a few steps, knock on the door, back down to the sidewalk, then do it again. She called it her workout: "You get in good shape doing this, let me tell you." It was just past noon on a gorgeous late-summer day. The park across the street was overrun with dogs and babies, and commuter trains occasionally rumbled down the adjacent rail path, hurtling towards or escaping from the city's core. Campaign signs clung to fences, grew from flower beds, and peeked through front windows like nosy neighbours. The election was only a few days away, but it wouldn't matter if it was held the following year or in a decade's time—the results would be the same.

A snapshot of Liz on this day, from bottom to top: black walking shoes, a white skirt adorned with a black flower pattern, black sweater over a white collared shirt, a black backpack slung over her shoulders, black-framed glasses, grey hair in a bob. She looked like your favourite high school English teacher.

Her knocking or ringing of the doorbell often went unanswered or ignored, and so she would slip a brochure into the mailbox or place it inside a screen door, where it was likely destined for the blue bin along with the rest of the junk mail. Once in a while a person might answer, albeit cautiously or irritated—one man said he'd worried Liz was a Jehovah's Witness. Who else showed up unannounced at your home at this time of day?

She was always gracious, and grateful, when given the opportunity to explain herself. She kept it brief; her pitch usually lasted less than twenty seconds—*I'm Liz White, I'm running for the Animal Protection Party of Canada, and I know I'm not going to win*—but, sometimes, a conversation would follow. She was especially happy when a dog came to the door; she seemed more comfortable with pets than people.

"My kind of voter," Liz said, bending down to meet a small scritch-hunting mutt named Bunny as the owner looked on approvingly.

"She likes you—she knows you're on her side," the woman said, then apologized for already having cast her ballot in advance.

It didn't matter. Liz White was not going to win. And she was okay with that.

Having reached the end of the street and the last of the houses, Liz and I retreated to a nearby café. We hadn't seen each other in about a year and a half, so we found a table outside and made small talk for a while, catching up on one another's lives over the racket of passing streetcars. I told her how work was progressing on my book—or not progressing, to be honest—and she told me about how the campaign had gone so far. A wasp flew figure eights around my coffee cup; I had to stop myself from swatting it away, unsure of the party's views on violence towards insects, even the stinging kind.

I'd first met Liz more than a dozen years earlier, in the summer of 2008. I was a staff reporter for a Toronto-based national newspaper, only a couple of years out of university and way out of my depth. The Great Recession, coupled with the fact nobody wanted to pay for news, had pushed an already precarious industry to the breaking point, and I figured I had another year or two before I found myself in law school or following in my parents' footsteps to teacher's college. I might as well spend what little time I had left writing stories that interested me.

As that year's federal election approached, I pitched one of my editors the idea of profiling a no-hope candidate—someone running for office who had absolutely zero chance of winning. To me, it was a story about motivation: I was interested in what compelled a person to devote themselves to a goal they knew they'd never accomplish, to knowingly pursue failure. Who does that? What was the point?

I don't remember why I chose Liz; maybe it was the fact that she wasn't the usual Marxist-Leninist or lonely Communist one found on the ballot, or maybe it was the fact that hers was basically a single-issue party, and that issue barely resonated with voters. Sure, people liked animals, but they liked a robust economy even more. I was also living in her riding, so knew full well she had no shot at being competitive, let alone winning. She had a better chance of being eaten by a tiger. In any case, she agreed to be profiled, and I spent a few days with her in the lead-up to the election, hanging out at the party's rescue cat–adorned headquarters near the city's East Chinatown, accompanying her to an all-candidates debate, and following her on the campaign trail. I especially recall one Sunday spent knocking on doors in an apartment complex in St. James Town, a diverse vertical neighbourhood in the city's downtown. She showed up on her bike with a knapsack stuffed full of campaign literature destined to remain unread. Before we went inside the first building, she excitedly recounted how, the previous day, she'd stopped canvassing in order to chase down an injured baby squirrel; after catching it (the ungrateful rodent bit her four times), she stuffed the creature into her bag and took it down to the Humane Society, where she'd once worked. She was hopelessly devoted to the cause.

"It's just something I have to do," she once told me. "It's just something I can't turn my back on. I just can't."

It was easier for people to turn their back on Liz; I saw a lot of it that day in 2008. The party was still relatively new—this was only her third time running for office—and, unfortunately, it didn't seem to be garnering much support. It could simply have been that she was canvassing in a low-income neighbourhood, and voters living there had more pressing concerns than the seal hunt and the thorny ethics of testing products on animals. Then again, the party platform could have been pretty much anything. It was one thing to run for an established political party; it was an entirely different matter to run as a fringe candidate. But that's what it took to bring about change, she said. "It doesn't happen in the old, staid, dried-up, burnt-out parties. That's not where change happens. Change happens on the edge." She didn't consider herself to be a fringe candidate, she added. "I think of myself as change."

Change took a long time, as Liz knew well. She'd been involved in politics since she was a teenager, in the 1960s, when she volunteered for the campaign of a politician running in Willowdale, where Liz grew up, on Toronto's northern boundary. Her interests soon expanded beyond her neighbourhood: Later that decade, she joined the protests against the Spadina Expressway, a proposed freeway that threatened to cleave the city in half. She took to the streets alongside a motley group of activists that included the urbanist Jane Jacobs, who'd recently moved to Toronto.

While her activism went back to her childhood, her devotion to animals came later in life. Liz landed at the Humane Society in the late eighties. She took the job at the insistence of a friend, not out of any particular concern for the plight of animals. It's not that she was ignorant—years earlier, she'd been given a tour of a slaughterhouse where an uncle worked: "It wasn't that I wasn't horrified when I was there," she told me, "but I didn't say, 'Oh my God, I can't eat meat anymore.'" She admitted that she once considered vegetarians "kooks." But her time at the Humane Society changed her; she began to understand the threats animals faced, and how it was up to people, people like her, to protect them. Looking back on the person she used to be, she sometimes sounded like a born-again Christian reflecting on her life before finding Jesus: "I don't know what kind of person I was before."

Working at the Humane Society was a memorable experience, though perhaps not always a good one. She'd arrived at a tumultuous time in the organization's history. "It was a wild place to work," she recalled. "People appeared and disappeared. You'd come in and a desk would be cleared." Eventually, it was her turn to disappear, which turned out to be a blessing in disguise. "The best thing that ever happened was that I got fired." She regrouped with some other exiles from the organization, and plotted their next move. "We all sort of gathered and decided that we wanted to do things differently," she told me. The Animal Alliance of Canada was founded in August 1990, and Liz White became its first director. She was forty years old.

The Humane Society, with its multi-million-dollar budget, and finely tuned fundraising machine, it was not. The staff went unpaid for the first several years. "Everybody bit the bullet and did what they had to do," she said. There were victories, but it often felt like one step forward, two steps back. Still, Liz and her colleagues were both stubborn and like-minded, a dangerous combination; they shared the same goals, no matter how difficult they'd be to achieve. For most of them, Liz said, ensuring the welfare of animals was "a passion. You wake up in the morning thinking about it, you go to bed at night thinking about it, you work all day thinking about it. It's who you are, as opposed to what you do." But they wanted to do more. After spending more than a decade lobbying and working behind the scenes, it was clear to Liz that they had to become directly involved in the electoral process in order to achieve their goals.

The Animal Alliance Environment Voters Party of Canada, as it was originally called, became a registered political party on December 10, 2005. It was the first political party in North America that focused on animal rights. Liz ran in her first election six weeks later—the party's sole candidate. She received 72 votes, 30,802 fewer than the winner. Most people would be discouraged, but not Liz. She ran again two years later, and was doing so yet again, when I came across her story.

I returned to the newsroom and wrote it all down—thousands of words. My article was published a few days before the election, under the headline "Who Are You Calling Fringe?" The subhead read: "Canadians will not wake up to an Animal Alliance Environment Voters government on Wednesday, and Liz White will most assuredly not be our prime minister. That's not stopping the Toronto-Centre candidate from giving this election everything she's got." A photo of Liz appeared on the front page of the section. I was proud of the profile, and I was also right: She received 187 votes.

Still, she continued to run, election after election, year after year, in different ridings across the city. Her life, or at least the second half of it, became about the pursuit of what she called "improbable change." She might have described it as impossible.

In the end, I didn't leave journalism—improbably, I managed to survive multiple waves of layoffs before jumping to a larger, more financially secure newspaper. And even as I wrote hundreds more stories, I never forgot *her* story.

And the morning after each election, I'd dutifully look up the results in whichever riding Liz had run. The vote totals she mustered—215, 233, 159—did not come close to the amount of work she had put in, countless hours for a vote total easily counted. But she was not discouraged. "Change is really hard for most people," she once told me. "It's like a ship going through the water, and you're trying to get it to turn around and go in the opposite direction. It's a huge effort to make that happen." She'd be working towards this change for the rest of her life, this she knew. "I'm going to die at my desk," she said. And so, onward.

This book is about people who have devoted their lives to things that might never happen. This book is about people, like Liz White, who are pursuing goals that seem impossible to achieve, or goals they know will never be reached in their lifetime. They are living to see a day that will likely never come.

Think about it like this:

When you open a book, you know how many pages it contains.

When you sit down to watch a movie, you're aware that it will eventually end.

When you listen to a song, you expect a final note to sound.

When you are waiting at the starting line, before beginning a race, you know its length—not only the actual distance, but roughly how long it will take to finish. The people you will encounter in this book—artists and astronomers, fortune hunters and physicists, and one man pushing for the end of us all—are running a race they know they might never finish. In some cases they are unsure where the finish line is located. In some cases they are unable to say whether there even *is* a finish line.

In other cases, to strain the metaphor further (although it's one I heard several times over the years), they are running a relay race—presently gripping the baton but ready to hand it off to the next person, who might never cross the finish line, either, but hand it off to someone else, again and again and again, into the distant future.

And yet, when the starting gun sounded, they all took off.

Let me put it another way: Would you keep reading this book if you didn't know how long it would take you to finish? Would you keep reading this book if you knew you'd never reach the final sentence? That you'd have to pass it along to someone else, who would continue on from the comma or period on which you stopped? Of course not.

My interest is not scientific, but human. What makes someone strive for something—in many cases the thing they want more than anything else—knowing they'll only be disappointed in the end? Why would someone devote their life to a dream they know will be impossible, or at least very unlikely, to achieve? It's as if I dedicated myself to writing this book knowing I'd never finish. Which, admittedly, I often felt over the past six years.

I've long been interested in exploring the strange ways people spend their lives. You only live once, so how we choose to fill our precious days—what to do with your time on earth until the sand runs out—is one of the most interesting questions there is to answer. Why become a doctor, why become a chef, why become a boxer? Why become an unelectable politician? What does it mean to spend a lifetime straddling the line between perseverance and delusion, between tenacity and obsession? Who devotes their future to a future that will probably never come?

I thought I'd try to find out.

This book is the culmination of hundreds of interviews and more than 100,000 kilometres of travel across several continents, from the deserts of Arizona to the forests of Norway, from a possibly civilization-saving space mission launched on the edge of the Pacific Ocean to a remarkable gathering of rocket scientists who want to take the human race beyond the stars.

What follows is not exhaustive or meant to be all-encompassing. There are many other people I could have profiled in the following pages. This book is simply a chronicle of my abiding interest, as a journalist, in people who have displayed incredible devotion. Who have refused to quit. Or who are starting an adventure others will one day finish.

I've thought a lot about a conversation I had at the outset of this project. One of the first people I spoke to was Seth Shostak, a senior astronomer at the SETI Institute, the American organization that leads the search for extraterrestrial intelligence. I'm captivated by the idea of life outside our solar system, and have often told people that my own hope is to live long enough to reach the day it's confirmed that we are not alone in the universe. But mine is a childhood fascination; Shostak had devoted most of the eight decades he'd spent on the planet to something he might never witness. And yet, he told me, he had no regrets. What he did was part of something far larger, far greater, than a single life could contain. He knew doctors who had spent their careers researching a cure for cancer. Did the fact that there was still no cure mean they had wasted their lives? Of course not.

"It's like building cathedrals in the Middle Ages," he said, the first utterance of an analogy I heard many times over the years. "It might take four, six, ten generations to finish the darn thing. You might think there isn't much incentive to get started because you'll never see the completed project."

This book is about the people who start, finish be damned.

The election to select members for the 44th Canadian Parliament was held on September 20, 2021. The next morning, I went online to check the results of my riding. Liz White received 183 votes. It might be a breach of journalistic ethics to admit this, but I was one of them. Standing in the polling station, looking at her name on the ballot, it was the least I could do. It brought her one step closer to a finish line she would never cross. And when I spoke to her next, there was no point even asking if she planned to run again. I already knew the answer. Onward.

ONE

THE LISTENERS

The centre of the search for intelligent life in the universe was a nondescript two-storey building in a nondescript commercial park in a nondescript section of Mountain View, California, a nondescript city about an hour south of downtown San Francisco. I arrived at the SETI Institute around lunchtime one Monday in late January. It had been drizzling on-and-off all morning, and the parking lot was mostly devoid of life. The neighbouring companies had names (CaaStle, Kaleidescape, NeuCyte) that didn't betray their work, but, to be fair, if you weren't familiar with the institute's decades-old mission, you'd probably be confused by its name as well. The logo was stencilled on a window next to the main entrance—the first letter a backward *S* that had been fashioned into a question mark. It represented uncertainty, a guess, a riddle without a solution: Are we alone?

It was, in my humble opinion, the greatest question we can ask ourselves, and I'd long been interested in the work done at the institute to answer it. All my life I've been fascinated with outer space and the mysteries it contains—what other civilizations and species might be out there, waiting for us to find them. When I began writing this book, I knew that I'd end up at the institute, that it was a necessary pilgrimage to make. Now that I was here, I could hardly believe it. I took out my iPhone, snapped a photograph of myself reflected in the logo, and went inside.

I climbed the stairs to the second floor—the institute shared the building with a robotics company that made, from what I could tell, souped-up versions of the Roomba vacuum-cleaning robot—and presented myself at reception. It was pin-drop quiet; only a handful of employees were working in the office on this day. Nearby stood a cardboard cut-out of the pioneering astrophysicist Frank Drake, the institute's patron saint. On the wall behind him, in bright white neon, was the equation, formulated to estimate the number of detectable civilizations in our galaxy, and widely considered to be the second-most famous in all of science, that bears his name:

$$N = R_* \times f_p \times n_e \times f_l \times f_i \times f_c \times L$$

A few moments later, I found myself face to face with Seth Shostak, the institute's senior astronomer, and one of its most visible public figures. He'd been involved in the search for several decades, and was probably the institute's longest-tenured employee. Not that his job had changed much over the years.

"What we're doing now is basically the same thing as we would have done twenty, thirty years ago, except the equipment is a little more sophisticated," he told me with a shrug. "You've got better electronics, better computers, better software, but the idea is still the same: Let's see if we can eavesdrop on the aliens."

His cluttered office was a testament to the peculiar path his career had taken. Among the awards and citations hanging on the walls were illustrations of extraterrestrial landscapes; photographs of radio observatories; a sign pointing the way to Roswell, New Mexico's "UFO crash site"; a "registered claim & deed for lunar property"; a bust of a bug-eyed grey alien; and a framed *Time* magazine cover asking the same question he'd spent the last several decades contemplating: "Is Anybody Out There?" To Shostak, it was an obvious yes. But, lacking concrete proof, it was now up to people like him to gather evidence and present it to the world, a messenger of the stars.

When I'd entered his office, my eyes were immediately drawn to a framed still from *Destination Moon*, which had been released in 1950, and which tells the story of America's first trip to the lunar surface, and to a vintage poster of the 1951 sci-fi classic *The Day the Earth Stood Still*, in which an alien visitor named Klaatu, accompanied by a giant robot named Gort, arrives to deliver a warning to our planet. Shostak, who served as a scientific advisor on the less-than-classic 2008 remake starring Keanu Reeves, had spent much of his life trying to find Klaatu.

The posters also told Shostak's origin story; it was cinema that first sparked his interest in space. As a boy growing up in Arlington, Virginia, he spent his free time making 8 and 16mm films with a friend. Kubrick he was not. They were "intended to be science fiction," he recalled, "but people laughed at them. And since they laughed at them we decided we were making comedies." It's easy to imagine a life spent in movies, but his father, who headed up the electronics branch of the Office of Naval Research, would not have approved of his son going off to film school, Shostak told me somewhat wistfully: "It would have disappointed him greatly." Instead, he studied physics at Princeton, then earned a doctorate in astrophysics at Caltech. After graduation he spent a few years as a research associate at the National Radio Astronomy Observatory, where his hunt began. In his quasi-memoir *Confessions of an Alien Hunter*, Shostak recalls aiming the observatory's Green Bank Telescope, during the brief moments it wasn't in use, at nearby stars in the hopes of getting a signal. He compared these attempts to "feeding pocket change to a slot machine on the off chance of hitting the jackpot." He later spent about a dozen years in the Netherlands, working at a small university and conducting research at a state-of-the-art radio telescope spearheaded by the pioneering Dutch astronomer Jan Oort.

Not long after his return to the United States, Shostak joined the SETI Institute at the behest of Jill Tarter, one of its founders, whom he'd first met in Holland when they'd used the Dutch telescope to probe the heart of the Milky Way for artificial signals. He'd never left.

"SETI addresses a question that *everybody* is interested in, not just a handful of academics," he said. "Whatever the reason, everybody wants to know if there's anybody out there."

That included me. It had been almost five years since we'd first spoken, when Shostak was one of the initial people I'd interviewed for this book. At the time, he bet me a donut that we'd "find ET" in the next few decades. He was now eighty years old—his voice was softer than I remembered; he spoke a bit slower—but he remained optimistic: "We have equipment now that can find a signal produced by a society that was, more or less, at our technological level. So we can find our peers, if you will. We haven't yet, but on the other hand, it could happen tonight."

A moment later the phone on his desk rang, the third time in the last hour someone had tried to reach him. Once again, he ignored the call.

One summer day in 1950, over lunch in the cafeteria of the Los Alamos National Laboratory, near Santa Fe, New Mexico, the Italian-American physicist Enrico Fermi posed a simple question to his colleagues that, decades later, had proven stubbornly difficult to answer: Where are they? His namesake paradox—that the universe should be teeming with civilizations, many of which are likely older and more advanced than our own, and therefore might have achieved the capability of interstellar travel, yet we still lack any evidence of their existence and, as far as we know, have not been paid a visit—was the question those in the field of SETI (Search for Extraterrestrial Intelligence) have spent their lives trying to answer.

Later that decade, in the September 19, 1959, issue of *Nature*, the Cornell physicists Giuseppe Cocconi and Philip Morrison, the latter of whom had worked on the Manhattan Project at Los Alamos with Fermi, published a short article called "Searching for Interstellar Communications." In brief, it argued that advancements in radio telescopes meant scientists now had the tools to probe for alien civilizations. "[T]he presence of interstellar signals is entirely consistent with all we now know, and that if signals are present the means of detecting them is now at hand." They concluded that "a discriminating search for signals deserves a considerable effort. The probability of success is difficult to estimate; but if we never search, the chance of success is zero."

"It was obviously not an article that could be easily put into an astrophysical journal or something like that because we didn't have results," Morrison, who died in 2005, later recalled. "It was a speculative thing." This speculation divided his colleagues. "Most felt it was not a good idea, probably rather foolish, certainly completely speculative, and hardly worth discussing. On the other hand, a number of people were much intrigued by it."

At the same time Morrison and Cocconi were preparing their article for publication, Frank Drake was preparing to conduct what is widely considered to be the first modern SETI experiment, Project Ozma. Beginning on April 8, 1960, at the National Radio Astronomy Observatory in Green Bank, Drake used a recently built twenty-six-metre radio telescope to "listen" for signals from two nearby stars, Tau Ceti and Epsilon Eridani—which coincidentally had been identified by Morrison and Cocconi as among the first stars that should be probed. His ground-breaking research, which took place over the course of several months and lasted a grand total of two hundred hours, found nothing.

The following year, the National Academy of Sciences organized its first-ever SETI meeting; scientists who made the trip to Green Bank included Drake, Morrison, and Carl Sagan. (The group became known as the Order of the Dolphin after the work of one of the attendees, the neuroscientist John C. Lilly, whose research involved communicating with these aquatic mammals.)

A few days before it began, mostly as "a way of organising the meeting," as he later put it to an interviewer, Drake wrote an equation on a blackboard. The Drake equation told us that the number of possible civilizations in our galaxy depended on myriad factors—from the fraction of stars that have planets, to the number of planets that could support life, to whether that life became "intelligent," to whether that intelligent life developed technology that we on Earth could detect, to the length of time a technologically advanced civilization actually produced detectable signals. Drake's original estimate put the number of such civilizations in the Milky Way anywhere between 1,000 and 100,000,000, though later in life he settled on 10,000. If Fermi was asking where they were, Drake was reassuring him: Don't worry, they're out there, somewhere.

This kind of speculation is instinctive—we look around and think "Why am I here?" Then we look up and wonder: "What's out there?" Even though SETI has not existed as a scientific discipline for that long, it might be considered one of the oldest sciences, as it attempts to address a mystery that has been troubling humans for as long as we've been aware there exists a vast world beyond our own.

And as long as SETI has been around, there have been people questioning whether or not we should pursue this line of research. Almost a year after Morrison and Cocconi's article appeared in *Nature*, and a few months after Project Ozma began, the Nobel Prize–winning physicist Edward Purcell delivered a lecture at the Brookhaven National Laboratory, on Long Island, New York, entitled "Radioastronomy and Communication Through Space."

Said Purcell of the search for extraterrestrial life:

"[I]n my view, this is too adult an activity for our society to engage in, on a large scale, at the present time. We haven't grown up to it. It is a project which has to be funded by the century, not by the fiscal year. Furthermore, it is a project which is very likely to fail completely. If you spend a lot of money and go around every ten years and say, 'We haven't heard anything yet,' you can imagine how you make out before a congressional committee."

Purcell had no idea how right he would be.

When I asked her to share the story of how she came to devote her life to the search for intelligence elsewhere in the universe, Jill Tarter, the SETI Institute's co-founder, told me about Florida.

Her family would regularly travel from their home outside New York City to see relatives who lived in Manasota Key, on the Gulf of Mexico. Sometimes, late at night, when the world had gone dark, Tarter and her father would take a walk by the water. He'd worked in an observatory as an undergraduate, and mulled a career in astronomy at one time, and so would point out the various constellations, Tarter told me, as they looked up at the army of stars.

"I just remember thinking that there would be some other little creature with a parent, walking along some ocean on some other planet around one of these stars. And the sun would be a star in their sky."

Years later, when she was a graduate student at UC Berkeley in the early seventies, a colleague handed Tarter a copy of *Project Cyclops*, a landmark 1971 report about how to best search for intelligent life. Spearheaded by Barney Oliver, another Green Bank Dolphin, it recommended that SETI become "an ongoing part of the total NASA space program, with its own budget and funding." A suitable budget, it was estimated, would be $6 billion to $10 billion, with no promise of success.

"The search will almost certainly take years, perhaps decades and possibly centuries," its authors wrote. "To undertake so enduring a program requires not only that the search be highly automated, it requires a long term funding commitment. This in turn requires faith. Faith that the quest is worth the effort, faith that man will survive to reap the benefits of success, and faith that other races are, and have been, equally curious and determined to expand their horizons. We are almost certainly not the first intelligent species to undertake the search."

Reading the report, it dawned on Tarter that the little girl walking along the beach had not been the only person on Earth looking up at the stars, wondering what else was out there. "I realized that this is *the* question that humanity's been asking itself forever."

I thought of Tarter now, sitting in a small conference room adorned with a full-size mural of her standing in front of the institute's Allen Telescope Array (ATA), in northern California, the construction of which she championed and which I planned to visit later in the week. A plaque near the door read: "Jill Tarter directly or indirectly impacted almost every SETI endeavor underway today." (She was also the inspiration for the radio astronomer Ellie Arroway in Sagan's 1985 novel *Contact*, one of my all-time favourite books, about the discovery of a signal from an advanced extraterrestrial civilization. It was later turned into a just-as-great film starring Jodie Foster, the viewing of which, when I was a teenager, was a formative experience in my own burgeoning interest in SETI. Tarter retired from the institute in 2012, and at the time we spoke was now in a role she described to me as "chief cheerleader for all things SETI.")

I was here to interview Bill Diamond, a goateed, bespectacled man in his sixties wearing a SETI-branded fleece. The current president and CEO, Diamond arrived at the institute in 2015 after a successful career in business and tech that had taken him across the United States and around the world. Growing up in the Boston area, he'd always had an interest in space: He'd studied physics and astronomy, owned all of Sagan's books and watched *Cosmos*, read the sci-fi classics. So he knew how fortunate he was to be in his role. It wasn't that running the institute was the best job on Earth; it was the *only* job like it on Earth. "I'm not aware of any other entity in the world with more or less the same mission," he told me. That mission was to explore a subject once "confined to the realms of philosophy and religion" but now "solidly within the domains of science to answer. And that question is: Are we alone in the universe? Is there any other life out there as we look up at the stars? That quest, the answer to that question, is what we do at the SETI Institute."

But it's always been an arduous quest, and perhaps never more so than when he joined the institute. It was a time of turmoil, though Diamond diplomatically described the period as "some upheavals, some financial struggles and other issues." To be fair, SETI and financial struggles are synonymous, as Edward Purcell had predicted.

NASA began funding SETI in 1975, though not at the *Cyclops*-like levels those in the field wanted; the initial program was a rather tiny affair, operating out of the federal space agency's Ames Research Center, which I'd driven past on my way into Mountain View the previous day. It was a small team and money was tight; indeed, the program was actually defunded for a spell in the early eighties. (Funding was restored thanks in part to the lobbying efforts of Sagan, who, in the October 1982 issue of *Science*, published a letter urging "the organization of a coordinated, worldwide and systematic search for extraterrestrial intelligence" that was co-signed by a number of Nobel laureates and other leading scientists; even Purcell added his name.) This haphazard, precarious existence, one reliant on the whims of oblivious politicians, was not conducive to what should have been treated as the greatest search in human history. Which is why a group that included Frank Drake, Barney Oliver, and Jill Tarter joined forces to form a separate, independent, non-profit organization. The SETI Institute was founded on November 20, 1984; Tarter wrote the charter, and was named its first employee.

The institute still relied on NASA grants, however, which meant oblivious politicians still controlled much of their funding. The darkest day in the institute's history came in 1993, when the United States government, led by an overzealous senator, Richard Bryan of Nevada, eliminated all SETI funding—axing tens of millions of dollars that had been promised for the rest of the decade. Few wanted to fund a program that was literally turning up nothing. "[M]illions have been spent and we have yet to bag a single little green fellow," said the senator, proving he had no clue what SETI actually did. "Not a single Martian has said 'Take me to your leader,' and not a single flying saucer has applied for FAA approval."

It was a catastrophic turn of events for the field, and for those who had made it their life.

"When Congress cut funding to the field in 1993, the final nail in the coffin, when Richard Bryan and all of that happened, it didn't just terminate a project," said Andrew Siemion, the Bernard M. Oliver Chair for SETI Research at the institute. "The effect of that was far, far more expansive than just that one program ending. It ended the progression, the continuity of research, the continuity of knowledge within the field broadly—it ended all of that."

"After Senator Bryan terminated the funds, I told my husband not to leave me alone with any sharp objects," Tarter told me. With the taps shut off, the institute had to find new ways to survive. "We've been raising money since '93 to keep this going."

The institute, at the time of my visit, employed 138 staff, including scientists and educators and administrators, on an annual operating budget of $28 million. But what was often described to me as "pure SETI"—the actual search for extraterrestrial intelligence that gives the institute its acronym—had become just a small part of their larger mission, and remained the one area that received no government funding.

"Pure SETI is funded entirely through philanthropic resources," Diamond said, seemingly both proud and irked that the researchers in this field had to fend for themselves.

And yet, the people I spoke to said SETI's future was brighter than at any time since federal support had disappeared. Yes, funding was still an issue, and probably always would be, at least until some evidence was found. But there had been an injection of resources in recent years thanks to a few deep-pocketed benefactors, most notably the Russian-Israeli billionaire Yuri Milner, who in 2015 announced a $100 million initiative called Breakthrough Listen to help find intelligent life elsewhere in the universe, and the American tech entrepreneur Franklin Antonio, co-founder of the semiconductor giant Qualcomm, who'd become a huge supporter of SETI before he passed away suddenly in May 2022. The word *huge* might not be strong enough: It was announced, a couple of months before my visit, that Antonio left $200 million to the institute.

"It's really a game-changer," said Diamond, who appeared to be still wrapping his head around the sum. "The long-term financial sustainability of the institute itself is secured in many ways."

I said goodbye to Diamond and made my way back to reception. Before leaving, I went over and snapped a photo of the neon Drake equation. When Drake had devised the formula, more than a half century before my visit, only the *R* variable had been known: the yearly formation rate of life-supporting stars. While progress had been made in the subsequent decades, the equation had still not been solved. True, astronomers had become confident in the value of f_p, the fraction of stars that have planets—it's likely most of them—while observations made by NASA's Kepler space telescope suggested that between 20 and 50 percent of these planets might be capable of supporting life, bringing us closer to answering n_e.

We also, unwittingly and unfortunately, might have been on the verge of solving L, too—the length of time that a technologically advanced civilization, like ours, lasts. As humans proved with every passing year, L could be a rather small number. There might have been hundreds or thousands of such civilizations—long, long ago, in a galaxy far, far away—that already died out. Or perhaps another space-faring species will come looking for us only after we're gone. SETI was not just a search for who, or what, but a search for when.

Humans don't last long, in the grand scheme of things. I never had the chance to talk to Frank Drake, for instance. I'd been given his email, and sent him a note during the early stages of researching this book. "I've spoken to many, many of your peers in the community, but, ultimately, it's you I'd most love to talk to," I wrote. He never replied. My heart sank when I learned of his death, in September 2022, at the age of ninety-two.

A couple of months later, the institute arranged a celebration of his life. The two-hour service was filled with speeches from his family and colleagues, including Seth Shostak, who'd first met Drake in 1974. Even Bill Nye the Science Guy sent in a tribute video.

People told stories about his childhood in Depression-era Chicago, tales from his time at Green Bank, the early days of SETI, and anecdotes from his years at the institute. He was remembered as a devoted father, a quiet and kind man who adored ice cream and wine and orchids and opals, a man who had a deep love for "all things wondrous and mysterious in our universe," in the words of his daughter, Leila.

One of the tributes came from Jonathan Lunine, chair of the astronomy department at Cornell, where Drake studied and taught, who called him "a visionary who saw the search for extraterrestrial intelligence not as a curiosity but as an essential demonstration of humankind's coming of age in the cosmos." He recalled attending one of Drake's public lectures, back when Lunine was in high school, which had cemented his own interest in astronomy. Now, more than forty-five years later, Lunine was recording his remarks from his office, which had once belonged to Drake. The blackboard behind him was filled with chalk equations, figures and graphs, the mad language of science. If I looked at it just so, I could almost see the faint traces of Drake's handwriting, like the light of a distant star.

After a couple of days in Mountain View, I drove north to Berkeley. On my first morning in town, I had coffee with Dan Werthimer on the edge of the UC Berkeley campus, at the eclectic home he shared with his wife and their son. When I'd asked for directions, Werthimer, chief scientist at the Berkeley SETI Research Center, told me to look for a bright green house with an elephant in the yard. I thought he was joking, but it turned out there was a reason he'd once been featured in an article titled "How Quirky Is Berkeley?" Inside, a lot of the decor was *Star Trek*–themed, and specifically Spock—there was Leonard Nimoy on plates in the kitchen, on a clock, on a cookie jar, even on a pillow on the couch where I sat, drinking coffee, as the family's two dogs pawed around my feet.

"A lot of us watched *Star Trek*," Werthimer said by way of explanation. By "us" he meant those in SETI, which had become obvious early in my research. Whenever I interviewed someone in the field, and asked how they'd first become interested in outer space and the question of extraterrestrial life, rarely did they fail to mention Gene Roddenberry's pioneering series and its portrayal of a universe brimming with intergalactic species. (Preference for the original seasons or *The Next Generation*—a beloved part of my childhood—was pretty split, though I was pleasantly surprised when someone finally chose *Deep Space Nine*.)

Werthimer's story was similar to others I'd heard: *Star Trek* and Carl Sagan and Isaac Asimov; days spent pondering the all-consuming question: Are we alone? "But I didn't really know how to address it until I got good at electronics and computing." He added: "You can't really do much in SETI unless you know how to build stuff."

When he was in high school, Werthimer was a member of a group that called itself the Homebrew Computer Club, an oddball collective of tech geeks and Bay Area misfits who got together to show off their DIY CPUs, trade parts, and swap tips. The club's ranks included Steve Jobs and Steve Wozniak, the future co-founders of Apple, among other eventual Silicon Valley luminaries. "Everybody in that club got pretty much filthy rich," Werthimer told me the first time we spoke. "Except me."

There's a universe in which Werthimer followed his peers from the club into the tech world. He sometimes thought about the life he might have led. He was a scientist, after all, and what was this alternate timeline other than a hypothesis left untested—what could have been, what might have been, what never was. He would never know.

Instead, he went into SETI. Perhaps it had not brought Werthimer unfathomable riches, but he'd enjoyed as successful a career in the field as is possible, short of finding proof of an advanced civilization. Besides being Berkeley's chief SETI scientist, he'd co-founded and served as principal investigator for SETI@Home, which harnessed a worldwide network of personal computers to help process data harvested by the Arecibo Observatory in Puerto Rico, a ground-breaking project that came to an end not long before the radio telescope, for many decades the world's largest, collapsed in 2020. It was SETI@Home that had introduced me to the field: When I was perhaps twelve or thirteen years old, while visiting family friends, I spotted a strange screensaver

on their desktop monitor. *What is this?* I asked. *We're helping look for aliens*, I was told.

After a couple of coffees, Werthimer and I headed for UC Berkeley, home to one of the only SETI research programs in the world. It was still fairly early in the morning, and students were just beginning to emerge. As we walked through campus, Werthimer played tour guide, pointing out various landmarks and regaling me with stories of his time as a student. "It's got a great history. I came out here in the sixties to get tear-gassed."

We arrived at Campbell Hall, the home of the school's physics and astronomy departments; outside the entrance was a row of parking spaces reserved for Nobel laureates. Werthimer took me up to the roof—we could see all the way to San Francisco; the Golden Gate Bridge and Alcatraz in the distance—and we then headed downstairs to one of the labs. He flicked on the lights.

"So, this is where we build the SETI equipment," he said. The room was empty. "Astronomers are not up yet."

There were electronic parts on shelves, cluttered desks, old spectrometers, wires and circuit boards and all sorts of things whose use I would never understand. Looking at the mess, it struck me that Werthimer had never really left the Homebrew Computer Club.

"The way that I go about doing astronomy is trying to figure out: Is there some new instrument that we could build to probe some new parameter of space that nobody's looked at before where you might find something? I'm not very good at doing astronomy. There are these theoretical astronomers that do a lot of math and work out the theory behind black holes. I can't really do that. But I'm good at building instruments. So I figured out that I could combine my skills in electronics and computing with SETI."

To demonstrate this, Werthimer showed me a project he'd been working on in South Africa's Karoo desert, an array whose 350 telescopes were constructed "out of plywood and PVC plastic pipe." I expressed incredulity that such a scientifically advanced project could be built out of items found at your local hardware store. "These are low-frequency telescopes," he explained. It was not specifically a SETI array, he added, but rather one looking into how the first galaxies and stars were formed.

Elsewhere in the room was a jumble of parts from his PANOSETI (Pulsed All-Sky Near-Infrared and Optical) project. The idea was to set up "100 telescopes poking out in different directions," he said, showing me one of the devices, so that they could "cover a big chunk of the sky." This would allow them to "make a movie of the sky at a billion frames a second—so every nanosecond we take a picture," which would enable them to look for laser flashes and other hard-to-find signals that might be out there. No one had explored the sky at such short timescales before. "What's kind of cool about astronomy is if you just probe the universe at some new timescale or some new wavelength [. . .] there's phenomena to be discovered."

"That's one way to make a discovery in astronomy—just probe something that nobody's looked at before," he added. "Maybe we won't find ET, but we'll find something."

SETI, when it came right down to it, was a shot in the dark. Or, listening for a shot in the dark. Werthimer agreed. Despite almost a half century of experience, which culminated in being awarded the Drake Award in 2021, he remained unsure what he, and his peers, were accomplishing.

"There's this problem in SETI: We probably don't know what we're doing," he admitted. "We don't know where to point our telescope. We don't know if they're sending radio or optical or invisible or gamma rays. We have no idea what might come out of another civilization. There's thousands of different ideas! We don't know *when* they might be sending a signal, what kind of modulation. There's like eleven different unknowns. And there's no way that humans can even scratch at that."

After some more time in the lab, we went to the nearby offices of Breakthrough Listen, where Werthimer had served as founding director. It had recently been announced that the project was moving its headquarters to Oxford, though it was keeping this outpost at Berkeley, which, between the university and the SETI Institute, had long made the region the epicentre of the field.

That said, not everyone involved in SETI lived in the Bay Area. There was Jason Wright, who'd founded the Penn State Extraterrestrial Intelligence Center in 2020, and Shelley Wright (no relation to Jason Wright) at UC San Diego. There was Michael Garrett at the University of Manchester, who'd told me "the thing that gets me out of bed in the morning is looking for extraterrestrials." At Harvard you had Paul Horowitz and Avi Loeb, the latter a talented self-promoter who'd made a name by theorizing that 'Oumuamua, the first interstellar object known to have visited our solar system, which had been identified in 2017, might be a spacecraft. (Loeb, who later published a book about it, *Extraterrestrial*, did not think much of the SETI community: "They have an inferiority complex," he told me. "They're trying to keep as quiet as possible. And every time they collect data they're doing their best to report that there is nothing in it." Many of his peers, I suspected and some confirmed, did not think much of him.) In all, Seth Shostak guessed that "the total number of people in the world who are looking for intelligent extraterrestrials might be a dozen. Maybe two dozen. That's it." Werthimer thought that was an overestimate: "You can count the main people on one hand."

Part of the reason for this was that, for many years, SETI was an object of ridicule, even among fellow astronomers. Horowitz, a professor emeritus in Harvard's Department of Physics, told me about a book that came out in 1995, a few years after Senator Bryan successfully cut funding, written by a SETI believer-turned-skeptic named Ben Zuckerman. It was called *Extraterrestrials: Where Are They?* At one point during our conversation, Horowitz put me on hold, found the book on his shelf, opened it to its title page, and read the inscription: "For Paul, to help you see the light." He laughed. "The light was we're not going to find them."

Andrew Siemion, who in addition to his work at the institute served as director of the Berkeley SETI Research Center and principal investigator for Breakthrough Listen, recalled getting funny looks as a grad student when he said he was pursuing SETI: "There was snickering. Like, well, you know, he's not really doing science."

Things have improved over the years, he said, but "working in SETI requires a certain resignation towards any kind of normal, professional career in astronomy."

The history of SETI was one of frustration. It was not simply that nothing had been found. (Unless you believe the Earth had already been visited by aliens, which, in SETI circles, was not exactly a popular opinion.) Those in the field could live with the silence—most expected it, in fact. It's that the people and organizations orbiting them, whether colleagues in academia controlling their careers or politicians controlling their budgets, had never felt the same devotion to the field as they did.

Training the next generation of SETI researchers—those more likely to witness a breakthrough—had proved especially daunting. They left for more stable jobs, more stable funding, better opportunities. "Only a few of my students have stayed in SETI," said Werthimer. "And I don't blame 'em. How are you going to get a job just saying, 'I did my Ph.D. looking and I didn't find anything'?" As painful as it was to hear, his advice for students was to pursue SETI on the side. "SETI is fragile," he said. "It's not a good thing to go into for a career. You're not going to get promoted. People just think it's kind of wacko."

Fortunately, not everyone took this advice to heart. In the Breakthrough offices I met one of his former students, Sofia Sheikh, likely one of the youngest SETI researchers in the world. Originally from a small town in South Carolina, she'd gotten involved in the search while an undergrad at UC Berkeley, when Breakthrough Listen was first getting off the ground. ("I read about it on Reddit.") There were a lot of students interested in going into the field these days, she said, there just weren't enough jobs or funds to go around.

"From my perspective, being able to do SETI is purely a curiosity-driven question," she said. "It's kind of a privilege to work on this as a topic and a job. I think we try to link it to some big overarching question about the importance of humanity, or these religious questions about 'Why are we here? Can we make connections with other beings?' All of these deep human questions. That's true for some people. For me, it's more like: This is really cool." She laughed. "It's cool that we have sort of reached a point where we can have people just thinking about these weird, wacko topics like SETI. And I get to be one of them."

They were born into a world whose greatest mysteries were in the stars. They listened to the sky and the fact they heard nothing, loudly, was a siren song they couldn't resist. They were obsessed with Isaac Asimov and Arthur C. Clarke, Stephen Hawking and Carl Sagan, *Star Trek*—but never *Star Wars*. Some of them were children of the space race. Others were simply taken by the enormity of the cosmos. Sometimes it was just a voice in the back of their head, wondering.

"Somehow, the universe has given rise to an entity that can ask questions about the universe itself—the universe that gave rise to that entity," Andrew Siemion said, the first time we spoke. "Ultimately, do we live in a universe in which intelligent life has arisen only once? Or do we live in a universe in which intelligent life has arisen, and is arising, many, many, many, many times?

"It was just so incredibly obvious to me that that was the biggest question, the most interesting question, most exciting question, that you could possibly explore in astronomy."

What drew them together was what separated them from everyone else: While the rest of the world went about their days, wondering what they could do *here* on this planet, they wondered what they could find *out there*, on other planets, in the vastness of the universe. What drew them together was the fact they knew they might never find a thing, and still they searched, intergalactic beachcombers looking for a single, specific grain of sand.

"You might not succeed in your lifetime," Jill Tarter told me, "so it takes a certain kind of person that enjoys the process of getting there—waking up in the morning to try and figure out how you can do the search better today than you did yesterday."

She was comfortable with the fact she would not live to see her life's dream come true, as were most of her peers. SETI, as a scientific pursuit, was in its nascency. There was still so much work to be done. I was constantly reminded that we'd only looked at a trivial cross-section of the universe. How trivial? Tarter wanted to find out, so, years ago, she commissioned a study. If the universe was the same size as all the oceans on Earth, she said, we would have searched the equivalent of a hot tub. (When she first ran the numbers, it was only a cup. "That should have sent us all screaming away from this," she told me.)

Instead, they were running towards it. Would they find success? Seth Shostak, of course, was endlessly optimistic. ("Seth Shostak always says it's going to be a few years away," Werthimer told me. "But he's been saying that, also, for forty years.") Sofia Sheikh, younger than most of her peers, told me that "if there's a radio beacon pointed at Earth, I think we will find it in our lifetime. Now that's a pretty big *if*." But there were so many different ways of detecting other civilizations, she knew, and the odds suggested we would still be looking decades, if not centuries, from now.

"People have been thinking about this question for thousands of years, and it's kind of naive to think that your generation is somehow special compared to the generations that have gone before you," said Werthimer. "It might be a generation a billion years from now."

Even if they'd begun their work knowing they'd likely never see an end, I felt a deep sadness whenever I read old interviews with the field's pioneers, almost all of whom are gone. Someone told me a story that, before he died, Carl Sagan was asked to name one thing he'd regret not having lived to see. His answer? Finding life elsewhere in the universe. I felt the same way. When I read *Contact* for the first time, it wasn't awe I felt; it was envy. His characters knew the answer.

When I asked Bill Diamond what kind of people are attracted to the search, what commonalities they shared, he said that it wasn't just an "unrelenting curiosity"—everyone involved in SETI possessed that in spades. Rather, it was that they were "motivated enough by their curiosity to pursue questions to which there may not be any near-term answers," he said. "Questions that they realize they may not be able to answer, or at least anytime soon."

"The people that have worked in this field generally have some kind of pathological situation that permits them, or encourages them, to continue to do it," said Andrew Siemion when I asked him a similar question. "We all weigh the relative probability of making some detection or getting some sort of payoff with what we individually view as the importance of the question. Thankfully, I think, for the human species, at least a few of us in the subject of SETI do that calculation and think it to be an important thing to continue to work on, even in the face of the reality that we probably won't succeed."

I didn't understand how it wasn't considered even *more* important. How there weren't hundreds—thousands!—of young scientists entering the field; how NASA wasn't breaking its budget on SETI missions; how the world didn't come together to forget about our problems *down here* and unite to focus on *out there*. It was silly, of course. I knew the answer, but still I asked. It was strange: Sometimes I felt I wanted to know the answer more than the people I interviewed. How did the search not drive them crazy? I was usually embarrassed to ask this outright, so I'd couch my questions around ideas of motivation and disappointment and uncertainty, hoping they'd pick up on what I was really asking: How didn't they let the search take over every part of their life?

"In order to stay sane in this," said Penn State's Jason Wright, "you have to focus on the search and not the discovery."

"If you define success as finding ET," Dan Werthimer told me, "then that would make your life pretty miserable, I think."

One morning, I arrived at the gates of the Hat Creek Radio Observatory, about twenty miles outside the town of Burney, in the Cascade Mountains of northern California. The gates were unlocked, and partially open, but I wasn't sure if anyone was here; I hadn't received a response to my last email asking what time I should show up and where I should go. It had taken me more than four hours to drive here from Berkeley, a long way to go for nothing.

Outside the main gate was a large blue-and-white sign, adorned with the SETI Institute's backward question mark, ordering visitors to put their mobile phones in airplane mode and to shut off Wi-Fi and Bluetooth. Paranoid, I even turned off the car radio, then proceeded slowly down the winding drive, unsure what I'd find at its end.

For a long time, humans thought more about communicating with aliens than listening. Previous generations of scientists devised different ways to alert the universe to our presence. Centuries ago, long before we designed telescopes that could detect faint radio signals floating through space, it was suggested we dig enormous ditches—perhaps twenty miles across—that would then be filled with kerosene and set alight. The thinking, rudimentary as it was, was that ET would see the flames and come calling. Earlier, the mathematician Carl Friedrich Gauss proposed the construction of giant geometric shapes—three squares and a right triangle—that would be visible from space, and would signal to any advanced civilization that the residents of this planet understood mathematics. Another idea involved manufacturing giant mirrors, which would catch the sun and reflect its rays back into the solar system, where the massive beam of light would hopefully be spotted by another civilization.

"They were all cool ideas at the time, and now we kind of laugh at them," said Werthimer, who'd outlined these various attempts to me. "So what that means is that what we're doing now, two hundred years from now, people are going to say, 'Dan was such an idiot. Why didn't he use tachyons?' There will be some new physics, or some much better ways to do this kind of stuff."

In more recent years, both the Pioneer and Voyager missions sent probes outside our solar system containing information meant for intergalactic eyes: at the insistence of Carl Sagan, Pioneer 10 and 11 (launched in 1972 and 1973, respectively) carried gold-aluminium plaques that showed renderings of human bodies and a map to the planet from which the craft originated; Voyager 1 and 2, both launched in 1977, included the famed twelve-inch golden records that contained even more information than the Pioneer plaques—besides 115 pictures it included music and greetings in almost sixty human languages.

Whether this was a good idea might only be answered decades from now. There is disagreement in the SETI community about the merits of listening versus reaching out, and signalling our presence—*passive* versus *active* SETI. There are moral and ethical concerns about the latter. For instance: What happens if we tip off a hostile alien species? What if a visiting alien species brings with it disease or parasites that our bodies cannot tolerate? What if looking for intelligent life leads to the end of our own? In 1974, Drake harnessed the Arecibo Observatory to send pictorial messages towards a cluster of 300,000 stars. Although broadcast as a series of ones and zeroes, any alien who translated the transmission into its graphic form would learn basic information about our species. Soon after, the British radio astronomer Martin Ryle sought a ban on the practice with the International Astronomical Union. "He felt we were notifying the universe of our existence and they were going to come and eat us," explained Drake.

Shostak, for one, considered such worries overblown: "Any extraterrestrials with technology advanced enough to threaten us will surely have antennas larger than our own, instruments that can pick up the television and radio signals broadcast willy-nilly since World War II," he wrote in a 2015 *New York Times* op-ed titled "Should We Keep a Low Profile in Space?" "We are already shouting into the jungle, albeit with less volume than a deliberate signal. But the dangerous creatures may have good hearing."

Here in Hat Creek, scientists just listened. I reached the parking lot, which contained several cars—a good sign. But the door to the main building was locked. I knocked, went to check my email before remembering I couldn't access my inbox, and then knocked again.

A moment later I was greeted by Alexander Pollak, a gregarious fellow in his mid-thirties who served as the science and engineering operations manager for the Allen Telescope Array. He unlocked the door and welcomed me inside, apologizing as he headed back to his office to finish up a meeting. He invited me to look around. Among the charts and plaques was a photograph of the Orion Nebula, a riotous cloud of pinks and reds, with a quote from Jill Tarter in the upper left-hand corner: "We, all of us, are what happens when a primordial mixture of hydrogen and helium evolves for so long that it begins to ask where it came from."

Pollak soon re-emerged from his office and took me outside to tour the array. Before departing, he double-checked that I'd turned off Bluetooth and Wi-Fi. The instruments were extremely sensitive, he said. What would happen if I forgot, I asked. Just interfere with the signal? He replied in a thick German accent: "You would actually break it."

Outside, I felt like I'd stepped into the opening scenes of *Contact*. A battery of telescopes, most pointed at the sky, were spread out before us, while Burney Mountain, one of the range's highest peaks, closer to space than any of us below, stood snow-capped in the distance. I stood there for a minute and just listened.

The observatory dated back to the late 1950s, when it was established by UC Berkeley, which eventually partnered with the SETI Institute in the early 2000s to build a new array. Armed with funding from the Microsoft billionaire Paul Allen, the array was supposed to be cutting-edge, but was instead plagued by issues; Berkeley pulled out of the project, only 42 of the planned 350-odd telescopes were built, and those that were built only sort-of worked, depending on who you ask. ("It never really worked," said Pollak.) Funding was spotty, and there was a period when the array was essentially mothballed. One person told me things were so bad that raccoons were living inside the telescopes. When I mentioned this to Pollak he said no raccoons had been found, just squirrels.

We approached one of the telescopes that was currently offline. Pollak pried open the hatch so that I could see the instrument's guts. There were no animals to surprise us. The last several years had been devoted to a major refurbishment of the array—at the time of my visit twenty-six of the forty-two six-metre antennas had been upgraded, twenty of which were used at any given time.

"We took all of them apart, we refurbished them, I worked out what the problems are, and then we rebuilt them from scratch. And now they're far more reliable."

The original feeds had been replaced by more sensitive second-generation "Antonio feeds," named after the SETI philanthropist Franklin Antonio, who'd helped design them. The signals bounced off the reflector and were captured in the feed and sent through a fibre-optic cable back to the main building, where they were subsequently digitized. The new feeds were made of copper and gold plated, and reminded me of a saw shark's snout—each edge corresponded to a different wavelength, and allowed researchers to search at up to fourteen gigahertz. The larger the range, explained Pollak, the more places you can look. The feeds were enclosed in thin glass and vacuum sealed to keep the temperature well below freezing.

"Because the signals which we look [for] are so weak, you have to reduce any noise," he said. Imagine being in a loud restaurant and trying to listen to someone whispering on the other side of the room. "The way we reduce the noise is by cooling everything down."

We wandered over to the shop where Pollak assembled the feeds. They used to be assembled in the Bay Area, but were so fragile they sometimes didn't survive transport. Now they arrived in parts, IKEA furniture for geniuses. "Every nut and bolt will be assembled here," he said. It was time-consuming, painstaking work. Fortunately, the pandemic provided a lot of time.

He'd arrived in Hat Creek in 2019, a continent and ocean away from home. Pollak grew up on a farm about an hour outside Stuttgart. As a kid with an interest in technology and the universe, he'd install SETI@Home on old computers. He attended a nearby university for engineering, and imagined after graduation he'd get a job, settle down, and start a family. Instead, inspired by a professor who'd done a Ph.D. in radio astronomy in the United Kingdom, Pollak headed for Oxford, where he eventually earned his Ph.D. After finishing a post-doc, he met with a former colleague who was now at UC Berkeley, and who mentioned that Andrew Siemion was looking to hire someone to fix the ATA.

"My speciality is basically fixing broken telescopes," Pollak said. "I'm good at figuring out what doesn't work, and making it work."

He had never heard of the ATA, but he flew to California over Christmas at the end of 2018 to visit Hat Creek. "It was in very rough shape," he said. "I was like, 'Oh my God, I'm not sure if I want to get into all of that.'"

Still, he took the job. He intended to live and work in Berkeley—he had a position at the SETI Institute, and also as a visiting scholar at the university with the Breakthrough Listen team—but the pandemic forced him to remain in Hat Creek.

He was joined by a new hire, Wael Farah, who'd just arrived from Australia to help refurbish the ATA. When the pandemic struck they closed the gates and spent two years fixing the array: Farah concentrating on the software, Pollak on the hardware. Two years of solitude, in pursuit of what would likely be silence.

For Farah, who grew up north of Beirut, the search wasn't just about knowing whether there were other beings out there in the universe; it was about knowing ourselves. If people understood the scale of the universe, he believed, it might shift "how they perceive themselves and how they perceive others," he told me. And if he was able to prove there was intelligent life elsewhere in the universe, he continued, it might make those living here treat their fellow humans better. "Why are we starting wars? Why are we fighting over land? We should do better because we're such a minuscule sand grain in this huge, vast universe. So if you ask me why SETI is an important endeavour, I'd say this is why: It's a reflection of ourselves."

Pollak and I wandered across the field and back into the main building, where he took me through the signal processing room, filled with machines and devices and sensors and other things whose use he patiently explained and which I nonetheless struggled to understand. Here's the computer controlling the array; here's the weather station monitoring the outside environment—high winds can damage the telescopes; here's the oscillators controlling which frequency is being observed; here's the station clock, ensuring everything is running in sync; here's the digitizers that take the analogue signals and, er, digitize them. Eventually, we ended up in his office, where large screens hanging above us provided an overview of the entire array—which telescopes were operational, which were dormant, and where they were pointing. If a strange signal were detected, I asked a bit sheepishly, would it be like something out of a Hollywood movie, with flashing lights and blaring sirens? *Aliens detected. Aliens detected.* No, he said, "sadly not like Hollywood."

Confirmation would be a long process. Back at the SETI Institute, Bill Diamond had been quick to emphasize that if they did find something, we'd know about it. The institute wasn't some shadowy, deep state organization funded with dark money. It would not be another Roswell (if you believe in that sort of thing). While they'd need extraordinary evidence—which meant a signal would need to be verified by multiple observatories—before making the news public ("I personally need to be very careful about calling a press conference," Diamond said), it would ultimately be made public. There's already a working group of people at SETI who meet to discuss "post-detection protocol."

"There's growing interest, both among policy-makers, among journalists, writers, scientists, anthropologists, people who do social sciences, in starting to address this," he said. "We should think about how we handle this information, how we disseminate this information, what impacts it might have on society, on science, on government, religion, philosophy. So there is this awareness that, as we think we might be getting closer to at least a partial answer to this question, we should be prepared."

Pollak and I sat there and spoke for another hour or so, but I was conscientious of his time. He'd only recently returned to Hat Creek the previous month after a year spent operating the ten-metre telescope at the Amundsen-Scott South Pole Station. He showed me photos of the aurora australis, the southern lights, as he shared stories from his time on the bottom of the world. Living in Hat Creek had prepared him for Antarctica. "It gets a bit lonely up here," he said. (Farah was now back in the Bay Area.) Still, when he thought of that moment—the decision to come to California—and everything that had happened since, he had no regrets.

"It's the most fun project I've worked on so far," he said. "And the chances that we find something? Who knows. Maybe it takes generations. I am not planning on finding anything in my lifetime. But we should still look. It's one of those things: We have the privilege and the ability to look, so we should look." Throughout history, he continued, humans have always considered themselves to be special. We've thought of Earth—and, by extension, ourselves—as the centre of the solar system, the centre of the galaxy, the centre of the universe. But, he added, "we know every star, pretty much, has planets. So our solar system is not special. So it's far more likely that, hopefully, there is life out there. How that life looks, I have no idea. But it would be very sad if we would be the only planet to develop intelligent life."

The field was undeniably advancing. "Whatever experiment you're working on today blows away what you were working on five years ago," Seth Shostak told me. They were getting better, smarter, at searching. "We're pushing the envelope on what we're doing," said Paul Horowitz, "and at some point that envelope's gotta envelop a source out there." A slate of new and upgraded telescopes were in the planning stages or about to come online. "The chances of finding something is just getting better and better," said Pollak.

Would finding something actually change the world? Probably not. Polls suggest that two-thirds of North Americans believe intelligent life exists in the universe, so we already walk around, in our day-to-day lives, convinced that we are not alone. Confirmation, be it a techno-signature or an artifact, wouldn't necessarily lead to the collapse of society. All the big questions—why are we here, what else is out there, what happens when this is all over—would remain. We'd still look at the stars in wonder and awe—perhaps, knowing we are not alone, with more awe.

I said goodbye to Pollak and went outside, where I found myself alone again. On the way to my car I took a detour back towards the array, to take a few more pictures, to look at it one last time. When I'd come up with the idea for this book, this moment, what I was seeing now, was one of the first images that came to mind. Like finding myself at the entrance of the SETI Institute, it was slightly unnerving to finally be here. I was confident I'd never return. Would they find a signal? Of this I was less certain.

Whatever happened, they would keep listening. Standing there, in the chill mountain air, I thought back to what Wael Farah had said when I'd asked him if he thought they'd find proof in his lifetime, and whether he'd be disappointed if they failed to do so.

He leaned back in his chair and ran his hands through his hair. He'd come a long way to get here—not light years, but far enough. From Lebanon to Australia to California. What we were talking about made that journey seem like the distance between grains of sand on a beach, where a little girl and her father are looking up at the stars.

"I don't live my life thinking that I'll find aliens today, or tomorrow, or next year," he said. "I live my life, I live my every day, thinking that I, hopefully, have done something, even if it's a tiny step, towards that direction. That's my philosophy, at least. That's how I think about it."

TWO

THE PATH

A life is marked by choices, not all of them your own. A simple decision could have enormous ramifications years from now, while what seems like a major fork in the road might ultimately have little bearing on your future. It could be who you marry. Where you decide to go to college. The friends you make as a child. Or, it could be something more mundane: Turning left instead of right. Answering the phone instead of letting it ring. Going to bed instead of going out on a Saturday night. And that's just when we have agency. After all, our lives are often shaped by the whims of family and friends, strangers we pass on the street, or people we'll never meet. Our hands might be on the ship's wheel, but we are at the mercy of the wind. Because of this, some put their trust in fate, while others believe we are guided by a higher power. And then there are those who believe it is all simply random, the universe drunk at the craps table, rolling the dice.

Jeremy Holden thought about this sometimes, the decisions he'd made or hadn't made, and the decisions made for him, and how they all led him deep into the rainforests of Sumatra, where he crossed paths with a woman who set his life on a course he'd followed for more than thirty years.

"My whole life would be different, so I owe an awful lot to her," he told me the first time we spoke, his voice marked by appreciation and a touch of acrimony. "And I owe everything to an ape that most people don't believe exists."

From Singapore I flew to Kuala Lumpur, then caught another flight across the Strait of Malacca, its waters dotted with dozens of enormous container ships that from above looked like my son's bath toys. Before too long the plane touched down in Padang, West Sumatra, a bustling city of a million people pushing against the Indian Ocean. I waited at the gate after disembarking; a few minutes later a man I assumed could only be Jeremy followed down the bridge. I hadn't spotted him before we boarded in Malaysia, so this was my first look at the person my wife was counting on to keep her husband alive for the next week: lean and tall, about six-three, with short salt-and-pepper hair and intense brown eyes, wearing a black T-shirt, jeans, a white and grey striped scarf, heavy brown boots, and a few days' worth of stubble. I was flabbergasted, flipping through our passports in the customs line, to learn he was fifty-seven years old; he looked to be in his mid-to-late forties. "I don't feel fifty-seven. I don't act fifty-seven," he later said. "I don't have the bank balance or the credibility or anything of a fifty-seven-year-old."

After securing our visas we picked up our packs from the baggage carousel, exchanged a wad of American dollars into a thick stack of rupiahs, and hailed a taxi.

My trip might have ended here. The cab driver wove in and out of traffic, treating the pavement markings like my aforementioned son treats the outlines in his colouring books. Jeremy was untroubled. Eventually, we made it to our hotel, a five-storey structure that was one of the tallest buildings in the city. Jeremy said it was once the site of another hotel, which had collapsed in the devastating Sumatran earthquake of 2009, which killed more than eleven hundred people across the island. This new building was probably built to a higher safety standard, he assured me. It was my forty-second birthday, and I wondered if I'd live to see forty-three.

In the early morning hours, I awoke to a sensation I hadn't encountered since a night spent sleeping in a waterbed, decades ago: a gentle rocking back and forth, back and forth. I lay there in the dark for a few moments, thinking to myself that this felt like an earthquake. Was it a train rumbling past? I didn't recall seeing any tracks near the hotel when walking back from dinner the previous evening, though I hadn't been paying close enough attention to say for certain. In different circumstances I might have guessed that I was drunk, only I'd had but a solitary celebratory birthday beer with the meal. As the shaking of the bed grew more violent, like a scene out of *The Exorcist*, it dawned on me that, yes, this was an earthquake. The next thirty seconds were a blur: I tried the lights and leapt out of bed, or I leapt out of bed and tried the lights. Nothing. I stumbled to the door and threw it open—in the hallway, guests were streaming towards the stairs. Definitely an earthquake. I shut the door and fruitlessly tried the lights again, and then used my iPhone's flashlight to find my pants, shirt, and shoes. Was I supposed to brace myself in the doorway? Hide in the bathtub? I thought back to the quick shower I'd taken before heading to dinner—was there even a bathtub? Before I could investigate, there was an urgent knocking. Jeremy was standing in the hall. "We have to go," he said.

Down four flights of stairs and out through the lobby. I assume by this point the shaking had subsided, but I cannot say for sure. A number of guests milled just outside the hotel's entrance, but Jeremy didn't stop until we'd scurried down the driveway and crossed the street, where we sat on the curb. Jeremy motioned to the folks who were standing outside the hotel. This is what happened in 2009, he said. People evacuated, but some were still standing too close to the building. It collapsed on top of them. As we sat there, I noticed a steady string of cars and motorbikes heading east; hotel guests were seemingly leaving, too—families hurriedly packing up their vehicles and heading off into the night.

We weren't sure what to do. I checked social media and quickly found news of the quake, which measured 7.3 on the Richter scale, and then pulled up a map of the affected area on Google—a red dot showed the epicentre to the west of us, while a blue dot denoted where we were sitting in Padang. We were very, very close.

We were also very, very close to the ocean. My brain decided that now was a good time to replay all the videos of tsunamis I'd watched in quiet horror over the years, the black water rushing onto land and drowning everything in its way. I looked around for something to hold on to—a tree, a street sign, an electrical pole—but the waters never came. (A few hours later, reading a Reuters story about the quake over breakfast, I learned that a tsunami warning had in fact been issued to residents—that's why so many people were fleeing for higher ground—but since Jeremy and I were not on the Indonesian cellular network, I assumed that's why neither of us received the alert. Thankfully, there was no tsunami.) I texted my wife and friends to tell them I was safe; my wife took the news distressingly well. As we waited, Jeremy and I discussed what the quake might mean for the rest of our trip—if the roads were damaged, we might be unable to leave Padang. Had I travelled halfway around the world for nothing?

After about an hour we decided to risk going back inside. At reception, the only other foreigner I saw was demanding a refund. Some people were sleeping on couches in the lobby, in case they had to flee again. We climbed the stairs back to our floor and said goodnight. I lay in bed, trying to ignore what felt like the occasional aftershock, until I managed to fall asleep.

Our driver failed to show up the following morning. Jeremy paced the lobby, trying to find us another ride, growing increasingly frustrated at this turn of events. We had a long journey ahead, and our options were limited. After several phone calls, he secured two seats for us on a minibus. My stomach sank at the news; Jeremy had told me all about the minibus the previous day, when smugly explaining why he'd arranged for a private car—minibuses were full of kretek-smoking men and carsick women and wailing babies. He'd once taken a long minibus trip with a television producer; the ride was apparently so bad the producer said he'd pay any amount of money, whatever it took, to get off and find an alternate means of transport. You didn't want to travel by minibus, no matter the circumstances. "Minibus is no good," Jeremy said, the only time I saw anything approaching fear in his eyes.

The minibus showed up an hour or so later. There were eight people in the vehicle for a trip that took about eight hours. Perhaps because the bar had been set so low, I found the minibus itself to be perfectly pleasant, though my knuckles were white almost the entire time. We followed the same twisting two-lane highway for the majority of the drive, on which the centre line was merely a suggestion, or perhaps just there for aesthetic reasons. Cars tried to overtake vans which tried to overtake trucks, one game of chicken after the other with oncoming cars. Darting between the larger vehicles were the motorbikes that transported not just lone riders and couples, but entire families—one, two, I even spotted three young children on a single bike, wedged between their parents, a baby balanced on the handlebars like some kind of living hood ornament. At one point a motorbike commandeered by three kids seemingly the same age as my eldest son, who was still a decade away from getting his learner's permit, zipped past us and disappeared down the highway. (Perhaps the jet lag was causing hallucinations, I thought.) The only real safety measures came from the men who stood in the middle of the road, often before tight curves, alerting drivers when it was safe to proceed; they collected well-deserved tips in cardboard boxes and empty cans. How would the Canadian embassy in Jakarta break the news of my death to my wife?

After a while I became numb to the danger and was able to look out the window at the towns and villages and countryside speeding past, the mosques and houses and tea plantations and rice paddies and forests, recently harvested coffee beans and cinnamon sticks drying on blankets on the side of the road. "Thirty years I've been coming along this road, and it hasn't changed," Jeremy said from the seat in front of me. He pointed out places he'd explored, and what you might find if you went searching there—here was the only place you could find this type of lizard; over there was the only hillside where a certain plant grew.

We reached the village of Pelompek, in the province of Jambi, as the sun fell. In the near distance stood the highest peak in Sumatra's Barisan Mountains: Gunung Kerinci, the 3,805-metre volcano dominating the landscape like a sleeping giant—one of almost seventy on the island. Jeremy studied the mountain briefly: "No smoke coming out of it, that's a good sign." We'd planned to climb later in the week—Jeremy raved about the views from its peak, to which he'd climbed many times—but upon arriving at the guest house where we were staying the night we learned the giant was awake, active, and thus off-limits. An earthquake and now a volcano; I wondered what the third natural disaster would be.

It was thoughts of something unnatural, or at least unknown, that chased away sleep that night. Jeremy had spent decades searching for a creature the world did not believe existed, and had agreed to bring me into his world, to this place, to help me understand what possessed a man to devote much of his life to a quest he knew he'd never complete, a knight forever tilting at windmills. It was that question that had spoken to him when I'd first reached out, three years earlier. He wanted to understand, too.

In the morning, we wandered down the road to the home of Doni Effendi, Jeremy's long-time guide, who would be joining us on our expedition, along with his son-in-law, Sonny. We sat in a circle on the carpeted floor of the house's main room, where sweets and drinks had been set out, and I tried to follow along as the old friends, speaking Indonesian, caught up on one another's lives. Afterwards we travelled back into the village for supplies—dry noodles, tins of tuna, chips—before hiking to the gate of Kerinci Seblat National Park, where one of the park officials recognized Jeremy and gave us a break on the entrance fee. At a total area of almost 14,000 square kilometres, the park was roughly twice the size of Ontario's Algonquin Provincial Park and a third larger than Yellowstone National Park. The animals found in its borders could fill a zoo—tigers, elephants, tapirs, clouded leopards, gibbons, sun bears, golden cats, muntjac deer, and hundreds of birds. Jeremy did his best to lower my expectations: Nothing was easy to spot in the wild, he said. Large mammals? Forget about it. "You will not see anything," he cautioned. Perhaps sensing my disappointment, he continued: "Having said that, there is this thing about beginner's luck."

We reached the base of the Gunung Tujuh without spotting any animals of note. Jeremy had described our day's climb as "not a big deal" back at the guest house. But, reader, it was a big deal. If we'd forgone porters and hiked up the mountain with our packs as I'd originally insisted—mine came in at about 15 kilograms, according to the digital scale at the airport check-in counter—I would have died, there is no doubt. Even carrying just a daypack, my legs and lungs were burning within minutes. We had 2,000 metres to climb.

The pain was worth it: We arrived at Lake Gunung Tujuh, the lake of the seven mountains, the highest caldera lake—crater lake—in all of Southeast Asia. It was as if someone, eons ago, had blasted the top off a mountain and filled the hole with water. A light rain began to fall as we arrived at the shore, so I took shelter under a small gazebo and stared out at the water. I felt completely exhausted, and asked Jeremy if we were close to camp. "No, we've got a long way to go," he said. I appreciated the honesty, even if I wanted to cry. A few minutes later the porters arrived with our packs and camping supplies. We'd arranged for a pair of local fishermen to ferry us across the lake, and so we piled our supplies into two narrow canoes that had been tied together side by side, and pushed off from shore.

The lake was calm, the rain and waves gentle—the antithesis of the drive to Jambi the previous day. Here and there, small plastic bottles bobbed along the surface, traps for the fish that called these waters home. The fishermen paddled in silence; sometimes Doni or Sonny took a turn. We reached a bank where the fishermen had built a small camp, moved our supplies into a different pair of similarly linked canoes, and continued our journey. The water was a rich emerald, and cold. Several of the peaks surrounding the lake were hidden by mist, which rolled down the slopes towards the shoreline and stopped, as if afraid of the water. "I do miss this forest—there's nothing like it," Jeremy said. "This is also some of the oldest forest in the world—it's considerably older than the Amazon." He was silent for a moment, letting this sink in. "We are slipping back into the past now. What you're looking at wouldn't have changed if we were here 10,000 years ago—other than the plastic oars." I told him that the theme from *Jurassic Park* had been playing in my head. He nodded. "If something stuck its scaly head up out of those trees, it wouldn't look too out of place." There weren't any dinosaurs out in the rainforest, but something else. "There is something here that's undescribed by science, and it walks on two fucking legs," Jeremy said.

He pointed to the peaks he'd climbed, the places he'd searched, the areas he still one day hoped to reach. He gestured to various ridges and slopes, some scarred by violent landslides, plotting out where we'd go in the coming days—that one too hard, that one too steep, that one requiring a full day's trek, which would mean sleeping on the summit. "I got lost on that mountain," he said of one, and pointed to another far distant peak, towards where we were paddling: "Up there, there's an undescribed flower that looks like Audrey Hepburn. Only two people in the world have ever seen it—him and me," he said, nodding at Doni.

He'd been searching these forests and peaks for years. A renowned wildlife photographer who had captured some of the rarest plants and animals in the world on film, Jeremy had once established a robust camera-trapping program around the lake. It was a natural arena, and a perfect stage for catching animals on film. "If you look at this landscape, you've got the lake—barrier. This mountain wall—barrier. So anything moving 'round has to come through that little bit of forest there," he said, pointing to a gap between two peaks. There was also a river near where we would set up camp, another natural barrier. He used the topography to his advantage, he explained—to "look where it can't go, and then we totally block off where it can go." He believed the creature didn't stay in one place, and so would have to travel through the area at some point. Eventually, one of the camera traps would get the photograph—of this he'd been "100 percent convinced."

After almost two hours, we reached the far shore.

"We have arrived," Jeremy said.

He arrived in Indonesia in the summer of 1994. He was twenty-seven years old.

"I came out here not really knowing why I'd come here," he told me over dinner on our first night in Padang. The plan was to spend six months touring the country, a vast archipelago between the Pacific and Indian Oceans, but when Jeremy arrived in Sumatra, the largest of the country's more than 17,000 islands, he changed his plans. This is where he'd remain.

During his travels he met a tourist who'd recently seen a tiger. If you want to see one, too, the man told Jeremy, go to Kerinci. It wasn't a place familiar to most Westerners; when Jeremy consulted his travel guide, he found a single paragraph about the national park—all the more reason to go there.

He made his way to Pelompek and found lodging in a guest house in the rainforest but, after checking in, discovered you needed to supply your own food. He turned around and began the long hike back to the village. On his way, he passed a white woman walking in the opposite direction—an unusual sight. "I said hello and she completely ignored me," he recalled. On his way back to the lodge after buying supplies, he overtook the same woman on the road, but this time said nothing. He arrived back at the guest house and was writing in his journal when, not long after, the woman turned up.

Debbie Martyr, when I had lunch with her a few weeks after my return from Sumatra, in Borough Market, near her London flat, acknowledged that, yes, she'd initially been rude to Jeremy. "He said hello to me, very friendly. I was being snobby." At the time, the region was experiencing a tourism boom, and she figured he was just another Westerner there to find himself. Debbie, on the other hand, was there to conduct serious research.

She'd first visited Indonesia in 1989, when she took a break from her journalism career to travel throughout Southeast Asia. In Sumatra, she hiked to the top of Mount Kerinci, the volcano from whose summit you could see the national park below. As she surveyed the surroundings, her guide pointed out where the region's fauna could be found: In the forest over there you had tigers; over here was rhino territory; that's where the elephants gathered. And over there, he said, is where you'd sometimes find orang-pendek.

"What's orang-pendek?" she asked.

Drawn from the Indonesian words for "person" (*orang*) and "short" (*pendek*), it is the most common term for the hairy bipeds that have been part of Sumatran legend and rumour for centuries. Marco Polo referred to them in his journals. The Kubu, a nomadic Indigenous group that lives on the island, have long told stories about an ape-like creature living in the forest. During the brutal era of the Netherlands East Indies, Dutch settlers saw it, too. The manager of a coffee plantation, who came across the creature while lost in the forest, described it in 1917 as having "thick square shoulders" and skin that "looked like black earth." He was certain that "it was not an orangutan; I had seen one of these large apes a short time before at Artis [the Amsterdam Zoo]. It was more like a monstrously large siamang [gibbon], but a siamang has long hair, and there was no doubt that it had short hair." Another Dutchman, a few years later, claimed that "the lower part of its face seemed to end in more of a point than a man's; this brown face was almost hairless, whilst its forehead seemed to be high rather than low. Its eyebrows were the same colour as its hair and were very bushy. The eyes were frankly moving; they were of the darkest colour, very lively, and like human eyes."

I read many accounts, both historic and contemporary, of orang-pendek sightings. Sometimes the creature was described as the same size as an adult; sometimes half the size. Sometimes it was muscular, like a gorilla, other times pot-bellied. The colour of its fur was a rainbow of possibility: yellow, black, brown, red, blond, silver, grey. But it always walked on two feet.

After coming down from the volcano, Debbie started collecting stories about orang-pendek, though most of these were second- or third-hand: A friend had seen it, or the friend of a friend, or a cousin or an uncle. The guide who'd told her about it in the first place—he'd had an encounter, too. She even started venturing into the forest to look for the creature. It could, she believed, be true. "As a journalist it didn't come across as a stupid story—just as a vague story," she told me.

When she returned to England she continued her research, digging into the decades-old Dutch reports and other historical records, and contacting various experts and academics for help. "I hate unanswered questions," she told me. Still, it soon became clear that if she wanted to prove the orang-pendek existed, she'd have to go and look for it herself. So she did. She took a leave from her job and went back again in 1993 to conduct more interviews and fieldwork. Debbie was not convinced the creature was real; she was open-minded, but skeptical. She didn't want to draw conclusions before reaching the end. "I treated it as a journalist would," she said. "It wasn't like: I believe there is something here. It was: This is just too interesting."

When she crossed paths with Jeremy the following year, after returning to Indonesia for good, convinced there was a story here and armed with both a newspaper and radio contract to tell it, Debbie didn't let him know the reason she was in Sumatra, not right away. It wasn't something you blurt out to someone you've just met. And so Jeremy was left wondering who this woman was, and what she was up to.

"She was obviously highly intelligent, highly capable, didn't fit into any of the types of traveller you would imagine to find," he told me. "So I was intrigued." She'd wander off into the forest every day, he recalled, and behave "mysteriously" upon her return. Finally, one day, she showed Jeremy an acetate sheet with the image of a footprint, and asked: "What do you make of that?"

At this point, Debbie finally told him about orang-pendek, and what she was doing in Sumatra. He did not believe her right away, or believe her at all for that matter. "I've always been very skeptical about these kinds of things, and the travelling I'd done had shown me that almost everywhere has a Bigfoot-type story," Jeremy told me. "It's almost something that human beings need—to think that there's this closely related 'other' that lives in the wilderness." Confronted with another such story, he kept his guard up. "I was very patronizing," he said, "because I had heard about these kinds of things in other countries, and I didn't believe in them at all. I just didn't think something like that could still exist."

Still, when Debbie learned that he was a photographer, she invited him to come along on her search. It was an adventure. Why not say yes? And so, together, Debbie and Jeremy headed into the rainforest to find the mythical beast.

There was one problem.

"It became very clear that she didn't have a clue what she was doing in terms of looking for animals," Jeremy said. Debbie's hunting technique could perhaps be blamed on her background as a journalist—she followed the story. If someone told her about a sighting over there, over there is where she went. She was always following the animal, always trailing in its wake. This wasn't the wisest approach to finding a creature that had resisted discovery for centuries. "This animal, if it hasn't been discovered, there's a very good reason for that," said Jeremy. "It's very aware of what's going on in the forest. And us tramping along, used to being on London footpaths, suddenly crashing through the forest, Debbie chain-smoking kreteks like she did—we were fucking never going to get close to this thing!"

Instead of remaining a step behind, the key was to get out in front. Jeremy had an idea: He suggested they use a pincer trap technique—the idea being you send two people ahead if you suspect the creature is there; either it will confront the two people or, more likely, double back to where the third person is waiting.

The very next day, September 30, 1994, they were following prints up a ridge when suddenly they heard monkeys "going nuts." When animals are agitated, it often means a predator is nearby. "And then suddenly, underneath the sound of the monkeys, was a single note"—Jeremy vocalized it for me: a deep *OOO*. "And I can still see this—it's burned into my brain—Debbie and the guide looking at one another, that quick look, to say, 'That's our animal.'"

Because of the terrain, the pincer was impossible; instead, their guide Augustam, better known as Buya, went up and around, leaving Jeremy and Debbie sitting on a slope of a small valley. Jeremy thought the sound had just been a monkey—"I really, honestly didn't believe there was anything to find"—and therefore he wasn't paying attention when she saw it.

Debbie recounted the moment in the BBC documentary series *The X Creatures*: "It walked straight across the valley in front of me, thirty metres away. So close, and so clear. I didn't expect it. I certainly didn't expect to see it that clearly. And just walking between these two trees, vegetation to about hip level. This gorgeous, graceful, very strongly built primate, a big ape, walking out of a legend and into broad daylight, lit up by the sun. And the disbelief of seeing this thing, and if I'd seen it concealed in undergrowth, I could have said, 'Well, I saw something.' But I didn't see 'something.' I saw an orang-pendek walk across the valley, just thirty metres away from me."

Jeremy, unfortunately, hadn't seen it—he'd been daydreaming, he admitted, so his only view was of her reaction, which was to break into tears. "What I saw was Debbie have a breakdown," he said. "It took a few minutes before she could even really explain to me what happened."

When I asked Debbie about this moment, decades later, she told me she still wasn't sure why she'd reacted the way she had. Her best guess, she said, was that it was because "something I thought was dead turned out to be living." The sight left her unable to move. "I had a camera in my hand. I didn't take a picture."

Surprisingly, Jeremy didn't feel like he'd missed out; in fact, he still didn't really believe the creature existed, despite the behaviour and testimony of his two companions (Buya saw it, too). It was, he explained to me, "a case of cognitive dissonance." He'd witnessed their reactions, but he couldn't believe there was a bipedal ape walking around in the jungle. It was impossible. Right?

A few days later, Jeremy and Buya investigated another possible sighting, in a different area, while Debbie was in bed back at the guest house, having fallen ill. The men were walking through a field, towards the forest, when they came across a footprint. "I thought it was a human footprint and I was perplexed as to how it could be there, because . . . nobody lived on that particular mountain." Buya examined it, and told him it belonged to an orang pendek. Jeremy was, of course, skeptical; if Debbie had spotted one just the other day, and now there was evidence they lived on this mountain, too, how come it wasn't spotted all the time? They kept walking, and discovered it wasn't a solitary print: "I found a trail of these footprints going towards the forest," Jeremy recalled, as well as signs something had been feeding—half-eaten potatoes, banana pith, broken ginger stalks, like it was shopping at the market or dining at a buffet restaurant, grabbing a bit of everything, taking a bite, and tossing it away.

As they approached the treeline they heard birds mobbing something. Jeremy had heard birds do the same back in England if they spotted a hawk or owl, "so I knew there was something there," he said. "I could tell by the way these birds were extremely agitated." Then, about a dozen metres away, a loud, aggressive vocalization. Jeremy looked at Buya, whose hands were shaking, and asked: "What the fuck was that?"

Jeremy ran along the edge of the forest for about fifty metres, then slipped in among the trees, hoping to head the creature off—the pincer movement they had planned. He'd just stepped into the forest when he saw a big banana plant sway. He ducked down into the vegetation. A second later something passed by, several metres away. He was alone with the creature.

"The first thing I felt," Jeremy told me, "was fear. Because it was a wild animal, because I was very close to it, and also because it was clearly something I didn't know. But not only that; it was something that shouldn't exist."

It was like nothing he'd seen before. When he'd been in northern Sumatra he'd spotted orangutans in the wild; they were bipeds, but walked comically. This animal's gait was eerily smooth. "It was walking like a human being," he said. "I could see that it was upright and very fluid and straight and not shambling." He thought that "there was something ghost-like about it."

As for what it looked like?

"It was probably 1.5 metres tall, and extremely thick-set and well-built," he said. "It was a formidable animal." Its head was turned away; Jeremy suspected the creature was looking in Buya's direction. He couldn't see below the animal's waist, but from his vantage point got a sense of the creature's size. "That was one thing that really shocked me: I did not expect it to be as big as it was. It was still only under five feet, but nevertheless it's very bulky in its arms and its neck and everything. I didn't make a squeak because I thought, fuck me, if that thing turns around, if it's got a face like a human, I'm going to piss my[self]. But, also, what would be my threat level to it at this distance? It could cover that ground in like a second, and I might have had my head separated from my body." As he put it to me while discussing the encounter on a different occasion: "My feeling was that it was a big male that didn't give a shit."

The initial fear was soon replaced by his naturalist's instinct: What was this? The first thing to flash in his mind was *Australopithecus*, a group of primates that lived during the Pliocene and Early Pleistocene, albeit in Africa. Whatever it was, and even though the encounter was brief, he was certain it could not be confused with another known species. He put it this way: If you saw a Ferrari and a Rolls-Royce for a split second, could you tell which was which? Of course. "It doesn't sound a very impressive amount of time, but it was certainly long enough for me to take in an awful lot about this animal, and certainly to know, without any shadow of a doubt, that what I'd seen was something that's unknown to science."

The creature took off, and Jeremy was alone once again, crouching on the forest floor. "I'm not a very social person. I'm quite happy alone. But I must admit: At that moment, after I'd seen the animal and it had gone, the one thing I had to do was see another human being and tell them what I'd just seen. I've never felt that before so strongly in my life." Buya appeared, and Jeremy, still dazed, told him what he'd seen. The whole experience, from discovering the first footprint to his sighting, was over in less than an hour.

Across a nearby gully, the men could hear another group of birds mobbing the creature. Jeremy and Buya decided not to pursue; they didn't want to scare it any further, and thought it best to return later with Debbie so they could employ their pincer strategy again.

They headed back to the town, where they ran into Debbie—apparently feeling better—straight away: "I remember she just took one look at the pair of us and said, 'Oh my God, you've seen it.'"

"I look at him and he's like this," Debbie told me over lunch, making a dumbstruck face. "So, needless to say, Madame News Editor goes: 'Did you get the picture?' You know what the useless bugger said to me? He looked at me accusingly and said: 'You didn't tell me how big it was!'"

The big question was: Now what? Debbie had been looking for the creature for years and had finally seen it with her own eyes; Jeremy was new to the search, but had been altered by what he'd experienced in the forest. How could they share what they'd seen with the world? *Should* they share what they'd seen with the world? They sat around a table back at the guest house and mulled the next steps. Whatever was to come, they would do it together: "We all clasped hands over the table and agreed that nobody would do anything without the agreement of everybody else," Jeremy told me.

Not long after, Jeremy's tourist visa expired, and he left Sumatra. For a while, he considered not going back to Indonesia. *This is a secret that you have been vouchsafed*, he said to himself. *Just walk away. Leave some mystery in the world.*

"I believe very strongly in things being gifted," he told me. "I thought, 'I don't deserve this. This is something David Attenborough hasn't even seen.' And so I felt extremely humbled to have been gifted the sighting of this thing." Initially he was against publicizing his sighting, he said. The more people who knew about it, the more people who actually saw it, the less precious his gift became. "To have a story which people can't believe, but yet I know to be true, is a fantastic thing on a selfish level." He compared it to being "like a miser sitting on his pot of gold. I can gloat over having it and not having to share it."

But he had another thought, too. It was about a hike he had taken with Debbie not long after their sightings. They found themselves at the top of Mount Kerinci, with a majestic view of the countryside, stretching into the distance. Looking out at the sea of trees, they discussed how many creatures might be out there. Later that day, in the forest, they came across an illegal logging operation, too remote for the authorities to stop. Now, as he wondered whether he should return to Sumatra, Jeremy was struck by a "crusading notion." If proven real, the orang-pendek could become a mascot, "a conservation hammer" that could "stand as an ambassador for the rainforest." It would replace the rhino or tiger as the symbol for the precariousness of nature. "Forget the panda!" Jeremy said. When people talked about undiscovered things in the rainforest, this was more than could ever be hoped for—not a frog or bird, but a bipedal ape! He was certain that the world, once it knew of the creature's existence, would rally to save it. It would become a turning point in the battle to save threatened ecosystems—not just in Sumatra, but around the world.

"If something like that—an upright, bipedal, intelligent, large-bodied primate—can exist unknown, then what the hell else is in the rainforest?"

He often thought back to that conversation with Debbie on the mountain, and the decision he faced in the weeks after. He wondered how he would have reacted if someone had revealed to him, like a clairvoyant, what the next several decades of his life would look like. Would he have gone back if he'd known what the future held? "I had, at that time, no notion of spending a lifetime doing this," he said.

It was as if he'd been hiking in the rainforest and come across two paths: He could continue on, keep travelling, return to England, start a life. Or he could go back to Kerinci and see what the universe had in store for him.

"I do sometimes wonder," he once wrote to me, referring to this moment, "what other versions of me have become in other alternate quantum universes."

He jotted down a postcard to Debbie. He'd come to a decision. He would return to Sumatra.

"It's like nobody's been here at all. Nobody."

It had been four years, thanks to the pandemic, since Jeremy had last visited, though it might as well have been the first time. The camp was just a rumour, something that might have once existed, but proof of which was now hidden by tall grass and plants. At first, I figured we must still have to hike to another site, but no, Jeremy said, this was it. Nature had reclaimed a small slice of its kingdom.

The fishermen tossed our packs onto the shore and departed. Doni disappeared into the forest carrying a machete and later emerged with large branches, which he and Sonny fashioned into a makeshift cooking stove and a shelter frame, covered by a blue tarpaulin, under which they set up their tent. A small, moustachioed man in his late forties who was never without his camo bucket hat, Doni, who usually had a machete in one hand and a kretek in the other, was the de facto camp director, ensuring our expedition remained on the rails; Sonny, who barely spoke a dozen words to either Jeremy or me during our time together, a black toque often pulled down just above his eyes, had seemingly accompanied his father-in-law just for the paycheque.

Jeremy and I set up our tents, then he led me to a shallow stream, as clear as glass, from which we could collect drinking water. That first night, I left to go fill my water bottle in the creek. It was only a few dozen metres away, and I wore a headlamp. Yet somehow, after only a few steps, I made a wrong turn. Quickly, incomprehensibly so, I was lost. For a few minutes I had no idea where I was. Panic rose in my chest like a cough. Everything looked the same. I had to stop myself from yelling out. I knew I hadn't gone more than a hundred metres—it would be mortifying to call for help, so soon after our arrival. But everything was cloaked in a bottomless black, the black of a black hole,

Vantablack, and the forest was so thick I couldn't see the burning embers from the cookfire or, when I stopped walking, hear any voices—the pounding in my ears was too loud. I forced myself to commit to a direction and somehow stumbled my way back to the camp, where I kept quiet about my ordeal. No one said anything about my empty water bottle.

We fell into a rhythm. Rise with the sun. Languid conversation over kopi, so sweet that the first time Doni handed me a steaming mug and I took a sip, I insisted we'd picked up hot chocolate by mistake. Breakfast was a plate of the lake's tiny fish, fried to a potato chip–like consistency, or a heaping bowl of egg and instant noodle in a spicy broth. Just as we were finishing our meal, the gibbons would begin to hoot, a riotous, primeval call and response between the males and females that is older than the forest—I eventually spotted a couple of these animals, at a distance, high in the trees. After breakfast Jeremy often retreated to a small clearing that he used as a makeshift photography studio; afterwards we'd go for a hike through the rainforest, my eyes peeled for signs of orang-pendek. We'd return to camp in the late afternoon, and read and talk until dinner.

The darkness came early, the cicadas announcing their presence just as the sun fell. Sonny went to bed, while Doni busied himself around the camp, cutting firewood or washing the dishes. There was no cell service, of course, and I had not been disconnected from the world like this my entire adult life. I saw fireflies for the first time since my childhood, tiny stars weaving bright patterns above my head, just out of reach. It rained occasionally, and I'd lie under the tarp and slowly read the one book I'd brought with me, or gaze at the water. But it always seemed to be thundering—if not overhead then in some distant valley, its rumble travelling over the peaks and arriving at the crater lake like a warning. When it was close, the sound was like nothing I'd ever heard. It wasn't the simple boom, a single crack in the sky, that I'd heard my entire life. Here it thundered in paragraphs, almost as if the heavens were speaking, trying to convey some ancient message whose meaning I couldn't grasp. It seemed to roll and twist and bend, like sonic origami. When it was close, it was louder than my thoughts. There was one night the sound was so great and terrible and beautiful I thought it might collapse my little tent. Oddly, it was seldom prefaced by lightning.

The rainforest was otherworldly—and treacherous. On our first hike through these lush environs my boot disappeared into a deceptively deep puddle only minutes after leaving camp and, after rescuing it from the sucking mud, I had to continue along with a soaked sock. Doni led these excursions, his machete slicing a path through the brush. Our route never made sense to me. It felt like an old *Family Circus* cartoon—we were going up and back and down and left and right, and yet always heading farther away from camp. The paths we followed didn't look like obvious paths to me, but Jeremy would point to a broken stem or a barely there animal print as if they were brightly lit street signs. After a while, I began to see the signs, too.

There were leeches everywhere, although I rarely saw them before they'd attached themselves to my body. When we returned to camp, I'd spend a few minutes picking them off, leaving tiny red dots on my skin. I'd invariably miss some, and find their smushed, bloodied corpses on my legs when I unzipped my sleeping bag in the morning. It was better than dealing with rats, though, which Jeremy promised me were in great abundance.

"There's an amazing diversity of rats," he said with glee. "You'd be amazed how many species!" That included a particular type of "giant rat" he'd seen only once, like the orang-pendek. "It was fucking enormous!" He proceeded to tell me a story about the time he brought an American friend to Kerinci—a big guy, "like Chris Hemsworth," who turned into "jelly" after hearing something scratching the side of his tent. "He honestly thought it was a tiger," Jeremy laughed.

He had a seemingly endless supply of such stories. No, really. "I've got a story for everything," he told me, and he meant it. We spent more than a week together and he never repeated the same tale. There was the time he spent three months in a prison in Balochistan; the time he was arrested in Liberia on suspicion of being a spy; the time he drove for hours talking to the corpse of his friend, who had just been killed by a soldier. By his count he'd been struck down by typhoid six times, and malaria more than a dozen. ("He should be dead five times over," an ex-girlfriend, Kelly Whitlock, who lived with him in Sumatra, told me.)

"I am aware that a lot of what I say can just sound like bullshit," Jeremy admitted. "To be honest, I don't have the imagination to come up with some of this stuff."

In my previous life I served, at different times, as the books editor of Canada's two national newspapers. This meant I've had the great privilege of interviewing many of the world's foremost writers. Yet I'd met few people who were as naturally talented a storyteller as Jeremy Holden, whose tales veered wildly between funny and frightening and fantastic. His stories could fill a volume of their own, so here are a few out-of-context teasers for what I hope are the memoirs he writes one day:

"Maybe the stupidest thing I've ever said in my life: 'You want this camera you have to chop my hand off.' In West Africa that's exactly what they do!"

"I ended up being a figure of fear in that prison. The prison chief stopped coming to work because I terrorized him so much."

"I remember looking at the desert lit up by the red lights of the truck, thinking, 'This is the last thing I'm going to see.'"

"I ended up spending four days on the top of this mountain, laying in a tent, just thinking I was going to fucking die—well, actually, hoping I was going to die."

"We had someone, a mullah from the mosque, come every day to try and convert us to Islam. I met him later in prison. Because he stabbed someone."

"Halfway through, the doors burst open and there's the Chinese army!"

"When I first had malaria in India, I could speak in rhyme."

Every night, after he'd finished his stories, when the lake was calm and the sky was dark, Jeremy would set out into the forest to look for frogs. One thing I have yet to mention is that Jeremy was one of the most distinguished photographers of rare frogs in the world, and had published books about the frogs of Cambodia, where he currently lived. It was never the plan to become a photographer who specialized in frogs, as well as carnivorous plants. But he had long felt a responsibility to document, to prove, to remember things that most people had no idea existed—"this hidden diversity that no one knows about," as he put it. If he didn't, he thought, no one else would. "I'm showcasing these things, these small forgotten things, to the world."

His friend Murray Collins, an interdisciplinary environmental scientist turned entrepreneur whose company supports the conservation and restoration of forests, and who met Jeremy when he himself came to Sumatra to look for orang-pendek, described Jeremy to me as "a gentleman explorer" who "embodies the very, very rich traditions of exploration, but in the oldest form—so turning up and plunging yourself in it, entirely on your own, without any backup, and putting yourself in the middle of nowhere, and discovering things. He's really the kind of character that you would probably more likely see in a book from the nineteenth or even eighteenth century—some explorer going off with the idea of identifying new species of plants and animals in some remote part of the world." He continued: "That's what he's here to do. That seems to be his driving force. He's a seeker of things."

Sometimes I would accompany Jeremy into the forest as he sought things to photograph. He had an uncanny ability to spot tiny frogs, resting on a leaf, camouflaged, or latching onto a tree trunk, his flashlight moving from plant to tree to plant faster than my eyes could follow. He kept an eye on the path and an ear open for the chirrups and trills that might reveal their location, though, he cautioned, "they're never quite where they sound." He showed me a frog he claimed had only been seen by perhaps five people in the world, and another he said was yet to be identified by science. "I don't actually know what this species is," he said, cupping the bright green creature and depositing it in a clear plastic bag, which he left on the trail to collect on the way back to camp. He found stick insects and small lizards, too. Once, I spotted a beetle of some kind covered in white fuzz. "That's pathogenic fungus—good spot," he said to me. "It can control the brain of the insect." I'd just finished watching *The Last of Us*, about a zombie apocalypse caused by a similar fungus, before leaving for Asia. The forest was filled with things I'd rather not know about.

On our first night hunting frogs, we wandered down the main path, away from camp, until we hit a small stream. "We're now in tiger territory," Jeremy said. "We're in orang-pendek territory." Not long afterwards, the forest fell quiet. Jeremy said he didn't want to alarm me, but this is what happened when a tiger was around. I thought he must be joking but, no, he was serious, though not panicked. Still, we immediately turned around and followed the path back to camp, our headlamps cutting parallel paths in the darkness. I'd heard tigers only attack from behind, and so I glanced back from time to time, looking for a pair of eyes piercing the darkness.

"People often say you're so brave to go into these forests," he later told me. "No! Bravery and courage only can occur if you're doing something that you're scared of doing. You can't be brave if you're doing something that you want to do."

Personally, I did not want to be eaten by a tiger. But we made it back without incident, said goodnight, and retreated to our tents.

I woke up a few hours later with the immediate understanding that something was in our camp. An animal, I was certain, moving back and forth between Jeremy's tent, a few feet away, and my own. At one point, sensing it was right outside, I unlocked my iPhone, and by the glow of its screen saw the tent's thin nylon moving in and out, just above my head, as if something was pawing at it. The terror I felt at this sight was so profound as to be hilarious, which lessened the horror of the moment and allowed me, eventually, to fall back asleep, despite the fact that whatever beast was stalking our camp was still outside. The next morning, over breakfast, Jeremy cut me off before I could finish asking if he'd heard anything. Rat, he said.

On another night, we became hopelessly lost. The search started promisingly enough—I spotted the first two frogs before Jeremy, and crowed about it as if I'd spotted orang-pendek itself—until we took a path that branched off the main trail. At least Jeremy thought it was a path. When it came to an end, rather suddenly, Jeremy was confused.

We started walking this way and that, trying to pick up the trail, looking for broken branches and tramped-down grass. We kept passing what I thought was the same enormous tree, its gnarled roots bursting from the ground like a Lovecraftian monster. I asked if we should call for Doni. We did not have walkie-talkies or any other means of communication. I wasn't sure how far away from camp we were, and whether our voices would carry from wherever we were all the way to the lake. Plus, it was late, and Doni might be asleep, although Jeremy said he wouldn't go to bed until we'd returned.

We kept walking, and eventually passed the giant tree again, as if we'd made a perfect circle. I was completely disoriented, like I'd just stepped off a carnival ride. I was certain the ground sloped towards the lake, but we'd be walking downhill and Jeremy would insist we were heading away from camp. I did not understand how this was possible. I also remembered something Jeremy had told me a few days earlier: "Some people have this internal compass, and some don't. I don't have it at all."

We started breaking branches to mark our way. My voice grew more insistent, more pleading. *Maybe we should call Doni?* It was not that I thought I would die, but it was raining, and I did not relish the thought of huddling under a tree, in the forest, until sunrise. My brain couldn't fathom such an experience. Something would have snapped. I might have gone insane. *Are you sure we shouldn't call Doni?*

"HO!" Jeremy shouted.

Nothing.

"HO!"

Nothing.

"HO!"

In the distance, faintly, a response: "Ho!"

It took another twenty minutes before I saw flashlights cutting through the trees. Doni and Sonny were grinning when they found us. Jeremy seemed sheepish. I was jubilant. On the way back we discovered our mistake—we'd gone down a path that Doni had made the morning of our arrival, when he went into the forest to gather wood, not the trail Jeremy was familiar with and thought we were following. By the time we arrived back less than two hours had elapsed, but I felt like we'd been gone a week. I crawled into my tent. Jeremy said goodnight, and then headed back into the forest, to find the right path.

When he was a boy, living in a small town north of London, Jeremy built a museum in his bedroom. It comprised a rabbit's skull he'd found, some fossils, not much else. "In a way," he told me, "I'm almost the same person I was at four years old, obsessed with the natural world."

His was a childhood spent outdoors, bottle-digging and mud-larking and metal-detecting, collecting flowers and bones and the detritus of years past—Roman coins and penknives and pottery shards. "I was always in trouble for not turning up for Sunday lunch," he recalled. If there is a theme to his life, it's searching. "I've been doing this my whole life: looking for things."

He would not find what he was looking for in Bedfordshire, where he lived with his younger brother and mother and father, "a man of no imagination" with whom Jeremy had a strained relationship: "It's not as if we hated one another or something," he said. "It was just we didn't really have anywhere that fit together." His father was into classic cars; Jeremy was into romantic poetry—John Clare was a particular favourite. "I was quite a maudlin little kid when I think about it." When he was about nine years old, he was featured in the local newspaper in an article about the antique bottles and clay pipes he'd dug up around town (the headline read: "Jeremy digs digging"). His parents used to describe him as "a little old man," he said.

Perhaps that's why he still had such a strong attachment to childhood—he was living his life in reverse, in a sense. As a child, he seemed older than his age; in his middle age, some might have said he was acting like a child, though I found it to be more about trying to maintain a connection with the things he loved when he was younger. To this day, he told me, what motivated him was "impressing my eight-year-old self. That's the person I want to impress: the eight-year-old that never dreamt that he was going to do these things."

He brought up Peter Pan several times during our conversations—not because he wanted to remain "a feckless child forever," as he put it, but because he'd always resisted the trappings of adulthood. He didn't want to get married or have kids or spend his waking hours working a nine-to-five job like so many of the people he'd left behind in England. The things that interested him as a child still interested him now, and "getting married and having kids means you have to leave those things behind," he said. It was the prospect of having to abandon that part of himself—not spending the night alone in the rainforest, or coming face to face with a Sumatran tiger—that terrified Jeremy. Peter Pan represented freedom, and it was clear Jeremy equated being an adult—at least in the traditional sense—with the loss of it. "Many people tell me, 'I wish I could do what you do,'" he said. "And my best friends often say to me, 'Oh God, I'm so envious.'" He scoffed. "You wouldn't last five minutes in my shoes. You'd be a shrivelling, cringing wreck." The freedom that he'd built his life around, the freedom that his friends and others claimed to envy, was an "abyss" that only certain people could traverse, Jeremy being one of them. "There's no barriers on my freedom, which is exactly how I like it."

But to find that freedom in the first place, he realized at a young age, he had to leave home. And so when he was still in high school, Jeremy and some friends set out for the Carpathian mountains, in Romania, "to hear wolves howl." At the time, the farthest he'd been from home was Malta, where his father, a Second World War veteran who'd served in the Royal Air Force, had been stationed during the war. The plan was to take a bus all the way to Thessaloniki, in northern Greece, and then head to Romania, but they wound up in Istanbul. The city was a "revelation," said Jeremy. One of his motives to travel had been "to travel back in time," and what he found in Turkey, he said, was "what I'd always dreamt about: seeing the past." He bought a wolfskin at a market and forgot about the wolves in Romania. Instead, the friends travelled by train east across the country, to Urfa, a city near the Syrian border that was visited by so few Westerners that Jeremy claimed the young Englishmen made the local newspaper. Eventually, sick with Giardia, Jeremy made his way home to England, the wolfskin rolled up in his sleeping bag. The trip had lasted three weeks, but it changed him forever. "I was fucking hooked," he said.

He kept going—a loop of leaving and coming home. Every time he travelled, his approach was to journey one country to the east: "I didn't ever want to fly over a piece of land that I hadn't travelled." He lived on a kibbutz in Israel and toured India. Leave home, come home.

He knew he couldn't do this forever, although he wanted to. He decided to go to university. He considered zoology, but in the end chose photography, "which kind of gave me a passport, like a journalist," he said, which, for a young man wanting to see the world, proved impossible to resist. After graduating, he ventured out into a labour force still reeling from the effects of Thatcherism. His options were limited. He'd worked as a postman during university, which helped pay for his travels, but it wasn't what he saw himself doing long-term. So he told his parents he was leaving once again. "My parents were absolutely devastated that after getting a degree I was just going travelling," he told me. His father scoffed at his son's plans, and insisted he was just delaying the inevitable—adulthood. You can't live in Neverland, after all.

"He said, 'You're going to be at square one.' I said, 'Well, I'm at square one now. But I've got to do something.' No one's going to knock on the door—'Is Jeremy Holden there? We need someone to go off to explore the Sumatran rainforest. We have a feeling he might be up for it.'" What he knew in his heart he had to do, he continued, was "to go out and make something happen. And when people say to me: 'How did you get this life? How did you get this job?' I say: 'You don't get it. You have to make it.'"

Debbie and Jeremy returned to Sumatra in 1995 armed with funding from Fauna and Flora International (FFI), a British conservation organization that had agreed to cover the cost of an expedition.

"Our scientists have reported back to us and they think there is something in this," FFI's Dougal Muller told *The Guardian*. "We believe there is something there or we would not be funding this trip. If it's what we think, it could be a very significant find." (Jeremy also secured $10,000 from the BBC, which resulted in an episode in the aforementioned but eminently forgettable documentary series *The X Creatures*.) The pair, "two crackpots from the UK with no scientific credentials," returned to Kerinci and picked up the trail where it had left off.

Jeremy recalled those years with a mixture of nostalgia and frustration. In a sense, they were the best years—a period of his life when proving the existence of orang-pendek seemed a matter of when, not if. They had money—never a lot, but enough—and the backing of a widely respected NGO. They were immersed in the country, its people and culture, and most of all the quest. But he and Debbie also had different ideas as to how best to conduct the search, which was code-named Project X. Jeremy, for his part, preferred to stay in one place for as long as possible: "The more time I spend in an area, the more I understand it. The more I find. The more I can photograph. That's what I'm about." Debbie felt otherwise: "My problem always with Jeremy was: Okay, we've been here for three months [. . .] we haven't got a photograph, we need to move somewhere else."

Weeks turned into months turned into years. While Jeremy had two more "aural encounters" with orang-pendek, there was never another physical sighting. This, in turn, caused him to reflect at length on the significance of the one occasion he said he'd seen the creature.

"I don't want to get woo woo and say it's scripted, but it felt scripted," he told me. "So I have to look at it as: Why? Why did it happen? And why did it suddenly go flat? And the thing that I come up with, as a consolation, is this life I've had would not have happened but for that." What he meant by this was had they returned to Sumatra in 1995 and proven orang-pendek existed, "it would have been, 'Right: Thanks very much you two amateurs.' And I would have been a postman back in England, Debbie would have gone back to editing a newspaper, and that would have been it. So *not* finding it kept the whole thing going."

But it could not keep going forever. Jeremy could handle the lack of results—there was a seemingly endless variety of rare animals to photograph to keep him occupied—but Debbie was losing steam. As her interest in finding orang-pendek waned, a new interest emerged: the Sumatran tiger. Here was a creature that was actually known to exist, and one that could use her help as much as a bipedal ape that perhaps did not. Estimates put their number at less than six hundred in the wild, and the tigers, which are smaller than their mainland Asia counterparts, were listed as "Critically Endangered" by the International Union for Conservation of Nature. "Debbie saw herself as like the next Dian Fossey," said Jeremy, while Debbie told me that her pivot to tigers was partly related to the orang-pendek: "If we can focus on the tiger, and try to reduce the poaching, it means we're going to have people in the forest. And who knows? They might go and see this bloody animal!" In 2000, she founded and became manager of FFI's Kerinci Seblat Tiger Protection Project, and had led conservation efforts to save these giant cats ever since. (On the day we met for lunch in London, I recognized Debbie because she was the only person around whose shirt sported the picture of a tiger.) In 2015, she was named a Member of the Order of the British Empire. Even Jeremy had to admit she made the right choice: "If she hadn't started that, Christ knows whether there'd still be any Sumatran tigers." Not that she had kept away from the search completely; right before Jeremy and I had left Padang, Debbie messaged him about a recent orang-pendek sighting she'd found to be credible.

Jeremy, meanwhile, reached a crossroads in 2005. Funding for the project had dried up. Debbie was off saving the tigers. What was he going to do? He was in his thirties and chasing ghosts. He might have ended the search then and there if not for a trip to the Indonesian island of Flores to visit the cave where *Homo floresiensis* (Flores man) had been discovered a couple of years earlier. For Jeremy, definitive proof that a hominin, previously unknown to science, had walked the earth just 50,000 years ago, and only a couple thousand kilometres away, was a sign that orang-pendek could still be out there. He couldn't possibly stop now.

The problem was money. He'd moved to Phnom Penh, Cambodia, and the only way he could afford to come back to Sumatra was as an advisor or on-camera personality for low-budget documentaries and hokey reality-TV shows with names like *MonsterQuest*, where he'd play the role of a "hapless kind of fool," as he described it. He recounted his experiences with these shows with a sort of cheerful hatred, but conceded they served a purpose: They paid for him to return to Sumatra. And as long as he was in Sumatra, he had a shot at finding orang-pendek. "However unlikely, there's always a chance of walking through the forest and discovering a skull, finding footprints," he said. "As long as you're somewhere where the animal might be, there's always that chance."

He wasn't the only one looking. Orang-pendek had long captured the imagination of naturalists, biologists, and cryptozoologists. (The term *cryptozoology*—the science of hidden animals, from the ancient Greek *kruptos*, for "hidden"—was coined by the French zoologist Bernard Heuvelmans, whose 1955 *Sur la piste des bêtes ignorées* (*On the Track of Unknown Animals*) remains a landmark.) Even when Debbie and Jeremy were in the field, there were usually others looking for the creature, too.

Jeremy knew he had to step up his search. What he envisioned, in order to finally catch the creature on film, was an extensive camera-trapping program—something that would keep watching the rainforest even when he was back in Cambodia. Such a project would not come cheap. The question was who would fund it. The answer came when he received a call from a friend, who mentioned he knew a wealthy individual interested in learning more about Jeremy's work.

Christopher Foyle was best known for running the century-old bookstore chain that bears his family name, but he was also a renaissance man—adventurer, philanthropist, writer, entrepreneur. He maintained a wide range of interests (cryptids and UFOs and the paranormal among them) and was involved in a wide range of projects—particularly those that coincided with said interests.

"Life was always an adventure with my husband," his widow Catherine Foyle told me when I returned from Sumatra. "His mind was always like: What's there? What's beyond? What's possible?" What he thought was possible was a creature living in Sumatra. "My husband, I think, was convinced that orang-pendek existed."

Catherine said she had "nothing but admiration" for Jeremy, who she first met while travelling through Cambodia with her husband. "His number-one quest was to look for this creature. I respected him. I didn't think in any way was he a lunatic."

The next time Jeremy was back in the United Kingdom, he met Foyle at The Ivy, the swanky restaurant in London. Foyle asked what he'd need; Jeremy, who had hastily scribbled out a budget on the train trip into the city, estimated it would take £250,000 to cover three years—that would go to FFI, who'd need to co-sign the project in order for them to obtain the necessary permits, medical insurance, and equipment, as well as pay a team. While Jeremy asked for a three-year commitment, he was confident it would only take a year. Foyle cut him a cheque.

"People say you don't get any second chances," said Jeremy. "That was the second chance."

Early one morning, I emerged from my tent to find Jeremy setting up his camera on the shore. The landscape that day was a Bob Ross painting come to life: The lake was ice-still, the forest had seemingly turned a richer shade of green overnight, the sun cast a warm glow on the mist-cloaked water, and the peaks were partially hidden by a curtain of ghostly clouds. I sat with Doni as he tended to the cooking fire, watching Jeremy work from a distance. He wanted to capture "the glory of the forest," he said, even though he'd taken this same photo countless times over the years. He adjusted his tripod, squinted through the viewfinder, and framed the shot. You could have told me this was the first and last time he'd have the opportunity to photograph this scene, so complete was the care with which he approached the task. It was clear to me then that he loved this place, dearly.

Even if orang-pendek was the reason he returned, he had forged a connection with everything else that called the park home. During our week in Kerinci, he went to great lengths to educate me about the plant life, animals, and insects that we encountered or heard in the distance while traipsing through the forest. It was as if he wanted to convince me of the specialness of this place.

On another morning, as the sun was beginning to lighten the sky, I heard what I thought was crying. It was not an obvious, dramatic boo-hoo-hooing, or gulping sobs, but the sniffling went on for quite a while, and I had the distinct, uncomfortable sense that I was listening to someone weep.

Later, when Jeremy emerged from his tent and joined me for kopi, he offhandedly mentioned that he'd "lay in this morning feeling bleak." He'd been thinking of everything that we hadn't seen or heard, the species that seemed to have disappeared since his last visit to Kerinci. "We haven't heard the red-billed partridges," he said. There was also an endemic shiny whistling thrush that called the lake home—something that was once common but had seemingly vanished. "We didn't see a single one on any of our walks," Jeremy said. "I didn't hear one, either."

It was for reasons like this that he constantly worried about Kerinci's future. Its status as a national park meant little—it had become increasingly under threat during the years he'd been working here. On our walk from the guest house in Pelompek to the national park gates, for instance, we'd passed swamplands once frequented by elephants, which had since disappeared from the area—a 2019 estimate put their number between 900 and 1,350 in all of Sumatra, a 50 percent drop in a decade. There were farms and tea plantations and illegal logging camps and palm oil operations blighting the park, and poachers were active. In many places the treeline had been pushed back, receding like a bad hairline, forcing the animals that relied on its cover higher into the hills. It didn't matter that UNESCO had included these rainforests on a list of "World Heritage in Danger."

"There's been no effort on the part of the Indonesians to honour that accolade and protect this place," Jeremy said. "I haven't ever seen a ranger in the forest that I haven't been paying to accompany me."

There was a simple reason for this: The economics outweighed the environment. Or, as he put it to me succinctly: "Tigers don't vote. People do." Although Indonesia was a G20 nation, and cut the poverty rate in half in the first two decades of the century, the area where we were searching was still very poor, and orang-pendek were not materially improving the lives of people here (and nor were any other animal). He feared even Lake Gunung Tujuh, remote though it may have been, was not safe from development: "I dread to think when they eventually build some kind of road up there." He imagined a day when the crater lake would be surrounded by homes and filled with motorboats.

Which is why he needed to prove orang-pendek already called this place home—before it was too late. He didn't want to prove it existed for fame, or put it on display like a real-life Carl Denham, but to protect it. He wasn't doing this for "personal glory," he said. "I thought this was something we could use to make a difference. Because what more evidence do you need about the rainforest having things that we don't know than that?"

One day, we set out on a long hike to one of the peaks overlooking the lake. Eating breakfast before we left camp, I studied the mountain, trying to visualize our path, though I hadn't the faintest clue. Jeremy said there'd be tricky sections, but, from where I sat, it didn't seem like it would be that challenging a climb, especially when compared to hiking to the lake earlier in the week.

Several times over the course of the next seven hours, I thought I might plummet to my death. It rained, on and off, and although the tree canopy acted as a giant umbrella, I was soaked for most of the day. The forest floor was muddy and spongy, and I stumbled down the path like a toddler learning how to walk. Meanwhile, Doni led the way through the forest like a cat, often walking with both hands clasped behind his back as if out for a stroll in the park, while I reached out for every branch and tree root so as not to fall on my face. I was constantly out of breath. As we went higher up, the path began to take us across systems of tree roots suspended off the ground like rope bridges, or something from an Ewok village. My legs went through so many holes that Jeremy joked that's how we'd finally discover the creature—I'd crash through the roof of an orang-pendek lair. There were a few segments of the climb when I found myself pressed against the hillside, inching along, grasping at vines, struggling not to fall off the side of the mountain, though the mist made it hard to tell how high the drop would be. I mentally composed emails to my book editor about how I'd haunt them from the afterlife.

We found the bones near the summit. A rope snare, simple and unforgiving, set on the path. It clasped a femur. Doni climbed down into a crevasse off the side of the trail where the rest of the animal's bones had fallen after the body had rotted away. He picked up the skull of what looked like a dragon horse and handed it to Jeremy, who studied it in the light. "It's a serow skull. Fucking cunts." The serow is a rare, goat-like mammal found in parts of Southeast Asia; a protected species in Sumatra, where it was threatened by habitat loss, there were no solid estimates as to the number remaining in the wild. "See, look, they set that trap." He pointed to the snare. "No one's come to check it." This, he said, was what worried him most about being away from Kerinci—the moment someone like him wasn't here, someone devoted to protecting this place, poachers would feel emboldened. "Fucking cunts." He kept saying this, over and over again. I'd never seen him this upset. "There won't be many of these animals up here, so killing one is a big fucking loss." He couldn't tell how long it had been since it died, but he knew the death had been unpleasant. "How many days does it take an ungulate like that to die?" It wasn't as if they were trying to snare a serow—the snare could have caught anything that had been wandering down the path, tiger or tapir. While Jeremy sorted the bones and photographed the skull, Doni searched the area and found a dozen more snares, which he disassembled. When we got back to camp, he turned one into a clothesline from which we hung our waterlogged belongings.

We continued on. Not far along, we found the Audrey Hepburn flower Jeremy had first mentioned to me while we were crossing the lake. "There she is," he said. They were lovely, small delicate things—the pitcher cup and wings were a pinkish red, while the bonnet-like lid was white. He called them Audrey Hepburn after one of her outfits in the film *Charade*; never having seen the movie, I said they looked like handmaids, and took a few photos to send to Margaret Atwood. I was only the second Westerner in the world to see one, Jeremy said. He set up his tripod and camera. "This flower has never been photographed alive." He'd gone from blinding rage to ecstasy in a matter of minutes.

Besides Audrey Hepburn, I saw numerous things that had only just or were yet to be identified. There were still new species being discovered in the rainforest on a regular basis. So why not an orang-pendek? I'd spoken to Bigfoot researchers and Loch Ness hunters, and had always left these conversations with a profound sense of skepticism. This was different. I believed Jeremy when he described his encounter, and I believed there could be an undiscovered creature similar to orang-pendek somewhere in Sumatra. Or could have been. Even Jeremy had to admit, with the rapid loss of habitat, it's possible the creature he saw back in 1994 no longer existed, or had been pushed into a corner of the rainforest where it would never be found.

"The race is on," he said. "You've already seen how fragmented these areas are getting. How much longer can it continue to live here? Something that's shy and hidden away is exactly the kind of thing that can disappear without anybody ever knowing it was there in the first place. So that's my worry: that it will never get discovered."

His worry was not misplaced. In my heart, I knew an orang-pendek would probably never be found. But there was always a chance. The rainforest was great at hiding things, as I discovered first-hand.

A couple of days after our trip to the summit, later on in the morning I'd heard the crying, Jeremy and I were on a hike when I spotted a pair of birds, of a type I hadn't seen before, in the trees above us. When I pointed them out, Jeremy broke into a smile.

"Oh, there you go. This is the bird I was saying [had] disappeared." It was the shiny whistling thrush, alive after all. "Oh, that's good, that's good. They're beautiful things."

On our way back to Pelompek, we hiked past the guest lodge where Jeremy had first met Debbie, where he'd first heard about orang-pendek, and where, in a sense, his life truly began. It had not seen a guest in many years; the building was a burnt-out husk—its walls crumbling, its roof collapsed, tall grasses snaking through the windows and missing door. But as we walked its perimeter, Jeremy brought it to life: "This was all surrounded by trees. There were monkeys. It was fucking amazing." Here is where they had an orchid garden; here is where he would sit, writing in his journal; here was where he heard about orang-pendek for the first time, sitting at a small table, with a candle burning in the dark.

"We were sitting right there," he said, as we stood inside the lodge, where they spent the first few years of their search. "This is where Debbie first told me the word 'orang-pendek' [. . .] This was the whisper."

Later that day, I was writing on the verandah of the guest house in Pelompek, listening to the call to prayer through the loudspeakers of the mosque down the road. Jeremy was sitting with the proprietor's family, down a short flight of stairs, next to the lodge's kitchen, engaged in an animated conversation. At one point, he called me over. The owner had just shown him a picture of an alleged orang-pendek footprint he'd snapped on his phone. It was clearly made by a bear, a common mistake. "Christ knows the number of times that I went to see orang-pendek evidence on the strength of a local report and found bear footprints," Jeremy said.

But then an older woman sitting nearby piped up to say she'd seen it as a girl. She was walking with a friend through some farmland that bordered the forest when they came across a strange creature. "She says it was as tall as she is now, and about as fat," said Jeremy, translating the story for me. It was dark, and had long hair. "She said it walked very slowly on two legs." The woman mimicked how the animal walked, and how it had behaved, placing one hand on a branch and raising its other arm above its head, "like a warning." Then, "it just kind of strolled off."

It was a classic sighting.

"When you start talking to the local people, and you ask them about it—it's not a fable to them," he said. "They'll say, 'Oh yeah, my daughter saw it when she was washing some dishes.' It's always something like that."

As for me, I did not have the privilege of seeing an orang-pendek walk out of the rainforest. My closest encounter occurred the morning after Jeremy and I had gotten lost. I'd barely wiped the sleep out of my eyes when he said he wanted to show me something. When he'd gone back into the woods, after I went to bed, he'd discovered broken stems of wild ginger, just like he had the day of his sighting. We trekked back down the main trail, past the false path we'd turned off the night before, until we arrived at a stream. "I could see something had been down here," he told me. There were indeed several ginger plants, and one had clearly been disturbed—torn open, its pith turned brown, meaning it had been like this for some time. "Try and break this open," he asked me, pointing to another stem. I tried, and could barely do it. "It's not easy to do, right? And it takes quite a bit of dexterity." Could it be a gibbon? I asked. "No," he said. "Gibbons don't come down to the ground." Was it an orang-pendek? Probably not. But I was not to get any closer than this.

Standing there, I tried to imagine what it must have been like for Jeremy. What was it like to have an experience—a profound, life-altering experience—and be met with not just doubt or skepticism, but suspicion and incredulity? It must drive you mad. Jeremy was friends with countless biologists, he said, and "a lot of them don't ever ask me about this because, I think, quite frankly, they're embarrassed to hear me tell the story and not want to believe it."

There were times during our conversations when Jeremy seemed despondent, when he tossed around the word *failure* and admitted proving the creature's existence was not going to happen. After all, the camera-trapping program had turned up nothing. Then the pandemic had kept him away. To complicate things further, Christopher Foyle died in 2022 and Jeremy wasn't sure how he would continue funding the search.

"The greatest achievement in my life was seeing this animal," Jeremy told me. "And my greatest failure is not having validated it, because that was the job I set myself to do."

It wasn't that he had regrets. He'd had a fantastic career, one that had taken him around the world. He was a pioneering photographer in the use of camera traps, and had developed a reputation for getting shots of animals that had never, or rarely, been caught on film: the saola in Vietnam; the large-antlered muntjac; the Sumatran rabbit. "All through my career, I've been looking for these things that have never, ever been photographed before. And I've got them. But the one thing that I've been doing not as a job, but as a personal quest, I've failed at." It didn't matter to Jeremy how many rare animals he captured on film if the one creature he'd set out to find remained elusive. "If I don't achieve that then it becomes a massive personal failure. And my epitaph will be 'The man that failed in his life's quest.'"

But there were just as many times when he was defiant, when he insisted it didn't matter if orang-pendek remained a myth. "Even to this day, when I meet people that are skeptical, I never feel threatened or angry," he said. "If someone doesn't believe, I actually get an upwelling of secret pride." No one could take away the wild life he'd led, the memories he treasured, the stories he could tell. This was the path that he'd chosen. When I looked at the arc of his life, I realized the most monumental decision hadn't been whether to return to Sumatra to continue the search; it was to embrace the uncertainty, the unpredictability, the possibility of failure—to choose a path not marked on any map. If his encounter with the creature had a cost, the life he'd led since was a price he was willing to pay. He knew what he'd seen, even if he might not live to see the day the world saw it, too.

"If it gets discovered or not, it's not a failure," he said as we walked back towards camp, leaving the ginger plants behind. "And that's what I will take to my grave—that knowledge that I've seen this. I was gifted this. If there is such a thing as fate and intervention to give people a certain type of life, I was fucking blessed." He stopped, then turned to me and smiled. "But it would still be nice to have it found, and to be able to say: 'See, I told you.'"

And with that, Jeremy Holden headed down the path once again.

THREE

MIDDLE CHILDREN

i.

Proxima Centauri, the closest star to our sun, is located 4.2 light years from the Earth. A light year, in case the term isn't obvious enough, is the distance light travels in a year, and converting one into a common unit of measure boggles the mind: 9.46 trillion kilometres—that's *trillion* with a *T*. Light travels fast—over 1 billion kilometres per hour—but even at that speed it would take, um, 4.2 years to reach Proxima, the smallest member of the Alpha Centauri triple star system. We cannot go that fast. The swiftest spacecraft ever built is the Parker Solar Probe, which reached speeds nearing 692,000 kilometres per hour when making its closest approach to our sun. *Voyager 1*, which began its journey in 1977 and in 2012 became the first human-made craft to enter interstellar space, travels a leisurely 61,000 kilometres an hour. At that pace it would take about 75,000 years to arrive at Proxima, which was discovered in 1915 and paradoxically means "nearest" in Latin—not exactly a weekend getaway. We shouldn't pack our suitcases quite yet.

Fortunately, my trip to Tucson, a paltry 3,500 kilometres away, took far less time. An early morning flight from Toronto to Denver; a brief layover, and then onward to Phoenix; lastly, after picking up my rental car, a two-hour drive towards the Mexican border at a snail-like 120 kilometres. I arrived at my hotel before dinner.

I'd come to Arizona for a spaceship convention, specifically the seventh symposium organized by the Interstellar Research Group (IRG), the pre-eminent gathering in the world—and possibly the galaxy—for those who've dedicated their lives to leaving this same world behind.

During the long drive through the desert, a fittingly alien terrain, I'd had time to consider my motivations for coming here. Unlike learning of the existence of intelligent life on other planets, which as I've said was on my personal bucket list, I've never really had any desire to go into space myself. But I wanted to know that we could, that at some point in the distant future our species wouldn't be limited to the Earth, that we'd eventually leave the nest. To put it another way, while I never imagined myself Columbus, sailing west towards the Orient, I completely understood why Ferdinand and Isabella funded the voyage. The trip across the Atlantic, however, looked like a walk around the block compared to the intergalactic endeavours being pursued by those gathered in Tucson.

When we think of space travel, we generally think about the distance to the moon (384,400 kilometres) or the time it will take a manned mission to reach Mars (approximately nine months). But to speed past the gas giants Jupiter and Saturn, to wave goodbye to Uranus and Neptune and tiny Pluto, to venture beyond the heliosphere and push through the Oort cloud and see for ourselves what lies beyond—well, the distances are simply overwhelming. And the scientific and technological challenges—the design and construction of a suitable vessel, the physics necessary to make it work, the energy required to launch and operate it, not to mention the financial cost that weighs everything down—are overwhelming, too. "Starflight is not just very hard," wrote the astronautical engineer Eugene Mallove and the physicist Gregory Matloff in their pioneering textbook on the subject, "it is very, very, very hard!"

And yet all the people I encountered throughout the weekend—from the sober-minded scientists to the eccentric engineers—wanted to try. It pained me how much they wanted to try. As Colin Warn, a young mechanical engineer from Seattle who I met for dinner my first night in town, said to me: "It's fucking interstellar travel. Why wouldn't we want to do it?"

I am a lifelong fan of both stars—*Trek* and *Wars*—and have read my fair share of science fiction, so I figured I was adequately prepared for the conference. After all, I know the difference between an impulse engine and a hyperdrive, and at one point in my life could have told you the class of a particular *Enterprise* on sight. But, after checking into the Marriott in downtown Tucson, I experienced a small panic attack while studying the list of presentations scheduled over the next several days.

"Deceleration of Interstellar Spacecraft Utilizing Antimatter"

"Reconnecting Plasmoid Propulsion"

"Pulsed Plasma Rocket: Developing a Dynamic Fission Process for High Specific Impulse and High Thrust Propulsion"

"A Gravitational Wave Transmitter"

"Phenomenology and Capabilities of Mutually Guided Laser and Neutral Particle Beams for Deep Space Propulsion"

Individually I understood what these words meant, but when assembled in this order they might as well have been ancient Greek. All of a sudden, and for the first time in many years, I regretted not having taken a science class since grade ten.

"The flood of ideas that you're going to see tomorrow is going to be pretty amazing," said Kenneth Roy, one of the IRG's founding members, as we sat in the hotel lobby the day before the presentations. (The title of his talk was comparatively straightforward: "The Solar Shield Concept: Current Status and Future Possibilities.") The symposium grew out of a weekly dinner party that Roy and his wife began hosting in Oak Ridge, Tennessee, a small city just west of Knoxville, in 2004. The couple had been involved in the local science-fiction community for years, and the dinners attracted others who shared their enthusiasm for all things out-of-this-world: physicists and scientists and engineers and authors. Not content to simply discuss and debate the latest in space news and research, attendees started producing (and publishing) their own scientific papers, and devising (hypothetical) next-generation extraterrestrial missions. An event was the next logical step. The first-ever Tennessee Valley Interstellar Workshop, as it was originally called, took place at a decidedly terrestrial DoubleTree hotel in Oak Ridge in 2011.

"We were thinking it was going to be a one-off," said Roy, a retired engineer sporting a closely cropped grey goatee and bald head. "I never would have expected this."

The symposiums, growing larger each year, soon attracted the leading names in the interstellar community, and the group, which began to hold events outside the Tennessee Valley, rebranded as the Interstellar Research Group in 2020. Its ultimate goal was "establishing outposts throughout the solar system" and "achieving a pathway to the stars." One of the founding members, Les Johnson, a science-fiction author and senior NASA official at the Marshall Space Flight Center in Huntsville, Alabama, who I spoke to before the conference, once said that "when interstellar travel finally occurs, we want to be a footnote." (When I caught up with Douglas Loss, president of the IRG, he scoffed at his colleague's small thinking: "Footnote? Hell, we want to be a chapter!")

Kenneth Roy knew he wouldn't be around to read the book, whenever it was written, but he could still help write it. These gatherings allowed him to "give back to the future," he told me. He believed in his group's mission, that it was vital work. To Roy, interstellar travel was not simply a scientific question but an existential one, as well. "The universe is probably littered with the one-planet graves of civilizations that made the very rational choice not to go into space. Each one discovered, investigated, and remembered by the civilization that made the irrational choice," he said, quoting the writer Randall Munroe. "It's comfortable just to hang out here on planet Earth. But it seems like there's a universal dictate that you either expand or you stagnate and die. We have got to expand."

I was scarfing down a quick breakfast in the hotel restaurant before the first day of presentations, and the waiter wanted to talk about starships. He'd spotted the pass around my neck, and had connected it to the posters for the symposium plastered around the lobby: a sleek IRG-branded spacecraft, floating through a red-and-purple nebula in the star-splattered cosmos, destination unknown. He was a science-fiction fan, he said, and looked forward to the day when his sons commuted from planet to planet in rocket ships. "Not my sons," he corrected himself. "Their sons." Probably not their sons either, I told him. We're talking many, many generations from now, if ever. His face fell. "Daaaaamn," he said, then walked away with my dirty plate.

I wanted it to happen soon, too. To me, interstellar travel went hand in hand with the search for extraterrestrial intelligence; they were two sides of the same coin. If alien civilizations weren't broadcasting their existence to us, or if the folks I'd met at the SETI Institute were unable to detect any signals, it made sense to literally go out and look around. Sticking to our solar system was like buying a house and never leaving the backyard. The universe holds infinite possibilities. We should see what else is out there.

While the *why* was blindingly obvious to me, the symposium sought to answer the *how*. Over the course of two and a half days filled with warp drives and wormholes, I sat through hours upon hours of lectures and discussions—there were almost thirty presentations in total. (Only two were delivered by women; the conference skewed heavily towards facial hair.) This did not include seminars ("Terraforming Planets: Why and How?"; "The Challenge of Closed-loop and Bioregenerative Life Support for Long Duration Space Exploration"), working groups, keynote speeches, and more than a dozen technical posters on display in a small room off the lobby like a grade-school science fair featuring only the most gifted (or madcap) students.

I left a tip for the waiter and made my way to the ballroom, finding a seat in one of the back rows. There were two giant screens at the front, framing a podium with the IRG logo affixed to it. I'm not sure what I'd expected, but the decor did not feel particularly futuristic:

Anyone walking by the room might have assumed a gathering of chartered accountants.

Perhaps an accountant with an interest in Bussard ramjets sat among us, but the room was mostly filled with physicists and astrophysicists, biologists and astrobiologists, planetary scientists, philosophers, futurists, astronomers, engineers mechanical, nuclear, computer, electrical, and aerospace, and at least a couple of sci-fi authors who were mining the symposium for new material. It felt like a *Star Trek* convention, but one attended not by fans but actual Starfleet engineers. My anxiety started its countdown to liftoff. A weekend surrounded by some of the smartest people I'd ever meet—literal rocket scientists—talking about some of the most complex concepts imaginable? This was no place for an English major. All I could do was mainline coffee and try to follow along.

The day began on a strange note. The second presentation that morning—and first of interest to me—was delivered by Marc Millis. (The subject: "Breakthrough Propulsion Study—Assessing Interstellar Challenges and Prospects.") I'd spoken to Millis the previous fall; a genial man in his early sixties, he'd spent years leading NASA's Breakthrough Propulsion Physics Program at Glenn Research Center in Ohio, and had also founded the Tau Zero Foundation, a non-profit devoted to advancing interstellar flight. His hopes for the field were refreshingly modest, and I'd appreciated his level-headedness when it came to a subject that could quickly veer into quackery: "If the topic is being researched in a credible and impartial manner," he'd told me, then "that will be success even if I do not see a breakthrough in my lifetime." But now he opened his talk with an unexpected announcement: "This is actually my last career presentation. I will be retiring at the end of this month and I don't expect to do any more work along these lines." (When someone in the audience asked him about it, Millis doubled down: "I don't expect that I'm going to dabble in these topics anymore unless it's at a fictional level.") For someone researching a book concerned with perseverance, it was an ominous start.

A presentation marking the end of a career was immediately followed by one announcing a new player in the field. Alan Stern had as much credibility as anyone in the room—he'd been the principal investigator on the NASA New Horizons mission to Pluto which, for a time, was the fastest craft ever launched. Whereas the Apollo missions took three days to get to the moon, New Horizons did it in eight hours. "At that blinding speed," Stern said, "it would take over a million years to reach Alpha Centauri. Clearly we need better propulsion."

Which brought us to Helicity Space, a start-up where he now served as an advisor. The California company—"We're all about going faster and farther," he said—was developing a "game-changing" reusable fusion drive that Stern described as "electric propulsion but on steroids," the largest of which could conceivably propel an expedition that arrived at the triple star system in 117 years.

"We think this is kind of a no-brainer," he said, "other than the fact we have to develop and prove this technology."

Ah. This was the rub. The presentations were long on theoreticals, short on practicalities. Everything needed to be developed, everything needed to be proven—not on the page, but in the real world. The math always worked, we were assured; the calculations just had to be brought to life. Confidence, irrational or otherwise, was not in short supply; if I'd taken a shot every time someone claimed their work was *not* science fiction, I'd have died of alcohol poisoning.

With the propulsion systems that Helicity was in the process of developing, Stern vowed that an unmanned interstellar mission—"launched in the twenty-first century, arriving in the twenty-second century"—would soon be possible.

"And that's not science fiction," he said.

Ever since Lucian went to the moon almost two thousand years ago, we've been dreaming up ways to explore the universe. In 1638, Francis Godwin took a Spaniard "to the moone" in a chariot pulled by a flock of geese; some sixty years later Daniel Defoe employed a winged chariot to make a similar voyage. Cyrano de Bergerac, in his attempt to reach the lunar surface, constructed a "Machine which I fancied might carry me up as high as I pleased" and launched it, and himself, off a cliff.

Jules Verne imagined using an enormous gun to blast humans into orbit, Edgar Allan Poe sent a man from Rotterdam to outer space in a gigantic balloon, and H.G. Wells invented a substance called "cavorite" to fuel a journey to the heavens.

Since these early beginnings, interstellar travel has become a foundational part of modern science fiction. When I arrived at the symposium's registration table, I was handed a small gift bag. In addition to a laminated map of the solar system—handy, if I ever found myself lost in the cosmos—it contained copies of a couple of books: *The Founder Effect*, an anthology about a group of spacefarers venturing into the universe, and a novel called *Saving Proxima*, which I read in my downtime and which was more digestible than the majority of the symposium's presentations. It tells the story of an interstellar rescue mission: SETI researchers discover a broadcast originating from Proxima Centauri b, an exoplanet orbiting the star. After years of messaging back and forth, they learn the humans living there (long story) face a fertility crisis that threatens their survival, and so the earthlings launch a spacecraft called the *Samaritan*, containing tens of thousands of human embryos and a small crew, to save their cosmic counterparts.

It was highly unlikely that we'd receive a similar call for help anytime soon, so there was no urgent need to devise the technology. But that missed the point. The question wasn't: Why should we pursue interstellar technology now, said the aforementioned IRG co-founder Les Johnson, who happened to be *Saving Proxima*'s co-author. The question to ask was: Why shouldn't we?

"It's part of the nature of science," said Johnson, who in addition to writing was a space propulsion technologist and technical advisor at NASA's Advanced Concepts Office. "You want to understand what you don't understand. And sometimes that means you have to go look in places you don't ordinarily look in order to understand what's going on." That said, his curiosity was not purely scientific. "I look at this beautiful planet that we live on and I view it as a rare garden in the universe. And the rest of the universe might have other interesting places to see." He continued: "You get me out on a starry night, looking at the stars, and I'm called. I don't know any other way to describe it. I'm not crazy. It's not little voices talking to me. It's just, Oh my gosh, look what's out there! How can we *not* go explore this?"

It's one thing to fantasize about exploring the stars in fiction, it's another thing to make it a reality. The Scottish polymath William Leitch first recommended using rockets to power off-world exploration in his 1861 essay "A Journey Through Space" (though, to be fair, he also suggested hitching a ride on a comet); the first major book (at least in English) to address the subject of spaceflight, *The Conquest of Space*, was published in 1931.

"To the imaginative mind viewing the star-filled heavens and the luminous glow of the planets there is present continually a world of mystery, and the suggestion of tremendous adventure beyond the Earth," wrote its author, David Lasser. "Since the day when man discovered the planets to be worlds similar to our Earth two questions have filled his mind: How can I get there? And what will I find?"

For Lasser, who co-founded the American Interplanetary Society the same year *The Conquest of Space* was published, the answer to the first question was, as Leitch had proposed, rockets. But by the time the Space Race was underway, only a couple of decades later, researchers were already contemplating what it would take to go further.

"It was realized as early as the early 1950s that rockets were not the ultimate solution to space access," Jim Woodward, a leading physicist in the interstellar community, told me. "Blowing gargantuan amounts of garbage out the tailpipe of something to lift a small payload into orbit was not the future of space travel."

In the late 1950s, after the Russians successfully launched Sputnik, the British physicist Freeman Dyson (whose daughter, Esther, a trained cosmonaut, gave one of the keynotes in Tucson) spearheaded Project Orion, which examined the possibility of using a series of nuclear bombs to propel a spacecraft. (If you've read or watched *The 3 Body Problem* you'll have a sense of what this looks like.) The idea was deemed intriguing enough to be considered a possible backup in case the Apollo program's Saturn V rocket fizzled out, but in the end it never progressed beyond studies; the Limited Nuclear Test Ban Treaty, signed by President Kennedy in 1963, restricted the testing of nuclear weapons and thus "dampened the prospects for Orion," wrote the physicist Gregory Matloff. "[T]he success of Saturn V doomed it." Dyson and his colleagues in the field also had to deal with interstellar naysayers like Edward Purcell—yes, the same Purcell who poured cold water on SETI research. "All this stuff about travelling around the universe in space suits," he said in 1960, "belongs back where it came from, on the cereal box." Still, despite the setback, Dyson was confident it was only a matter of time before humans traversed the stars, predicting that "barring a catastrophe," humans would embark on their maiden interstellar voyage in two hundred years.

At the end of 1972, humans left footprints on the moon for the last time; the following year, on the other side of the Atlantic, a small team connected to the British Interplanetary Society (BIS) launched Project Daedalus. Named after the Greek craftsman who designed the wings that his son Icarus used to fly too close to the sun, the project's goal was to design, using current or near-future technology, a mission that would reach Barnard's Star, almost six light years away, in a human lifetime. They published their final design, a nuclear fusion–based propulsion system, in 1978. (A follow-up study, Project Icarus, was launched by the BIS in conjunction with the Tau Zero Foundation in 2009.)

At the same time the British team was moving ahead with its study, the trailblazing sci-fi author and physicist Robert L. Forward was making a case for American involvement. In 1975, he stood before a subcommittee of the U.S. House Committee on Science and Technology, as it was then known, to push for an interstellar program that would see probes travel outside the solar system by the year 2000, with human-manned missions to begin twenty-five years later. It was an audacious goal, but Forward understood the reality. There would be no progress without funding, which he believed had to be on par with the U.S. lunar program. "To travel to the stars will take years of time, gigawatts of power, kilograms of energy, and billions (if not trillions) of dollars," he conceded in the pages of the *Journal of the British Interplanetary Society* the following year. "Yet it can be done—if we wish to."

Three decades later, with the likes of Jeff Bezos (Blue Origin), Elon Musk (SpaceX), and Richard Branson (Virgin Galactic) increasingly important players in the space industry, it was becoming likely that private citizens, not politicians, would lead the way. I was reminded of this when, in Tucson, I ran into Pete Worden, a retired U.S. Air Force brigadier general and former NASA administrator. For almost a decade he'd run the space agency's Ames Research Center, during which time he'd helped launch, in partnership with the Defense Advanced Research Projects Agency, the 100 Year Starship project, which sought to make interstellar travel a reality within a century's time.

"It's a dream that I've had since I was a kid," he'd told me the previous year. "For me, I don't need any more justification than that. It's sustained me for seventy-one years now."

After retiring from NASA he became executive director of the Breakthrough Initiatives, the Russian-Israeli billionaire Yuri Milner's ambitious suite of long-shot, but well-funded, scientific challenges, which not only included Breakthrough Listen for SETI but Breakthrough Starshot, a $100 million research program devoted to interstellar travel. This made Worden one of the most popular people in Tucson; every time I spotted him it seemed he was surrounded by conference-goers trying to have a word with him about their work.

We sat for a while in the lobby one afternoon, talking about the progress he'd seen in the field over the years, which had transformed from "speculative, fruitcake stuff" to a "professionally accepted" subject worthy of scientific pursuit. What hadn't changed was the need to find money. "One of our objectives is to try to get other high-net-worth funders," he said.

Abandoning the quest to the private sector, and the whims of billionaires, felt short-sighted. This was a bigger project than any one person could fund. Which politician would make the modern-day version of Kennedy's 1962 speech at Rice University that promised the world a man on the moon? ("The most hazardous and dangerous and greatest adventure on which man has ever embarked," the president said.) True, it wasn't as if NASA didn't dedicate funds to interstellar projects—many of those in Tucson had benefited from the agency's Innovative Advanced Concepts program—but it represented a tiny percentage of their overall budget. Why wasn't interstellar travel (along, of course, with SETI) NASA's number one priority? Forget Mars—Mars is boring; you can see it with the naked eye. We needed to embrace bigger thinking. We needed universal thinking.

But universal thinking requires a different mindset. You might start off with a dream—interstellar travel, within your lifetime. At some point, you realize the scale of the challenge, and eventually you must make a choice. You can continue down this road, knowing you'll never reach the end, or you can stop. It's much easier to stop. To continue requires sufficient motivation. Instead of thinking about yourself, you start thinking about the people who will come next, and your goal becomes helping them one day achieve the goal that you will not. You design the spaceship, but you don't get to take it out for a spin.

To people like Les Johnson, this was a feature, not a bug. It didn't bother him that although he could describe it on the page he'd never see a Proxima Centauri sunrise; that he'd devoted so much of his life to something he wouldn't get to experience himself.

"There is more to life than just me," he said. "And I think that the goal of enabling people that I'll never meet, descendants of people living today, to be able to walk on a planet circling another star, and explore it, and see more of the universe that I believe was created by a God—to me, it only makes sense. So I've never felt sad that I won't see it." He paused, then asked me a question: "I don't miss being alive in the time of the dinosaurs, do you?" I most certainly did, but bit my tongue and let him carry on: "I wasn't here then, I won't be there in the future. I'll just do what I can today to make that future happen."

The patience of these people! It was humbling, I had to admit, and made me question my own values. I wanted to be a reasonable person, but I wanted a fucking warp drive, too. It *was* unfair! The mountains had been climbed, the oceans had been probed, the islands all mapped. There was nothing left but the stars. And they were inaccessible to us. Unlike with SETI, where I remained optimistic there might be a breakthrough in the coming years, I was certain that no one alive today would still be around when we finally touched down on Proxima Centauri. If its denizens needed saving anytime soon, they were on their own.

When I bemoaned this point to Matthew Gorban, a bespectacled, curly-haired doctoral student from Baylor University I was having breakfast with one morning in Tucson, he mentioned an anonymous quote that summed up my feelings exactly: We are the middle children of history, it goes. Too old to explore the Earth, and too young to explore the stars.

"That really resonates with me," he said, then added: "It *is* a little bit depressing."

At twenty-five, Gorban was the youngest of the conference's presenters (topic: "Controllable Mass Propellantless Propulsion Drive: A Gendankenexperiment") by at least a couple of decades. I'd reached out to him because I'd wanted to talk to someone at the start of their career, someone who'd gone into the field knowing success would only come afterwards; someone who was standing at the starting line knowing they'd never reach the end. He would not be zipping around the solar system in spaceships anytime soon. When I'd emailed him a few weeks prior to introduce myself, and tell him about the book, he'd written back excitedly: "It's funny, I believe I have spoken those exact words 'won't be accomplished in my lifetime' before." Now, as we lingered over second cups of coffee, I asked him again: Why was he starting a race he knew he'd never finish?

"My dreams of going into space and exploring the cosmos are so strong that even if I can't do it, I want that to be a reality for someone else at some point," he replied.

To help make that a reality for someone else, at some point, at some unknowable time, he was approaching his life and his work in a very deliberate way. Imagine all human knowledge is represented by a circle, he said. Physics, which he studied, was one part of the circle, and his own research was just one tiny section within that. What he wanted to do, in his life and in his work, was simply enlarge that circle, even if just a bit. If he could accomplish that much, help humanity inch ever closer to the stars, it would have been worth it.

"We're not going to be making these leaps and bounds where the circle now becomes twice as large," he told me. "That's not how science works, that's not how the pursuit of knowledge works. It's these incremental steps. And someone's got to make that first step, so that someone can make that second step."

Maybe my problem was that I thought there was a finish line. That once the goal was reached it would be over, a box that we could check off and move on: interstellar travel, complete. But Gorban believed that was not how we should look at it. There was always going to be a next step. There was never going to be an end. We'd never acquire all the knowledge in the universe. There would always be new science to pursue, new technologies to perfect. Think of the automobile, he said. We didn't stop at the Model T.

"Nothing is ever going to be done," he told me. "That's not how we work. Humanity's not ingrained with the ability to stop. We don't know how to stop. And I think that's what really drives me. Even if I may not be able to say I'm going to make a space engine that can take us to Alpha Centauri, that was never the end goal. Even if I want to get to Alpha Centauri, it's always going to be: How can I improve this better, to go even further? We always want to go further and further."

While interstellar travel was the focus, the symposium ran the gamut of far-out ideas and concepts, from constructing habitats made out of mushrooms to cryopreservation to using solar shields to combat climate change to the benefits of building a radio observatory on the far side of the moon. (I had no doubt the folks in the SETI community would appreciate this last one.) One day at lunch I listened to a lieutenant colonel deliver a talk about the United States Space Force; when he polled the room about what this branch of the armed services needed to have by 2040, answers included ion blasters and a Death Star.

While the presentations were brain-melting, the conversations during coffee breaks, at mealtimes, and after-hours were just as interesting. One night at dinner I sat beside Mark Shelhamer, a professor at the Johns Hopkins University School of Medicine and director of the school's Human Spaceflight Lab. ("A medley of Marks," he said when I introduced myself, and then grabbed me a bourbon; I was quite fond of him.) For several years he'd served as chief scientist of NASA's Human Research Program at the Johnson Space Center, and was in Tucson to deliver a keynote address on the effect of interstellar travel on the human body. (Specifically: "Challenges to Crew & Mission Health & Performance in Ventures Beyond Near-Earth Space.") At conferences like this, he told me, all the discussion revolved around spaceships. No one actually thought about how, and if, humans could survive such a long journey.

"There's a tendency to talk about how to build a better rocket, how to do something faster, how to concentrate on the technology and the engineering and the machinery," he said at the start of his talk a couple of days later. "The people should not be an afterthought that you stick in after all the engineering design work has been done."

At another point, on the first day of the symposium, I found myself debating the merits (and legality) of salvaging space junk with IRG president Douglas Loss and a few others during a recess.

"Everybody's talking about material in space that needs to be deorbited," said Loss. While he thought it would make perfect "feed stock" for future missions, the problem, he continued, was that "everything, down to every bolt, is owned, by treaty, by the country that authorizes it to send it. So you can't just grab that bolt and reuse it, unless they agree to it."

"Suppose you did it," said Jeff Greason, a veteran electrical and aerospace engineer, and the chairman of the Tau Zero Foundation. "You grabbed an expended second stage, but it doesn't belong to your country. Great. They take you to court. What are the damages? It's an expended asset! It has, if anything, a negative economic value."

"Except that if you take it and reuse it you've created economic value," Loss pointed out.

"What you do is you grab somebody else's junk and you de-orbit it," said Greason. "You do that enough times and the precedent has been established." Loss laughed, but Greason went on: "If you're at all smart about it, you would establish the customary practice that permits international salvage. The real problem is there's no customers."

The goal, said Loss, should be to produce "modular" spacecrafts from pieces already floating in orbit. "Need an Earth-sensing satellite? Oh, well then you need modules A and G and F. We'll just bolt them together, and there you go."

"It's even better, because in the geo-graveyard orbits, which are part of valuable real estate you'd like to clear, the mass up there is literally mostly solar panels from old geo-satellites," said Greason. "And the number-one thing you need on the moon is more solar panels." He added: "They're degraded—they're 50 percent or less of their original power capacity, but they're right there."

"Fifty percent less is still 50 percent," said Loss. "If you could figure out a way to approach the governments who have responsibility for them and say: You have these—we won't call them assets—these things in orbit that you are getting very bad international publicity from. We will take them off your hands for a very low price. You just pay us ten dollars on the kilo."

"There's a company in the U.K., Astroscale, that's doing this now," said Andrew Higgins, a mechanical engineer from McGill University in Montreal who was sitting with us, and whose presentation the following day was on "Dynamic Soaring as a Means to Exceed the Solar Wind Speed." He was not convinced it was a realistic option. "I'm pretty pessimistic on this. Go try and sell your iPhone 6 on Craigslist and see what you get for it."

"You'll get something," said Greason.

"Not much," said Higgins.

"But you'll get something," said Greason again.

Coffee cups empty, we went back to the ballroom. Greason was presenting soon. I'd first come across his name in the 2002 book *They*

All Laughed at Christopher Columbus, by the journalist Elizabeth Weil, about American rocket designer Gary Hudson's quest to create a single stage, reusable spaceship; Greason had overseen the propulsion team at Hudson's company, Rotary Rocket, and now ran his own shop.

"I need to review some things that you already know, but it sets the context for where I'm going with this," Greason said as he kicked off his talk on "wind-pellet shear sailing." "Interstellar travel is fundamentally a problem because the energies involved are huge," he said, as a slide labelled "Interstellar Travel Review: An Energy Problem" appeared on the screens. Current popular ideas, whether beamed energy or anti-matter or fusion, were not feasible from an energy or financial perspective, he said. His idea—and Jeff, if you're reading this, I'm so sorry I've dumbed it down to this degree—was to harness the velocity difference ("shear") between two streams of matter, in this case aerographite pellets and interstellar winds, to propel a spacecraft. "The magic answer here is if you're running into two matter streams, and you are running into them at different speeds, you want to extract energy from the fast one, and you want to push on the slow one." Think of it as an interstellar roadway, with the fuel (i.e., the pellets) sent ahead first. (In my defence, I just want to point out that one of his slides read: "If you find this confusing, you aren't alone.") Greason ended his presentation by outlining a proposed mission, at the bargain price of $600 million, that would take a ship, reaching 20 percent the speed of light, to Alpha Centauri in twenty-seven years, with data transmitted back to Earth four years later. "Thirty years is a short enough time that the principal investigator of the project can still be alive to collect the Nobel Prize," he said.

I caught up with Greason again after the first day of presentations was over, and we spent an hour in deep conversation about his life and work, and the path that had brought him here to Tucson. I was still feeling scrambled by what I'd seen, and it's possible he saw it on my face.

"People who are not technically educated often see it as this big, magical enterprise that's beyond them," he told me. "That's just not true. If you really understood high school physics, you can check most of the things that were talked about. It's not that abstruse. You just have to not be afraid to dive in and do the math yourself." (I did not tell him that I had not taken high school physics and therefore could not do the math myself, even if I lived to be three hundred years old and witnessed the dawn of interstellar travel.) With that in mind, how could we determine what showed legitimate promise—the technologies that my great-great-great-great-great-great-grandchildren might one day have at their fingertips—and what would remain in the realm of science fiction? After all, Greason said he had a good "bullshit detector" when it came to this stuff.

"Every idea is interesting, but not every idea is useful," he answered. "The trick is: You don't ever want to throw things out just because you haven't seen them. You don't want to throw things out just because it sounds like it couldn't work. You don't want to throw things out just because it seems too good to be true, although too good to be true is at least a big yellow flag which should prompt you to look closer, because most things that look too good to be true probably are—but not certainly are. You don't even want to throw them out because they're challenging the orthodoxies of physics.

"Challenging orthodox physics should be encouraged," he added, "because if you don't challenge it you don't make any progress. But that doesn't change the fact that most people who challenge physics will lose."

Still, there was a difference between challenging physics and ignoring science altogether. And I couldn't help but notice that there was a slight spiritual bent—a belief in faith, a sense of wonder—underlying some of the presentations, this feeling that some of the speakers seemed to value reverie over reality. The words *Alpha Centauri* were often spoken in reverential tones, as if in reference to some far-flung celestial paradise, and anytime someone mentioned *C*, the symbol for the speed of light, I recalled parishioners in my childhood church uttering "amen."

"I have noticed that there is a surprising number of people in the interstellar community that are quite religious," said McGill's Andrew Higgins when I caught up with him again after the conference. It sometimes reminded him, he told me, of his childhood growing up in the American Midwest, at the top of the Bible Belt. "Everybody wants to be part of something bigger than they are," he said. "For most people that need is satisfied by religion." In the interstellar community, however, you had researchers who believed in mathematics and science. And then you had a group pursuing what Higgins called "alt physics"—although *miracles* was perhaps a better word. "There's kind of a bifurcation between these two communities," Higgins told me. "And I've noticed, particularly among the community of people that work on these alternative physics approaches, there's a remarkable number that are people that are pretty open about their Christianity, which in hard science and engineering fields is usually not the case." He mulled it over: "I don't know what to make of that. I've always suspected that people that are religious might have a belief that maybe God's willing to make a special exception for us. Maybe God has woven into the fabric of reality a little something that we might be able to get purchase on that actually would allow us to go to the stars."

Even as a non-believer, it made sense to me. If prayer was all it took to get to Alpha Centauri, you'd find me in church every Sunday. But, as was made incredibly clear to me during my time in Tucson, we were going to need much more than that.

After saying goodbye to Jeff Greason, I took a walk to clear my head and try to digest everything I'd heard. The air was dry, the sun was falling, and the streets were filling up with college students emerging from their dorms like drunken cicadas. The city felt a bit like Mos Eisley spaceport, a bustling urban oasis surrounded by desert. Coincidentally, when I got back to my hotel room later that night a *Star Wars* movie was playing on TV. I put down the remote and let my brain focus on X-Wings and other vehicles that didn't require a graduate degree to understand. But although I'd seen the film countless times before, the spaceships now seemed different to me, like watching a magic trick after learning how it's done. Do you have any idea how much energy it would take for an Imperial Star Destroyer to make the jump to hyperspace?

Eventually I fell asleep—a deep, dreamless slumber, like I'd been put in cryogenic storage on a starship speeding through the galaxy.

ii.

"We built beautiful cathedrals, hundreds of years ago, and they took multiple generations to achieve—in some cases multiple centuries," said Harold "Sonny" White, an aerospace engineer on a video call with me from his office in Houston. "The teams that were building the basement, the foundation, they never saw the finished product. They could only imagine in their head what it might look like. But they knew they had to do their part, however small it was. They knew they had to do their part so that the next generation after them could do their part, and the next generation could do their part. Through the willingness to contribute, in that way, across time, they were able to realize something incredible. So, to me, the whole noble goal of enabling interstellar flight—I don't know if we'll get it done in fifty years. I don't know if we'll get it done in five hundred years. But I know it's something we need to strive for."

Which is why, one morning that same week, White invited a group of interstellar strivers together to discuss how to make it to the stars. A NASA veteran who served as the agency's advanced propulsion theme lead, he was now director of advanced research and development at the Limitless Space Institute, a Texas-based non-profit whose motto was "infinite possibilities come to those who believe."

"It certainly takes a lot of imagination to try and think about what's beyond what we know and what we understand," he told the roughly two dozen people gathered on Zoom. "We're out in the unknown and there's no textbook, if you will, to help figure out some of the things we're trying to figure out."

The occasion was a chance to hear from the first-ever recipients of the institute's Interstellar Initiatives Grants—another example, like the Breakthrough Initiatives, of private money stepping in where public money was lacking. The hope, said White, was that this funding would help the institute achieve its mission: "Our pinnacle objective, our big, hairy, audacious goal—I call it a North Star, if you will—is to ideally enable interstellar travel by the turn of the century."

Over the next six hours the scientists and engineers from around the world, who'd been awarded between US$100,000 and US$250,000, gave brief overviews of their work. There was "centrifugal confinement direct-drive fusion propulsion" and "origami photonic crystal snails with machine learning" and a talk about "assessing the viability of vacuum-based propulsion with hydrodynamic quantum field theory," something called HELIO-X, which was "inertial confinement fusion code for advanced space propulsion," and, oh yeah, wormholes. Specifically "traversable wormholes."

The first of the Limitless presentations was delivered by a man named Philip Lubin, who'd received a grant for a proposal titled "Directed Energy for Revolutionary Space Propulsion and Power Projection," and whose work I was already familiar with, even if I couldn't fully understand it. White gave a brief introduction, then turned the floor over to Lubin, whose head and shoulders appeared in front of a blue-tinged silhouette of the Earth, like a bearded, bespectacled alien appearing on the viewscreen of the *Enterprise*.

"I will, in the spirit of going incredibly fast, also go incredibly fast through these slides," Lubin said. Then, for the next twenty minutes, he provided an overview of direct energy propulsion, which one of his slides championed as the only known path to interstellar flight.

The interstellar community sometimes struck me as a coalition of mad scientists, each working on their own wild theories and pet projects. While they sometimes dismissed the work of a peer—why was I bothering to talk to *him*?—for the most part they all seemed supportive of one another's work. They were, after all, pushing the same boulder up the hill, and the more muscle they assembled the faster they'd reach the top. But whenever I asked who was the closest to success—who might actually achieve the dream—it was Philip Lubin's name I most often heard. One leading figure in the field described him to me as "the modern-day Goddard," conjuring the name of the inventor of the first liquid-fuelled rocket.

And so, a few weeks after leaving Tucson, I made another trip—cross-continent, not interstellar—to California.

Because I'm Canadian, and thus celebrate Thanksgiving in October like God intended, when I booked my flight it didn't occur to me that my late November trip would coincide with America's version of the holiday. The campus of UC Santa Barbara, where Lubin worked as a professor of physics and served as the director of the Experimental Cosmology Group, among other roles, was gorgeous and very much deserted. I walked along the Pacific Ocean, which hugs the campus, and eventually made my way to Broida Hall, where the physics department is housed. Lubin told me to meet him in Building 937, one of several beige modular units that had been set up outside. "The world gets changed here," read a sign next to the front door.

I had spoken to Lubin several times at this point, but this would be our first time meeting. My visit to Santa Barbara was only necessary because he'd skipped the IRG symposium at the last minute, though I got the sense he hadn't been terribly sad to miss it. (As Andrew Higgins, who'd once spent a year in Santa Barbara working alongside Lubin, told me: "Phil is always emailing me saying, 'Andrew, get rid of all this science-fiction stuff at the symposium. We have to make this a more serious meeting.'") In a drab conference room that reminded me of where I took driver's ed classes, Lubin was cramming in one last meeting before the holiday. Joining him in person were a couple of colleagues: Nicholas Rupert, his team's engineer, and Prashant Srinivasan, a project scientist. Appearing on the screen at the front of the room were perhaps a half-dozen grad students and postdocs whose faces materialized and vanished at random.

"We have an author," Lubin said, introducing me, "so we have to be on good behaviour."

The group spent the next several hours discussing projects, ranging from a rover they were working on for NASA to planetary defence, another of Lubin's myriad interests (if you want to know more about this subject, skip to chapter 8). If this was an example of good behaviour, I could not imagine what the meeting would have been like if I hadn't been present. They were "no holds barred. You can say anything, within certain limits," Lubin told me afterwards. "It gets nasty sometimes." Lubin's role was a mix of traffic cop and therapist—"He has the patience of a saint," said Srinivasan—and he sported a gruff, no-nonsense demeanour, though it was obvious he was well-attuned to his team's needs, and genuinely welcomed their insight. A dictator he was not. "Phil lets everybody have their say," Srinivasan told me during a break. "He values everybody's point of view." He was almost seventy years old, but he might have been the only person whose energy didn't flag over the course of the afternoon.

Afterwards, the four of us headed to a dinner at a nearby Thai restaurant, where the men quizzed me about my book and Canadian Thanksgiving traditions, and asked what I'd thought about the IRG conference in Tucson the previous month. As Higgins had warned me, Lubin was not exactly a fan of the event.

"I'm never going to one of those again," he said between bites of basil chicken, then made a crack about warp drives. Many of the participants, he continued, "are more, I would say, dream-based than physics-based, and that's why I have a hard time. For me, it's just mathematics—either it works mathematically and physically, or you're saying I have to invoke a new theory of physics." He called such folks "crystal" people. "There's all kinds of people out there who approach this from a highly non-scientific point of view, and it's all sort of PR-driven." They made promises that wouldn't—that couldn't—be kept. They were purveyors of science fiction.

Lubin, on the other hand, traded in fact. He was a serious scientist, not a showman. It wasn't as if he kept quiet about his interest in interstellar travel—when you googled his name a top result was his TED Talk, "How humanity can reach the stars"—but he preferred to work in obscurity, or at least out of the spotlight. Having "too high of expectations can be a very detrimental thing," he said. "That's why I'd rather keep a lower profile," he added, "rather than have people say, 'Come on, man, it's been five years. Why aren't you ready?' Well, we never said we'd do it in five years."

I could tell that Rupert and Srinivasan, his colleagues, were wary of me lumping Lubin in with the crystal people; I felt them sizing me up over dinner, trying to figure out if I was going to portray their boss as a quack or a crank. (To be clear, he is neither.) It was obvious they were protective of the man and his work, and also in awe of him, too. At one point earlier that afternoon, when Lubin had momentarily left the classroom, Srinivasan leaned forward across the table, and motioned for me to do the same, like he was about to tell me a secret.

"I must say that he is a visionary, and he is ahead of what we think is possible."

At one time, Philip Lubin wanted to be an astronaut. He was serious about it, too, making it so far in the selection process as to be invited down to Johnson Space Center in Houston for a final round of trials. For one of the tests, to determine how they handled small spaces, the candidates were forced to spend an hour curled inside a personal rescue enclosure—a spherical escape pod measuring a claustrophobia-inducing thirty-six inches in diameter. "I went to sleep inside there," Lubin recalled. "It was very comfortable. It was quiet and dark and peaceful and no one was bothering me."

Although he was ultimately rejected for medical reasons, and knew that he would never go into space, Lubin still wanted others to have the opportunity to do what he could not.

"There's something inside of us which is driven to explore," he told me the first time we spoke. "Sometimes not-so-good consequences come from that. But I think there are more noble reasons." One of them was to distribute ourselves throughout the galaxy, especially if it turned out we were the only intelligent life around. Our efforts, at the very least, would serve "as a memory that we were there," he said. He knew it was illogical, especially if we were on our own—why leave evidence of our existence if there's no one else around to remember us? But just because something is illogical doesn't mean it's not worth pursuing, he said. "People are illogical creatures, you know? Why do we like art? Why do we watch the sunset? The sunrise? Why do we lay down on a grass field? Why do we fall in love?"

Why did Lubin do the things he did? He could trace it back to a time before he was born. He grew up in Los Angeles, the son of a secretary and a postal worker. His father hailed from a small town in Lithuania and was able to escape just before the start of the Second World War. His mother came from Odessa, and moved to America around the same time. Both his parents were Jewish, and many of their relatives were murdered in the Holocaust. "There's a whole lot of trauma in our family," he said. "Most of our friends were concentration camp survivors." He was certain that the intergenerational trauma he absorbed during childhood shaped how he approached science later in life. He used math and physics as a shield, in a sense, to protect himself from "the reality of the world," which had come across to his younger self, he told me, as "this very dark, dangerous, easily disturbed place that could explode at any point." In these two disciplines Lubin said he found "an idyllic world that I wish existed for everybody," and he came to view one of his goals in life as making sure something like the Holocaust never happened again.

"One cannot close one's eyes," he told me. "One has to be a sentinel in life, and always look for those things which are terrible for others."

Lubin began devouring back issues of *Scientific American*, *Popular Science*, and *Popular Mechanics*, and soon developed a fascination with electronics and electrical systems. He haunted rummage sales and scouted surplus stores for old military equipment, radios and transistors that he could take apart and put back together, among other things. "I loved to blow up things as a child," he said.

Despite his bookish nature, he never intended to go to college. "College was for other people, and I wasn't one of those people," he told me. His parents believed he wouldn't be accepted, anyways, because he was Jewish. Instead, he signed up for the military, but his plans were thwarted when his parents refused to sign the enlistment papers—they had lost so many people in the war, after all—and since he was only seventeen, he could not join on his own.

One day, near the end of his senior year, he ran into a guidance counsellor, who pulled Lubin aside and asked what he would do when high school was finished. When he learned of Lubin's lack of plans, he pushed him towards a local community college; Lubin reluctantly enrolled.

"I would lock myself in the library, or lock myself in my room, and just read, read, read," he said. "I didn't go to dances and didn't participate in the normative things." Instead, he listened to classical music, and built motorcycle engines for fun. (At one time, he owned a Kawasaki Mach IV, once described as the most terrifying bike in the world. It wasn't that he had a death wish, he told me. "It was that life is fatal to everybody, and you need to push your boundaries and see how far you can go.")

He was an excellent student, and his teachers encouraged him to transfer to a more academically rigorous institution. He wound up at UC Berkeley, where he earned degrees in both math and physics, and then applied to grad school. He couldn't afford to visit any of the campuses (with the exception of nearby Caltech) before making his decision where to go, so Lubin flipped a coin—Harvard or Princeton—and set out for Massachusetts.

The next few years were spent bouncing from coast to coast and starting a family. (He had four kids, who at the time of my visit ranged from in their early thirties to mid-forties.) After two years in Cambridge he returned to Berkeley, where he earned his Ph.D., and then did a stint teaching at Princeton, before coming back out west and eventually landing at UC Santa Barbara, where he founded the Experimental Cosmology Group. (Most of Lubin's papers were in the field of early universe studies, exploring the Big Bang and how everything came to be: "A lot of it is this existential question: Where do we come from? Where are we going? Why are we here?")

It was an existential question that led him to interstellar travel. What would we do if the Earth was threatened? At Berkeley, Lubin had befriended Luis and Walter Alvarez, the father-son duo who were first to theorize an asteroid strike had killed off the dinosaurs. Lubin wondered what would happen if the planet was threatened by such an event today. How would we defend ourselves? He was attending a planetary defence conference in 2009 when he came up with the idea of a direct energy–based system—lasers pointed at the sky. It didn't take him long to realize you could potentially propel spacecraft using the same technique.

Light doesn't just illuminate; it "carries energy and momentum," as Lubin put it. Turn on a flashlight and point it towards the wall in a darkened room; it's not just brightening the room, it's pushing the wall. His idea: What if you took a laser—on Earth, in orbit, on the moon—and focused it on a craft outfitted with a light sail? (Light sails, or solar sails, have long been a popular concept in the interstellar community; way back in 1610 the German astronomer Johannes Kepler wrote to Galileo that "given ships or sails adapted to the breezes of heaven, there will be those who will not shrink from even that vast expanse" and the history of interstellar research is littered with similar proposals.)

Of course, you'd need more than a single source; you'd need many, many lasers, synced together. Group them in a giant array the size of, say, a small city—a phased array—and direct it towards a tiny, lightweight craft outfitted with cameras and sensors and other technology necessary for rudimentary exploration. You're in business. Relativistic speed is possible.

In a talk, Lubin put it like this: "This is a lot like sailing on the ocean. When you're sailing on the ocean you're pushed by the wind. And the wind then drives the sail forward through the water. In our case, we're creating an artificial wind in space from this laser array, except the wind is actually the photons from the laser itself—the light from the laser becomes the wind upon which we sail."

In theory, you'd be able to propel the craft—and again, we aren't talking about something that can carry humans, at least not yet—to about 25 percent the speed of light. This meant, theoretically, we could reach Proxima Centauri in less than twenty years.

"There's zero uncertainty about the physics in Phil Lubin's work," Andrew Higgins told me. "Whether they can make the phased array, the light sail—that's all engineering problems. But the physics is known."

This was a versatile technology that Lubin believed should be pursued even if it wasn't used to travel to the stars anytime soon. He offered some examples: It could allow for faster travel within our own solar system; it could remotely power space stations or off-world bases (say, a colony on the moon or Mars); it could be a tool for removing space junk; it could be used for planetary defence.

It was actually Lubin's work in the field of planetary defence that caught the attention of the interstellar community. On February 14, 2013, UC Santa Barbara issued a press release for a project called DE-STAR (Directed Energy Solar Targeting of Asteroids and ExploRation), which could theoretically help defend the Earth against objects hurtling towards us from space but could also, Lubin knew, power an interstellar space mission. The next day, in what could only be called a cosmic coincidence, the Chelyabinsk meteor exploded above Russia. Lubin immediately became a sought-after speaker on the subject, giving dozens of presentations in the months that followed.

It was through these talks that Lubin was introduced to Pete Worden, the NASA bigwig with a reputation for out-of-the-box thinking I'd met in Tucson, and who laughed when recalling his initial encounter with Lubin: "At one of the 100 Year Starship meetings, Phil Lubin came up to me and said, 'Look, I understand you guys are interested in interstellar stuff. I know how to do it.' I don't know if you've talked to Lubin? He's a very confident guy." Lubin subsequently sent Worden a paper titled "A Roadmap to Interstellar Flight," which had built on his DE-STAR concept, here called DEEP-IN (Directed Energy Propulsion for Interstellar Exploration).

"The human factor of exploring the nearest stars and exo-planets would be a profound voyage for humanity, one whose non-scientific implications would be enormous," Lubin wrote. "It is time to begin this inevitable journey far beyond our home."

At the time, Lubin thought Worden was still with NASA. "I'd never heard of Breakthrough before," Lubin told me. "I'd never heard of Yuri Milner." But he soon came to understand Worden was now employed by a deep-pocketed benefactor with a lifelong interest in interstellar travel. When the two men later met, in January 2016, Lubin said that Milner came into the room carrying a marked-up copy of the "Roadmap."

"This has always been a dream of mine since I was a child," Lubin recalled Milner telling him. "And now you've shown me how to do that."

Milner must have liked what he'd heard at the meeting, because Breakthrough Starshot was announced in April. Taking place fifty-five years to the day since Milner's namesake, Yuri Gagarin, became the first human in space, the press conference was a star-studded affair, as least as far as space travel is concerned: Joining Milner and Pete Worden on stage in New York were Freeman Dyson of Project Orion fame; the Harvard astrophysicist and alien hunter Avi Loeb; astronaut Mae Jemison, who was running 100 Year Starship; Ann Druyan, who was not only Carl Sagan's widow but had been responsible for the golden records on Voyager 1 and 2; and, most famous of all, the theoretical physicist Stephen Hawking. (Lubin was sitting in the audience.)

Milner, wearing a black sweater under a charcoal blazer, and standing at a lectern, began his speech by outlining the history of space exploration, from landing a man on the moon to the launch of the Voyager probes. A photo of Alpha Centauri appeared on-screen behind him, and he underscored just how far away our "neighbouring star" actually was. If the first Voyager probe had left our planet when *Homo sapiens* first walked out of Africa, he said, it would only now be arriving at the star.

"So how do we go faster?" he asked. "And how do we go further? How do we make this next leap?"

The answer was Breakthrough Starshot, a mission that would one day, hopefully, maybe, possibly, send a fleet of laser-propelled nanocrafts—a postage stamp–sized "StarChip" attached to a light sail, totalling just a few grams—farther in the universe than humans had gone before. As Milner spoke, a computer animation showed a phased array somewhere in the desert blasting a beam of light towards a light sail, propelling the nanocraft into the cosmos, never to return.

"For the first time in human history we can do more than just gaze at the stars," he said. "We can actually reach them."

By the time I visited Philip Lubin in Santa Barbara, more than five years had passed since that day in New York. Breakthrough Starshot was still a going concern, unlike, it seemed, 100 Year Starship, whose website had not been updated in four years. But the dream to go fast was progressing rather slowly. Interstellar flight would only be achieved inch by inch, experiment by experiment, as was made clear to me when I visited Lubin's cluttered lab later in the week.

"All this junk needs to be thrown out," said Prashant Srinivasan, who'd offered to give me a tour, as we stood amidst the mess. That might have been as challenging a task as interstellar travel. "Phil is very attached to it."

Srinivasan might not have been attached to the junk, but he was attached to this place. It was a holiday, but it soon dawned upon me that he'd have been here regardless of my presence. He vibrated with the zeal of a true believer.

"I believe that there's a conservation principle," he told me. "In physics, conservation principles are laws. There's a conservation of energy. There's a conservation of momentum. I believe there's a conservation of happiness." Working here, in this lab, with Lubin and the rest of his colleagues, made him unspeakably happy, even if he never saw the phased array come online, or a nanocraft propelled beyond our solar system. "I don't really care much about the ultimate outcome. It is what it is. But it's the process and the journey, and the fact that I believe in what I do and I think it is meaningful. It may not bear fruit today. It may not bear fruit fifty years from now. It may never work." Whatever the outcome, he said, "I don't see this as work. It's a way of life."

In the middle of the lab he showed off a small array, though to me it looked like a robot undergoing an autopsy; wires spilled out in all directions.

"To achieve any kind of propulsion or remote transfer of energy, we need a lot of optical power," he said. "There's no single source that generates such high power. The only way to achieve large flux, or optical power, in a certain area is by combining many sources." I followed what he was saying, but he kindly simplified it for me. "Think of, let's say, the ocean. You do observe the occasional large wave. That happens because several smaller waves are superimposed such that their crests line up, and then you create a large wave. The exact same principle applies here. The key is superposition." One thing on top of the other—this I understood in a way that the material in Tucson escaped me. "Our entire approach here is to generate superposition of all these sources," he said. "It's called constructive interference." This was done, he continued, "with a single source. A single laser. You split it up, amplify the power, and with some control electronics, you align the phases, as in you align the crests, to obtain constructive interference at a target that is very far away."

This phased array, and the immense power that it would require, was one of many puzzles that those involved in Starshot would need to solve in the coming years and decades. At the press conference, Milner had shown a list of all potential challenges the mission faced, which ranged from "sail integrity under thrust" and "maintaining functionality during decades in space" to "interstellar dust," which I admit I'd never considered before.

So, yeah, there was a lot of work to do. While his team was focused on the array, in the years since the press conference Lubin had come to realize that even with Milner's funding, and grants like the one he'd received from the Limitless Space Institute, plus an anonymous benefactor, it was still "a much harder technical problem than any individual philanthropist is going to be able to fund," as he'd put it at dinner. "In terms of the interstellar capability, we have a lot of technology development to do. We've shown that everything seems to work more or less as we thought it would. But the cost is much, much beyond what we can afford."

In the meantime, Lubin had other things to occupy him; interstellar travel wasn't the only thing he cared about, unlike many of the folks I'd met in Tucson, who had a one-track mind when it came to this stuff. He'd begun the work, but that didn't mean he needed to finish it.

During his Limitless presentation, Lubin showed a slide that outlined the project's timescale. "A path to the stars, in our lifetime," it read. It showed what he wanted to achieve in the next five years; what he hoped to achieve within a decade; what might be achieved in twenty to fifty years, if all went according to plan. Despite the title of the slide, he knew that at some point he'd need to pass the baton off to someone else. The first time we spoke he was already talking about succession plans.

"I do not expect to be alive when the system becomes operational," he told me. "This is not a short time-scale project. This is a human lifetime project. And I do pretty much firmly believe I'm not going to be around. And that doesn't bother me at all. I'm okay with that."

Standing here in his lab, among the wires and lasers and assorted junk, it occurred to me that this was the cathedral basement that Sonny White had spoken of. This was the foundation. Tucson had been a foundation, too. None of us who'd been there would ever see the finished project, but brick by brick, an edifice would be constructed out of the graphs and formulas, the math and physics, the mystery and magic, and maybe a touch of the divine. This might be a chapter, but the book was still being written. This might be where it started, but this was not where it would end.

FOUR

WITHOUT A TRACE

If you follow Highway 26 east out of Owen Sound—a town nestled against an inlet on the lip of Georgian Bay, on the edge of Lake Huron, in the northeastern-most reaches of southwestern Ontario—driving past strip malls and a shopping centre, gas stations and big-box stores, a car wash and a car dealership, into the countryside, past a golf course and an airport and farmers' fields sprinkled with off-white sheep and golden bales of hay, the morning sun right in your eyes, until you hit the Irish Block Road and a tidy red-brick Baptist church, and turn south down an unpaved lane, the gravel pinging the undercarriage of your car like hail lashing up from the ground, past scattered houses and weathered barns, until the tops of the trees on either side join together to form a tunnel and the light fades, and you reach a dead end and, after parking, head down a twisting path that winds through the forest like something out of a fairy tale, the mosquitos whispering in your ear, eventually, after walking some distance, you'll arrive at a crevice that cuts deep into the earth.

I stood at its rim, one humid summer afternoon, and looked down. The crevice, part of the Niagara Escarpment—a long cliff that bisects this part of the province, down to and past the falls for which it was named—had been used as a dump for many years, long ago. And although most of the trash was now covered by a carpet of dirt and stones, felled trees and fallen leaves, there was still evidence of its former life—crushed beer cans and scraps of rusted metal, deflated tires and jagged barbed wire poking out of the ground like tree roots growing in the wrong direction. It also might have hidden, according to Matthew Nopper, who stood beside me, the body of a young woman named Lisa Maas, missing for more than thirty years—a young woman he had never met. The search had consumed him for five years, but Lisa Maas's story had haunted him for much of his life.

A tip had drawn Matthew to the crevice. Beginning the following morning, a group would spend a week excavating the site, in the hope of finding Lisa's body. Matthew, a former reporter with the local paper who now worked at a big-box home improvement store I'd passed on the way here, had conducted a preliminary search the previous summer, but this one would be on a much larger scale, with dozens of volunteers and several pieces of heavy machinery to help comb through the archaeological layers of refuse. He'd been waiting all year to come back to the crevice and, less than a day before the search was to begin, vibrated with the nervous excitement of a fighter about to step into the ring, a mix of focus and tension. Forget about waiting until tomorrow; I half expected him to jump down and start digging through the garbage with his bare hands.

"To put her here makes so much sense. Of course, it doesn't mean she's here," he said, almost as a reminder to himself, as we surveyed the pit below. "I have to keep telling myself that. Because, if not, you're in for a big fall when you don't find her. Five years we haven't found her. So, yeah, I've got to come back to reality, that she might not be here. Just watch your step."

A minute later, we reached the bottom. The temperature was several degrees cooler, as if we'd walked into a root cellar. We were maybe twenty or twenty-five feet below where we'd just been standing, and the ground sloped away another ten or so feet at its deepest recesses, into the shadows. The moss-covered rock face rose up on either side, and the space was perhaps fifteen feet across at its widest point. All around was a camouflage of greens and browns. Glass crunched under my hiking boots, but the earth was soft and springy, as if I were walking across a trampoline. Back in the day kids came out here to drink, and Matthew—fifty and long past his bush party days—picked up a recently chugged can of Molson Canadian, proof this was still a popular spot for at least some local teens. It was secluded; the police wouldn't bother you here. After Lisa's disappearance, it was never searched.

Looking around, and back up to the surface, the cedar and hemlock trees standing watch, I realized the enormity of the task. It was overwhelming, Matthew agreed. Where to start? There were rumours that Lisa was wrapped in a green carpet, or tarp, and Matthew had found green fibres while searching here the previous summer. "There's another one," he said, picking a thin green thread out of the dirt and holding it up to my face. It could have been from anything, he knew, and he laughed, aware of the absurdity of the situation: "Only someone, or people, who were so far down the rabbit hole that they can't see out would actually think to do this. Because no reasonable person would think this is possible. No one who's reasonable. I'm so far down the rabbit hole now."

We spent maybe half an hour in the crevice, picking through the garbage, not really looking but not not looking, either. It was possible Lisa was here—*felt* possible, at least. It was a morbid thought: We might have been standing exactly above where she was buried. She had to be somewhere; why not here?

It was a question Matthew had been asking himself for years: Why not here?

"What's your gut telling you?" I asked.

"I don't know," he answered, his voice barely a whisper, then said it again: "I don't know. I've learnt to not be too hopeful—but be hopeful, if that makes any sense. I mean, if I didn't think there was a possibility she was here, I wouldn't be here digging. So, yes, I think there's a possibility she's here. It's also possible we're in a completely wrong area and she's nowhere near here."

"We used to say," he added, a moment later, "when we used to dig in other areas: 'How can she not be here?' How can she not be here—I don't say that anymore, but I still feel that way."

Later that night I walked into a pub in downtown Owen Sound possessing the inspired name of The Pub. It was, I'd been told, the oldest drinking establishment in town, its lineage traced back through different monikers, but its storied legacy had not attracted many customers on this evening; the few men huddled near the back looked up from their half-drunk pints and eyed me warily as I sidled up to the bar. Matthew had cautioned me, on our drive back from the crevice, that we might not be welcomed: "It's a little bit of a rough bar." He was only partly joking. Recalling his warning, I paid for my beer, retreated to an empty table near the front, sat down, kept my eyes on my drink, and minded my own business. This was one of the last places Lisa Maas was seen alive before she disappeared.

On the evening of July 16, 1988, Lisa left the pub and, after a couple of stops, went with a girlfriend to meet up with a male companion, who drove the two women to a nearby party. In the early morning hours of July 17 Lisa left the party with the man, who brought her back to his house so she could pick up her car. She was last seen, investigators were told, driving off in her green 1976 Plymouth Fury at around 4:30 a.m. Her car was found, abandoned and ransacked, two days later. She was twenty-two years old, and five months pregnant.

"[E]verybody's scared to talk," one of her friends told *The Globe and Mail* not long after she disappeared. "Whoever hurt Lisa knew her. Someone was either waiting for her in the car or she picked someone up. I know Lisa wouldn't stop on a back road in the middle of the night to pick up a stranger."

The subsequent investigation produced little in the way of results; no one was charged with a crime. There were no answers, only rumours.

Some people feared Lisa had been the victim of a serial killer—a girl named Lois Hanna had vanished in nearby Kincardine a couple of weeks before Lisa. In 2008, an Owen Sound *Sun Times* reporter learned police originally had a list of seven suspects—including Lisa's ex-husband, from whom she'd recently split after two years of marriage, and her ex-boyfriend, with whom she'd reportedly argued a few hours before her disappearance—but, over the years, they were both ruled out as suspects, and the list was whittled down to a single name.

Matthew did not care about names; he cared about Lisa. The police could handle the investigation into those allegedly involved in her disappearance; he just wanted to find her. The problem was that the possibilities were practically endless. There were so many places she could be. After we'd left the crevice, Matthew had driven me around the back roads and concessions Lisa had likely travelled that last day. Each of these spots contained a thousand places to hide a body. "Every farm has, probably, an old well from the 1800s that isn't filled in," he said. "If you knew about it, because you're a local kid, you could walk on, throw something down it." We drove by the house where he suspected Lisa was murdered; the secluded laneway where a farmer came across her car; past the ditch where her driver's licence was found on the side of the road three weeks later. I got the sense Matthew drove these roads frequently, retracing her path, following a map of absence, one he knew by heart.

The head had hardly settled on my beer when Matthew arrived, along with Nick Oldrieve, his co-organizer in the search. The last time I'd seen Nick had been more than a year earlier, when I accompanied the men on another search in another town for another lost girl. It had not gone well—a key piece of equipment went missing—but he remained unflappable, and his last words to me on that day rang out in my ear: "You can't stop us," he'd said. "There's no stopping us."

I accompanied them to the bar, offering to cover their tab, and Nick immediately started interrogating the barkeep about two men—whose names I won't mention here since they have never been charged with any crime relating to the disappearance of Lisa Maas, but, more importantly, because I've been warned they are scary individuals and I don't need that in my life. I knew that Nick and these men were on bad terms, but he couldn't help but ask: Had they been here lately? After all, this was apparently one of their favourite drinking establishments. Listening in, I remembered something Matthew had said about his younger partner: "He has balls." This sometimes got him in trouble.

"Multiple people have called the police on me," said Nick, a bit too proudly. Having squeezed no useful information from the bartender, we were back at the table, looking out onto streets that were deserted on this Friday, just after 9 p.m. The stereo played a nostalgic mix of nineties rock and pop, much of which I hadn't heard since high school, the volume increasing as the night went on. A Heineken sign buzzed radioactive green in a front window. One of the coin-operated pool tables near the entrance was soon surrounded, and our conversation was punctuated by the occasional crack of colliding billiard balls as the two men outlined their plans for the largest search in the history of their organization, Please Bring Me Home.

"This is, without a doubt, the most difficult search we've done," said Matthew. "It's going to be terrible. But it has to be done. It has to be done."

Nick was the executive director, and Matthew the director of operations for the group, which the pair founded, along with their colleague Melissa Harwood, in 2018. Unlike other amateur sleuths and internet detectives, they were not interested in solving crimes. To them, it wasn't the who or the what that drove their obsession but the where. As in: Where would they find a body? They sought closure for families who had been living in a state of limbo, between certainty and uncertainty, often for decades. A case could conceivably be considered cold after a few weeks, if not a few days, but Please Bring Me Home tended to go back further in time: cases from the sixties, seventies, eighties—men and women who had been forgotten about, except by dogged family members, or perhaps friends, who'd kept their names and memories alive.

Since its founding in Owen Sound, the organization had expanded across Canada—taking on cases the police no longer had time, or interest, in pursuing. What they did was one part P.R.—they were the "squeaky wheel," Nick said, ensuring these cases remained in the public eye—and one part investigations, which had resulted in several successful searches. Its roster of volunteers ran the gamut from paralegals and private investigators to K9 handlers and fire fighters to anthropologists and psychologists to forensic archaeologists and paleopathologists. Nick and Matthew often expressed incredulity at the number of people who freely offered their time and expertise—helpful, as they operated on a shoestring budget—and at the staggering number of requests for help they'd received. There were a lot of missing people out there waiting to be found.

Lisa Maas was their first case, however, and remained the organization's North Star—the person they wanted to bring home more than anyone else, even if every passing year dimmed this possibility.

"No matter how much I try and focus on these other ones," Nick said, "I always end up going back to [Lisa]. She's the one that made it all happen." He continued: "I made up my mind, the second I started to look for her, that we're doing this until a conclusion is reached. You have to have that mindset, I think. You can't just do it until it gets hard." He couldn't quite articulate what it was about the case that compelled him—and others—to spend so much time and energy looking for Lisa, only that he felt a responsibility to keep doing so. "I feel that if we didn't do it, then nobody would."

One of the first games children play is hide-and-seek. We are hardwired to find the missing. But a group like Please Bring Me Home could not have existed until fairly recently. It's not that amateurs couldn't attempt to out-police the police; it's that they would be at a profound disadvantage from the outset. How do you know where to start? How do you know where to look? How do you know who to talk to? The internet provided a platform and a forum—as long as there have been message boards, there have been amateur sleuths meeting online to discuss theories and connecting with people who shared the same interest. Who hasn't dreamt of working as a PI? The internet allowed you to conduct investigations from your kitchen table—access to old newspaper clippings and databases and archives. Social networks were an accelerant; now those researching these cases had access to entire familial, social, and professional circles. You could reach out to the niece of a woman who'd gone missing in 1975, or send a note to the teacher of a boy who disappeared in 1998. There was no longer such a thing as a cold case; at worst, they were all just lukewarm.

It was also clear that the growth of groups like Please Bring Me Home could be attributed to the exploding popularity of the true crime genre—TV shows and books and podcasts—during the previous decade, a popularity I imagined was at least partly fuelled by the rise of online detectives.

"There's a really growing fascination with missing persons, and I think that's just human nature," Matthew told me, the first time we spoke. "The human mind likes to make sense of things. It likes to put things in order, right? And it can't do that with a missing persons case. You get to a brick wall and you can't see beyond it. And the human mind hates that." He continued: "You look out at a night sky and you see those stars, and five hundred years ago, a thousand years ago, when you didn't know what those were, you tried to make stories about what they could be. Same thing with missing persons. You try and speculate about what could be, what could have happened. You want to make sense of it."

I reached the dead end, just before eight the following morning, and parked my car on the side of the road. There were already roughly a dozen people milling about, drinking Tim Hortons coffee and chatting in small groups. The searchers had only learned of the location the previous evening—Matthew and Nick didn't want anyone involved in Lisa's disappearance to know ahead of time that they were meeting at the crevice.

Matthew, wearing heavy black boots, baggy blue jeans, a blue T-shirt underneath a neon orange-and-yellow safety vest, red-and-black work gloves and a dark blue Under Armour baseball cap, had a stack of waivers for volunteers to sign, insurance in case someone tumbled into the crevice or was run over by a tractor. Nick, wearing brown boots, black Nike tearaways, and a blue-grey T-shirt, was handing out knee pads. Both men wore shirts emblazoned with *Please Bring Me Home*, Lisa's name, and the date she was last seen.

Everyone soon gathered in a semicircle around the two men. Nick thanked the volunteers for coming and began outlining the plan for the week, detailing how the search would proceed. Although he had come around to the merits of searching here, Nick was less optimistic than Matthew about the chances of finding Lisa. "Based on our past, it's more possible that we're not going to find a body today," he said. "But at this point, thirty-three years later, anywhere that we look that is within the area that Lisa went missing, that has never been searched, holds the possibility."

"A lot of tips have led to this area," added Matthew. "It's not just a random location." Back in 1989, police searched a dump in a nearby town, but nothing was found. Matthew told the volunteers that someone close to the main suspect was later heard saying police had searched the wrong dump. Three decades later, Nick and Matthew were led to this crevice by a person they claimed was "a very close friend of the main suspect."

Matthew revealed that they'd found a small black leather purse here the previous summer. It was falling apart, and empty, but it matched the description of the one Lisa had with her on the night of the party, and was the main item discovered missing from her car. Unfortunately, they couldn't find any photographs of Lisa with the purse to confirm it was hers. "We also can't confirm it's *not* hers," said Matthew, though to him that wasn't the point: The purse would get people talking, he believed, and that could be as helpful as an anonymous tip. In his view, news of the purse would do one of two things: "The people who know that it's not her purse might go, 'Those fuckers, they think they found Lisa's purse?' And say something to the wrong person, who will tell someone else, who might tell us. And if it is her purse? They'll go, 'Holy shit, they found it!' It'll work both ways."

In any case, the purse was still in their possession.

"We did try to give it to the OPP"—the Ontario Provincial Police—"and they did not want it," Nick told the volunteers. "Take that as you will."

The police, and their apparent disinterest in the search, were sore points not only for Nick and Matthew but also for many of the volunteers I spoke to over the course of the weekend. I was also surprised by the lack of a police presence. "They've made up their mind where they think she is," Nick told me. "They've made up their mind who did it. Anything against that, they won't listen." Although they said they shared everything they found with investigators—even if, like the purse, their findings weren't embraced—it was not a two-way street: "They won't tell us a damn thing," scoffed Matthew. They'd considered trying to obtain police files regarding the investigation through an access to information and privacy request, he said, "but the OPP gets around that by saying it's an active case."

"I would deem us the experts on Lisa's case, above law enforcement," Nick said. "We know that case like the back of our hand." All they were asking for, he said, was "some give and take." It was the lack of give that bothered him. "Let us do it, and just stay out of our way," he said.

As the group made its way towards the crevice, with rain threatening and the muted rumble of thunder off in the distance, I found myself hiking alongside an older woman, Michelle Weiss, who, it turned out, had known Lisa in childhood. She told me that Lisa's father had owned a jewellery store in downtown Owen Sound, which I already knew, and that Lisa's nickname was Mouse, which I didn't, on account of the fact she didn't crack five feet or one hundred pounds. "Just a tiny little thing," said Michelle, but "she had a big heart."

Michelle was here along with her sister, Cindy Hamel, who was outfitted in a hot-pink tank top and tan overalls, her brown hair in pigtails, with the ends dyed pink, and tucked underneath a black ball cap. Throughout the search, I often spotted Cindy behind the wheel of a Massey Ferguson tractor that had been loaned to help move garbage from the top of the crevice to an industrial-sized dumpster that had been left on the edge of the forest, near the dead end.

A decade earlier, Cindy had launched her own investigation into Lisa's disappearance. It wasn't just that she didn't want Lisa to be forgotten, it was that she knew people had information. "I just don't understand how people could sit this long on something and never say a word," she told me. She created a Facebook page, on which people started discussing the case, trading theories, naming names. It was through this forum that she'd first connected with Please Bring Me Home. For the search, she'd gotten her employer to donate the heavy machinery, and to give her and some colleagues paid time off to help excavate the crevice, though she would have been here regardless. "I am in this now right to the end," she told me. "'Til the day I die."

The volunteers were drawn from two worlds—those who'd known Lisa, or her family, or who lived in the community, where this remained one of the most infamous missing person cases, and those who learned about Lisa from Please Bring Me Home. But everyone seemed to have a slightly different reason for being there. I spoke to Joan Monk, a close friend of Lisa, who still blamed herself for Lisa's disappearance—she'd spent some of Lisa's last day with her at the beach, and was supposed to go to the party, but had a baby at the time so stayed home. There was Dave Burr, a soft-spoken farmer who'd actually discovered Lisa's car before she was declared missing; Marg Thomas, a bellicose older woman who seemingly knew everyone involved in the case, and wasn't shy about telling anyone who'd listen what she thought had happened; Jim and Dave Hanna, the brothers of Lois Hanna, the missing girl from Kincardine, who I didn't see stop working the entire weekend; and Beth Purkis, a woman who'd driven two hours to be here and who had, in her youth, dreamt of becoming a criminologist after two friends were murdered. She was now an investigator with Please Bring Me Home.

"I think most people just want to try and make a difference," Matthew told me at one point, when we were talking about what compelled someone to go looking for a body. "I mean, that's all we want to do—is try and set a wrong right. Is try and return someone to their family. And I think that's probably what most people want to do. I think most people internalize it and think, what if that was my daughter? What would I do, thirty years later? You wouldn't stop. You would never stop."

If that was one of my sons, I told him, I don't know how I'd ever sleep.

He nodded. "I have nightmares thinking about that—about what if it was one of my boys that went missing. Like when my dad went missing, just for those few hours, it was the worst evening of my life. And that was an evening! What happens when an evening turns into thirty years? It's heart-wrenching." What Please Bring Me Home tried to do was offer families—if not exactly closure, then at least the possibility of it. "These families have hope that someone is out there looking. Even if we don't find them, we're out there. We're asking questions when everyone else has stopped."

Matthew Nopper arrived in Canada from England when he was eleven years old, his father enticed across the Atlantic by a job in publishing. When his parents later split, his mother moved Matthew and his sister to a town near Owen Sound. It was the year after Lisa Maas went missing.

Matthew was at a house party when he heard Lisa's name for the first time. Another partygoer told him the story of the missing local girl, which had already moved from tragedy to urban legend, and made Matthew an offer straight out of Stephen King: "They actually said to me, 'Do you want to go look for a dead girl?'" They took him to an abandoned farm, not far from where he later learned Lisa's car had been found, to look around. They didn't find her, of course, but her story, and the stories about what might have happened to her, stuck with him.

"There were all these rumours about what had happened to her," he said, "lots of talk, quietly, at kitchen tables and back rooms," about the many places people thought she might be found: "She could be in a foundation. She could be in the footings of a bridge. In a dump. In a well. In a crevice in the Niagara Escarpment. In Georgian Bay. Fed to pigs. It goes on and on and on and on and on. I've said this a bunch of times: She can't be everywhere and be nowhere. She has to be somewhere."

He graduated from high school and went away to school. Eventually, he became a reporter, and moved back home to work at the local paper, the *Sun Times*. He married and had kids of his own. And he never stopped thinking about Lisa Maas. He can't quite explain why. It's sometimes hard to make sense of the things that haunt us. But his life, at least, had settled into a routine. Until September 2012, when his father disappeared.

"All I knew was there was a note, and Dad was missing. And so I got in my vehicle with my wife, and we drove down the two hours to east of Newmarket, where they lived. We got there and all hell had broken loose. The police were searching. It was just a horrible scene, just a soul-crushing scene. I just couldn't stay in that house. I couldn't stay in that house. I had to get out and try and do something. And we didn't know where he was. His vehicle was in the driveway. So for all intents and purposes, he left on foot or he got a ride from somebody—but we didn't know who he'd got a ride from or what happened. He could well have been in the forest, so I went searching. I went with a flashlight and tried to find my dad. Which then, of course, took me back to Lisa. Looking for Lisa all those years before. And now I'm looking for my own dad. The police ended up finding him. Not in the forest around there. He had gone to a hotel. He had actually called a taxi. A taxi had picked him up, taking him to a hotel. And that's where he ended his life. Yeah. So thankfully I didn't find him. While I wanted to find him, I wanted to find him alive. So I'm glad that he didn't take his life in the forest. So that got me into looking for missing people."

He laughed then, a sad, terrible, incredulous laugh.

"Four years later, Nick Oldrieve is in the newspaper. And he thinks he knows where Lisa Maas is buried."

When we arrived at the crevice I found a spot at the top, off to the side, near where a rope handrail guided searchers down to the garbage-strewn floor. It was the perfect vantage point to watch the excavation unfold. From where I sat, if I looked over my right shoulder, I could also make out, through the foliage, the rusting body of a car in the distance. Matthew had told me the story the previous day, but it was recounted to me numerous times over the weekend, one of those strange tales that flourish in every community. Back in the early 1960s, it was said, two men stole a car—some versions had them robbing a bank. In any case, the police gave chase. They turned down the concession I'd driven that morning, but instead of stopping at the dead end had barrelled into the forest, and followed the pathway through the trees, trying to outrun the cops. They must have been unfamiliar with the sharp turn in the path that you encountered once you reached the crevice and the cliffs it abuts, because they went straight over the edge. Somehow, the men survived. The car was never removed—too difficult a salvage, I guessed, though I liked to imagine it was left as a warning to the teens who partied here. It factored into Lisa's disappearance, too; one person told Matthew that "Lisa will be no more than one hundred feet from the car."

Every so often a lone hiker, or a group of hikers, would come walking down one of the trails that criss-cross the area; some would stop and chat, asking what was happening; others would pass by without saying a word, probably confused by the strange forest gathering. A couple with a dog emerged from the woods and asked what was going on. The man didn't flinch when he heard Lisa's name, but the woman remembered. "I hope you find her," she said.

Besides the Massey Ferguson tractor, there was a telehandler—imagine if a forklift and a crane had a baby—with an extendable boom that could reach into the crevice, and an ATV parked over near slats of bottled water, on hand in case someone had to be sped out for medical attention, though while I was there it was mostly used to bring in coffee and pizza. The lip of the crevice, where Matthew and I had stood the previous afternoon, was marked with caution tape. About ten volunteers were below at any given time, sifting through the garbage, which they placed in huge one-ton bags. When full, they'd attach the bags to a cable connected to the telehandler, which would lift the trash to the surface. It was then moved to a palette, and, when the palette was full, the tractor would drive it down the path to the storage bin, where the garbage would be examined again, in case the searchers had missed something the first time around. A bright orange bucket was kept on hand for bones, which would later be sent to the University of Toronto to be examined by a forensic anthropologist. ("It's not our job to determine if it's animal or human," Nick told the volunteers. "If you find bone, it goes in the bucket. If you think it's bone, even if you second-guess yourself, just throw it in the bucket.") Any items of clothing were to be kept separate, as well.

The volunteers began to dig. They dug by hand and by shovel, with axes and hatchets, hoes and spades. They dug with purpose. Once the search began, a quiet descended over the crevice, other than the thud of metal hitting dirt, as they looked for Lisa.

"I always try and visualize it as if it will happen," Matthew told me. "What will it be like? How will I act? How will other people act? What will we do? Will she be in that carpet? Will she be in something else? How will we find her?"

They worked quickly, tote after tote filled with trash and brought up, banging against the crevice walls as it made its way towards the top, raining debris on the searchers below. They pulled out the hood and trunk of a car. Rubber boots. Licence plates from before I was born. An empty wallet. So many animal bones—filling the orange bucket again and again. Tree roots, gnarled and stubborn and preventing searchers from digging further down, were either chainsawed away or wrapped with chains and ripped from the earth by the telehandler, producing an unsettling sound like Velcro being pulled apart. After about two hours Nick emerged, his face smeared with dirt. He'd been hopeful, at the outset, that they could finish clearing the crevice in two days, but already he was reassessing this timeline: "All we've done is unearthed more and more garbage." A break was called; there was coffee and Timbits. The searchers steeled themselves for the hours to come. Already, some of their energy had been sapped.

"You understand the scale of it once you're down there and you start moving stuff," said Matthew. "There's just so much of it. So much."

"What are you thinking?" asked Nick.

"It's going to take six days," Matthew replied. "And, even then, we might not get it all."

They went back down, like grizzled miners returning underground. Deflated tires. Barbed wire. A gun brought momentary excitement, until it was determined to be a toy. And then: a green tarp.

It was hard to tell how big it was, being buried in the earth, but it definitely looked large enough to hide something. It was exactly what Matthew had been looking for—almost certainly the source of the green fibres he'd found last summer and had shown me the previous afternoon. Everyone stopped digging and gathered around as someone tied a chain around it. I clambered down the boulders to get a closer look. Joan, who'd been with Lisa that last day, stood anxiously beside me. The telehandler began to pull, and for a split second I was sure this was it—that they'd found Lisa. And then, as the tarp emerged from the dirt, it was apparent it was only a couple of feet long, much too small for a body. Matthew waved his hands in disgust and turned his back.

"Come on, Lisa, show yourself," Joan said, shaking her head. "Show us where you are."

The search ended around three in the afternoon, though people stuck around for beers. Nick ducked out early—it was his thirty-first birthday, and he had dinner plans. Having been talking to him for the better part of eighteen months at this point, it did not surprise me to learn he'd chosen to spend his birthday in a crevice, sorting through garbage, looking for a body.

Nick was born in 1990, the same year that Matthew first went searching for Lisa Maas. Although he was raised near Owen Sound, he was unfamiliar with the missing girl; by the time he was in high school, the story of her disappearance had begun to disappear, too.

He moved away after high school, and got into social work. This led to jobs in group homes and youth detention centres, two places where residents often try to go missing. At one of his jobs he was put on the "crisis team," which meant he was tasked with tracking kids down when someone broke curfew, snuck out after hours, or simply couldn't be found. He discovered, to his surprise, he was good at this part of the job, and, he claimed to me, the crisis team boasted a 100 percent success rate finding kids within twenty-four hours during his tenure.

He later moved back home to Owen Sound, thinking about how he could turn his new-found skill into a career. He offered his talents to local organizations like the Children's Aid Society that might need someone like him, and even secured a meeting with the local member of Parliament to pitch his services. No one was interested.

Instead, Nick started working as a personal support worker for people with brain injuries. In his spare time, he'd scour local Facebook pages, where people often posted if they were looking for someone. Along with a couple of friends, he would attempt to track the missing person down—becoming, in some ways, a quasi-bounty hunter, except there was nothing in it for him besides satisfaction.

One day, a few years later, Nick logged onto the Canada's Missing website, a national clearinghouse for the Royal Canadian Mounted Police's National Centre for Missing Persons and Unidentified Remains. It was there that he spotted a listing for a woman from just outside Owen Sound he'd never noticed before, one whose name he didn't recognize, and who had been missing for a long, long time: Lisa Maas.

"It blew my mind," he said. "This is ten minutes from my home," he remembered thinking. "How is nobody talking about this?"

Up until this point his focus had been active searches—people who had been gone for a day or week. The idea of a cold case had never really occurred to him. How could someone remain missing for years, never mind decades? Nick and a couple of friends began talking to acquaintances, family members, and others in the community who were alive when Lisa vanished, even going so far as to call up her father, out of the blue, to pepper him with questions about his daughter's case. Not everyone was co-operative, and after efforts to search a property he was convinced would provide evidence into her disappearance was stymied, he went to the media, claiming to know where to find Lisa Maas. Not long after reading the story in the newspaper, Matthew emailed Nick. "We've been joined at the hip ever since," he said.

There were times the work was frustrating, when it seemed impossible. We can put a man on the moon, the men often said to each other. So why can't we find a missing person? It was demoralizing and motivating at the same time. "Looking the families in the eyes, you see how desperate they are," Matthew said. "They feel so lost. And I think that's what drives me most." It could be rewarding, sure, but it wasn't enjoyable. He wished this work wasn't necessary, but, he added, "if no one's going to do it, then I'll just do it myself. That's kind of what it is. Someone has to do it."

Before the search resumed on Sunday morning, Nick borrowed my phone and read, to the gathered volunteers, an article that had just been published on the *Toronto Star*'s website a few minutes earlier. The headline was: 'As long as you've got a breath in your body': Lisa Maas's father is still searching for his daughter—and her killer." I noticed more than one volunteer wiping their eyes as he read the story, which detailed the current search and the discovery of the purse the previous summer, and included an interview with Lisa's elderly father, Ken. (Lisa's mother had died the previous year; Ken, who declined to talk to me but was a staunch supporter of Nick and Matthew's search, died in 2023.)

"It's constantly on my mind," her father told the reporter. "I have her picture that I look at every day, along with my wife's picture. Those are all part of my life and will remain with me until my passing."

Nick finished reading, and the group headed back towards the crevice.

The search continued much as the day before. They found a pair of women's slip-ons; a plastic spider; a shotgun trigger; old glass bottles. It often felt closer to an Earth Day clean-up than a search. At one point someone yelled out that they'd uncovered a skull, but they meant animal—dog or cat, likely. Don't say the "s-word," cautioned Matthew.

"Isn't it just a little crazy that two guys who've never met the girl ever in their lifetime are doing this?" remarked Shelley Pearce, another one of Lisa's childhood friends, who'd joined the search on this day. She was dumbstruck not only by the turnout, but by Nick and Matthew's dedication to her friend's case. "They leave their families for days and days on end to come do this."

When she took a break from driving the tractor, Cindy Hamel joined me at the top of the crevice to watch. It was an emotionally draining experience, she said. "I went home last night and I cried. I look at these guys—I look at Jim, I look at Dave. They have a sister that's missing. And here they are looking for a girl they don't even know." She began to cry. "These are the kind of people we need in this world, you know? Just to give up your weekend, and give up your time with your family and your friends, to come out here and dig in dirt. This is what I wanted. This was the outcome I wanted, and now I'm looking at it."

Nick joined Cindy and me a few moments later, emerging from the crevice and plunking down another purse on one of the boulders. "It's the third one we've found down there," he said. It was black leather, matching the description of the one Lisa had with her the night she disappeared. The faded label read *Handbags limited*. It was empty.

As the day wore on, the optimism seemed to fade. On Friday when I'd first arrived at the crevice there was a genuine feeling Lisa might be found; by lunch on Sunday the search felt like a chore that just had to be finished. Even Matthew admitted the chances were getting slimmer. "Of course, the further we dig down, the less chance she's here. That's the reality, unfortunately." That said, he added, "We have to keep going. We can't just say, 'Ah, you know what, she's probably not here.' Probably not is not good enough. She has to definitely not be here."

"If we don't find anything, we don't find anything, but that doesn't mean we're not going to go to the next spot," said Cindy. "You've got to overturn every stone or you're never going to find what you're looking for."

There were volunteers who confided in me that, although they'd come to help search, they never thought Lisa was actually in the crevice. One person told me that she and a few others were heading to a different site later on Sunday, planning to search a location that had appeared to her in a dream. Everyone seemed to have their own pet theory as to what had happened to Lisa that night and where she was buried, or how she'd finally be discovered.

Most, however, seemed to have settled on who was responsible. During breaks, I'd hear small groups discussing different suspects, what they thought they knew, and what they knew they thought. Some people who had been involved in the search online, through Cindy Hamel's Facebook page, were meeting for the first time in person, trading names and stories. Everyone had a theory. Many people worried that the suspects, knowing the search was happening, had sent people to monitor. Maybe there was a mole. One woman had gone for a walk but came back a short time later, creeped out by the woods: "You know that feeling when you think someone is watching you?" she asked me.

Later that afternoon, Nick emerged from the crevice looking a bit like a raccoon, his eyes ringed with dirt. He was exhausted, and took a seat beside me on the rocks. He, too, understood the search would likely prove fruitless, and as we talked, watching those working below, I could tell he was thinking what might come next. He'd been checking his phone since the *Toronto Star* article had gone up that morning and had received several messages from other people who wanted to help. He was already planning new places to search. That was the problem, I thought. There would always be a new place to search. It was like finding a needle in a haystack, although more difficult—at least, in that case, you know the needle is there.

"I would welcome a needle in a haystack," Nick responded when I pointed this out. "I would just be smacking [it] until I get the needle in my hand. Jump on it. Roll around. You'll find it. But this is what it takes. It takes literally going down to the actual bone." He went back down to continue digging.

People slowly trickled out of the crevice as evening approached, and I began to say my goodbyes—I had a three-hour drive back to Toronto. Matthew wasn't among the volunteers who were having a well-earned beer; he was still down below. When he looked up at me, after I'd called down to say I was leaving, his face seemed a mask of embarrassment and frustration. They had failed. They had not found Lisa Maas.

"It was a tough five days," he emailed me later, after the search had ended. "Some emotional moments, especially near the end when we, and Lisa's friends, realized Lisa wasn't coming home this time."

Standing there at the edge, looking down as Matthew continued to dig through the dirt, the last person in the crevice, I knew he was disappointed. But I knew I was looking at a man who would not stop.

As I drove away, I thought back to the previous afternoon. The volunteers were celebrating the end of the first day of searching, standing around the tractors, cracking beers that seemed to appear out of thin air. Someone handed me a phone and asked that I take a group shot; I counted down from three, and instead of "cheese" people called out "Lisa." A few minutes later, I found myself standing with Matthew and Cindy, who were discussing the green tarp. How it seemed like the search had come to an end. How close they felt to Lisa at that instant, even though it turned out to be yet another dead end.

"Just for a brief second, I thought . . ." Matthew said, his voice trailing away.

"We'll find her," Cindy told him.

Matthew was quiet for a moment, and then answered.

"She's there," he said. "We'll find her."

FIVE

ACTS OF BEAUTY

When Bonnie Morton was five years old, her father decided to try his hand at farming, so he moved the whole family from Gananoque, the small town in eastern Ontario where they lived, down the highway to an acreage outside the village of Lyndhurst. They rented the land. They rented the house. They rented the cattle. They rented the equipment. They had no idea how to farm, and any money they lucked into went towards bills and upkeep. These were lean years in a childhood all too familiar with lean years.

She married at twenty, and soon became a mother. Then, darkness: cancer, and a hysterectomy. Her husband wanted more children, and when he learned she could not provide them, he was no longer her husband. She began a new relationship. She had been with her partner a few years when the violence began, but in what could only be considered a small mercy, he too eventually decided he would rather not be with her. She found herself living in a cabin in the bush near the town of Pembroke, about an hour north of Ottawa, alone with her son, cut off from the world. There was no electricity. There was no running water. At times, there was no heat. She was used to this—she'd sometimes lacked these things growing up, too. They also lacked an outhouse, the facilities having been taken over by a family of porcupines. "It was kind of a battle between me and the porcupines," Bonnie said. "I won. So we had a place to go to the bathroom." Another small mercy. But she had no money either, for heating oil or food, and she had a growing boy to feed. Pride wouldn't let her ask her parents or siblings—a twin sister, a kid sister, and two younger brothers—for help. Instead, she made do. "You gotta do what you gotta do to live," she said. It was a simple mantra, and she clung to it like she clung to her son. As a girl, she'd often allowed herself to think about the future, about what she might do with her life if given half a chance, but those daydreams had abandoned her, too: "I was too busy trying to survive to be able to dream."

Survive she did. She planted a vegetable garden, and stored what she grew in the root cellar. She restored an old well, though in hindsight wonders if drinking its water had been wise. When her son needed boots, or a hat, or mittens, to keep him warm during the cold Canadian winter, she snared rabbits and muskrat and marten and stitched their pelts together for clothing. She learned to fish, and she hunted with an old rifle that she'd used on the farm for skeet shooting, the report echoing through the trees like a shout, a reminder that she was still alive. She lacked a hunting licence and paid no mind to the seasons. You've got to do what you've got to do to live.

One day, she was apprehended by the game warden. An inevitability, perhaps, but frustrating all the same. She was presented with two options: She could either go to jail or accompany the warden to town and sign up for social assistance. She agreed to go with him, even though she was sure she could provide better for her son alone in the woods than in town on welfare. In the end, it didn't matter much: Her partner returned and said he wanted to try again. "It sounds strange, but at the time I was prepared to put up with the beatings so that my son could eat," she said. They headed west, but the violence followed her across the country. Before, it had been "a few slaps here and there." Now, it grew worse, and culminated in death threats. "He put a shotgun to my head and told me if I ever tried to leave him he'd kill my son first, and then me." Bonnie went to her employer and told him what had happened, although he could already see it on her face. Her boss gave her a final paycheque and then drove her home, where Bonnie ran inside and packed what she could. They then picked up her son from school and drove to the train station. She used her wages on two tickets that would take them as far away from their old life as possible. It didn't matter where.

They stepped out onto the platform in Regina, Saskatchewan's gritty capital city. It was 1981, she was thirty years old, and starting from scratch once again. A new life for a woman who had already lived so much.

She was still at the station when it occurred to her that she did not know a soul in town. She had not told her family about the abusive relationship, and did not want to call them now, anyway, worried they would tell her partner where she'd fled. She broke down crying when a concerned taxi driver asked if she was all right. She was not all right. "Just hang on," he said. "I think I know somebody who can help you."

There were no women's shelters in the city at the time, so the taxi driver took them to a motel and told her to talk to the owners. Inside, as she began explaining her situation to the man at reception, she started crying again. The man excused himself and went to find his wife. When the couple returned, the man took her son outside, while his wife listened to Bonnie's story—what had brought her to Regina, and what she was trying to forget. "You can stay here," the woman said.

They lived in the motel for three months. The owners vouched for her, and helped her find a job as a cook at a local greasy spoon, despite the fact she was not a good cook. The wife would watch her son during the day while Bonnie worked. Finally, she saved up enough money and they moved into an apartment of their own. The motel owners bought her a pullout couch, as well as a kitchen table and chairs. They gave her a bed and sheets and towels and old pots and pans people had left at the motel over the years. And when she offered to pay them back for everything they'd done—she still cried, all these years later, when she reached this part of the story—the motel owners refused her money. "They just told me, in place of paying them, just to pay it forward."

And so that's what Bonnie Morton, one of the most ferocious advocates for the poor and downtrodden Canada has ever produced, spent her whole life doing.

"At the time, I didn't know what 'pay it forward' meant."

We were sitting, Bonnie and I, in an idling car outside the motel where she once lived on a warm day in late spring. Or at least the place where the motel had stood. As she turned off Victoria Avenue, Bonnie let out a startled cry: "It's all gone! Holy jeez." The Siesta Motel was no more; in its place a barren field, bulldozed level. Anything might have once stood here.

Since there was nothing to see, we sat there for a while, in Bonnie's Kia Soul, discussing her arrival in Regina all those years ago, how she began to piece together a new life, and how in those early weeks and months "time seemed to drag so slow." Even with the kindness she'd received from the motel owners, it was hard going. Not long after their arrival, her son was diagnosed with muscular dystrophy. Between shifts at the diner where she worked and the partial social assistance for which she was eligible, she was barely able to make ends meet. When her son required surgery, Bonnie was forced to take a leave of absence. Her boss was kind, but the recovery was more arduous than anticipated, and since social services would not pay to have someone come watch her son while she worked, Bonnie remained at home, by his side. Eventually, Bonnie's boss called and said he had to give her shifts to someone else. She tried to find other work, but in job interviews was constantly told she should be at home with her boy. She felt trapped, she told me. "I swear, I was getting close to having a nervous breakdown."

She met with social services to see what might be done. As luck would have it, she'd just been assigned a new social worker, fresh-faced and fresh out of school, who had not yet grown cynical about the system in which he worked. He asked her: Have you ever considered returning to school? She said no, that she wasn't smart enough. He said: Let's give it a try. Not only would finishing her education be helpful, but there were financial resources available to students that Bonnie otherwise didn't qualify for. She agreed—at the very least it would get her out of the house during the day. After learning she was not even reading at a fifth-grade level, the social worker found her money to hire a tutor, and sent her to an ophthalmologist, who diagnosed Bonnie with dyslexia. She enrolled in an alternative high school and eventually received her diploma.

During her last year of school, it was announced students would no longer be provided with free bus passes. Bonnie, as well as most of her classmates, relied on the passes to get to school; not only that, if you were late too many times you were expelled. The students rebelled, with Bonnie leading the charge: "I had a big mouth and I was pretty angry," she said. The principal gave Bonnie time off so that she could dedicate herself to activism—teachers were against the loss of the passes, too—and so Bonnie went around the city rallying students against the decision. Eventually, the passes were returned to disabled students and those with children in daycare. She had fought, and she had won, and she had loved it. An injustice, at least in her eyes, had been overturned. Not long after, a supervisor from the Ministry of Social Services told Bonnie that they would "rue the day they ever educated" her. They were right.

Unbeknownst to the supervisor, Bonnie had been radicalized years before coming to Regina. If her activism had an origin story, it was written back in Ontario. As was common at the time, her school had a dress code, and the girls were required to wear skirts or dresses. One particularly cold winter morning, not knowing how long she'd have to stand outside waiting for the bus, Bonnie decided to wear a pair of slacks that she had sewn (she made all her own clothes). At school, she was accosted by a classmate, the school council president, who chided Bonnie for her sartorial choices. (It should be noted here that her prim and proper twin sister had stuck to wearing a skirt.) He told Bonnie to take off the pants. She said no. Later that day, Bonnie was called down to the principal's office and given a choice: take them off or serve detention. She chose detention.

That night she discussed the matter with her father, who'd received a call at work from the school informing him of his daughter's disregard of the rules. He was furious, but Bonnie kept calm. She knew that she was in the right. She'd read the student handbook—it didn't say girls couldn't wear slacks, she insisted, "all it said was clean clothing appropriate for school." Why weren't slacks appropriate? Besides, she told her father, the boys (and some male teachers) were notorious for standing under the stairs, which were open between treads, and looking up as the girls walked down. That changed her father's mind. "You keep those pants on!" he told his daughter, much to the chagrin of Bonnie's mother, who must have sensed her husband was helping forge an activist.

She wore pants again the next day, and the next, and the next. For three weeks she wore slacks to school. At first, the punishment remained detention. But she'd begun proselytizing to the other girls, arguing how unfair it was that they all had to wear skirts—in the dead of winter; standing shivering at the bus stop!—while the boys enjoyed the warmth of pants around their ankles. This was an act of rebellion, mutiny against the school administration, and could not stand, so they moved Bonnie down to the basement—full-time, not just for detention. Teachers sent down classwork for her to complete, but she mostly hung out with the custodian, she told me. "When I had no work to do, the janitor and I played cards."

Eventually, a school assembly was called to deal with the issue once and for all. Bonnie and the school council president would debate the matter, each presenting their side of the argument, and then a vote would be held. The student council president wore a kilt for the occasion—being a smartass, he said if girls could wear slacks, boys could wear dresses and kilts. All eyes were now on Bonnie, who had nothing prepared. "I just looked at him and I said: 'You can wear a kilt any time you want to school. Your knees are better looking than mine!'"

A small riot ensued. Over the pandemonium, Bonnie made her case: "I looked at the girls and I said: 'Just remember: It's men telling us what to wear.'"

Bonnie won in a landslide—it seems school officials had overlooked the fact that the school's student population was largely female. She also won a reputation as a "shit disturber," she said. But, more importantly, she gained an understanding of the cost of doing what's right, and what might happen if you tried to change things that people didn't want changed.

"When you stand up, and you're doing something that's against the status quo, you need to remember there might be a price to pay for that," she told me. "And that was my first lesson on the price to pay."

Like the Siesta Motel once did, Knox-Metropolitan United Church also sits just off Victoria Avenue, in the heart of downtown Regina. It's a lovely old pile, and dates back to 1912, when part of the current building was rebuilt after being levelled by the Regina Cyclone, the deadliest tornado in Canadian history, though its roots stretch back to 1882. One morning, Bonnie offered me a tour. The church had been her second home for many, many years, an outcome that still surprised her.

"I never thought my life would be in a church," she told me. "My family finds it hard to believe." Raised Anglican, she'd stopped going to service after being terrified by her childhood parish's fire-and-brimstone minister, who she swore once pointed straight at her and hollered that she'd burn in hell. A few years later, she said, "when I needed the church, when my first marriage broke down, it wasn't there for me." She decided she wouldn't be there for it.

Bonnie's tiny stature and kind face, framed by spectacles and shoulder-length grey hair that called to mind a grandmother you'd meet at a knitting club, concealed a boundless energy and righteous fury, both of which were in evidence on this day. She led me down long, darkened hallways adorned with serious portraits of the church's former ministers up winding, creaking staircases, and past Sunday school rooms and community meeting spaces (a Toastmasters group was gathered on this day) and the auditorium and finally the sanctuary, a marvellous room brightened by stained glass windows and framed by an immense organ. It was empty, and quiet, and dust motes floated in the morning sun. "There was a time when this church was packed right to the rafters, but that's probably the truth about all churches around here," she said.

I took a moment to linger in the stillness. Since I'd started writing this book I'd thought a lot about the relationship between faith and perseverance. Faith, after all, is a sort of perseverance; perhaps heaven is an impossible goal. I was raised Catholic, and went to church every Sunday morning for the first dozen-odd years of my life, until my mother, disgusted by the sexual abuse scandal and the Vatican's response, stopped forcing my brothers and me to go. Even though religion didn't follow me into adulthood, the conversations I'd had on the subject of perseverance—people spending their lives pursuing the improbable, if not the impossible—often brought me back to those quiet hours attending Mass. Everyone I spoke to was holding on to something. I found something incredibly comforting in their willingness to believe. In their devotion.

We left the sanctuary and continued our tour. The church's layout was positively labyrinthine, and even Bonnie, who'd spent more than thirty-five years haunting these halls, was still confused by elements of the building. ("That door takes us downstairs, I think," she said at one point.) The places she knew best were the two cramped rooms, near the front entrance, that housed the office of the Regina Anti-Poverty Ministry (RAPM), where Bonnie spent the majority of her career fighting for the city's neglected and ignored.

This had not been the plan; it was supposed to be law school. After high school, Bonnie enrolled in the local university's Department of Justice Studies. As part of her degree, she was required to do a field placement. She worked for legal aid and then a private firm, and realized she'd watched too much *Matlock*. She also concluded that the legal system perpetuated poverty, which meant it was actively working against people like her. She wanted no part of it. Perhaps she could fight, and help, in a different way.

During her freshman year, she received a phone call from a man named Bob Gay, the reverend who headed RAPM, which had been based out of Knox-Met since 1971. They had met about a year earlier, when Reverend Gay had come to Bonnie's high school to talk about his experiences as Regina's downtown chaplain, working with the city's poor. After his lecture, he asked to meet with Bonnie, having heard about her fight to save student bus passes. Bonnie never thought she'd hear from him again, and so was surprised by the phone call. He told her he was hiring, and wanted to know if she knew anyone who might like to work with him. Bonnie said she'd think about it and would definitely let him know if someone came to mind. He phoned back a few hours later and explained that, actually, he was offering her a job. She was tempted, but there was a problem, she said—she wasn't religious.

"I don't need you to be religious," he replied. "I need you to believe in justice."

"Well, that's me then," said Bonnie.

She believed in justice, but readily admitted that she did not accept the job for entirely noble reasons; she took the job because she needed the money to help cover her son's medical expenses. She certainly did not expect, when she started at RAPM in December 1987, that she would spend the following decades in those cramped offices, fighting on behalf of those who were now in a place she'd once been. She did not know that this would become her life's work. At first it was just a paycheque, but it wasn't long before the job became something more profound. "It had become a passion," Bonnie said. "And I think I must have been in this ministry for a couple of years before it dawned on me: I was doing what the hotel owners wanted me to do. I was actually paying it forward."

It helped that she enjoyed the job immensely. There had been times in her life when she woke up dreading the day ahead. She'd worked in factories and grocery stores and as a chambermaid—jobs that had her dreaming of retirement. "I thought, 'Oh man, sixty-five can't come quick enough.'" Now, when she'd wake in the morning she couldn't wait to get to the office. It wasn't unusual for her to work straight through her lunch hour, she told me, and then late into the night after dinner. These long hours never felt like an imposition. It felt like she was doing something good—not just with her life but to improve the lives of others.

Her work focused on three things: advocacy for low-income folks, mostly those who rely on social assistance; educating the public on issues relating to poverty; and challenging systemic discrimination, meaning lobbying the government for legislation that helped, not harmed, the poor.

When it came to the latter, she quickly developed a reputation for making life difficult for politicians who made life difficult for her clients.

"When they knew that Bonnie was calling, or Bonnie was showing up, I think that they would shake in their boots," Barry Rieder told me. A community minister in Toronto's Jane-Finch neighbourhood, who first met Bonnie in the mid-nineties, Rieder described her, with the utmost affection, as full of "piss and vinegar" and consumed by "justifiable anger, and righteous anger—not for herself, but for those that are oppressed and marginalized."

"She doesn't put up with any shit, no matter where it comes from," said her long-time friend Nicole Desormeaux, who was also a former client. "She doesn't put anybody up on a pedestal. Everybody, in her eyes, is equal. And she fights inequality."

It's a fight Bonnie had been waging, when I first spoke to her in the fall of 2020, for more than thirty years. During this time a bleak situation had grown increasingly bleaker, the result of austerity budgets slashing away at social spending; rising housing and energy costs; wage stagnation; inflation—the list went on. And it seemed to be getting worse by the day, with the pandemic pushing vulnerable people past the breaking point, and pushing people who thought they'd had a safety net towards the breaking point. Eliminating poverty was a Sisyphean task. Every time Bonnie and her colleagues made progress, every time a small victory was won, the boulder would inevitably roll back down the hill. It was often pushed by those in power. There was always some new hurdle being placed in front of the people she'd devoted her life to helping. And there were always excuses being offered by politicians and those who made the decisions: "Every time you meet with them they'll say: 'We need to study it,'" Bonnie complained to me. "You've literally studied poor people to death. Literally."

It was a source of endless frustration—not only this reluctance to address the issue in a meaningful, life-changing way, but this misunderstanding of what poverty was, and why people fell into its clutches. It wasn't incompetence, proof of laziness, or lack of ambition or misfortune or poor luck—though the latter could play a role. Instead, it was an agreement society had made, a bargain with a system that lavishly benefited a very small percentage of the overall population, provided the majority of people just enough not to question what was going on, and harmed a sizable group stuck on the bottom rung of the economic ladder. Poverty wasn't an unintended consequence of this system, Bonnie argued. It was by design. "We have it because we have an economy that benefits from poverty. It's not a choice. I didn't wake up one day and say, 'God, doesn't poverty look great—I aspire to be poor.' My parents didn't say that." And yet, Bonnie continued, "we've taken poverty, and the concept of poverty, and we've made it a personal failure."

She spoke from experience. For years she hid from her family the fact that she'd required help, opening up about this part of her life only when she learned one of her brothers felt ashamed that he'd had to go on welfare. She knew it was hypocritical to tell clients to go on social assistance and yet hide the fact she'd once done the same. It was another lesson she'd learned in her childhood: "Our father said welfare was for others, not for us."

It was not being poor that filled her with shame. "I was proud of who I was when I was poor and growing up on the farm," she told me. Even though things were tight, they made do. They survived. It was relying on others, the act of asking for help, that was the hard part. "All of a sudden it's like there's something wrong with me," she said. "What's wrong with me that I can't compete in this world?" She knew, now, how foolish it was to think this way—Bonnie had provided for and protected her son under some of the most challenging circumstances imaginable—but she also knew it was a sentiment that most people shared. Welfare was seen as the result of wrong decisions, and poverty as a moral failing. She rejected this with all her heart. The fact we allowed poverty to exist was the moral failing. She reminded people of this with every email she wrote, which all signed off with RAPM's motto: "The existence of poverty is shameful—to be poor is not!"

One morning, a week before Palm Sunday, the Rev. Bonnie Morton welcomed the Knox-Met congregation, some of whom had joined her in person and others who were streaming the service on YouTube. A number of candles rested on the altar, which she'd lit upon entering the nave, as well as a vase of pink flowers and a trio of rainbow flags. Behind her, the choir benches were empty save for two masked singers and an organist dwarfed by the massive instrument. Standing there, she looked very much at home, and at peace, even if I knew her body was coursing with nervous energy.

"I still get a knot in my stomach every Sunday," she'd said to me. "As soon as I open my mouth, though, it starts to go away."

Despite warning Bob Gay that she wasn't religious when he offered her the job at RAPM, Bonnie drew closer to the church over the years. She was especially taken with Bob's philosophy that it was easier to ask forgiveness than seek permission—the clergy as troublemakers: "I have really taken that one to heart," she told me. She became a lay minister in the United Church of Canada in 2011, the same year Bob died. But more than a decade later, she still found herself struggling to define her spirituality. "I wouldn't say I'm religious," she said. "The word 'religious' has a very negative connotation to it. For me, I would have to say that my faith, once more, has been reawakened."

After running through a series of typical church announcements, from a rummage sale to a roast beef dinner, Bonnie turned to the day's reading, from the Gospel of John. Jesus visits Bethany, the home of Lazarus, at this point already back from the dead. A dinner is held, during which Mary anoints his feet with perfume and dries them with her hair, an act that incenses Judas. The disciple accosts her: Why not sell the perfume and donate the proceeds to the poor? (In truth, Judas just wants to sell the perfume because, as keeper of the group's purse, he can steal whatever they earn.) Leave her alone, Jesus tells him. You will always have the poor among you, but you will not always have me.

Even though everyone sitting in the sanctuary and watching at home probably already knew this, Bonnie explained how she'd spent decades working at RAPM. "My thirty-four years in this ministry have been spent working for, and calling for, the elimination of poverty." Many times over the years, she said, she'd had this passage quoted to her by those she was hoping would provide help. "Can you imagine being in meetings with some politicians," she said, "and that's what you get? 'Doesn't your scripture tell you you will always have the poor with you?' It's an excuse by those in power, when they're not willing to discuss or to progressively address poverty issues in our communities." And so what was she to say about a piece of scripture that had been weaponized against her so many times?

The subject of Bonnie's sermon on this day was "brazen acts of beauty," which was how she described Mary's anointing of Jesus. They were acts, undertaken without any ulterior motive, that made a difference in someone else's life. They were not always simple, or safe for those carrying them out. These acts often required bravery, or boldness, or trust. Sometimes they were great, and sometimes small. Sometimes you wouldn't even know how much your actions had helped. "But know you have done exactly what God tells you to do, and that which Jesus has shown us examples of how to do it."

After recounting some acts she had recently witnessed in the community—Regina families opening their homes to people fleeing the war in Ukraine, for instance—Bonnie said she wanted to share a couple of brazen acts of beauty from her own past. The first was the story she'd told me about the young social worker who'd set her life on the path that ultimately led to where she was today. "I heard later that this man also got a lot of internal flack for what he did to help me," she told the congregation. "But without that help, I'm standing here to tell you my life would look a whole lot different than it does today. He was brazen, his acts were courageous, and they were full of beauty."

The second story was longer, and although I'd heard it before, she told the congregation that she was telling it publicly for the first time. In the early nineties, Bonnie was asked by the University of Regina, where she was finishing her degree, to travel to Londonderry, in Northern Ireland, to study whether an exchange program could, and should, be set up between her school and Magee College, part of Ulster University. At the airport in Belfast, she was greeted by a man in a clerical collar, who introduced himself as Fr. Neal Carlin. "I said, 'Oh, a Catholic priest coming to pick up a little Protestant woman in the middle of the violence.' And I'm like, 'Oh, this might not go well.'"

Her worries were for nought. She was cared for, and she was made to feel welcome. She worked for her room and board, planting trees and cleaning and cooking for Father Carlin and attending classes in the evening. One night, she was awakened by voices and movement out in the hallway. Dressed in her flannel nighty, and armed with a cricket bat, she left her room to investigate. In the dark, she spotted Father Carlin, flashlight in hand, leading a group of young people up the ladder to the attic—Irish Republican Army members being sought by the paramilitary, she later learned, whose parents had gone to the priest for help. "I know I witnessed a truly brazen act of beauty, filled with trust, bravery, and love," she told the congregation. (Bonnie said that when she returned to Londonderry years later, and saw Father Carlin again, he gave her permission to share this story. He died in 2021.)

An act did not need to be as significant or brave as what she'd witnessed in Northern Ireland. It could be volunteering for the church feeding programs, she said, or visiting people in the hospital, or sending cards or flowers to those who might be lonely. Even the smallest act made a difference. "Let us leave here today as faithful followers of Jesus, following Mary's example, and continue doing our forms of brazen acts of beauty whenever and wherever we can. Remember: We are God's, and Jesus's, army to go out and do good."

She raised her arms aloft. "As you leave his place, may you be awe-struck by the beauty of this world. May you laugh, and may it be contagious. May you overflow with love for those around you. May you be effusive with hope, and quick to point out joy. And in all of your living and breathing and being, may you find yourself full to the brim with God's holy spirit. In the name of the lover, the beloved, and love itself, go in peace, full to the brim with the blessing of God, to carry on brazen acts of beauty."

To carry on. To continue. To go forward. Onward. One of the traits that connected those I interviewed over the years, the people I travelled around the world to meet, was this incessant forward momentum—the refusal to acknowledge an ending, or an understanding that their end was someone else's beginning. And so I was surprised when I received an email from Bonnie, late one night, telling me that she was retiring. It seemed impossible—I read the email several times, to be sure—but her ending was drawing near.

It arrived on a breezy Sunday afternoon in June, outside the Saskatchewan legislature, an imposing Beaux-Arts building on the edge of Wascana Lake, where I stood alongside a group of fifty-odd people—friends and family, colleagues and clients from RAPM, fellow ministers and other community members—who'd gathered for Bonnie's release of covenant. In layman's terms, her retirement, after decades of service. As I chatted with the people around me before the proceedings began, the atmosphere was less like a retirement party and more like waiting to view a solar eclipse, or catch sight of a comet that comes around only once in a lifetime.

The ceremony began with a blessing, followed by prayers and speeches and readings from the Gospels. I was particularly moved by the words of Julie Graham, a long-time friend and colleague, who paid tribute to Bonnie's decades-long struggle against "the systems that grind people down with intention." She compared Bonnie to the prophets of old, and said that in the pursuit of justice for the oppressed it was the prophet who reminded everyone else, when they wondered if change would ever come, that, yes, it was possible. "The prophet's there to remind us of that continued possibility, even if it stretches beyond our lifetime. Even if thirty-four years of very dedicated ministry has not been enough. And yet, in many ways, it is enough. Because Bonnie has offered us all that she can."

When it was time for Bonnie to be released from service, the four symbols of the Regina Anti-Poverty Ministry were brought to the front—a loaf of bread, a Bible, a placard, and a stack of pages. Standing behind a microphone that went almost over her head, holding the placard that read *Stop Poor Bashing*, Bonnie explained what the symbols meant.

The bread, she began, is "the sustenance and life that we all need and that we all should have but we don't. And RAPM fights for that—to ensure that no one goes hungry." The papers represented policy and regulations, she said, which are a tool used in the ministry's quest for justice. The Bible acknowledges RAPM is a ministry of faith, and that they are guided by the lessons in the Bible, like resisting evil and seeking justice. And the sign? These came out, she explained, if and when "the powers that be"— the politicians who worked in the building behind her—failed to act, or failed to listen. "And we stand, and we march, and we have our voices heard."

"For me, these symbols can't be separated out— they go hand in hand, one to the other." She began to cry. "I hold these symbols dearly." She ended her speech by thanking her colleagues and the people she'd worked with over the years, especially her clients, "for the gift of enabling me to live into my passion of seeking justice, and allowing me to have the thrill of resisting evil, and challenging it."

Later that afternoon, everyone gathered at a church a few kilometres away for coffee and cake. Video screens set up in the auditorium played a slideshow of photographs from throughout Bonnie's life and career. A local TV anchor hosted the proceedings. There were more prayers, and more speeches, and letters written by those who could not make it were read out: "It will never be possible to tell the number of lives you've touched," said one. Another, from a high-profile

Saskatchewan politician and federal Cabinet minister, praised Bonnie's "amazing tenacity" and "relentless determination to make our society more caring, more fair, more inclusive and more humane."

When I'd had breakfast with Bonnie the previous day, she'd told me she would likely cry if people said nice things about her. There were many nice things said about her: "Bonnie is filled with a spirit of justice and truth. She's a force of nature." "She's made me and everyone around her braver." "Bonnie is living proof that not all heroes wear capes." "She taught me how to fight hard for the people that I serve."

After the speeches were over, Bonnie took the stage. Her speech was different from the one she'd delivered earlier that day. As she outlined the reasons why she'd decided to take a step back from her activism, it almost felt to me like she was speaking to herself, as if trying to rationalize her decision, although no one (at least no one I spoke to) was questioning it.

She'd had numerous health issues in recent years. Cancer. Panic attacks. A pacemaker. She was seventy years old, and her body was telling her it was time. "And my doctor, and my cardiologist, and my husband," she'd told me earlier. "It was taking a real physical toll on me—not just a psychological toll."

The psychological toll, she explained, was that she struggled to leave her work at work. She'd return home at the end of the day, to her modest little house on a tree-lined street, and feel immense guilt thinking of the people she couldn't help—those who didn't have what she had, or the families who had to spend the night in separate shelters. "Do you know what it's like splitting a family when they're already in crisis? That hurt. Because I couldn't get it fixed." She began to cry; it felt like everyone in the room was about to run onstage to give her a hug. But despite the toll the work took on her life, she said, she could not—would not—look back on her time with RAPM, or her time in Saskatchewan, or any of her life, in fact, with regret. "Everything I've gone through, all the crap that's been thrown at me, it's given me the strength to be who I am, and to do what I do."

The party began to disperse in the early evening. I was on the verge of heading back to my hotel for the night when Mike Lamb, a former roofer who'd become one of Bonnie's long-term clients and a friend, took the stage and began to sing an old Garth Brooks song, "The River," to the half-empty room. It was one of her favourites.

"You know a dream is like a river / Ever changin' as it flows / And a dreamer's just a vessel / That must follow where it goes." The room fell quiet. His voice was reedy and slightly off-key, but strong. Bonnie stood near me, staring at the stage, as if no one in the world existed outside Mike. "I'll never reach my destination / If I never try / So I will sail my vessel / 'Til the river runs dry."

In my many conversations with her friends, colleagues, and clients, it became apparent that the breadth and scope of Bonnie's work, and life, would be impossible to sum up in a book, let alone a single chapter. Her hats were many: social worker, psychologist, lobbyist, advocate, activist. Her stubbornness was legendary, as was her heart. "She walks with a heart that's overflowing with compassion," Harriet McLachlan, her colleague on the board of the national advocacy organization Canada Without Poverty, told me. As for her obstinance? "There's a certain lived experience that you have when you're younger that marks you, that shapes you, that makes you the person that you are. And I think the kind of early experiences that Bonnie had, in her younger life, just shaped and formed and marked who she is as a person. You just don't give up . . . It's just not even a thought to give up. It's like how do you stop a tsunami? Do you stop a tsunami? No, the waves are still going to come."

The bigger the heart, however, the bigger the heartbreak. Bonnie had fought for decades, and yet victory remained elusive. One might argue she'd lost. To take on poverty, homelessness, inequality—symptoms of a system that parried all attempts to change it—was to embrace a life of failure. You had to find comfort in small fixes, in moral victories. As McLachlan said: "Our hope is that poverty will be eliminated. Our hope is that there would be no people who are homeless . . . Are we going to be able to achieve that? No. But we need a goal to move towards."

Unlike with the other people featured in this book, whose goals were for the most part tangible, the idea of poverty was nebulous and constantly shifting. Being poor meant different things to different people. But we knew what was required to end poverty—we had a map to the destination. Bonnie Morton could live to see the day, if we wanted her to.

"I know that we're not going to be able to build a completely equal world. But a world in which nobody—nobody!—will go hungry or homeless, and that we, as citizens of the world, ensure that we do what we can to make sure that homelessness and hunger no longer exist in our communities—that's my vision," Bonnie told me. "And it's not ever going to happen in my lifetime."

Still, whenever she felt herself growing disheartened, she reminded herself of the victories she'd won along the way—because there were victories. Some of them were small, like the bus pass. But she had transformed countless lives, just as she had transformed her own. She had come a long, long way from Lyndhurst. She'd met prime ministers and won a slew of awards, she'd spoken at the United Nations, and travelled the world.

"I just never thought that I would ever have the wherewithal to do any of the things that I've been able to accomplish," she said. "It's definitely a different life than I ever, ever dreamed of." She had overcome so much, only to devote her life to helping others overcome, too. And despite the lack of progress and obstacles placed in her way, she still saw her ultimate goal—of a world without poverty—as one worth fighting for.

"It's a lifelong work," McLachlan said. "It is the thing that gives her breath. It's her life and it's her reason for being. It's just who she is." Helping people is "what she lives and breathes and walks and talks and dreams, probably," she continued. "When she comes to the end of her life, I think that she might have a long list of things that she would still like to do, but I think that she would die in absolute peace of everything that she's done and accomplished. I think that she could be very proud and very satisfied in the life that she's lived."

It turned out Bonnie didn't find retirement all that satisfying.

"The first three months of retirement just about killed me," she told me. "I am not a person to sit around." She was filling her days with sewing and quilting, a little bit of the fiddle. But she kept an office in Knox-Met, and continued to preach and serve on various boards, even if she was no longer part of RAPM. Bonnie was living proof that you can't quit a calling, you can't retire from a vocation.

She recalled how, not long before her retirement party, someone who knew her, and thus sensed the absurdity of the proceedings that were about to take place, asked her when she *really* was going to retire. The answer was obvious.

"I said: 'Well, I guess I'll retire when I take my last breath.'"

SIX

GOLD IN THEM HILLS

> *The sun seemed to rise very slowly as dawn struggled to claim its portion of the day. But the Superstition Mountains held onto all of its darkness for a little longer than usual, or so it seemed to Ron Feldman, who stood on his front porch watching the struggle of dark and light. He watched the same scene almost every morning until the sun peeked over the top of the mountain and bathed the huge monolith of volcanic rock in a sea of golden light.*
>
> *No different than a million years ago, the same light on the same mountain, thought Ron as he watched the sun envelop the Superstitions, bringing the distant dove coos and the repetitious call of the quail with it. Once in a while, a lone coyote could be heard. Yet, as expected as it all was, Ron never tired of it. There really was only one Sonoran Desert and he felt lucky to live in this part of the world.*
>
> —**RON FELDMAN**, *Deep Fault (2005)*

We'd only just set out from First Water Trailhead, in the foothills of the Superstition Mountains, and already Ron Feldman was annoyed. "Hiking is a nasty, four-letter word," he said, interrupting a conversation I was having with his wife, Jayne, regarding Weavers Needle, a thousand-foot rock column off in the distance that pointed skyward like a finger. "Listen: God didn't make horses so I had to hike—and I've hiked a lot in my life, especially in these mountains. And you know what?"—he didn't wait for an answer—"I'd rather be on the back of a horse!" He was just getting warmed up: "These people that go out and just hike?"—here Ron adopted what I can only assume he believed to be the dainty vocal affectations of a hiking enthusiast—"'Oh, I'm going to go take a ten-mile hike.' Well, if there ain't no gold at the end of that, or a possibility, then I ain't hiking."

I was not surprised by this outburst; Ron had demurred the previous afternoon when I'd asked him to take me into the Arizona wilderness to get a better sense of the place he'd spent so much of his life. ("I hate hiking!" he spat as we stood outside his home; his adult son, Josh, looked on, smirking at a scene he'd no doubt witnessed many times before.) And now, perhaps ten minutes down the trail, Ron was reminding me of this fact again. And again and again. "Hiking for hiking's purpose? Uck. It's beyond me."

But Ron Feldman, not being one for quitting, kept walking. It was early in the morning on an eye-blue day in late September, and the sun was hanging low in a cloud-spattered sky. The temperature was relatively low, as well—seventy-nine degrees Fahrenheit when we arrived at the trailhead—but crept upward along with the sun. Ron had warned me, when we'd first spoken about a year earlier, not to visit him during the summertime, that it was too hot, too uncomfortable, a sentiment he repeated as we made our way down the trail: "You will not be doing this in the middle of summer. If you do, you're stupid."

The landscape was a poem about a desert; there was a stark, almost otherworldly ruggedness to the terrain. It was here, in the shadow of the Superstitions, thirty miles east of Phoenix, where "the Sonoran Desert is at its glory," as Ron once put it to me. "Forget Phoenix and all that crap over there," he said another time. "That's wiped out. When you get to the Superstition Mountains, the Sonoran Desert lives." I had never before been in this part of the country, and although the region was experiencing a terrible drought, my eyeballs greedily drank in the surroundings. A devastating wildfire had swept through the area the previous year, and many of the saguaros, the giant cacti that dot the land like unlit candelabra, were charred, their normally green skin turned crispy like burnt marshmallow. It was the first time Ron and Jayne had come this way since the fire, and they marvelled at how quickly things were regenerating. The desert was a clash of beige and yellow and orange and green; paloverdes and pincushion cacti and tufts of Bermuda grass and mesquite trees and prickly pears—I'd always thought of the desert as a dead place, but there was so much life, if you just paid attention. Jayne pointed out purple verbena, and gave me a lesson about the benefits of jojoba, a waxy-leafed shrub whose oil is used in cosmetics. Ron barked at us to keep up the pace. The sooner our hike was over, the better.

I was starting to feel the same way; my scuffed off-white Converse, and horribly flat feet, were not designed for a trek through the desert. Ron and Jayne had wisely put on hiking boots before leaving for the trailhead earlier that morning. We must have seemed an odd trio to the occasional person we met on the trail. ("If you want to go on a twenty-mile hike, you can join these guys," Ron suggested as we passed a small group heading in a different direction.) I looked like I was ready for a night out at some hipster dive bar, while the Feldmans had come prepared: Jayne wore a faded green hat, turquoise T-shirt, and dark blue jeans, a plastic water bottle jammed into her back right pocket, while Ron, leading the way the entire time, wore lighter denim, with a plastic water bottle in his back left pocket, a black-white-and-blue plaid shirt, sunglasses, and a ball cap advertising the Tucson Festival of Books. His belt looped through a brown leather holster; peeking out was a Kimber semi-automatic pistol. Curious, I asked about the gun.

Jayne: "It will put you down."

Ron: "You don't want to get hit by it."

Jayne: "A twenty-two calibre—you might survive that. In fact, you probably will. A forty-five? You probably won't."

Ron: "And always remember: If you shoot somebody, make sure you kill 'em."

I made a mental note, and changed the topic of conversation.

Although he didn't enjoy hiking, Ron enjoyed playing guide, leading our small group further into the wilderness, narrating almost every step of the way. This was, after all, his backyard—he seemingly had stories about every peak in the distance, every bend in the path.

Eventually we reached the old wilderness line, and the place, in 1966, where Ron's journey—and one might argue his life—began. Standing here now, more than half a century later, Ron Feldman—treasure hunter, amateur geologist, serial entrepreneur, devoted husband, proud father, globe-trotting adventurer, prolific novelist, modern-day cowboy, and a dozen more possible descriptors—could still recall those first moments with clarity: "I got out of my vehicle and I immediately started walking down the path with my metal detector—that's how green I was." He mimicked moving the device side to side, hopelessly scanning for gold and other precious metals; for a moment, the decades shed off him like snake skin and he was that cocky and naive twenty-two-year-old again, hell-bent on finding one of the most famous treasures in American legend: the Lost Dutchman's Mine—something that generations of fortune hunters before him (and after him) had failed to do. "I was right *here*," he said.

I thought about how Ron must have felt at that moment, faced with a 160,000-acre mountain range, with its crests and canyons and caverns, and having no idea where to begin. He'd come with his younger brother, Gary; besides the metal detector they each had a backpack, bedrolls, and enough food and water to last a few days in the wild. He'd exhaustively researched the story of the Dutchman in preparation for this trip, but the mine, if there even was a mine, could be anywhere, a fact that quickly dawned upon him: "Everything I've studied is nowhere nearly enough," he told Gary. The desert seemed endless. I thought back to my conversation with Nick Oldrieve a few months earlier. In the case of the mine, it wasn't just a needle in a haystack; it was a barn filled to the rafters with haystacks. Most people, faced with the magnitude of the task, would have gotten back in their vehicle and sped out of the Superstitions, never to return. Ron Feldman made the desert, these mountains, and the treasure, his life.

If there was a treasure—of this, Ron did not doubt—it was not, he was now certain, anywhere close to where we stood today. Other

Dutch hunters, as they were known, disagreed. Ron pointed out a hillside in the distance. "There was a guy—Crabby. No, it wasn't Crabby. He camped right up in here, in these rocks, for years. And he believed the Dutchman was up in here. I mean, so many people did, and I did too—the first twenty-five years I became an expert on where the Lost Dutchman was not. I followed everybody else's information, and I did the same mistakes."

We walked past dry riverbeds and scorched cacti, little lizards skittering across the path and disappearing between the rocks. Ron told me to keep an eye (and ear) out for rattlesnakes. There were also scorpions and tarantulas and mountain lions, he said. And then you had to factor in the weather. "This is the only place you can literally go into hypothermia at night and then die of heatstroke during the day," one long-time Dutch hunter warned me, a sentiment that had also been shared with me by Ron's eldest son, Jesse, a few days earlier: "Winter, summer, doesn't matter if it's hot, cold, or just right. You can find yourself dead really quickly." It made no difference how beautiful the desert looked; the Superstitions could kill you a thousand different ways.

Ron: "I guarantee you that every week the helicopters are up here rescuing somebody."

Jayne: "Weeeeeeeeeeeell, that's an exaggeration."

Ron: "Not much of an exaggeration!"

Still, I had designs on returning here by myself, maybe getting out to Weavers Needle and poking around—I had a free morning later in the week. Plus, no matter what Ron believed, the treasure might be close. According to a legendary Dutch hunter named Adolph Ruth, "the mine lies within an imaginary circle, whose diameter is not more than 5 miles, and whose center is marked by Weaver's Needle [sic]," although to be clear, he'd written this in a notebook discovered not long after his bullet-shattered skull was found in these mountains in 1931. Now that I knew what to expect, I'd come back better prepared. Maybe I'd rent a metal detector from a shop in town. I had visions of stumbling across a gold nugget—it would pay for my trip ten times over, I bet. I could forget about the book and quit my day job, if I got really lucky. Perhaps Ron saw the fanciful look on my face as I peered off into the distance. Or maybe it was simply that, as the mercury continued to rise, I was gulping steadily from the oversized water bottle I'd filled that morning. Whatever the case, it felt as if he wanted to further caution me against such foolishness.

"Feel that heat from that sun? Just figure being out here and it's thirty-five degrees hotter—it would bake you!" He laughed, though I was unsure if it was at the idea of my melting, and then turned his attention to Jayne: "Matter of fact, what's it been—fifteen years ago maybe? Twelve years ago?"

"I don't know what story you're going to tell," she replied with the patience of a woman who had heard them all before.

The story he told was this: A number of years ago, three treasure hunters came out here to find the Dutchman, map in hand. It was July, when daily the temperature averages more than a hundred degrees Fahrenheit. The men disappeared into the desert. They were never seen alive again. A few months later, a fellow Dutch hunter stumbled across their remains about a mile and a half from the trailhead. "All three died of heat," said Ron. "Just died! Shouldn't have been out here. I can realize that better than most, because I lived here—June, July, and August, never coming out of here. And it was like living in hell. I would never do it again. But I am so happy that I did."

When I was a child, our house backed out onto a small forest that eventually led to an executive golf course and the municipal airport. Surveying it as an adult, on Google Earth, I was struck by its tininess. To me, and the other kids on my street, it might as well have been the Amazon. Foxes were sometimes spotted darting between the trees, and I remember the occasional rumour of coyote. There was a shallow, winding creek where we raced paper boats and hunted for frogs and crayfish. During the day it was our playground, but you wouldn't catch us there after sunset. Who knew what horrific creatures it contained?

At birthday parties, when friends and classmates poured into our backyard for pizza and ice cream cake, it was the site of a scavenger hunt. My father would provide a hand-drawn map and share an initial clue, often in rhyming couplets. Reading it aloud, we would parse its meaning until, suddenly, someone would scream that they had solved the riddle. The answer would lead us to a particular tree somewhere in the forest, where we would run around, frantically searching, until one of us found the next clue, perhaps in the trunk's hollow, or tucked into a low branch where an eight-year-old could reach. And then we would go after the next clue, and the next, onward until the end. There we would discover the loot bags—some candy, maybe a whistle or deflated balloons. To us it might as well have been gold, a pirate's hidden bounty. Over the years, I began to look forward to the search more than any present.

Later, one of my most treasured books was a tattered paperback copy of a novel called *Moonfleet*, which my mother pressed into my hands when I was perhaps ten years old, like a secret. It had been one of her favourite childhood books as well. Set in the mid-eighteenth century, it told the story of an orphan boy, John Trenchard, who lived in the titular English coastal village, and his attempts to find a valuable diamond that, legend had it, was stolen from King Charles I by a local pirate and hidden somewhere in the community. ("Since man first walked upon this earth, a tale of buried treasure must have had a master-power to stir his blood," wrote its author, J. Meade Falkner.)

In university I discovered the legend of Oak Island, which had obsessed, and brought ruin and sometimes death, to generations of treasure hunters on a small island off the coast of mainland Nova Scotia. An elaborate series of shafts and traps have puzzled and confounded searchers, and speculation ran rampant as to what might be found when the island's mystery was solved: the Holy Grail or the Ark of the Covenant; manuscripts that reveal Francis Bacon authored Shakespeare's plays; a treasure from the nearby Fortress of Louisbourg buried by the French before the British captured the colony. Maybe the gate to hell.

This is a short way of saying that, for almost as long as I could remember, I'd had a thing for lost treasure.

These memories were unearthed, one morning, as I was sitting in the shade outside the Mammoth Mine Rock Shop, in the small city of Apache Junction. Before me rose Superstition Mountain, over five thousand feet at its highest point, the western peak of the range that shares its name. Driving there the previous morning, I'd felt the pull of the mountain, just like innumerable treasure hunters over the decades. This was, Ron boasted, the best view of Superstition, and during my four days in town I did not find one better. "Once you've been here, you'll be back," he promised me before my trip. "I've travelled the world, but this is my home, and always will be." Even after living within its reach for more than fifty years, he often sat here, as I sat now, simply looking at the mountain, contemplating the life he had led. "It takes me back in my memories," he said now.

Ron didn't have time to sit with me and reflect on the mountain this morning; he was getting the store ready to open the following week, the unofficial start of tourist season. The shop sat right off Apache Trail, a prime piece of real estate, and business was booming. Part of the allure was no doubt the man behind the till: "I would say 50 percent, at least, of the customers that come down here know who I am."

As I sat there unhelpfully, transfixed by the mountain, Ron wrestled with a huge jaw crusher—it was over one hundred years old, but he warned me that the device, built to break down rocks, could still eat my hand. He carefully moved it from the bucket of a small front loader and, along with one of his employees, slowly shifted it into position on the covered patio outside the shop's entrance, next to an ancient minecart sitting on a section of track that went nowhere. Afterwards, the men struggled to hang a large rusted steel bucket from one of the canopy's thick wooden beams. Across from me, on the other side of the patio, was an old green wagon, the wheels painted fire-engine red, along with two rectangular wooden bins filled with various rocks and minerals that were pushed together in the shape of an L.

The inside of the store was an eclectic mix of kitschy gift shop and local historical society. Along one wall hung a series of black-and-white photographs, dating from the nineteenth and early twentieth centuries, of the actual Mammoth mine, of which Ron was now a co-owner, and which was located not far away from the shop. On the facing wall were a couple of framed movie posters—*Riders of the Deadline*, starring William Boyd as Hopalong Cassidy, and *Lust for Gold*, with Glenn Ford and Ida Lupino—with a photograph of the desert at sunset, two saguaros in silhouette, hanging in between. Behind the cash: a faded map of nearby Zigzag Canyon. There were the usual trinkets and souvenirs one found in a place like this: wine stoppers and stuffed animals and bolo ties and jewellery made from silver and amber and tiger's eye. There were mismatched shelves and antique display cases holding all manner of rocks and minerals: bismuth and amethyst and serpentinite and Apache tears and pyrite hearts and chrysocolla and quartz and peacock ore and float copper and rhodonite and gastroliths and fluorite and tiny gold nuggets selling for twelve dollars apiece. A sign in one of the cases read: "Remember the Golden Rule: Whoever has the Gold Makes the Rules."

Along one wall, set out on a table adorned with a *Jurassic Park* banner, and under the mounted head of a T. Rex, was a not-insignificant collection of bones—the humerus from a triceratops, part of the femur from a T. Rex. Ron was eager to talk about dinosaurs, and spent several minutes recounting a rambling story about a fossil he'd sold that involved a trip to California and a baseball signed by Mickey Mantle. In another life, he said, he might have become a paleontologist.

But it was the Dutchman, not dinos, around which his life had revolved, and evidence of that life's richness was on display throughout the shop, more generally, and specifically on a small table near the entrance, under a wooden "Dutchman's Mine" sign, the head of a pickaxe etched with the word "Silverton," and various other mining ephemera. There, neatly stacked, were several piles of books, mostly written by Ron, with titles like *Crooked Mountain* and *Double Cross* and *Deep Fault*. There were a few dozen copies of his latest, a memoir called *Lost Dutchman Gold Mine: Evolution of a Treasure Hunter*, which I'd read on the plane the previous week. Ron grabbed a copy of the one title I hadn't been able to track down online and enthusiastically signed it for me, like an author meeting his biggest fan.

Ron Feldman's life could have been lifted from the pages of a novel, so it made a kind of sense that he'd poured his stories back into books. His fiction was a mix of Dan Brown and Clive Cussler, one of his personal favourites, and filled with lost treasure and shadowy conspiracies. Several of them involved an organization called HEAT, which stood for Historical Exploration and Treasures and was based on a real-life group of friends and fellow adventurers who were also Ron's co-investors in a number of mining claims. He'd used his decades in the Superstitions as the framework for fiction; in *Deep Fault,* for instance, a fortune hunter who conveniently shares Ron's name becomes tangled up with a group of government-hating survivalists who also might happen to know the location of the Dutchman. Ron, of course, saves the day. As charming as they were to read, bestsellers they were not; he'd worked with a small publisher for a time but now just self-published and sold the books here in the store.

"I ain't Stephen King," he said.

The legend of the Lost Dutchman featured as many twists and turns as one of King's novels. Not only had the mine vanished, so too had many of the facts. It was a tale that existed somewhere between history and fiction, and whose truth was buried deep in the past—perhaps never to be found. The story, or at least one of them, went like this:

In the early-to-mid-1800s, the Peraltas, a wealthy family hailing from northern Mexico, established several mines in Arizona, a place about which legends of golden cities and unfathomable riches had long been shared. The miners came into constant conflict with the local Apache tribes, however, and were eventually forced to flee. Some stories claim they discovered a particularly rich vein of ore but were slaughtered before it could be extracted. Some accounts maintain there were no survivors, while in others one or two people live to tell the tale (one version claims the Peralta family patriarch, Don Miguel, hid his two sons in "a brushy draw" in the moments before his own death). And this being lost treasure, there's also a mysterious map that would no doubt lead its owner to the fortune.

What can't be denied is that in the years after the Treaty of Guadalupe Hidalgo ended the Mexican-American War in 1848, and granted this part of Arizona to the victorious United States, prospectors descended upon the Superstitions. One of them was a German émigré named Jacob Waltz, who arrived in Arizona around 1864. (The Dutchman of legend is actually a *Deutschmann*, although, as the writer Robert Blair put it, "it is evident that much of the published biographical material of the life and times of Jacob Waltz is demonstrably false.") One popular story is that Waltz saved a man in a bar fight who turned out to be a Peralta, and who told him about the treasure. In any case, at some point Waltz allegedly found an abandoned mine that contained an "eighteen-inch wide quartz vein, so rich with gold that it would make millionaires of twenty men." He held the particulars close to his chest, and died in 1891, taking the location with him to his grave. That hadn't stopped treasure hunters, who had been coming to the area ever since to find what Waltz might have been left behind.

They didn't find gold, but endless frustration. There was little consensus about the history of the mine—let alone the location—and in the century after Waltz's death, theories and conspiracies blossomed, and speculation became indistinguishable from proof. Everyone who searched for the Dutchman seemingly had their own ideas, and in some historical accounts I read the author would stop to slag the writer of another book who dared propose a different premise. It was, as the saying goes, a riddle wrapped in a mystery inside an enigma. "The issue is there's so much manipulation and lying that has gone on, all the way back to the beginning of the story," Jesse Feldman told me. "And then, of course, it just goes awry from there, because the next generation has that information to deal with."

I'd been introduced to Jesse earlier that morning, though in less-than-ideal circumstances. An author like his father (I'd spotted his book, *Jacob's Trail: The Legend of Jacob Waltz's Lost Dutchman Mine*, in the shop), he was stressed out because he'd just lost a chunk of his newest book, which was supposed to go to press imminently. He had been frantically retyping it from rough notes and fuzzy memory late into the night. Plain-spoken and calm, whereas his father was animated and excited, Jesse was decked out in a denim shirt and black cowboy hat, looking even more an outlaw than his father. Along with his brother, Josh, he ran the OK Corral Stables, which Ron founded in 1968 and which shared the property with the rock shop. He'd also followed his father into the *other* family business: Jesse was a treasure hunter of some renown—he co-starred in a couple of reality TV shows, including *Ice Cold Gold*, set in Greenland, and *Lost Gold*, set in Arizona, though I struggled to envision him enjoying show business.

His passion, rather, was history, and when it came to the Lost Dutchman he wanted to set the record straight, which might well have been as impossible a task as finding the mine itself. Over the years evidence had been manipulated, rumours and gossip perpetuated, trustworthy sources deemed as valuable as gold. The story of the Lost Dutchman was one of history's greatest games of broken telephone.

"What you have to do is reverse engineer this thing," Jesse said. "If you can do that, then you can begin to unravel and figure out what actually happened, and where the mine is. But, still, even then, I still argue you can't solve it. It's just the nature of the beast. It's a legend."

Storytime over, we watched as Ron continued to ready the shop for customers.

"He has a knack, I think, for figuring out these legends," Jesse said to me, then addressed his father: "You just keep at it, right? You don't give up."

"I'm very persistent," agreed Ron. "I don't take no for an answer."

We drove eastward, down the Apache Trail, an old stagecoach route that bisected the town and wound through the mountains like an asphalt river. Ron warned me, too late, that he was considered a terrible driver ("I hate to drive!") and that no one in his family would get into a car if he was behind the wheel. "I still, to this day, scare Jayne and my boys driving," he said, with evident self-satisfaction. "I'm talking about normal driving in town!" It would have been nice to have known this information beforehand, considering we were far from Apache Junction, and considering the number of switchbacks and hairpin turns we traversed, which Ron took on like an immortal.

We were headed towards Canyon Lake, and then onward to Tortilla Flat—the same stretch he'd driven decades prior, in his '63 Chevy with a burro named Phoenix in the back. It was a glorious desert morning, bright and hot and still, and as we rose higher into the Superstitions it was hard not to become distracted by the views. I found myself staring out the window, lost in the mountains, and for a few pleasant minutes pushed the vision of my body lying in a smouldering hunk of twisted metal on the canyon floor from my mind. "This is one of the most spectacular drives you'll ever be on," Ron said, gripping the wheel. "It, today, still absolutely churns my blood."

It unlocked his memories, too. We were not, I soon realized, simply driving through the Sonoran Desert, or the Superstitions, but Ron's life, the layers peeled back further with every mile he drove—here's where this happened; here's where that occurred. And not just a personal history, the things he'd seen and experienced first-hand, but myths and legends piled on top, like layers of earth—here's where this was supposed to have happened; here's where they say that occurred. The desert was a palimpsest, revealing traces of not only the life he'd led but the lives of those who came before him, as well.

Ron once told me that he'd been born in the wrong era, that he would have been more comfortable in some rugged nineteenth-century frontier town. Modern society—its rules and codes and ways of being—did not agree with him, or maybe it just was that he did not understand them. Living on the edge of the desert for almost sixty years could do that to a man. "What pisses me off a lot is the norms of society," he said. "Where society has gone, and their values, and their bullshit liberal-leaning cry-baby bullshit . . ." He let his words trail off, perhaps sensing I agreed with most liberal-leaning bullshit. "Just leave me alone. This world would be a better place if everybody just took care of their own little circle. I take care of mine. You take care of yours. If everybody did that, it would be a perfect world."

He described himself as a loner, or at least someone with no time for what he called "run-of-the-mill people." He explained how, over the years, he'd packed thousands of people into the Superstitions on horseback—a big part of the family business was outfitting others heading into the mountains. Sometimes he spent only an hour or two with customers; sometimes he went into the wilderness with them for days at a time. Either way, it meant a lot of small talk. "I get to talking to them, and I entertain them, and I enjoy them, to a point." That point usually came when he asked them what they did for a living. "Ninety-nine percent of the time they would say, 'Oh, I'm an engineer' or 'I'm an electrician.' The conversation almost ends right there." Rarely did he ever find anyone he "clicked" with, he said. "Most people don't interest me."

Fortunately, Arizona in the 1960s—and specifically Apache Junction—was like a different century, full of people who did interest him. It was the closest thing to a perfect world for a man like Ron. "This place was so much the Wild West it was incredible," he said as we sped towards Tortilla Flat. It was one of the reasons he'd finally written a memoir—to transport himself back "to one of the best times of my life." He quickly corrected himself: "I'm living one of the best times of my life now," he said. "But that just—" He suddenly yelped, a plaintive, primal sound, a cry for his younger self and the life he'd led in these mountains.

We were a long way from Buffalo, where he grew up. His childhood in upstate New York, looking back now, was not one that necessarily predicted the life of a treasure hunter. His mother was a homemaker who later worked in a doctor's office; his father was a car salesman by day, and by night a piano player who toured strip joints, dive bars, and other establishments of questionable repute. "The one thing that my father taught me was how to sell," he told me.

As a kid, he was drawn to tales of adventure and daring: "All my childhood," he said, "I was fascinated by stories of lost treasure and lost mines and sunken wrecks and so forth. But [in] Buffalo, you know, you don't get a whole lot of chances to do any of that." Of all the stories of lost treasure and sunken wrecks he heard, it was the Dutchman that stayed with him. "I always knew, someday, that was what I wanted to do. I wanted to go after the Lost Dutchman."

He told me his life story over lunch at the Superstition Restaurant and Saloon, in Tortilla Flat, an old trading outpost in the heart of the mountains. He'd been coming here for decades, and the restaurant probably hadn't changed much—it was straight out of the 1870s, with the exception of the Johnny Cash on the stereo coming a hundred years too late. The wood walls were covered in paper money—the place was famous for the dollar bills customers stapled to the walls at the end of their meal. We wondered how much there was. I estimated $50,000, and, when Ron expressed incredulity, lowered my guess to $10,000. When the waitress next checked up on us, Ron asked—the answer coming before he finished his question: $450,000. I took a closer look at the wall: The bills were four or five deep in some places, disintegrating and weathered, but currency all the same. When she left we discussed how one might pull off a heist and free the cash—an unmade sequel to *Ocean's Eleven*. He'd been in this area his whole life looking for a lost fortune when one was sitting here in this restaurant the entire time.

His family left upstate New York for California when he was seventeen. His parents wanted to leave the winter behind, and thought a move to the West Coast would provide more opportunities for Ron and his three siblings: "They believed this shit that California's streets were paved with gold," he told me. He hated California—he hated it to this day, and he spent a significant amount of our time together bemoaning and dreading a forthcoming trip. It was "too civilized," he said, although he conceded the beaches were nice.

Despite its many flaws, California had a history of gold, even if the streets didn't contain any, and there were old-timers still working the leftover claims from the Gold Rush a century prior. He started hunting some of the state's fabled treasures, but the Lost Dutchman remained in the back of his mind.

When he finally made it to Arizona in 1966, it was in search of a different fortune. Ron had been a fan of the 1950s show *Treasure*, which chronicled famous cases of buried gold and sunken wrecks and other such mysteries; one episode featured a man who claimed to be a descendent of the outlaw Jesse James, who was searching for a treasure around Safford, Arizona. Ron began corresponding with the man, and decided to go out to help with his search. But as they traded letters back and forth, Ron grew alarmed by the man's behaviour: "He was nuttier than a fruitcake," he recalled. After doing a little digging into his pen pal's past, it turned out the man was a complete phoney, a fact that rankled Ron to this day. "His name was Orvus Lee Howk!" Still, he'd done all the prep work for a trip to Arizona; why let it go to waste? "I said, 'You know what? Screw it. I'm going for the Dutchman.'" So he did. "And that was it. It was all over."

It was as if the Westerns he'd read as a kid had come to life. "It was living the dream," he told me. "It was the Old West. People strapped guns on their hips, and we rode horseback. It was wild. Hardly anything was here. Nothing. A couple gas stations, a couple hotels." What he did find were treasure hunters. The promise of the Dutchman seemed to draw every eccentric, romantic, and get-rich-quick confidence man to Apache Junction. It is not a statistic kept by the United States Census Bureau, but it is quite probable that if, in 1966, they had counted the number of treasure hunters in any one town, Apache Junction would have won, at least on a per capita basis, by a comfortable margin.

Not long after their arrival, Ron and his brother Gary came under the wing of a swarthy, bald-headed con artist named Robert Jacobs. Crazy Jake, as he was known, controlled everything that went on in the Superstitions, and knew the brothers had been poking around the mountains. "I have two men that live out there full-time, to watch what goes on for me," he cautioned the brothers the first time they met. But he also claimed to know the location of the Dutchman—a claim that proved irresistible to Ron, who spent the next year and a half living in the mountains, working on behalf of Crazy Jake, who he quickly learned was fool's gold, and who later served seven years in prison for fraud. (He died in 1994, though rumours that he faked his death persisted.)

In 1968, after breaking away from Crazy Jake, and after Gary had gone back to California, Ron bought a piece of land in the "middle of nowhere" and established the stables, a way to earn a living while still allowing himself to hunt the Dutchman. Maybe earn a living is a stretch. "If I had fifty cents a day, it was a lot," he told me. His parents, no doubt hoping their son's desert misadventures were just a phase, thought he was nuts, and his father was especially vocal in letting his son know what he made of his life choices. "It was just a different way of life to him," he said. "I wasn't selling cars." When Ron's parents visited for the first time, not long after he'd opened the stables, his father tried to convince him to come back home. "My father, I'll never forget when he visited me, he said: 'Why don't you stop this, move back to L.A. and get a goddamn job?' I said, 'That will never happen.'"

And it never did.

"There is something in a treasure that fastens upon a man's mind," Joseph Conrad wrote in his 1904 novel *Nostromo*. "He will pray and blaspheme and still persevere, and will curse the day he ever heard of it, and will let his last hour come upon him unawares, still believing that he missed it only by a foot. He will see it every time he closes his eyes. He will never forget it till he is dead."

The Treasure Hunter of the Year Awards have been presented annually since 1993, a tribute to the men and women—let's be honest, it's mostly men—who roamed the Superstitions in search of the mine. "We're giving 'em some recognition for what they've done all their lives," said the prize's co-organizer Bob Schoose, a long-time Dutch hunter with the voice of a grizzly bear that swallowed a chainsaw. It's also a prize that not everyone wants to win, he told me. "A lot of 'em are afraid to get the award, 'cause a lot of 'em, we're giving it to 'em and they're on their last legs—they usually pass within a year or two of getting the award."

When Schoose first came to Apache Junction, in 1965, a year before Ron (the two men later became best friends and co-investors in a number of mining claims), the mountains were crawling with Dutch hunters. Now, said Ron forlornly, the town was becoming just another suburb of Phoenix. "We are a dying breed," he told me. "We're dinosaurs." And so another generation of searchers was fated to pass into myth, the legend left unsolved.

"If you ever meet these treasure hunters in their seventies and eighties, you can see there's a desperation," said Wayne Tuttle, a prominent Dutch hunter and local historian, and co-organizer of the awards. How would it feel, he asked me, if you'd lost everything dear to you devoting your life to the search—family, marriages, friendships—"and then there's no closure at the end?"

While there might not be as many Dutch hunters as before, Tuttle said he still sometimes stumbled across their camps, or encountered them out in the desert with (illegal) ground-penetrating radar rigs, scanning for gold. And each year he organized the Dutch Hunter Rendezvous, which attracted hundreds of searchers from around the world, proving legends never really die.

"If you ever share a campfire with treasure hunters, guys that have been out there and have really put themselves through it, besides some of the tall-tale stories and the drinking, you'll realize there's a shared common thread," Tuttle said. "Maybe there's something in the DNA that does that. Those people are just who they are, and it's not about believing in something. It's just they're wired that way. And there are people that will search and never find a damn thing their entire life worth talking about, but they will have a thousand and one stories of their trips and adventures in the mountains."

I heard the line about treasure hunting being something in the DNA numerous times, including from Ron: "This sounds a little corny, but I think it's kind of in our DNA." Even if the science wasn't sound, there was no disputing that searching had been the most powerful motivating factor in his life. It brought him not only to Arizona, but had taken him on hunts across America and around the world, from

Florida's Treasure Coast to Loch Ness in Scotland. He had designs on looking for the Ark of the Covenant at some point, too. Searching was his passion, and treasure was an excuse to search.

"We are modern-day explorers," he said. "We have something that travels in our blood, in our DNA, that we have to go search for the unknown. And it's not the find, Mark. Not really. The find is always nice. It's the search. And that was the most important part of my life."

One of the reasons Ron never moved back to L.A. and got a goddamn job, as his father had hoped, was because, one day in the early months of 1972, a young woman—five-eight; brown hair; "friendly, open, kind, smart, and beautiful, all in one package"—arrived at the OK Corral Stables and asked to be taken horseback riding. Ron and Jayne were married the following year, on July 4. They built a life in Apache Junction—expanding the stables, opening a trailer park, welcoming children into the world.

The Feldmans lived on a family compound a few miles away from the rock shop, and I visited one afternoon. Jayne ushered me into the living room—where a large glass cabinet of curiosities, collected during Ron's treasure hunts around the world, took up the majority of one wall—and there was a beer in my hand before I knew what had happened. The Millers were cold, the chairs were comfortable, and Ron was feeling philosophical.

"Most people in the world," he began, as Jayne and their youngest son, Josh, looked on, "they're born, they get up, they go to work. They might have a family, or not. They eat, they crap, they get up, they go to bed. And when they're dead, they're not a part of nothing." He tipped his drink in the general direction of Superstition. "When I'm gone, I will be a part of something bigger than me, and it's that mountain and legend."

Speaking of the legend, Josh told his father, taking advantage of an opening in the conversation, he'd just heard from a man who had, surprise surprise, discovered the Dutchman.

"A guy called me last night," said Josh.

"Who?"

"Some wild-mouthed Alabaman. He wants to talk to you. He sent you an email, and you didn't reply. I assume he's a bit off his rocker."

"What's his name?"

"It's a weird name," said Josh, and shared it with his father. "He probably sent you an email like, 'I know where the Dutchman is!'"

"No, I reply to them all. All of 'em!"

"I don't know. But he's coming out here, and he wants to really talk to you."

This was a regular occurrence. Dutch hunting could be a lonely occupation—days and weeks and months in the wilderness, the ghost of Jacob Waltz your only company—so it made sense that those who pursued it sought connection, and kinship, with others who shared their obsession. And as one of the most high-profile hunters in the world, Ron had become a lightning rod for all manner of fellow searchers, even if many of them thought he was looking in the wrong place.

"It's fun, until it starts to waste too much of your time," said Josh, when I asked how he maintained his patience with these people. "You're willing to play with it for a minute, and then you're like, 'All right, I'm done,' after he gets into aliens or spaceships, or he had a vision."

One had to accept a certain amount of delusion if one remained a part of this world, added Josh, who'd appeared in the TV series with his brother. "Treasure hunting is not about logic. It's not logical at all. It's completely and totally emotional. So, since it's emotional, everybody's going to have their own theory and feeling about it. And they can! And you can question it, but it's not going to get you anywhere. How do you question emotion? If they want to believe that, they can believe that."

If everyone had their own theory, the fact remained that ultimately only one would be proven right. Treasure hunting was a pursuit where failure was the rule, not the exception—something that had never bothered Ron. I wasn't sure if I believed him, but he insisted he never thought about the history of failure that was the uncomfortable legacy of the Dutch hunting community. "I only thought of me being successful," he said. "That's what has propelled me through treasure hunting—being positive. Otherwise, if you were negative you'd never hunt for anything. Never!" Treasure hunters, he added, are "all positive, optimistic thinkers. You have to be."

That said, you had to let others fail on their own terms, added Jayne. For the half-century they'd been taking people into the mountains, the Feldmans' clientele had included many a Dutch hunter. "You take them into the mountains and you assure them that you're not going to tell people where they're going." They'd see the same people come back, year after year, pursuing a new theory or location. "We politely would not get involved in their search, because you didn't want to ruin their dreams," she said. "For a lot of them, you could look at them and say, 'You're absolutely crazy! What the heck are you doing out there?' And they would be back next year."

Ron told me that he didn't discourage any of his clients, even if he thought they were looking in the wrong place. It likely wouldn't have made a difference if he had. Treasure hunters were a stubborn breed. If they asked for directions and you told them to take a left at the next stop, they'd probably turn right—unless they had a map that was drawn by the city planner who built the street in the first place, and even then they still might not believe you. "Dutchman hunters have their own view," said Ron, "and I'm going to tell you something: There is, by God, no way you're going to change that view."

Ron knew from personal experience. He was convinced he'd found the location of the Lost Dutchman, but had struggled to persuade others. It was, he maintained, a mine called the Silver Chief. The irony was that it wasn't searching in the mountains that brought him to this conclusion; it was modern science. Using an XRF (x-ray fluorescence) spectrometer, he'd conducted a battery of tests on gold he obtained from various parts of the Superstitions and compared it to gold that purportedly once belonged to Jacob Waltz, and which had, after his death, been fashioned into a matchbox. Both the matchbox and ore from the Silver Chief, he discovered, contained similar levels of mercury. Of course, there was no definitive proof that the Waltz gold came from the Dutchman, and so it was easy for other Dutch hunters to dismiss Ron's findings, no matter how impressive they seemed to me.

"It cracks me up, because there ain't a lick of gold in it," said Bob Schoose, about his best friend's Silver Chief theory. He thought the mine would never be discovered because the legend itself was too lucrative—not to the hunters but to the community. Schoose himself ran Goldfield Ghost Town, right next door to the Mammoth Mine—its train's steam whistle provided a soundtrack whenever I was around the shop. "It's been a gigantic draw for tourism," he told me. "They don't want to kill the legend, because it makes a lot of money."

If the mine was found, said Wayne Tuttle, the Superstitions would become "just a hiking trail."

Another problem when it came to proving Ron's theory was that the Silver Chief was located in a federally protected wilderness area, which meant it was off-limits to any kind of mining, which in turn meant there was no way to go in and dig for the gold without the proper permits, and the proper permits weren't forthcoming. The feds, said Ron, "don't want to believe in the Dutchman, they don't want you to believe in the Dutchman, and they don't want to deal with us." The government had valid reasons for downplaying the legend, as several searchers had died looking for the mine—including a thirty-five-year-old Denver man named Jesse Capen, whose body was discovered in 2012, three years after he went searching; his mother told reporters her son had grown "beyond obsessed" with the story of the lost treasure, and after he went missing more than a hundred books and maps about the treasure were discovered in his apartment.

This all meant that although Ron and his sons had been "right on the cusp" of being able to prove it, they couldn't "get all the way over that crest, into actually proving it," Jesse Feldman told me that day on the patio of the rock shop. "It's not possible."

"What Jess says is absolutely correct," said Ron. "There are Dutchman hunters that I can introduce you to, hundreds of them. We could show them all the evidence and everything and they'll say, 'Ah, Feldman's crazy.' Because they believe we could not have found it, because they have." When it comes to finding the mine, he said, "nobody is going to believe the other guy has it." He'd seen Dutch hunters who'd searched away their lives and, at the end, instead of admitting failure, denied the mine's existence. "It's too painful to say 'I didn't find it.'"

Which is why the legend endured. Even if the number of on-the-ground hunters had dwindled, interest in the Dutchman remained high. Plus, there was no longer a need to move to Apache Junction—people could conduct their searches from the comfort of their own homes.

"Every year I hear from a hundred people that send me photographs, maps, clippings, everything else, of how they found it," said Tuttle. "I've had thousands of people tell me, 'I've found it.' But they don't have a physical piece of proof or anything. That actually does more to keep it alive than anything. The people repeatedly say they found it, and the guy from across the canyon is going, 'Nope, I've found it over here.' And then there's a guy somewhere else in the mountains going, 'Nope, I found it over here . . .'"

"Are you ever going to be able to definitively prove it?" Tuttle continued. "Probably not. Because I don't think Waltz left a signed piece of paper sitting there on the wall for us."

Dutch hunters could only dream of such a tidy resolution—directions, written in the Dutchman's hand, leading them to fortune. Instead, they've been driven to ruin, driven mad, driven to spend their lives searching for what, in the grand scheme of things, would only be a footnote in the history of these mountains, which would outlast any treasure they may hide.

"The mountains don't give a shit whether you live, you die, whether you found gold," said Tuttle. "They don't care. They're going to be there long after we're all gone and dust."

We arrived back at the mouth of the trailhead, and civilization, in the form of a parking lot. As Ron drove his truck down the long, snaking entranceway towards the highway, we noticed signs, at intervals of about thirty feet or so, along either side. Some said "no parking at any time"; others just said "no parking." There had to be dozens of them, all telling would-be parkers to look elsewhere. Ron and Jayne scoffed at this government intervention, a reminder that the wilderness was being infringed on in ways big and small.

"Who in the heck came up with this?" wondered Jayne. "What bureaucrat, sitting in an office somewhere . . ."

"They're trying to control people," said Ron. "The whole thing is control."

We found a small crew installing another sign when we arrived at the turn-off for Apache Trail. "I gotta talk to this girl," said Ron. He rolled down the passenger-side window and leaned over my lap, Jayne laughing in the back. "There was a sign back there that said 'no parking,' but it didn't say anytime—so when can you park at that sign?"

"Never," she replied.

I was reminded of something Jesse had told me earlier in the week: "It's a different world than it was when he first came here." Ron wasn't just searching for the Dutchman; he was searching for a world that was on the brink of disappearing, probably forever. Ron loved the desert, and this part of the world, fiercely. He was appreciative of what it had given him, and protective of it. His distaste for hiking was partly an act, but also a hatred well-earned from decades of doing that very thing in these mountains. If he wanted to be on a horse, so be it.

After we arrived back at the rock shop, Ron said he wanted to show me one of his claims. While the location of the Dutchman might not be decided, one way or another, in his lifetime, he'd still found gold. "I've searched for gold all over the country, and sometimes in others, and right here, in my backyard, is the most gold I've ever seen," he said, holding up a small, water-filled vial to the sun. "This is jewellery-grade gold." Flecks danced in the water like in a snow globe.

At the time of my visit, Ron controlled nineteen mining claims of varying profitability. There was the Mammoth, his store's namesake, which had been discovered in 1893 and produced millions of dollars' worth of gold over the years before falling into disarray; Ron and his co-investors purchased it in 2003 and revived the mining operations. Others sported names like Mother Hubbard, Tom Thumb, and the Black Queen, which was the main vein he worked these days, and from which the vial of gold he showed me had been mined. This is where he offered to take me now. "We can walk," he said. "It ain't that far—it's about two and a half miles one way. Are you okay with that? I like to hike, so it's no problem with me."

We did not walk to the mine. After driving down multiple dirt roads, stopping every so often to open a locked gate, Ron and Jayne and I arrived at the Queen, the excavation of which began in 1892. Mining season had yet to begin, so it was still under several feet of water, a desert oasis. As we walked down the slope of the man-made ravine, a great horned owl watched from afar. "To get down to the vein we've been working on, we have to pump this water out," said Jayne when we reached the pool's edge. I could make out the top of a tunnel just above the water.

"The tunnel is flooded right now," said Ron. "That vein is all the way down and underwater right now. Which is wonderful, because now high graders can't come and do anything."

"Hydraters?" I asked, thinking of water.

"High graders," he said again. "Stealing ore."

They would start pumping in a few weeks, when the weather grew cooler, but since we were here, Ron said, he might as well get a jump on draining the water, a process that took about two weeks. "So if you want to stay here for a minute, I'll run back and get a couple buckets and we can start." He laughed at his own joke. "It'll take us the rest of our lives."

SEVEN

ONCE WAS LOST

He worked as a clerk in a small department store, in a small town, in the southeast of England. It was a small life, and he often thought there must be more to it than this.

On his lunch hour, he would sometimes wander down the street to the local library and browse the stacks, studying the spines, waiting for something to capture his attention. Books were a passport to a bigger world. They allowed him to leave his life behind.

One day, he noticed a volume called *Vanishing Birds*, by the biologist Tim Halliday. He was not all that interested in the subject—his brother was a devoted birder; he liked them just fine—but something about the title spoke to him. He took the book off the shelf, went back to the store, took a seat in the lunchroom, and began to read.

He soon came across a chapter comprising three case studies of birds rendered extinct thanks to the folly of man. The first section focused on the dodo and the solitaire, the flightless inhabitants of Mauritius and

Rodrigues, last seen in the mid-seventeenth and eighteenth centuries, respectively. The second told the tragic tale of the great auk, a grounded penguin-like creature that made it to 1844, when the last known pair were clubbed to death on a tiny island off the coast of Iceland.

The third changed his life.

On a warm afternoon in June, as we sat in the living room of his small flat in the town of Crowborough, in East Sussex, Richard Thorns picked up his copy of *Vanishing Birds*, although he probably knew the passage by heart, and in a soft, wistful voice read aloud to me what he had read on that day so many years ago:

"The area around the lower reaches of the Ganges and Brahmaputra rivers, previously called Bengal, now Bangladesh, is one of the most densely populated parts of the world. In the 19th century, Bengal was a largely unexplored wilderness whose rich and exotic wildlife attracted British colonialists seeking a substitute for the hunting and shooting which was so popular a pastime at home. It was extremely difficult country to cross, with areas of thick, tall grass intersected by innumerable slow-moving expanses of water. The grassland was the home of the tiger, the chief target of the sportsmen who used elephants to cross the difficult terrain and to provide a vantage point above the grass. The streams and the pools were infested by crocodiles, which, with the tigers, were chiefly responsible for the fact that this country had previously been virtually unexplored by man. The limpid waters were largely covered by pink and white lotus flowers and were the home of innumerable species of waterfowl which provided another target for sportsmen. The most beautiful and the rarest of all these waterfowl was the pink-headed duck."

Among the book's colour plates of avian ghosts, nestled between renderings of the great auk and the passenger pigeon, Richard found an illustration of four ducks floating by a cluster of flowering lily pads, their pink heads and long, slender necks reflected in the ice-still water, their plumage an outrageous combination of cotton candy and dark chocolate, with pink-and-white markings on their wings.

It was the most beautiful thing he'd ever seen.

By the time his lunch hour was over and he returned to work, to sell socks and underwear to customers, Richard had made a decision: "I don't want to be a shop's assistant anymore," he said to himself. He would do something incredible. He would live a big life. Right then and there, he made a vow to the universe: "I'm going to try and find it."

I learned about Richard Thorns, and his quixotic pursuit of the pink-headed duck, from a biologist and conservationist named Robin Moore. I'd long been intrigued by not only the subject of cryptozoology—animals we have scant proof exist, like the orang-pendek—but the subject of de-extinction, as well. Fuelled by advances in genetics, the movement to bring back disappeared species through science and technology—*Jurassic Park*, in real life—had made strides in recent years, and in my former jobs as the editor of two national newspapers' books sections I'd seen a small library's worth of titles chronicling the resurrection race come across my desk in a short amount of time: Beth Shapiro's *How to Clone a Mammoth*; M.R. O'Connor's *Resurrection Science*; Ben Mezrich's *Woolly*; Britt Wray's *Rise of the Necrofauna*. Reading these, it often felt as if it was only a matter of time before I'd spot a dodo or thylacine roaming down the street.

But there were also people who believed that extinction was just a word, not necessarily a fact, and that some things assumed to have vanished from our earthly realm were still out there, somewhere, waiting to be found. Animals that didn't need to be revived by science but by determination.

Which brought me to Robin Moore. In 2014, he published a book called *In Search of Lost Frogs*, which chronicled his exhaustive and sometimes successful quest to rediscover various tiny amphibians considered gone for good. The book sparked a worldwide campaign, sponsored by Global Wildlife Conservation (later rebranded as Re:wild), the organization where Moore worked, called the Search for Lost Species, which included a most-wanted list of twenty-five "extinct" animals it was thought might still be out there in the wild. Launched in 2017, it was a global scavenger hunt—perhaps fugitive hunt is a better description—with the goal of rediscovering as many creatures on the list as possible.

Most of my conversation with Moore was focused on his life and work, and his search for lost frogs, but at one point, when discussing the other folks participating in the campaign, he made an off-hand comment that caught my attention: "One of the people we're working with on the lost species has devoted his life to trying to find the pink-headed duck in Myanmar. A decade spent trying to find one bird!" He seemed genuinely stunned at this level of commitment.

I spoke to Richard for the first time a couple of months later. At that point, his search had been ongoing for a dozen years, although it had been far longer than that since he'd learned of the duck. After finding *Vanishing Birds* in the library, in 1998, it wasn't as if he'd gone traipsing off to Asia straight away. In the intervening years Richard had read everything he could about the duck and its dismal history, becoming perhaps the world's foremost authority on the bird—which, to be honest, was kind of like being the world's last pink-headed duck. It was a lonely existence.

While the pink-headed duck, which was first noted by biologists in 1790, was officially still listed as critically endangered by the International Union for Conservation of Nature, the last confirmed sighting in the wild was made in June 1935, by the British museum curator Charles M. Inglis, in the eastern Indian state of Bihar. (This date has been disputed, although subsequent observations in the 1930s and '40s were "possible, but open to serious doubt," according to the paleontologist Julian P. Hume, author of an essential paper about the duck.) The bird had the great misfortune of residing where it did. The combination of a fast-growing population, a devastating loss of habitat, and over-hunting spelled its doom, though it was never exactly considered common in the first place. "In fact it was always considered rare enough to be taken notice of," wrote Salim Ali in the Wildfowl Trust's annual report in 1960, "even by such sportsmen as seldom bother to vet their bags and to whom the significance of a duck is merely how it tastes!" By the time local governments attempted to save the species, in the mid-1950s, outlawing hunting or the poaching of its eggs, the pink-headed duck had not been spotted in the wild in years. "Everything about it was just too late," Richard told me mournfully.

A number of pink-headed ducks survived in captivity, although according to the French ornithologist Jean Théodore Delacour, "they were very stupid birds because they refuse to breed." Delacour was intimately familiar with the species, having two pairs in his private zoo in Clères, France. These were gifts from Alfred Ezra, the president of the Avicultural Society, who kept as many as sixteen pink-headed ducks on his estate, Foxwarren Park, coincidentally only about an hour's drive from Richard's home in Crowborough.

There exist a number of striking black-and-white photographs of the Foxwarren Park ducks, taken in the mid-1920s. Whether or not they look miserable, as Richard believed, is hard to say, but there is something incredibly lonely about the birds, as if they knew in all the world they had only each other. All were dead by 1938.

Ezra obtained his ducks from his brother, David, who served as "sheriff" of Kolkata, was director of the Reserve Bank of India, and, like his brother back in England, maintained his own personal zoo. David published advertisements in leading Indian newspapers signalling his interest ("Wanted—TO BUY. PINK-HEADED ducks and drakes") and promising bird-catchers one hundred rupees each, more than three months' pay, for each specimen. He apparently shipped many of these ducks back to Europe, though saved some for himself, and according to accounts the last-known living pink-headed duck died in his care in 1948.

Despite its inglorious, apparent end, this meant that, unlike, say, the dodo, which has been gone for centuries, the pink-headed duck was alive within the lifetime of people still alive today. There was a chance that the bird was still out there, Richard thought, even if it was a remote chance. What he knew was that doing nothing, and later regretting it, was not an option.

"My grandfather always wanted to go into the Amazon and try and find Colonel Fawcett," Richard said of the British explorer, who went missing searching for the mythical city of Z. "Even in his eighties, he was kind of lamenting that he never did any of these things. And I never really wanted to be like that. I never really wanted to be in my seventies or eighties, thinking, 'If only I'd gone to Burma to look for the pink-headed duck. If only I'd found it.'"

Richard and I kept in touch over the years, and he kept me abreast of his expedition plans, sometimes cc'ing me on emails chronicling his lengthy back-and-forth with diplomats and civil servants in the military junta running Myanmar, which Richard still called Burma, where his efforts were focused—a coup in February 2021 had complicated his return, turning his quest into what he described as a "wretched game of Burmese snakes and ladders." While our conversations and correspondence were always pleasant, there was not the possibility of joining him on a search—he preferred, he repeatedly and firmly told me, to work alone. I could, however, visit him any time I wished.

And so in the summer of 2023 I travelled to Crowborough, not long before Richard returned to Asia for the latest chapter in his search—which, he was sure, would lead to proof, once and for all, that the pink-headed duck still quacked.

There were only a few cars in the train station parking lot, but even if there had been hordes of people waiting on the platform, I would have singled him out immediately: Richard, who was in the final year of his sixth decade, wore a faded olive T-shirt, which emphasized a slight paunch, adorned with various images of the pink-headed duck, tucked into tight pink shorts. His hair, messily parted on the left side, might have once been light blond but was now going grey, and he peered through the windshield through a pair of thick glasses as he drove us to the town of Royal Tunbridge Wells, about fifteen kilometres away.

On the drive through the countryside he regaled me with his plans for after he found the duck—the book he would write, the speaking tours he would embark upon, regularly asking for my advice as to how he'd navigate the media maelstrom that would no doubt arise after the discovery was made. "I think I probably would have to leave the job, though that would suit me fine," he told me. "I like it, but I don't really want it to get in the way of what I really want to do." Richard was a driver for the National Health Service, ferrying patients from their homes to clinics, or between hospitals, and he was more than happy to share his adventures with the people he met on the job. "There are so many people who get in my ambulance now and say: 'Have you found the duck?'" He might have been the closest thing Crowborough had to a celebrity.

After arriving in Royal Tunbridge Wells, we walked the town's handsome streets down to the municipal library where he'd discovered the book. The library had since been renovated, but Richard quickly orientated himself among the shelves until he was certain he'd found the spot where his quest began. "This is where I would have been. And I picked it out. And it was *Vanishing Birds* by Tim Halliday." His mind seemed to wander for a second, as if he'd been transported back to that moment, time-travelling through the years. "It was this perfect storm," he said. "A lost world. A lost age. And a lost duck." He sometimes thought about what might have happened if he'd never gone to the library that day, or if he'd browsed a different shelf, picked up a different book. What if *Vanishing Birds* had been checked out? Maybe someone else would have gone trekking through the far reaches of Myanmar. I thought about Jeremy Holden, and the paths not taken. "I was lucky," Richard said.

We left the library, this time without a book, and walked over to the department store, now called Hoopers, where he'd worked. Richard started clerking there in 1980, when he was figuring out what to do with his life beyond play in bands. At Richard's insistence, and despite my misgivings, we snuck up a set of stairs marked "Employees Only," at the very top of which we found the break room, in the same spot as when he'd worked here so long ago. Richard was absolutely giddy. "That's where I was sitting!" he said, peeking through the glass and pointing at a table. "Just there!" I feared he was going to go inside, but just then a woman came out and asked us what we were doing here; Richard played dumb and said we were searching for the menswear department. It was obvious she did not believe us, and followed us back down the stairs to the ground floor. I was convinced she would call security. We scurried for the exit and hurried across the street to a restaurant.

Soon after, Richard's friend, the artist Anna-Marie Buss, joined us for lunch. They'd known each other for ages and, more importantly, she was "one of the few people who didn't take the piss out of me," Richard said, when he finally decided to go looking for the pink-headed duck. Come to think of it, he added, looking around, it was at this very pub where he'd told her about his plans to go looking for it. He'd called her, excitedly, saying that they had to meet up.

"Anna-Marie probably thought I was going to announce a new girlfriend," Richard said.

It was true, she replied. "I thought it was going to be he'd hit it off with one of the girls he worked with or something like that, something very trivial." Instead, Richard showed her the colour plate from the book that had captured his imagination. "I didn't actually believe that it was a real bird—it just looked so fake," she told me. Richard had brought along a map, as well, Anna-Marie recalled. "He said, 'I'm going on an expedition. I'm going to go and find this.'" She studied the map as he outlined his plans; it looked like he was pointing at the middle of nowhere. "I thought," added Anna-Marie, "that he was being very brave or very naive."

I'm not sure if I'd go so far as to say Richard was experiencing a midlife crisis when he made his decision to finally head to Asia to look for the duck, but it was clear to me that he'd become frustrated with his life. At the time, he was employed by a health-care temp agency that served a local hospital, where he worked as a porter, serving patients their meals. The commute wore him down to the point he eventually moved on-site into a residence for hospital workers, which, while solving his commuting issues and saving him money on rent, did not improve his mood.

"I remember you phoned me up," recalled Anna-Marie. "You were quite depressed at the time. And you said you thought that you could see ghosts in the corridor."

Richard nodded. "There was something like six ghosts," he said. "But Anna-Marie's right. It was getting me down. Of course, the plus side was that suddenly I had all this money." He'd saved a few thousand pounds; seed money for an expedition.

We ordered drinks and lunch and more drinks. Anna-Marie's partner, James, joined us partway through our meal. We discussed the ethics of de-extinction and Richard's various expeditions over the years as well as his future plans—where the duck might be and why no one had found it and how Richard would be the one to finally do it. When Richard left the table—either to use the restroom or grab us another round, I can't recall—I took advantage of his brief absence to ask his friends about him, hoping they might talk a bit more freely. I'd only spent a few hours talking to Richard; they'd known him for years. What made him tick?

James, an acupuncturist, considered my question. "I love Richard," he finally said. "He's a really interesting character. And I would put him, if you had a scale, like you do for other things, he moves somewhat along the slightly eccentric—"

Anna-Marie broke in: "Oh, most definitely! I would definitely put him as eccentric."

"He has that obsessive gene," said James, and then remembered something: "I asked Richard the question [. . .] not as a provocation or a downer: What happens—not if you don't find it, because if you never find it, it could always be there. What happens, emotionally, if you do find it? Not just in terms of the bird world and how that would spin out. But it's almost like it's become an obsession in his life, and the obsession has grown over the time we've known him. I see obsessed people in my clinic, and he would be one of those people I would just put a little note in his patient notes: 'There's a danger here of success.' Which might sound ludicrous."

No, I said. I understood what he meant. I'd heard it from others I'd talked to over the years. That the pursuit was what brought them joy. That there was a part of them, even if they didn't want to admit it, that never wanted to cross the finish line. That it was about the journey, not the destination. That they'd suddenly find their life empty, and without meaning, if they achieved their goal. Sometimes, I suspect, they even self-sabotaged to prevent themselves from succeeding. Not that I'd put Richard in this camp. His desire to find the pink-headed duck was pure, and real, and he was certain, at least outwardly, that he'd be proven right in the end. But, as he'd also said to me, "Nothing is as much fun as looking for the pink-headed duck."

In between the odd jobs and uninspiring work he'd had over the years, Richard completed a university degree in writing for children. "I thought if I wrote a book that was successful, I could raise enough money to not do anything else but look for the pink-headed duck," he told me. On my first night in Crowborough, he gifted me a copy of his second self-published novel, *Gravenhead*, an edition of which featured art by his friend Anna-Marie. "I really hope you enjoy it," he said as he pressed the paperback into my hands. It tells the story of a young girl named Morwen who discovers an old village, lost to time, under a lake not far from her home in northern Wales. It was easy, when I finally read it on the plane back to Canada, to catch glimpses of Richard in the novel. "Everything Morwen is doing, I'm doing as well," he told me.

That same evening, Richard and I went out for dinner at a decent Indian restaurant a few minutes from his home and, afterwards, we strolled for an hour or so through Crowborough's deserted downtown. We'd been walking for maybe ten minutes when he pointed across the street to an old white house on the corner: This is where he'd lived as a kid.

He hadn't wanted to come to Crowborough, he told me. But he had no choice. His father, a bank manager, moved the family here for work when Richard was thirteen. (His mother was a teacher.) "It was a terribly heart-wrenching moment," he said. Richard wanted to stay in Horsham, in West Sussex, where they were living at the time. "If I became a millionaire," he said, "I would go back to our house in Horsham."

Our conversations were peppered with asides like this: If I became a millionaire. If I found the duck. Of all the people I spent time with, or interviewed, for this book, Richard was the ultimate dreamer. It seems he'd been this way his entire life. "I've seen my old school reports," he told me, "and it always says: 'Richard spent his whole day with his head in the clouds. He's always dreaming.'" There was a part of me that read him as a textbook case of arrested development, that supposed he'd never quite shed his childhood wonder, which, even at a young age, tended to be transfixed by the stranger elements of the world.

"Ever since he was a kid, he's always been very fascinated by the mysterious, unusual, unknown," his brother, David, told me. "Lake monsters in Ireland, all that kind of stuff. The Tasmanian tiger. Dinosaurs. I think it's just ingrained."

Richard was still living in that old white house when Robert Ballard found the wreck of the *Titanic* in 1985, and he remembered being awestruck by the images of the doomed ship on the ocean floor that appeared in publications around the world. He believed that finding the pink-headed duck would be just as newsworthy, and now our conversation turned back to the question of what he would do—should do—once he found the duck. "Do you think now I should start thinking about getting in touch with a photography agency?" he asked. "Just to make sure that I can be looked after if the photos do come out?"

We finished our walk, drove back to his place, and said goodnight, but the subject was still on his mind the following morning. "The one thing that bothers me about the pink-headed duck that I haven't got the answer to is: What do I do if it turns up?" He worried that he'd be forced to step back and let the so-called experts take over, that he'd be pushed aside, ignored, told his services were no longer required. "I don't know at what point people are going to say, 'Right, thanks very much, we'll take it from here.'"

It's not that Richard wanted the duck's rediscovery to lead to riches or to fame. He wasn't a greedy person. But he wanted *something*—a reward for his years of dedication to the cause, a sign that it had all been worth it in the end.

"This is what I've given up a halfway-decent way of life for," he said. "It's cost me a lot of money, this. A lot of money." I asked how much, and he guessed, to that point, he'd spent £20,000 on the search over the years, a not-insignificant sum for someone who was not a wealthy man. "I remember somebody said: 'Oh, you could have bought a lot of nice things with that.' And I said: 'But I don't want nice things. I want to see a pink-headed duck.' *That's* the nice thing!"

Although I was ready to spring for a hotel, at Richard's gentle insistence I slept on a pull-out couch in his flat's living room. On its walls were paintings of the pink-headed duck—an anatomical sketch of the bird's field markings and shape in various hues of pink; two pink-headed ducks in flight—done by his friend, Sam Mackenzie, who'd searched for the duck himself while living in India in the mid-twentieth century. Richard had looked at these paintings, and the pictures and illustrations he'd collected over the years, more times than I could possibly imagine, and yet he didn't seem tired of them.

"Beautiful, isn't it?" he asked as we looked at one of the ducks. "Can you imagine seeing that on your camera? You never know. One day. Maybe."

Alongside the paintings were clippings culled from various world newspapers, which chronicled a sliver of the bird's troubled history:

"Elephants To Be Used In Hunt For Pink Duck."

"Rare Pink-Headed Duck Found After 3 Years."

"Pink Headed Ducks Still Exist In India."

(The only thing on display that rivalled the ducks was a frame displaying two tickets to Genesis; one at the Brighton Centre in April 1980 and another from Wembley Arena in December 1981. Richard loved Genesis almost as much as he loved the pink-headed duck.)

There was a bookshelf next to the sofa that could have used a couple of extra shelves, and before turning off the light I studied the titles, pulling out and flipping through those that interested me. There were several volumes devoted to other lost birds—the dodo; the passenger pigeon; the great auk—along with many whose subjects were more esoteric in nature: *Lost Animals*; *The Beasts That Hide From Man*; *Undiscovered*; *Mysteries of Planet Earth*; *In Search of Prehistoric Survivors*;

Vanished Species; *Extinct*; *Extinct Birds*; *The Lost Ark*; *The Menagerie of Marvels*; *Without Trace*. On one of the lower shelves I spotted a book I'd actually read: Rory Nugent's *The Search for the Pink-Headed Duck*, a chronicle of the American journalist's trip down India's Brahmaputra river, in the late eighties, in search of Richard's obsession. Nugent's search proved rather fruitless, though he left Asia convinced it was still out there, just difficult to find.

Almost as soon as the duck disappeared people started trying to find it again. The Bombay Natural History Society organized a major search in the 1950s. Illustrations of the duck were distributed to the society's membership, as well as hunters (who were more likely to actually come across it in the wild), showing the pink-headed duck side by side with the red-crested pochard, a much more common bird that might be confused for its missing counterpart. Salim Ali noted, in the Wildfowl Trust, that since the images were distributed, "the sporadic claims made from time to time of the duck being seen have ceased."

The bird would no longer be found in India, of this Richard was certain. (A "handful" of historical records also place the duck in Nepal and Bangladesh.) Instead, Richard focused his efforts on Myanmar, the troubled country to the east, where there had not been a confirmed sighting since 1910, when a dead duck, currently in the collections of the American Museum of Natural History, was found at a bazaar in Mandalay. "The truth is, next to North Korea, Burma's probably the most impregnable system to infiltrate," he said. "That's why the pink-headed duck is probably still there."

Richard wasn't the first researcher to reach this conclusion. Between 2003 and 2005, BirdLife International and the Biodiversity and Nature Conservation Association (BANCA) conducted numerous surveys of wetlands, rivers, and lakes in Myanmar's northern Kachin State. Before undertaking the initial search, the team distributed posters and flyers throughout the state's lowland areas, offering money to anyone able to show the survey team a living pink-headed duck. The reward went unclaimed. While the search teams found plenty of suitable habitat, collected reports of sightings, and experienced what might be generously described as two close calls (they preferred the term "unconfirmed sightings"), they did not find the duck.

Still, as they wrote in a 2008 report, "There are several reasons for believing that the species may still persist in the lowlands of Kachin State and, perhaps, elsewhere in Myanmar. Shyness, combined with rarity, possible nocturnal habits and the impenetrability of its habitats, means that the species tended to be under-recorded historically, and may continue to be so currently. Further surveys are required to confirm this."

Richard went on his first expedition the following year, concentrating on an area north of the city of Bhamo in Kachin State. Before he left Yangon, he met with the renowned zoologist, the late Tony Htin Hla, who'd been involved in the surveys a few years earlier; together they pored over maps in Richard's hotel lobby, Tony advising him on places he should look and areas he should avoid. "That moment, it was just brilliant," Richard said. "You didn't need to pretend to be David Attenborough, because what you were doing was the most exciting thing in the world."

There was actually a bit of Attenborough in Richard, who was a comprehensive chronicler of his quests. He recorded extensive footage of his searches and, upon returning to the U.K., edited them into short documentaries, with Richard serving as cameraman, audio technician, production assistant, cinematographer, director, and host. These were travel shows few people would ever watch, though he screened a couple of these films for me during my stay, and kindly sent me the others upon my return to Toronto. Together, these movies showed his evolution from a bumbling fish-out-of-water to a skilled amateur ornithologist who'd earned the trust of several global wildlife organizations.

"He's really grown his skills," said Christina Biggs, the lost species officer at Re:wild. "He's grown his instinct and his intuition. He's taken on the feedback of others. What he's lacking, he has sought out." Richard, she added, was "pretty unique" among the wildlife biologists and researchers her organization worked with. "Most of our researchers, even if they're not trained in that specific taxa, or that specific area, they usually have some type of science background."

The vow made by a menswear clerk living in a small English town had been fulfilled. Richard had indeed gone searching for the pink-headed duck, the bird that sparked an obsession all those years ago.

In retrospect, that was the easy part. Now he had to find it.

Spread out on the table before us was a map of northern Myanmar. I cannot say that I'd studied the country's geography before, and I was struck by its size. It is a large country, the largest in mainland Southeast Asia, and Richard had spent a long time thinking about where within its boundaries the pink-headed duck could be hiding. Small circles of various colours were affixed to the map in different spots, as were white rectangles on which he'd written the names of places pertinent to the search. A couple of areas had been circled in pen.

"You're not going to find the pink-headed duck waddling down Mandalay high street," he said. "It's going to be somewhere where nobody ever goes."

He was still focused on Kachin, the country's northernmost state, which "even now contains a mostly inaccessible terrain of elephant grass jungles, low-lying swamps, rivers and marshes that are, to this day, largely unexplored. Crucially, this environment still resembles the disappeared habitats that once existed in the Pink-headed duck's last strongholds of East Bengal (now Bangladesh), West Bengal and northern India."

This description came from *The Flyway in the Rains*, a detailed report Richard authored in 2023, which outlined his latest theory and search plans for a series of oxbows—bends in the river—where he thought the duck might still be found. While sightings of the bird had, historically, usually occurred farther south, Richard believed that for the species to survive it would have had to head north.

There'd been several unconfirmed sightings in this part of Myanmar over the years, as the BirdLife/BANCA surveys made clear. Richard had heard stories, too. He was always asking the people he encountered if they'd seen the duck, always carrying a picture of the bird, hoping to jog a villager's or fisherman's memory. The most memorable of these reports, he told me, came in 2016. Richard was sitting in a café with his interpreter and guide when a local man approached them and started tapping the picture of the pink-headed duck in the book sitting open on the table. Through his interpreter, Richard asked the man if he'd seen this bird. No, the man said, and started walking away. Quickly, Richard asked his interpreter to call the man back to the table. Richard posed the same question a different way: Have you *ever* seen this bird? Yes, the man said. It was very rare, but he had seen it, perhaps six years ago.

To be sure, a solitary duck does not a breeding population make. There had to be more—many more. Richard's current theory was that the birds likely bred during the monsoon season in the region of the Hukaung Valley Wildlife Sanctuary, the world's largest tiger reserve, which encompasses 17,000 square kilometres of rivers, wetland, and forest. In Myanmar's second season—the cold, dry season—the ducks followed a "flyway" down to the oxbows where Richard had now focused the search. "Both habitats are in extremely remote areas and each would provide advantages for the Pink-headed duck's three main areas of defence," wrote Richard, which were isolation, shyness, and nocturnal behaviour.

He'd produced the report with the help of his friend, Sam Mackenzie, who'd painted the ducks I'd admired in Richard's flat, and who served as a mentor of sorts. Mackenzie had spent a quarter century studying birds in that part of the world—mostly in Assam, a state in northern India, adjacent to Myanmar, where he'd once worked on tea plantations. As a "shooting man," as he described himself to me, his original interest in birds was not exactly scientific in nature. "I could eat them," he said. "In that time in India, food was very scarce. And so I used a shotgun rather a lot." The Brahmaputra, where the author Rory Nugent later searched for the pink-headed duck, bisected Assam, and Mackenzie spent his free time on the river looking for waterfowl. Mandarin ducks, Chinese spot-billed ducks, the white-winged wood duck—Mackenzie came to know them as well as any ornithologist, and his interests eventually transformed from culinary to conservation.

Mackenzie was confident that while the pink-headed duck was extinct in India, they'd be found next door in Myanmar, where there weren't as many people, especially in the remote north. "There's got to be a breeding site somewhere, locked away, where nobody has observed them," he insisted to me. "Even if we saw only one, that would immediately indicate that there's a breeding colony somewhere."

In order to finally observe one in the wild, Richard had acquired ten remote trail cameras, to be placed at the ten oxbows they'd identified as the most promising. The plan was to hire a local hunter to monitor these cameras over the dry season, when solitary males, looking for a mate, were most likely to visit the area. He'd also designed a floating feeding station, four of which would be placed at various oxbows and baited with dried mealworm infused with essence of crayfish; if a bird came close, the movement would trigger the camera. Richard showed me footage he'd taken near his home, of regular old ducks swimming up to the cameras to snack. It was rather ingenious, I had to admit. Some of the platforms were equipped with microphones, too. "We'll know what a pink-headed duck sounds like!" he said with glee.

When I later asked Christina Biggs of Re:wild whether she actually thought the pink-headed duck might be out there, she answered without hesitation.

"Absolutely," she said. "Oh, absolutely."

So much of Myanmar had never been properly explored, she explained, and the areas in which Richard was focusing his search contained the ideal habitat for ducks. Besides, species that were thought to be extinct were being found all the time. Just a few days before our interview, she said, the leopard barbel fish had been rediscovered in the Tigris River in Turkey; the previous month a trapdoor spider not seen since 1931 was found in a small Portuguese village; and the month before that a blind mole thought lost since 1936 was discovered alive and well on a beach in South Africa. In all, a dozen lost species had been found since Robin Moore launched his search in 2017. "There are continuing and constant examples of successful outcomes," said Biggs. "He's aware of those. He knows that it's possible."

Even Sam Mackenzie, many years ago, claimed to have "caught a butterfly in Uganda which they thought was extinct—quite by accident!" He discovered it sitting in a dung pile, he recalled. "That was quite exciting, I must admit." Although he was soon kicked out of the country by Idi Amin, the notorious dictator, his sighting proved that "things do crop up," he said.

At the time of my visit to Crowborough, the feeding platforms were already with Richard's guide, Lay Win, in Myanmar; Richard had brought them over the previous year. What he now had to do was get the cameras to Lay Win, who would then transport them north. It was not as easy as sending them by courier, or checking them with the rest of his luggage on a plane—Richard knew the military might not fancy a strange Englishman setting up camera traps around the countryside. The last thing he wanted was to be arrested as a spy. "I don't think a spying charge in Burma is very pleasant," he said.

And so, when I left Crowborough, there was no guarantee Richard's upcoming expedition would go ahead as planned. Still, he remained optimistic. "I don't want to use 'destined,' but if I wasn't meant to find this thing, why would I be in this situation now?" he asked as he drove me back to the train station. "There's got to be a reason for it. Otherwise, why would I be here?" He felt something great was about to happen, something that would leave the world "amazed." He predicted that if they were right—"and I think we are," he said—they'd have the pink-headed duck on camera by the following spring. "Ten months, maybe nine months, and then I think we've got it. And then we'll change history."

It was a kind of madness that had gripped Richard for the past several decades. It was clear to me that he was in love with a creature that would never love him back, in the sense that he would probably never come face-to-bill with a pink-headed duck. He loved something he had never encountered, and would likely never encounter. It was a love that was palpable, even if it was not tangible. It was like the ultimate high school crush.

"Have you read *Great Expectations*?" he once asked me. Of course, I said—it's one of my favourite novels. He went on: "I call it the Estella bird, because it just exists to break people's hearts. It's very tantalizing, out of reach all the time. It's like catching smoke." He put it another way: "It was put on the planet just to get revenge for its own existence."

There had been times when he tried to break up with it, tried to forget about his dream. "I don't want to end up like one of those old-timers, out in the United States, looking for the Dutchman's Mine. 'One last go!' I never really wanted to end up like that." (I didn't tell him about Ron Feldman.) There were times when he thought his quest was over, when he thought he would never return to Myanmar. Even if it wasn't necessarily a dangerous country, it was certainly politically unstable—from military rule to a brief period of quasi-democracy and back again. And it wasn't just financial sacrifices he'd made, but physical sacrifices, as well—in 2012 he was struck by a speeding motorcycle, which shattered his hand; the subsequent surgery left him with more than a dozen pins under the skin, holding everything together.

"There's a limit to what you want to really put yourself through," he told me. It's hard, he said, to travel across the world, spend weeks searching, only to return home to England empty handed. To be filled with doubt. To be reminded of the possibility that it would never happen. "It's a very crushing feeling to not find what you're looking for," he said. "And I'm quite an emotional person, so I tend to react quite badly."

And yet.

"I don't want to give up, put it that way," he said. There was this innate thing inside him, inside everyone, he believed, though it expressed itself in each of us in different ways. "Psychologically, the search for the Grail is in all of us," he said. "It's why we do what we do."

In Richard's case, it was partly a matter of faith. His late father had been a devout Christian, and Richard had marvelled at how stoically he'd handled his final days on earth. "I was intrigued that he could hold on to his faith all the way through this ghastly situation. So I thought I'd go and find out whether or not it was bullshit or whether there was something there." Richard's was a quiet faith. He didn't attend service, and considered himself a non-practising believer. But, in a way, his search was a show of faith, and the duck's existence proof of a higher power. "It's a strange-looking bird, but it's also incredible," he said. "How can you get this duck that's just got a brown that's almost a black, and a pink that's so beautiful? I mean, if there was any proof that there's a creator in this universe, the pink-headed duck is it."

He knew people thought it was impossible. People had mocked him. Told him that he was wasting his time. His mother had people laugh in her face—in church!—when she mentioned what her son was doing with his life. "What the hell, it doesn't matter to me," he said. "Because if it is found it will change history. It would be a *National Geographic* moment. And if anyone's gonna find it, I want it to be me."

And so, a few months after my visit to Crowborough, Richard returned to Myanmar once again. He'd arranged with a high-ranking official—code name: Bill Smuggs—to have a police officer meet him at the airport when he landed, to ensure he'd be allowed to bring the cameras into the country. He'd also sent a long email ahead of time, to Christina and Anna-Marie and all the others who comprised his team of supporters, outlining his itinerary and what he hoped to accomplish before his return. His message included special thanks to the "veteran of Asian avifaunal study," Sam Mackenzie, who "helped so much with the submission to the Myanmar government reps at the Consulate [*The Flyway in the Rains*] that piqued their interest so much. We would have been in the Kalaymyo area on the Indian border had it not been for Mackenzie!"

I WhatsApp'd Richard good luck but didn't receive a response.

At the newspaper where I worked, I followed the updates about rebels gaining ground in the north. The fighting was the worst in years, and there were rumours the junta might collapse. Richard was an experienced traveller but: A Westerner showing up with thousands of dollars of cameras and recording equipment right when the junta—run by paranoid fanatics—was losing its grip on power? I did not fear the worst, but I did worry. And then:

"Hi Mark, this is just to let you know I got all of the cameras safely through into the country. The police officer was waiting for me as I got off the plane . . . all went ok. I can't believe I don't have to think about the cameras, visas, customs, the Forestry Department and the logistics company ever again. It's been 18 months of bad thoughts, to be quite honest. But now we can begin."

The cameras were with Lay Win, and would soon make their way north to the oxbows. Richard included a photo of himself, outside the airport, standing next to a man I assumed was the police officer, holding an illustration of the pink-headed duck. He looked exhausted, but was smiling. The photo made me smile, too.

"Incredible news!" I wrote back, and told him we'd talk when he made it back to Crowborough.

But there was one more text: While he'd been out of contact in Myanmar, Sam Mackenzie had died. "He was one of the giants of the Pink-headed duck search efforts," he wrote. "I will miss my friend." If there was solace to be found, he told me later, it was that Mackenzie had received word the cameras had made it safely into Myanmar. Also: "Up there, he's probably found the pink-headed duck already. He's probably shot it. He's probably eaten it."

Richard returned to England, and before Christmas sent out a report detailing his trip and the next steps: Lay Win would make his way to Kachin State to set up the cameras and feeding stations; Richard would fly back to Myanmar in March to collect the results.

There was more than a small part of me that thought he would be successful this time. That he'd retrieve the memory cards from the cameras, and, once they were downloaded onto his computer, he'd finally see the sight he'd been waiting for: a flash of pink, a bird returned from the dead, like Lazarus, to live to see another day. Yes, my work would be for nought—I'd have to cut him from the book, after all—but I wanted this for Richard. He deserved it.

And then, in late February, another update.

He forwarded Lay Win's note to all of us: "I am very sad to inform you this information," his guide and friend wrote. He'd been unable to access all the oxbows they'd planned to search due to rebel activity in the area, and those he could visit were found to be "heavily contaminated by spoil from regional gold mining," Richard wrote. "This seems another battle to overcome, over every other bureaucratic obstacle—the contemporary habitat destruction itself." This meant that they had not been able to deploy the cameras nor the floating platforms.

"To me personally and I am sure to all the supporters of the Pink-headed Duck Project this really is a very hard blow," Richard told us. "How this latest setback at the survey site has made me feel is probably to be imagined."

But it was *only* a setback; Richard remained determined and wanted to "reassure one and all that we *do* keep going!" he wrote.

He was already thinking about where to look next.

EIGHT

SENTINELS

The sign said to watch for falling rocks. I drove onward into the Catalinas, racing the sun and ascending towards it at the same time. Tucson fell away, though I'd occasionally catch the city's lights below, often coming out of a hairpin turn, my hands throttling the steering wheel, praying that if a vehicle was heading the other way on the narrow two-lane highway its driver was taking the curve as carefully as I was. The road led higher and higher while the temperature dropped lower and lower; the flora became alpine, the cholla replaced by aspen. I was due at the top of Mount Lemmon, the highest peak in these mountains, before sunset, but every so often I turned into a pullout and got out of the car to take in the vista; dusk enveloped the desert spread out before me, stretching into the distance. The sky was infinite.

In Summerhaven, a tiny community of less than fifty people about eight thousand feet above sea level—it was once home to the highest-elevated golf course in the world—I pulled into the parking lot of the town's modest general store. A lightly bearded man in his early thirties, wearing jeans, a grey pullover, and a black-and-white trucker hat, was standing next to a black Nissan Rogue, waiting patiently. After we shook hands and exchanged pleasantries, Kacper Wierzchos got into his vehicle and turned onto the road, where I followed him even farther up the mountain as the sun continued its descent.

We drove for another ten or fifteen minutes, stopping so that Kacper (pronounced *Casper*) could unlock a cattle gate—the "road closed" sign didn't apply to us—and then a chain link fence—"authorized personnel only," warned one sign; "no headlights," demanded another—before arriving at a small collection of weathered buildings dotting the summit like an abandoned summer camp. We parked in front of two white marshmallow-like domes and got out of our cars, ninety-two hundred feet above sea level. "You might get an altitude headache," Kacper cautioned. I had not packed any Advil.

We walked towards the mountain's edge; it was still light enough to make out the campus of Biosphere 2, the scientific research facility, just to the north; a crowd of ominous-looking clouds were drifting towards us from the same direction. But except for the soft crunch of gravel under our feet, all was quiet; there didn't seem to be anyone else around. If it brought to mind the kind of place spies would gather to eavesdrop on the Soviets at the height of the Cold War, that's because many of the buildings were originally part of a radar station operated by the Air Force between 1956 and 1969, watching the skies for possible enemy bombers. Now the few people working here kept watch for other dangers.

We went into the larger of the two buildings—Kacper's home away from home. It was like a ranger's cabin crossed with a college dorm. "It's cozy, especially when it's snowing," he said. There was a tiny bathroom; a bedroom, barely wide enough for a double mattress; a utilitarian kitchen. Above a small table hung a bulletin board onto which assorted documents were tacked: names and contact numbers; a calendar; a brochure on the dangers of mountain lions; a NASA sticker, peeling from the board as if trying to escape; a sign warning employees to

"NEVER-NEVER-EVER-EVER attempt to clean, adjust, touch or otherwise disturb any optical surface in this telescope." A poster explaining the geological effects of impact cratering reminded me of what was at stake: "Shock pressures are greatest near the point of impact, where material may be melted and vaporized," it read. "At greater distances, a planet's surface may be shock-metamorphosed and fractured."

One of the walls was covered by a giant white board, its surface filled with evidence of the boredom—some might say a gentle madness—that sometimes gripped Kacper and his colleagues during their long, solitary shifts: notes to colleagues and half-formed thoughts, numbers and equations, inside jokes and crude sketches—a red Swingline stapler, a dinosaur, a passable attempt at what appeared to be Casper the Friendly Ghost, in honour of my host. In the centre of the white board, and written in all-caps, were the words *carpe noctem*—seize the night.

Pushed against the wall directly across from the white board was a plain wooden desk, at which Kacper took a seat in a simple black office chair.

"When you're sitting on this chair, you kind of forget that you might discover something that might wipe out civilization," he said.

From sunset to sunrise, on countless nights each year, Kacper sat alone at this desk and monitored the sky as part of his job as a senior research specialist—an observer—for the Catalina Sky Survey (CSS), which was the world's most prolific finder of NEOs—near-Earth objects. He was, to put it bluntly, an asteroid hunter, looking for things that could one day—hopefully, fingers crossed, many, many days from now—end us all.

"You never know what you're going to find," he told me. "You never know if you're going to find the next impactor, or a big NEO or the next great comet. You never know, with each night, where it's going to take you."

Where it had taken him was far away from home. Kacper was born in the city of Lublin, Poland, in 1988, though when he was a toddler his family moved to Spain, where he was raised. He'd been interested in space all his life—the comet Hale-Bopp, discovered in 1995, was an early obsession—and he got his first telescope when he was a teen. After telling me this, Kacper opened his laptop to show a "How it started/How it's going" meme he'd recently posted to social media: The first photo showed Kacper, fourteen or fifteen years old, wearing a black T-shirt adorned with various planets, standing next to a chunky black-and-purple telescope; the second photo showed him leaning against one of CSS's massive instruments. Most kids follow sports teams, or celebrities; Kacper followed the scientists and researchers at CSS. He knew them all—Eric Christensen, Richard Kowalski—tracking their discoveries like other kids track baseball statistics. "They were like rock stars," he told me.

While pursuing his Ph.D. in applied physics at the University of South Florida, Kacper wrote to Christensen, director of the CSS, and asked if he could do an academic placement at the survey. They said yes. All of a sudden, he was working alongside his heroes. "I was a little bit starstruck in the beginning," he said. "All these folks, I'd read about them, and now they're like my co-workers." When a permanent position opened up, he applied. Again, they said yes. He joined CSS full-time at the end of 2019. Even now, he seemed a tad shocked to be sitting here with me. "A lot of things had to work out right for me to work here," he said. "It's a dream come true."

The Catalina Sky Survey was founded in 1998, at a time when the threat of asteroids was being taken seriously for the first time, and politicians were asking NASA to keep an eye on the sky. "There was this sort of realization, at the political level, that there was a measurable threat of impact to the Earth," Christensen told me. "And that was graphically brought home with the impact of comet Shoemaker-Levy 9 on Jupiter."

The comet, which had been discovered in March 1993 by Eugene and Carolyn Shoemaker and David Levy, struck the largest planet in our solar system the following year. Christensen was in high school at the time, and he remembered looking at the impact's aftermath through a telescope in his backyard. "I wasn't really aware of how that was being turned into this new program within NASA," he said.

Catalina was one of a handful of surveys that came online around the same time, funded in part by NASA's Near-Earth Objects Observations Program. CSS was started by the American astronomer Steve Larson, who served as the first director, along with two of his undergraduate students at the University of Arizona—a powerhouse in the field of astronomy and planetary science. Mount Lemmon, where Kacper and I were sitting this evening, was not, in fact, its original site; the team first took over an old telescope on nearby Mount Bigelow that had been sitting idle for fifteen years.

"That was a photographic instrument," explained Christensen. "So the team would go up and expose film for an hour, and then run over to another building and develop those films. It was very hands on, very manual, and not particularly productive by today's standards. By the standards of the day, it was state of the art." It was also slow. "In those days, it was a great month if you found a couple of NEOs."

At the time of my visit, the CSS consisted of the telescope on Mount Bigelow, since upgraded, and two on Mount Lemmon—a 1.5-metre instrument, which did the bulk of the searching, and a smaller one-metre device that was mainly used for follow-up work, tracking NEOs that Kacper and his colleagues had already found.

"The surveys are the first line of defence," Christensen told me. "It's the first step in a long process."

The process began here, at this desk. Positioned in front of Kacper were six large monitors, stacked in two rows of three. Off to the side sat a bright red analogue phone. It looked extremely important, as if it connected the caller directly with the White House or Batman, and I was disappointed to learn it was just an ordinary landline. It did not feel like we were on the frontlines in the battle to save humanity.

Kacper turned on the computer, and the monitors came to life. He pulled up weather reports and radar maps, a clock alerting him of the times until sunset and sunrise, a live feed of the sky outside the telescope bay. On the monitor in the middle of the top row he opened up a map of the sky, divided into a grid of small blocks. The program, designed by Christensen, was called Covtool, short for coverage tool, though Kacper just called it "the planetarium." It was both an atlas and an archive, showing the searches that Kacper and his colleagues had undertaken over the previous few weeks, and where he plotted which section of the sky to search on a particular night. It looked like a Tetris board turned on its side: the blocks were coloured green, orange, blue, which corresponded to different dates over the last month (for instance, the green blocks signified searches undertaken on September 17, a few days prior.) "We try to cover the entire sky a few times each month," he said. I noticed a long diagonal block of greys and off-whites—this, Kacper explained, was the Milky Way. It would be a waste of time to look here—too bright.

He scrolled through the grid, 360 degrees of possibilities, looking for a spot that hadn't recently been surveyed. A certain area might have been skipped because, on that night, there were clouds in the way, or the moonlight was too strong. (CSS observers don't work on the days around a full moon.) Observers surveyed from north to south, but otherwise had free rein when it came to where to search on any given night, so if it was cloudy in the west, for instance, they might concentrate on the east.

Kacper selected a chunk of sky and clicked on the grid. The black boxes turned purple, then peach. Once he was done selecting a search grid for the night, the telescope would take over—automatically locking onto that section of the sky. Over the course of thirty minutes, it would take four photographs of the same area.

Next came the "validation." The observer retrieved the photographs and went over the results. Here, Kacper pulled up a photo on the monitor below the sky map, a grainy black-and-white image of outer space. There were little white dots everywhere, some larger than others, some brighter than others. The four photos taken by the telescope's camera, each one 10,560 pixels by 10,560 pixels, were superimposed onto one another, resulting in a mini, four-frame movie. This was where the search happened: If there was an asteroid or comet, the observer should see it move across the sky over the course of the four frames. If unsure, they could pull up a catalogue of past images of the sky to compare it with.

"Everything comes down to movement," Kacper said. The software helped identify possible NEOs, but it was up to the observer to decide. "That's the main reason CSS is so successful. We have a human, all the time, making decisions in real time."

He went through the images quicker than I'd expected. "That was clearly no. That's also clearly no. I see some stars here." He clicked the *N* key over and over again: no, no, no. The key, he said, was getting worn down, as an observer might look at four thousand images in one night. "On a good night, we find over forty NEOs here."

Sometimes they missed one, too.

"It's no secret: We all make mistakes and miss objects," Kacper said. "NEOs, very often they're very faint, and you're like, 'Oh, what if this is the one that strikes?' And you have to make the call: Is it real or not?" He continued: "I know I have missed objects, and I know that everybody has and it's part of the job. This is a system, and there's a human here, and sometimes humans make errors. You look at thousands of those a night, and it's not even fatigue—it's just sometimes they are so subtle, literally one or two pixels." It's like a magic eye image—you stare and stare and only after a while does the NEO reveal itself.

All measurements were sent to the Minor Planet Center, based in Cambridge, Massachusetts, which receives hundreds of thousands of observations each night, a number that "is constantly growing," the center's director, Matthew Payne, told me, "because surveys, like CSS, are constantly evolving. The technology is improving." If you read in a newspaper that an asteroid will make a fly-by of Earth, it's likely the Minor Planet Center has revealed this information to the public. That said, anyone is free to log on to the center's website and scan the NEO confirmation page. Transparency is important. "We aren't doing anything secret here," said Kacper.

Sometimes they'd find an asteroid only to learn it had been discovered decades ago and subsequently lost. This helped speed things up, explained Christensen: "If we detect an asteroid today, and start building the information about the orbit from today, it's going to take decades before we can get a very precise orbit," he said. "So if we can reach back and connect our observation to observations that were made earlier, then suddenly the work for building that orbit is essentially done. And that's going to be true going forward, as well. Future surveys that are detecting or re-detecting asteroids are going to benefit from the work that the Catalina Sky Survey [. . .] and those who have come before us have already contributed. It is a multi-generational effort."

As a message on the white board reminded me, at the time of my visit the Catalina Sky Survey was the undisputed leader in the field, discovering more NEOs than any other survey in the world. It was responsible for 1,056 of the 1,843 NEOs found in 2018; 1,069 of the 2,473 found in 2019; 1,520 of the 2,968 found in 2020; and 1,307 of the 3,122 found in 2021.

Keep going at this rate, I said to Kacper, and you'll eventually be out of a job. He laughed, softly. "Not going to happen in my lifetime, I don't think." There were an unfathomable number of things to find. The job would be measured in decades, not nights.

Kacper powered-off the monitors. Here's where I admit this was all a simulation, a performance just for me. The threat of lightning meant he couldn't use the telescopes. You might be disappointed; trust me, I was even more bummed out not to go asteroid hunting, especially having braved the road to the top of Mount Lemmon. But what can you do? If anything, it gave me a glimpse at the patience required to do this kind of work. This was the third night in a row Kacper hadn't been able to search. It was obvious how it might play havoc on your mental health, the loneliness and the repetition, the pressure not to miss something that could kill us all, no matter how remote the chance. The nights like this, where there was nothing to do but wait for sunrise and the next sunset.

Earlier, Kacper had taken me to see the telescopes, first the original now used for follow-up work, and then the 1.5-metre hunter, which he estimated was responsible for 90 percent of the survey's discoveries. The dome was shut because of the weather, so the instrument wasn't at its most majestic, but I still had to crane my neck to take it all in. This was the tool keeping us safe—or keeping some immeasurable future generation safe, at least.

"I always like to say that our job is like the job of a lighthouse keeper," Kacper said. They were alone, working at night, for days at a time, albeit on top of a mountain and not beside the sea. "And we all love it. Trust me, no one would do this if we didn't love it because, as you can imagine, the lifestyle is not easy. We're on a night schedule all year long, because the body would go crazy if you were changing from day to night, day to night, every time you have to work. So we sleep during the day all year long. Sometimes, in winter, you spend six days here by yourself without seeing a soul, and it's like, 'I want to go home!' But it's worth it."

To be the one to find an object known to no one else on Earth, even if only for a short period of time? This is what he'd dreamt of, years ago, peering at the stars through his telescope. Every discovery was "a little dopamine rush," he said. "We all are addicted to the thrill of the hunt, or else we wouldn't be here." The job, he admitted, was probably not good for his health. He suffered from insomnia, and took medication to sleep. When he went back to his house, outside Tucson, or came out to the survey, it was a two-hour drive each way. He often missed his wife. But he wouldn't trade it for anything in the world. "I wanted to do this," he said. "I wanted to experience the night."

So did I, although it seemed I wouldn't get the chance. Kacper and I sat around for a while, talking about his job and childhood in Spain and the time he discovered a comet, one of the happiest days of his life. But it became clear the weather wasn't going to improve. It was going to be a long night.

I drove back towards Tucson in the dark. It was hard to concentrate on the road, which was woefully under-illuminated by my headlights; I was looking out for boulders rolling down the mountainside to collapse the roof of my rental car, but my mind couldn't ignore the night sky, recalling what Kacper had said about the threat NEOs posed to the planet: "It's not a matter of if, it's a matter of when." My eyes were drawn to the endless darkness, punctuated by jewel-like pinpricks of light, and I wondered what might be out there, waiting for us to find it before it found us.

One of the cruellest things we do to children is teach them about dinosaurs. We buy them dinosaur toys and read them dinosaur books, let them watch dinosaur cartoons and dinosaur movies, dress them in T-shirts emblazoned with skateboarding T. Rexes. (It looks cute on my son.) The idea of giant lizards roaming the Earth—how could a young mind not become obsessed? For a time, I was obsessed, too. As a boy, I could name every type and every era, and knew which type lived in which era. Stegosaurus, pterodactyl, dimetrodon. Triassic, Jurassic, Cretaceous. I remember sitting in the basement of my childhood home, building tiny dioramas using my plastic toy figurines and finger paint; staged in cardboard boxes, the finished scenes would capture a triceratops valiantly fighting off a bloodthirsty T. Rex, or a lumbering brontosaurus attacking an ankylosaurus. (They were not always scientifically accurate.) One of my favourite books, which if memory serves I picked up on a trip to Toronto at the dearly missed World's Biggest Bookstore, was *When Dinosaurs Ruled the Earth* by David Norman, which is still on a shelf in my father's basement, and which I've read to my sons. As an eight-year-old, I'd have probably recognized Robert T. Bakker if we'd passed one another on the street. As I type these words, part of me still deeply regrets becoming a journalist and not a paleontologist.

And then we learn they are all dead, wiped out, extinct, never to return, with only their bones and birds—stupid birds!—here to remind us they once walked the Earth. It was a crime.

For a long time, there was a body (well, fossils), but the murder weapon remained unknown. I was once talking with the astronaut and physicist Ed Lu, the co-founder of the B612 Foundation, named after the asteroid from *The Little Prince*. B612 is a non-profit organization dedicated to planetary defence, which, if you haven't yet surmised, is the subject of this chapter. Like me, Lu loved dinosaurs as a kid, and memorized them all. The difference, he told me with a laugh, was that when he was young the books he read ended the same way: "And then they all died out and we don't know why." (I recently looked up what David Norman had to say about it in his book: "What could have happened to cause the disappearance not only of the dinosaurs but also of so many other groups of animals? Nobody can give a satisfactory answer.") It wasn't until he was in college, said Lu, that "this crazy idea came about: Maybe an asteroid could have done it."

In the June 6, 1980, issue of *Science*, Luis W. Alvarez, a professor emeritus of physics at the University of California, Berkeley, and three colleagues, including his son Walter, published a study called "Extraterrestrial Cause for the Cretaceous-Tertiary Extinction." In layman's terms: What killed off the dinosaurs.

Various hypotheses had been proposed over the years, they wrote, including "a magnetic reversal; a nearby supernova; and the flooding of the ocean surface by fresh water from a postulated arctic lake." These were all wrong. Instead, they'd found a layer, deep beneath the planet's surface, but above where most dinosaur fossils were found, rich in iridium, an element uncommon on Earth but often found in asteroids. This suggested that it wasn't disease or volcanos or flooding that led to the extinction of the dinosaurs but something extraterrestrial. Their hypothesis was that "an asteroid struck the earth, formed an impact crater, and some of the dust-sized material ejected from the crater reached the stratosphere and was spread around the globe. This dust effectively prevented sunlight from reaching the surface for a period of several years, until the dust settled to earth. Loss of sunlight suppressed photosynthesis, and as a result most food chains collapsed, and the extinction resulted."

Murder weapon in hand, the crime scene was later determined to be the 180-kilometre-wide Chicxulub crater, discovered under the

Yucatan Peninsula in the 1970s but not identified until 1991. And while there were still those who disagreed with the asteroid theory, in 2010 an international panel of scientists confirmed that a rock from the sky—albeit one that was fifteen kilometres wide, and whose impact was more than a billion times stronger than the atomic bomb dropped on Hiroshima—had indeed (and to children everywhere, tragically) wiped out the dinosaurs. Case closed.

"We now have great confidence that an asteroid was the cause," said Joanna Morgan of Imperial College London, a member of the 2010 team. "This triggered large-scale fires, earthquakes measuring more than 10 on the Richter scale, and continental landslides, which created tsunamis. However, the final nail in the coffin for the dinosaurs happened when blasted material was ejected at high velocity into the atmosphere. This shrouded the planet in darkness and caused a global winter, killing off many species that couldn't adapt to this hellish environment."

It's not as if the idea of something from outer space slamming into the Earth was unthinkable before the Alvarez theory gained traction. As long as there's been an Earth, shit has been hitting it. Most strikes go by unnoticed—thousands of meteors strike the planet every year, according to studies. But widespread damage does occur from time to time. In 1908, to cite one fairly recent example, a meteor exploded over the Tunguska River in Siberia, the 10-to-15-megaton blast flattening the forest for dozens of miles in every direction—an estimated 80 million trees were felled. It's an idea that had been explored in popular culture, too, long before the likes of Bruce Willis and Ben Affleck turned the scenario of a killer asteroid into a summer blockbuster. A few years before the Alvarez paper, sci-fi authors Larry Niven and Jerry Pournelle published the novel *Lucifer's Hammer*, about a comet strike that leads to the fall (and rebuilding) of civilization. "Orange holes glowed on the dark Earth, like cigarettes poked through the back of a map," goes one particularly memorable description of Earth, post-strike. "Hard to tell where each glowing spot was. City lights had disappeared across Europe, covered by clouds, or simply gone. Sea looked like land . . ."

So we knew what they could do, their awesome power and destructive potential. But for a long time, studying asteroids was a bit like being an asteroid: You were on your own. To be sure, there were scientists, like the Dutch-American astronomer Tom Gehrels at the University of Arizona, who pushed for the planetary sciences to take asteroids seriously. In 1971, he edited and published a compendium of papers about asteroids and other near-Earth objects, *Physical Studies of Minor Planets*, and in 1979 published the ground-breaking textbook *Asteroids*, coincidentally the same year the Atari game of the same name (no relation) was released. The following year he helped establish the Spacewatch program on Kitt Peak, about a hundred miles southwest of Mount Lemmon—the first survey of its kind.

"We are now on the threshold of a new era of asteroid studies," he wrote in the introduction of *Physical Studies of Minor Planets*. "There was a previous period of great activity on minor planets in the nineteenth century when time and effort of astronomers were devoted to discovery and orbit determination, and this work has been pursued by some until the present time. Physical studies, however, have not been popular, at least not among astronomers. The lack of appreciation is coming to an end . . ."

Gehrels's optimism was misplaced, or at least a bit premature: The lack of appreciation was not coming to an end. As I was regularly reminded by those in the field, even after the publication of the Alvarez paper, asteroids remained a tiny, marginalized subject in the larger universe of the planetary sciences.

"Asteroids were still the vermin of the sky," the astronomer Richard P. Binzel, who taught planetary sciences at MIT, co-edited the book *Asteroids II* alongside Gehrels, and was the inventor of the Torino Scale, which measures the impact probability and hazard of NEOs, told me. As a graduate student at the University of Texas in the 1980s, he said, "I had professors telling me I was wasting my time. 'Why would a bright young student like you waste your time studying asteroids?'" It was not seen as a respectable or promising field of study, nor particularly rich when compared to the other mysteries of the universe. Said

Binzel: "When you had black holes and quasars being discovered, why would rocks in space be interesting?"

(A pause, here, to define the terms: An asteroid is a round or irregularly shaped rocky body—a minor planet—mostly found in the main belt between Mars and Jupiter; a meteoroid can be a small asteroid, or a tinier object; a meteor is a meteoroid that has entered Earth's atmosphere; a meteorite is what's left to find, if it hasn't burned up completely upon entry. There will be a test at the end of this chapter.)

And if studying asteroids was a waste of time, the idea of worrying about whether one might strike the planet—well, that was the sort of thing that got you laughed out of the room. Even though NASA and the legendary astrogeologist Eugene Shoemaker organized the first meeting on impact hazards in Snowmass, Colorado, the year after the Alvarez paper was published (one of the discussion topics was whether it would be feasible to ward off an incoming asteroid using a nuclear weapon), it basically remained the equivalent of studying whether the Earth was flat.

"Whenever you mentioned impacts of comets and asteroids with the Earth, people who weren't in the field would just sort of roll their eyes and say, 'Oh really? Surely you've got something better to do?" said Don Yeomans, the former director of the Center for Near-Earth Object Studies (CNEOS) at NASA's Jet Propulsion Laboratory (JPL) in Pasadena, California.

"It was kind of dismissed: 'It can't be a serious hazard because we've never seen this happen on the Earth,'" said Paul Chodas, Yeomans's successor at CNEOS. He found this line of argument profoundly misguided—just look at the moon, which has countless craters! The surface of our planet would look the same, if not for erosion. "Every spot on the Earth has been hit by an asteroid at some point, just as every spot on the moon has been hit by something," Chodas told me.

So what changed, and when? Although the exact date depends on who you talk to, the vibes around planetary defence began to shift in the late 1980s and early 1990s.

On April 20, 1989, a story appeared on the front page of *The New York Times*, albeit below the fold, that announced: "Big Asteroid Passes Near Earth Unseen In a Rare Close Call."

"A large asteroid capable of wreaking widespread damage if it collided with Earth passed within half a million miles last month, the closest approach of such an object in 50 years, astronomers said today," wrote Warren E. Leary. The asteroid, which was calculated to be travelling at almost 75,000 kilometres per hour, and whose diameter was the size of a football field, had "crossed Earth's orbit undetected March 23 at a distance equal to twice that between Earth and the Moon."

Later that same year, the astronomer Clark R. Chapman—who later co-founded the B612 Foundation alongside Ed Lu—and the astrobiologist David Morrison published what is considered the first serious book about the risks of asteroid impacts, *Cosmic Catastrophes.*

"The greatest hazard of all is that civilization could be entirely destroyed any day by the unexpected impact of an asteroid or comet," they wrote. "We don't recommend that anyone run for cover right away. Yet our planet is a target in the cosmic shooting gallery of high-speed asteroids and comets. So far, fewer than a hundred projectiles, of the presumable thousands that could terminate civilization as we know it, have been discovered in the skies."

A few years later, in the fall of 1992, the British astronomer Brian Marsden garnered a considerable amount of press when he announced that the comet Swift-Tuttle might strike the Earth, though not until August 14, 2126. Although Chodas and Yeomans soon ruled out that the comet—which was called "the single most dangerous object known to humanity"—would collide with our planet, Marsden's initial observations still led to a lengthy write-up in *Newsweek*, under the headline "The Science of Doom."

The doom-mongering didn't stop. In January 1994, a few months before the Shoemaker-Levy impacts on Jupiter, Chapman and Morrison published an article in *Nature* that warned "there is a 1 in 10,000 chance that a large (greater than 2 km diameter) asteroid or comet will collide with Earth during the next century, disrupting the ecosphere and killing a large fraction of the world's population."

Finally, in 1998, it was speculated (again by Brian Marsden) that the nearly one-kilometre-wide asteroid 1997 XF11 could strike the planet in 2028. Although it was quickly determined that the asteroid posed no threat—"Paul Chodas and I pointed out, again, that that was an incorrect prediction," Yeomans said. "We could definitely rule out a possible impact"—that close call, combined with the close calls of the previous years, at last led to action. NASA asked Yeomans and the Jet Propulsion Lab to put together a small team to calculate the orbits and impact probabilities of near-Earth objects—basically, a group to determine whether or not something would slam into the planet.

"We were on the hook to do this properly," said Yeomans. "At that point, NASA was saying, 'Well, look, we need some place where we can get this straight the first time around.'" He laughed. "That's pretty much how we got our program started at JPL—headquarters had had enough of these predictions that turned out to be erroneous."

The same year that the Near-Earth Object Program Office—which later became CNEOS—was founded, the U.S. Congress tasked NASA, and by default, Yeomans's new group, with detecting and cataloguing at least 90 percent of all NEOs a kilometre wide or larger—the so-called planet killers. They had until the end of the following decade to complete this mission.

If NASA and politicians were taking notice of the threat, so was Hollywood. On July 1, 1998—two weeks before the announcement of Yeomans's group—Michael Bay's oil-drillers-save-the-world action blockbuster *Armageddon* was released. This was two months after *Deep Impact*, another (better) asteroids-will-destroy-the-world movie, arrived in theatres. (*Armageddon* was "the first 150-minute trailer," said Roger Ebert in his one-star review, and compared to it, *Deep Impact*, which he'd give two and a half stars, "belongs on the American Film Institute list.")

The Catalina Sky Survey was founded in 1998, too, and was eventually joined by the likes of NEOWISE and Pan-STARRS and ATLAS. In the years that followed the congressional mandate, the number of newly discovered asteroids larger than a kilometre exploded: from twelve in 1997 to forty-eight in 1998 to eighty in 2000.

But it wasn't just the planet-killers that kept astronomers up at night. In 2004, the discovery of the 340-metre-wide Apophis (the Egyptian god of destruction) reminded the world of the dangers of "smaller" asteroids—initially, it was believed to have a 2.7 percent chance of striking the planet on April 13, 2029. It might not wipe out humanity, but it would still be catastrophic. Although the odds of it hitting Earth were soon downgraded to zero, it was another reminder that the search should be expanded to encompass NEOs of every size. "You have to find them and do the predictions if you want to mitigate the hazard," Chodas told me. "The number one priority is detection."

With that in mind, in 2005 the U.S. Congress introduced the George E. Brown, Jr. Near-Earth Object Survey Act, which called for the planning, development, and implementation of "a Near-Earth Object Survey program to detect, track, catalogue, and characterize the physical characteristics of near-Earth asteroids and comets" larger than 140 metres in diameter. The Apophises of the solar system had been put on notice. (That said, Eric Christensen of the CSS acknowledged that 140 metres is "an arbitrary cut-off. If a 139-metre asteroid hits us, it's going to hurt just about as much as a 140-metre asteroid.") In any case, as I write this the search is ongoing, even though the goal had been to find 90 percent of these objects by 2020. They had a long way to go: In a 2024 update, NASA estimated they'd found only 44 percent of NEOs 140 metres or larger, and that the survey would take another thirty years to complete. Many of the people who started the search would not see it through to the end.

"The chances are quite good that we will not find any object of that size on an impact trajectory in the next century or so," Binzel told me. "The odds are in our favour. But we ought to know. We ought not to rely on luck, not rely on the odds, and let knowledge replace the roulette table."

"Luck is not a plan," he said. "We really deserve to know what's out there."

When you look at it on a map, Vandenberg Space Force Base resembles a nose sticking out into the Pacific, though, please take my word for it, it's not the kind of place that welcomes nosiness. I was very glad to be at the base, about thirty miles west of Mission Hills, California, as a guest of NASA, instead of driving up to the gates in my rental car to ask for a tour. There were serious-looking men with serious-looking guns who likely would not have taken kindly to such a request. But I'd made it past security without incident, and now, on this warm fall day, stood on the tarmac of Landing Zone 4, a short distance from the ocean, which stretched into the distance until it became indistinguishable from the sky.

I was joined there by several dozen other people—a mix of NASA employees, folks from the Johns Hopkins University Applied Physics Laboratory (APL), engineers of one kind or another, and various space agency bigwigs, many of whom I'd spoken to over the previous year about planetary defence. Above the landing zone, a few hundred metres away, was a large rectangular structure with "SpaceX" painted alongside an American flag, and at a safe distance from the building stood a Falcon 9 rocket, seemingly ready to blast off into the sky at a moment's notice. I was taken aback by its sleek frame; it seemed just an oversized version of the stomp rockets my son played with in the park near our home.

A crackling voice broadcast itself over a loudspeaker: "Please obey all clears . . . conditioning remains amber."

"Maybe we're going to get blown up," said someone standing nearby.

People scurried around the tarmac, exchanging greetings with friends and colleagues, taking group shots and selfies and videos I imagined they'd later send to their families back home. Everyone was laughing, or smiling. It felt like a party, though one at which the guest of honour was going to die.

At one point, I found myself chatting with Cheryl Reed, a former project manager at the Johns Hopkins University Applied Physics Laboratory, who I'd just met, and Ian Carnelli of the European Space

Agency (ESA), who I'd spoken to before. Both of them seemed astonished to be standing there.

"It's unbelievable," said Carnelli.

"It's *very* unbelievable," agreed Reed.

"It's emotional," he added.

"It *really* is," she said.

A minute later, Reed was pulled away for a group photo, and Carnelli and I were joined by a moustachioed man in his sixties. I recognized him right away, and extended my hand: It was Lindley Johnson, who ran NASA's Planetary Defense Coordination Office. You'd never have guessed, if you didn't already know, that of all the people gathered on the tarmac this morning, Johnson was the person who one day might hold the fate of the world in his hands.

Let's pretend, for a moment, that one of the near-Earth objects discovered by Eric Christensen and his team at the Catalina Sky Survey is determined by Paul Chodas and his colleagues at CNEOS to be on a collision course with the Earth. The man tasked with saving our planet would be the self-described "Kansas farm boy" standing in front of me now. And like Carnelli and Reed, he seemed surprised to be here today, and equally emotional.

"A lot of hard work by a lot of people went into getting here," he said.

"There were a lot of tears, I must say," agreed Carnelli. "So much work, so many hours, so many people."

So much work and so many hours, but no one here today had been striving for this moment longer than Lindley Johnson.

"I had a dream thirty years ago," he said. "The idea that we needed the capability to go up and intercept one"—by this he meant an asteroid—"I started talking about that thirty years ago."

When he was still in university, working on a degree in astronomy, Johnson joined the United States Air Force with an eye towards becoming an astronaut. ("I grew up in the Apollo era, so we all wanted to be astronauts," he told me the first time we spoke, several months before running into each other on the tarmac.) His postings included the North American Aerospace Defense Command and the Space and

Missile Systems Center, now known as Space Systems Command, where his roles included orbit analyst, tracking the satellites and debris encircling our planet, attempting to prevent collisions with the space shuttle. It was a job that prepared him well for his future career. "That's kind of a microcosm of what I do today," he said. "Preventing the Earth from colliding with natural debris."

In the early nineties, he was transferred to the Air Force Research Laboratory in Albuquerque, New Mexico, an assignment that brought him into contact with "the first generation" of NEO hunters, like Tom Gehrels. Before too long, Johnson began to see NEOs as a national security issue, one that the Air Force was uniquely positioned to address.

"A significant asteroid impact could upset the balance of things quite considerably, so I saw it really as something that ought to be part of the Air Force's space situational awareness mission," he said. "Not only should we be interested in what other nations are putting up there, but we should be interested in what threats are coming from outside."

Not long afterwards, Johnson was involved in a study called Spacecast 2020 whose purpose, as the name suggests, was to determine what space-related capabilities the Air Force should acquire by 2020. Johnson wanted to focus on asteroids and the threat they posed to Earth. "I was laughed out of the room, quite frankly," he recalled. "That was not what they were looking for." The Air Force, he was told, "needed to worry about threats from other countries, not the sky."

Only a week or two later, as Johnson remembered it, the comet Shoemaker-Levy 9 was discovered. In any case, no one was laughing now. When the Spacecast study was published in June 1994 (a month before the comet's impact with Jupiter) it included a paper titled "Preparing for Planetary Defense: Detection and Interception of Asteroids on Collision Course with Earth," which recommended that, "as opposed to accepting such a cataclysmic event as an act of God," the Air Force prepare for such a threat by establishing a project office "to detect, track, characterize and mitigate planetary debris of sufficient size to cause significant destruction of human lives and property should it impact the Earth." The paper ended with an appeal: "Mankind must now prepare for planetary defence."

Later in his career, Johnson helped set up MIT's Lincoln Near-Earth Asteroid Research program, another pioneering survey, which found more than half of the one-kilometre-or-larger NEOs discovered between 1998 and 2005. After retiring from the Air Force in 2003 with the rank of lieutenant colonel, Johnson joined NASA, where his roles included leading the Deep Impact mission to comet Tempel 1. All the while, he continued to sound the alarm about asteroids. "He was instrumental in bringing the issue of near-Earth objects to NASA," Don Yeomans told me.

And then came Chelyabinsk.

"That one caught us by surprise," admitted Yeomans.

On the morning of February 15, 2013, a meteor roughly twenty metres in diameter exploded approximately thirty kilometres above the planet's surface. The residents of the Russian city of Chelyabinsk had a front-row seat for the fireworks, which were brighter than the sun. It was the first asteroid event of the social-media age, and the footage, much of it recorded by dashboard cams, went viral: a fiery tear across the sky; a blinding flash; a tremendous bang; screams, shattering glass, and car alarms set off by the explosion, which, wrote Kate Howells of the Planetary Society, "released the same amount of energy as 500 kilotons of TNT—around 30 times more energy than the atomic bomb detonated at Hiroshima." It was a fairly small rock, all things considered, and it didn't even strike the Earth. What would have happened if it impacted in the middle of a major metropolitan area? What would have happened if it had been two hundred metres in diameter and not twenty?

"That really called the world's attention to the problem," said Megan Bruck Syal, a planetary defence physicist at the Lawrence Livermore National Laboratory in California. "But the reality is something like Chelyabinsk could happen at any time. We haven't discovered the vast majority of things in that size range."

With multiple surveys already attempting to track down similar threats, it was the subject of preparation that came into focus. And so

Johnson was soon presented with a choice: He could continue as an executive in NASA's Discovery program, or he could make building up the agency's planetary defence capabilities a full-time job. It was an easy decision.

"There was no question in my mind that I wanted to continue to build the planetary defence program to get it to the state that I really felt it needed to be—something that I envisioned way back in the nineties when I wrote the [Spacecast] paper," he told me. That said, he added, "I didn't do it for myself. I did it because I thought it was something that we, as a species, needed to prepare ourselves for. [To] get ourselves into a position that we no longer needed to fear what was an act of God in the past."

The Planetary Defense Coordination Office was established at the start of 2016. The office was tasked with identifying "potentially hazardous objects"—called PHOs—which are NEOs predicted to come within 8 million kilometres of Earth's orbit, and whose size—30 to 50 metres—would cause significant damage to our planet. It was a version of what Johnson had advocated for in the Spacecast paper decades earlier. Yes, it was a small team, and the resources devoted to planetary defence represented less than one percent of NASA's overall budget. But it was a start.

Years later there were still, Johnson knew, people who questioned why the agency bothered with hypothetical threats rather than devote more resources to practical missions. It was true that, more likely than not, the world would not face a killer asteroid anytime soon. But that missed the point. "It's a legacy for future generations," Johnson said. What he was doing was laying down the first bricks in a wall that, one day, might shield the planet.

"Hopefully we don't face any [threat] in the near term, but it's one we will face someday, there's no doubt about that," he said. "But I think we're finally getting ourselves in a position that we would be able to deal with it, should an impact be detected."

Which brought us back to Vandenberg Space Force Base. Later that evening, at two seconds past 10:21 p.m., if all went according to plan, the rocket in front of us would blast off into the night sky on a mission never before attempted by man. Attached to the Falcon 9 was a spacecraft that, once released from the rocket, would embark on a year-long collision course with an asteroid. The goal was to smash itself into the target and alter its trajectory. A kamikaze mission to save the rest of us, someday.

When you work in a field like planetary defence, one might think the main question that comes up is: Is there an asteroid out there, that we know of, on a direct course with Earth? When I brought this up with Matthew Payne, director of the Minor Planet Center, the clearinghouse for all observations and orbits of NEOs and other things beyond the clouds, he said that, curiously, no one really asked him that. "The main thing people fixate on is: 'What can we do about it?'" he said. "They all just want to know: If there is something coming, how can we stop it? What will we do? And, up until relatively recently, the answer had to be rather theoretical."

A decade before the gathering at Vandenberg, and on the other side of the country, Andy Cheng was exercising in the basement of his home on a frigid winter morning when he experienced an epiphany. At the time, Cheng was chief scientist for the Space Department at the esteemed Johns Hopkins University Applied Physics Laboratory, where he'd been working since the early eighties. The (lengthy) resumé of the Princeton- and Columbia-educated scientist included roles on the Galileo mission to Jupiter, the Cassini mission to Saturn, and the New Horizons mission to Pluto and the Kuiper Belt. The morning of his workout, however, he was thinking about how to pull off a different mission—one that had been struggling to get off the ground for several years.

"I've been thinking about planetary defence for a very long time," he told me the first time we spoke.

In the early 1990s he served as project scientist for NASA's groundbreaking Near Earth Asteroid Rendezvous, the first mission to orbit and eventually land on an asteroid, in this case 433 Eros. His involvement left a lasting impression. "I couldn't get away [from asteroids] after that," he said. Cheng later worked on the equally historic Hayabusa mission, led by the Japan Aerospace Exploration Agency, which returned a sample from asteroid 25143 Itokawa.

But asteroids were one thing; planetary defence was another.

"Even in the 1990s, there was what you might call a 'giggle factor,'" he told me. "People just did not take it seriously. They did not appreciate that scientists are actually concerned about this. This is real. This is not a joke." It was seen as such a disreputable field of study, Cheng recalled, that before giving a talk on the subject, his managers ("I won't name names," he said) asked him if he was sure he wanted to associate Johns Hopkins APL with planetary defence.

"Twenty years later," he added, "the situation has changed."

First, some background: In 2003, the European Space Agency proposed a mission called Don Quijote, in which a spacecraft named Hidalgo would smash into an asteroid. A second craft, codenamed Sancho, would measure how the collision affected the asteroid's orbit, among other things. While the mission never took off, having been deemed too expensive by ESA, it was admired by others with an interest in planetary defence, including Cheng, who contributed to a 2010 study published by the U.S. National Research Council entitled "Defending Planet Earth: Near-Earth-Object Surveys and Hazard Mitigation Strategies." It recommended that, "if Congress chooses to fund mitigation research at an appropriately high level," the course set out by ESA should be followed by NASA: "[T]he first priority for a space mission in the mitigation area is an experimental test of a kinetic impactor along with a characterization, monitoring, and verification system, such as the Don Quijote mission that was previously considered, but not funded, by the European Space Agency. This mission would produce the most significant advances in understanding and provide an ideal chance for international collaboration in a realistic mitigation scenario."

Which brought us back to Cheng, and what was going through his mind as he did his morning stretches.

"It just occurred to me one day that the way to get this kind of a mission going would be to modify the Don Quijote approach," he told me. "And the key modification is that you should do the test of a kinetic impactor on a binary asteroid. The reason being that if we did that, if you choose the right kind of target, then you can measure the deflection without a second spacecraft. You can do it from Earth with Earth-based telescopes." Instead of a mission that required two separate launch vehicles and two separate spacecraft, he continued, "you only need one. You effectively cut the cost in half."

This was the epiphany that Cheng experienced in 2011, and the birth of what became known as the Double Asteroid Redirection Test—DART.

The first step was to find an appropriate asteroid—no simple task seeing as the vast majority of them are solitary creatures. That fall, Cheng and a small group of colleagues identified an asteroid named Didymos, which had been discovered by the Spacewatch survey in 1996. Measuring about 780 metres in diameter, it would be coming close to the Earth—well, 10 million kilometres away—in the fall of 2022. More importantly: Orbiting Didymos, which means "twin" in Greek, was Dimorphos (also sometimes referred to as Didymoon), which is Greek for "two forms." This 160-metre satellite would be the target.

They settled on testing a kinetic impactor because, as Cheng told me, the National Research Council study had determined it was the "most mature" of all the methods that could conceivably protect the planet. (The study also considered the feasibility of "nuclear explosions," suggesting that *Armageddon* might one day be considered a documentary.) The idea behind an impactor is straightforward—hit the target and hope you've altered its orbit enough to, eventually, miss the planet. That's why detection is essential—if you strike the asteroid far enough away, even a tiny change could end up significantly altering its course.

"Our level of understanding of these objects, physically, is incredibly limited," said Richard Binzel. "And when you don't know very much you undertake relatively simple experiments, like hitting them, to see what happens." Just watch any young child when they pick up a new toy, he said. "What do they do? They hit it against the wall, or hit it against their head, to try to get a fundamental understanding of what the thing is. It's a very fundamental first step about learning things—you physically interact with them and see what new information you gain."

Cheng approached NASA with the idea, and also reached out to ESA, in case they still wanted to participate—it was their idea, after all. This led to the Asteroid Impact and Deflection Assessment, an international mission that consisted of two parts: DART, which would collide with Dimorphos, and AIM (Asteroid Impact Mission), which would measure DART's success using a combination of ground-based telescopes and a spacecraft. A key selling point, explained Cheng, was that each mission could proceed independently, should funding fall through; AIM, for instance, could still be the first mission to study a binary asteroid even if there was no impact to monitor.

In 2016, the AIM mission failed to obtain the necessary funding to proceed and was "considered dead," Ian Carnelli of the European Space Agency told me. The setback was devastating, he said, but ultimately temporary: Funding for the mission—now named HERA—was eventually secured in late 2019; it would launch three years after DART and reach the binary asteroid system in December 2026. "When AIM was not approved I cried, I think, for the whole evening," Carnelli told me. "When HERA was approved, I think I cried for over a week."

It helped that by 2019 NASA and Lindley Johnson had established the Planetary Defense Coordination Office and DART was going full-steam ahead, unlike in 2016, when the mission had still not been officially approved by the space agency.

"Until 2018, we weren't really sure if DART was going to go forward," said Justin Atchison, the mission design lead, who started working on the project in 2013. "We were never given the go-ahead to say, 'Yes, this will definitely be a mission.' And it was very stressful to pour so much of yourself into it [. . .] and then still be living in uncertainty."

This seemed par for the course when it came to space missions. Cheng, who was the DART investigations team lead, laughed when he told me he had "lots of experience working on projects that never actually get approved," and was thus used to operating in a state of constant unpredictability. Even the first time we spoke, about a year and a half out from the scheduled launch date, Cheng acknowledged there was still plenty of time for the mission to go off the rails. "In a space mission, a complicated kind of thing like this, nothing ever goes according to plan exactly. It doesn't work that way. There's always problems. There's things that go wrong. Bearing that in mind, things are going well."

For him, not for me. I'd wanted to visit Maryland to see the craft as it was being assembled, but the pandemic had complicated international travel. Cursing my luck for living on the wrong side of the border, I'd go down to my basement and talk to team members over Zoom instead.

"DART is something that looks so simple on paper," Nancy Chabot, the project's coordination lead and one of the first team members I interviewed, told me. "It looks like a Physics 101 kind of problem, right? Crash this much mass into it, going this fast, and that will deflect it by this much. But seeing how that actually plays out, on an asteroid of the sort of size that you would potentially need to use this technology on to deflect it from the Earth, is going to be very interesting."

"DART is an experiment," echoed Elena Adams, the mission systems engineer, whose slight accent betrayed her Russian childhood. "We're going to see if we can do this—if we can really move an asteroid. Hopefully, the answer is yes." But, looking at the bigger picture, it was about more than altering Didymoon's orbit, she said. "It's an experiment to see if we can save humanity and not become dinosaurs."

It was partly that element, she added—the blockbuster save-the-world-from-catastrophe aspect of the mission—that made it such a novel project. When it came to space research, Adams explained, the public always had the same questions: What was the point? What was the value? Why spend money on this, instead of that? Compared to most missions, DART was an easy sell. "I feel like the possibility of not becoming dinosaurs is a very straightforward reason why you would actually want to do something about it," Adams told me. "You would feel very stupid that you had this great space program, and the last thing we never knew what to do is how to protect ourselves from space rocks."

On the day I spoke to Adams, the team was doing some structural testing: in this case, shake the craft and see if anything falls off. The craft itself was a box that, once fully kitted out, measured 1.8 metres by 1.9 metres, and 2.6 metres tall—about the size of a semi-trailer, she said. It was equipped with long roll-out solar arrays (nickname: ROSA) which were each 8.5 metres long when deployed. When loaded with propellant, the entire thing weighed 610 kilograms. The craft might be simple, but Adams said that it was "riddled with technology" that had never been flown in space before. The idea wasn't just to slam into an asteroid; it was to test out stuff that might prove useful in future missions. "If there was a Christmas tree–approach to a space mission, we're definitely it," she said. "Every single ornament in the world has been stuck onto this Christmas tree." New solar arrays. New navigation system to help target the asteroid. Though it wasn't the main engine, it would also be an opportunity to try out NASA's Evolutionary Xenon Thruster–Commercial (NEXT-C) engine, a solar-powered ion propulsion system—though I'm sure the interstellar researchers I'd met at the IRG conference would turn their noses up at it. Images of the target would be sent back to Earth by the craft's "eye" and lone instrument, DRACO (Didymos Reconnaissance and Asteroid Camera for Optical Navigation), while the impact would be witnessed by the Light Italian Cubesat for Imagining of Asteroids, developed by the Italian Space Agency, which was hitching a ride on DART and would be deployed a couple of weeks before impact. The spacecraft would hit the asteroid going almost 23,000 kilometres per hour.

It all sounded impressive to me, and it had taken the team years to get to this point, so I asked Adams if she was sad they were spending all this time, money, and energy only to destroy the craft in the end. She looked at me as if I were an asteroid. "Are you kidding me? No! That's the whole goal! How often do you get to crash a $250 million dollar spacecraft?"

There was no guarantee that would happen, though. The asteroid was tiny, and they'd be coming in hot. Usually there'd be weeks to prepare before making contact, but not in this case—they were flying blind. "We're coming screaming in to the point that we don't even see Dimorphos until less than an hour out," said Atchinson, the mission design lead. At that point, it was predicted that the target would be just a pixel on their screens; some models said it would still be a pixel thirty minutes from impact. They had no idea what Dimorphos was made of (a rubble pile, a solid chunk of metal?) nor what it looked like (a dog bone, a sphere, a donut?). The team had been running simulations to account for all these different possibilities, I was assured. But anything could happen.

"The final five minutes are the parts I've played through my head so many times," Atchinson told me. "Usually at about 2 a.m."

What he dreamt about, even when he couldn't sleep, was "a final image where Dimorphos is taking up the full screen of the imager"—that would mean success. But there was, he admitted, "a reasonable chance" that they'd miss the target.

"Not hitting it is a very bad option," said Cheng. "That's mission failure."

There were some in the planetary defence community who were skeptical of DART, who thought the mission wasn't the best first step when it came to the ultimate goal of protecting the Earth. There were scientists who mused about gravity tractors; others talked to me about the possibility of lasers. I spent a couple of hours in discussions with a couple of colleagues about the benefits (and potential drawbacks) of using nuclear bombs. Some took issue with the idea of a kinetic impactor itself—that it required a long lead time, and could only deal with smaller asteroids. "If we ever find one coming our way, giving it a gentle push with a kinetic impactor is not the way we're going to do it," said Alan Harris, a senior research scientist at the Space Science Institute. "Get that thing away from me." There was also the chance, said Franck Marchis, a chief planetary astronomer at the SETI Institute, that using an impactor might make the problem worse—or create a new problem for someone else. "When you start deflecting an asteroid, there is still some chance that you will fail," he told me. "And then what will happen to this asteroid if you move it along the path, and instead of landing on the United States it will land on China?" When I mentioned the DART mission to Eric Christensen of the Catalina Sky Survey, he told me that he worried we were putting the cart before the horse: "The idea that we need to be able to push asteroids out of the way before we find out where they all are is getting ahead of ourselves a little bit," he said.

The DART team members felt otherwise, of course. To Cheng, a successful mission would mean that, when we eventually spotted a dangerous asteroid heading our way, we'd "be able to do something other than just try and evacuate the regions that are threatened," he said. We'd have at least one arrow in our quiver to fight back.

"We know it can happen—we just don't know when," he said. "It could be tomorrow. It could be a thousand years from now. But this is something we should be preparing to deal with."

"I think most people want to leave the Earth in a better place than they found it, and in this particular field, this is one of the more direct ways to do it," said Atchinson. "I think it's fair to say that, most likely, everything we learn from DART will go into papers and sit on bookshelves and not be needed for maybe decades." But, he continued, "even if there's a 99 percent chance we don't need it, knowing that it's not a problem if you do need it would be a good contribution."

Even if the book gathers dust on the shelf, there's comfort in knowing it's there, ready for when the day eventually comes that we need to read it.

Early one morning, several days after my visit to the Catalina Sky Survey, I took I-40 east from Flagstaff, Arizona, and, after abandoning the interstate at exit 233, followed a series of signs that you didn't want to encounter while behind the wheel of a car: Five miles to impact. Four miles to impact. Three miles to impact . . .

Here, the rock had already fallen. Meteor Crater, as it was officially known, is the world's best-preserved impact site and a physical reminder of the devastation that could be unleashed, one day, eventually, if we failed to remain vigilant. I'd come to see with my own eyes what the successors of the DART mission would one day, eventually, try to prevent.

My arrival at the visitor centre coincided with the departure of a tour, so I attached myself, remora-like, to the small group. Our guide was a twenty-something woman named Penny, who employed a wonderful, Yoda-esque syntax—it was as if she placed a fully formed sentence into a hat, shook it, and drew the words out one at a time. Standing beside the 638-kilogram Holsinger meteorite, the largest fragment found in the area, Penny gave us a brief history of the crater before we headed outside to see it for ourselves.

"To be accurate with information given here, 61,000 years ago was what we were informed the meteorite created this open site," she told us.

Tens of thousands of years ago, a rogue meteor, measuring forty-six metres in diameter and weighing an estimated 300,000 tons, hurtled towards our planet at a speed of 64,500 kilometres per hour, tore through the atmosphere, and slammed into the ground travelling 12 kilometres per second with the force of 20 million tons of TNT, or 150 times more powerful than the atomic bomb dropped on Hiroshima. The leading theory holds that it hailed from the asteroid belt between Mars and Jupiter, though the meteor might also have come from the tail of a comet passing through the solar system. Wherever it came from, said Penny, "4.5 to 5 billion years old this meteorite does age as."

Though there's no doubt the Indigenous communities that call the region home knew about the crater, it was first recorded by one of General Custer's scouts in 1871. In 1902, a lawyer and mining engineer from Philadelphia, Daniel Moreau Barringer, learned of the crater from an employee of the forestry service, S.J. Holsinger. Barringer believed it must have been caused by a meteor, which meant there must be a load of precious metals buried below the surface. He secured a mining claim from the government and hired Holsinger to oversee the operation; in 1911, Holsinger discovered the meteorite fragment on display in the visitor centre. That might have been the pair's best find. Though they dug dozens of shafts, on the crafter floor and its slopes, and though Barringer promised potential investors that the minerals he thought he would find would be worth upward of half a billion dollars, nothing of the sort was ever discovered. Barringer's outfit searched for two decades before he went broke in 1928; he died of a heart attack the following year. The crater, which remained in his family, opened to the public in 1950.

Penny led us through a set of doors, outside, and towards the rim. "No putting rocks inside your pockets—it is a federally protected site," she warned us. "So nobody's allowed to go out and go do their own meteorite hunting." If we wanted something from outer space, we could peruse the gift shop on our way out, where they sold fragments at different price points alongside copies of the movie *Starman*, starring Jeff Bridges, which was filmed here, and which I had never seen.

I'd seen photographs of the crater online, however, but it was no match for the real thing. It was as if a giant had taken an ice cream scoop and spooned out a portion of the desert. It was awesome, in every sense of the word. "It does still sit 2.4 miles around a circumference that you are looking upon the rim, 4,000 feet across," Penny told the group. It reminded me of a gigantic amphitheatre; indeed, I later read that 2 million people could sit on the crater's slopes, if the occasion arose. It was 550 feet deep, though at the time of impact "much much deeper down into the crater you would be seeing," Penny said; erosion had filled the crater in by at least 150 feet over the millennia. One day, it would be gone.

Remnants of Barringer's doomed mining concern littered the crater floor—a boiler, a winch—though I couldn't make out the shafts that had been dug over the years. The crater floor had been off-limits to the public since the 1980s, but that didn't stop a madman who, in 2013, scrambled down the slope and threw himself into one of the open shafts to "appease the gods." Penny pointed out the fuselage of a Cessna that crashed in the crater decades ago—the passengers survived—as well as a new addition to the landscape: the mannequin of an astronaut, which Penny and her colleagues had carried down into the crater just a couple of weeks back when Ed Lu from the B612

Foundation visited the site. The mannequin replaced a cut-out of an American astronaut that had been there for decades, honouring the fact that from 1963 until 1971 the crater served as a training ground for astronauts during the Apollo program, under the leadership of Eugene Shoemaker, who years earlier had finally proven Barringer's theory irrefutably correct.

I looked up at the sky and tried to imagine an asteroid able to cause such a wound in the Earth hurtling towards this spot. Life around the impact zone was devastated; the animals, including megafauna that roamed the land, would have been killed up to twenty-four kilometres away—those not vaporized would have been dispatched by rock or the hurricane-force winds, which swept as far as forty kilometres away. If something like this happened today near an urban centre, it would be catastrophic. I'd spent so long talking to folks in the field about exactly this kind of event, and here was the result before my very eyes. It had happened: with the dinosaurs hundreds of millions of years ago, and here tens of thousands of years ago, albeit on a much smaller scale. It would happen again.

"That's your information given to you all," said Penny. "Any questions?"

Tour over, I wandered around the perimeter for a while longer, taking it all in, then I got in my car and drove back to Flagstaff. The next day I returned to Toronto. And the day after that, October 3, a meteorite crashed through the roof of a house in the small town of Golden, British Columbia. The owner, a retired woman named Ruth Hamilton, woke up at the sound of her dog barking. This was almost immediately followed by an explosion. She thought perhaps a tree had fallen on her home. While on the phone with a 911 dispatcher, she discovered the 1.3-kilogram chunk of rock, described as "the size of a large man's fist" or "the size of a melon," between two pillows, near where her head had been moments before the crash.

"I was shaking like a leaf," she told a reporter. "You're sound asleep, safe, you think, in your bed, and you can get taken out by a meteorite, apparently."

The news went national, and then international. She later sent the rock to researchers at a university in Ontario, who concluded that it was about 470 million years old.

Ruth said she planned to keep it for herself.

I arrived in Buellton, a town in southern California's Santa Ynez Valley, on a Sunday. The DART launch was scheduled to take place in less than seventy-two hours. I knew enough about the history of rocket launches to know they didn't always happen when they were supposed to. There were many factors at play—some out of the team's hands. With that in mind, I checked the weather app on my phone incessantly, worried that I'd flown across the continent only for the launch to be scuttled by fog or lightning or even an earthquake—this was California, after all. (It turned out I'd have to wait a bit longer for that last one.)

Not long after checking into the Marriott, which was doubling as NASA's media centre, I caught up with Andy Rivkin, DART's mission investigations lead, who I'd interviewed the previous year. With his vintage *Asteroids* video game shirt, greying hair in a ponytail, and an unruly beard, he looked like a middle-age garage rocker, which, to be fair, he sort of was; a musician as well as a scientist, he wrote songs when he wasn't figuring out how to save the world. One earworm he'd recorded to commemorate the mission was called "The DART Song." (Sample lyric: "DART will visit the Didymos system / a one-way trip that won't be a fluke / so when hazards come we can resist them / without resorting to a giant nuke.") I asked how he was feeling about the launch. Things were going well, he told me, but it wasn't time to relax. "There's the desire to make sure this goes [smoothly], and then we'll handle the celebrating after that," he said.

He had just come from a briefing. There were so many briefings. Science briefings and technical briefings and investigation and engineering briefings and mission overviews and briefings about when the next briefing would occur. Each briefing had its own peculiarities and focus but shared a common refrain: Don't worry. This is just a test.

Everyone made sure to emphasize that the mission was taking place not because Didymos was on a collision course with Earth but because, you know, science.

I understood their caution. It seemed, during the years I was writing this book, that not a month went by without an article in some newspaper or magazine around the world warning readers about one close call or another.

"Skyscraper-sized asteroid to pass within 1.7m miles of Earth on Friday," screamed a headline in *The Guardian*.

"NASA tracks 5 'potentially hazardous' asteroids that will fly by Earth within days," announced *USA Today*.

"747-sized asteroid skimmed by Earth, and scientists didn't see it coming," *The Jerusalem Post* told readers.

Stories like these made it seem the planet was constantly being targeted. I realized they made for good copy, but I also knew that the majority of readers wouldn't understand that these were not particularly close encounters of any kind.

"An object the size of a bus passes between the Earth and moon every week," Richard Binzel told me. "It's entirely normal that these objects are passing by the Earth all the time."

Still, NASA did not entirely shy away from the apocalyptic, Hollywood-esque facets of the mission—one briefing kicked off with a trailer that could have comfortably screened before the latest Michael Bay flick, complete with booming baritone voice-over and swelling, dramatic music:

"In a galaxy where asteroids have pummelled planets for billions of years, now one planet strikes back," it began. "At the crossroads of science fiction and reality, DART is part of our plan to defend planet Earth against potential future impacts. The test to protect the future of our planet begins now!"

"It *is* the stuff of movies," said Thomas Zurbuchen, the associate administrator for the Science Mission Directorate at NASA, during one of the briefings. If the DART mission proved successful, he imagined, in some unspecified future, an armada of deflectors in orbit, ready to rendezvous with a NEO that was getting too close for comfort.

The evening of the launch, I drove the hour from Buellton back to Vandenberg Space Force Base, then walked from the parking lot through the dark to a viewing area called the Hawk's Nest. There were groups of people on picnic blankets and fold-out chairs, from NASA and DART and the mission's other collaborators. (Not all the DART team members had made the trip—Andy Cheng, for one, was back home in Maryland. Those who weren't in California, I was told, had been invited to a double-bill of *Armageddon* and *Deep Impact*, followed by the launch broadcast.) There were screens posted around the viewing area, on which regularly scrolled a chyron: "DART is a test. There are no known threats to Earth." Organizers screened the trailer for *Don't Look Up*, a Leonardo DiCaprio comedy streaming on Netflix in a few weeks, about a comet heading towards the Earth that's greeted with a collective shrug. The film's director, Adam McKay, delivered a brief videotaped message to the gathered crowd.

It was the first time I'd attended a rocket launch. The weather was cool and clear, and there was a charge in the air, like the minutes before a concert begins, before the lights go down and the first note sounds. Over the loudspeakers, a man and a woman provided a play-by-play, like baseball announcers, and every so often we'd receive updates from the mission control feed. And then, suddenly, the countdown began. The sky turned from night to morning as the rocket lifted off, and there was clapping and cheers and screams, so loud and sustained they muffled any noise coming from the launch pad. After a minute it went supersonic, faster than the speed of sound. And I stood there, watching the rocket pierce the clouds, until it became another star in the sky.

Not long after I returned from the launch, a tractor-trailer slammed into our car in a grocery store parking lot while my wife was running errands. My wife was fine; our car was not. The truck driver gave her a phone number, but then wouldn't return our calls. It was thousands of dollars of damage, but at least we were insured.

I tell you this story because, around the time it happened, I'd been thinking a lot about insurance, though as it related to planetary defence. It pains me to frame such an exciting field in these terms—Bruce Willis was an action hero, not a policy, goddamnit—but this was usually how those in the community chose to portray their work, whenever I pressed them on why, exactly, they were spending their lives doing what they did. Everyone was (fairly) confident that a civilization-destroying asteroid wasn't going to show up on the Earth's doorstep anytime soon—not in my lifetime, it was safe to say, and not in my kids' lifetime, either. This wasn't something we'd have to worry about in the near future, so why think about it now?

"It's like an insurance policy," said Andy Cheng.

"Most insurance policies don't ever get cashed in, but they are still worthwhile," said Andy Rivkin.

"You have fire insurance for your house," argued Jessie Dotson, an astrophysicist at NASA's Ames Research Center. "It's very unlikely that your house is going to burn down, but you've decided, well, it's worth putting this little bit aside, just in case, so I'll be ready if this big thing happens."

Ed Lu, of the B612 Foundation, recalled how, when he was a pilot in Honolulu, he'd regularly see a fire rescue crew training at the airport, even though they'd never had to deal with a crash. This is how, he said, we should think about planetary defence. "You can't play the odds forever and not eventually have your number come up," he told me. "It could be tomorrow. It could be a thousand years from now. You just don't know."

"Eventually, something is going to hit the Earth," said DART's Nancy Chabot. "The Earth has been here for 4.5 billion years, and it's going to be here for billions more years, and there's no way that we're going to go that long without things hitting [us]." The question, she continued, is: "Are we safe for the next one hundred years? Two hundred? A thousand? Ten thousand? Eventually, the Earth will get hit by something that's fairly large, because this is what happens in the solar system."

Whatever the timeline, the consequences of a strike, even if it wasn't on the same scale as the one that ended the dinosaur's reign, would be so severe that it would be "a betrayal" not to start preparing now, said Lawrence Livermore's Megan Bruck Syal. "There's a peace of mind that comes from having done the work, even though you hope you don't need to use it," she said. It just came down to striking the right balance, she added, between conveying "a sense of urgency" and "not frightening people."

The latter point was key. Those I interviewed were clear they did not want to be seen as doomers; there was a stark difference between issuing a clear-eyed warning and loudly proclaiming the end of the world was coming.

"We're not carrying sandwich boards down the street saying 'The end is nigh, repent,'" said Rob Landis, who'd served as a program executive in the Planetary Defense Coordination Office. "I'm not Henny Penny. I'm not Chicken Little. The sky is not falling." But, he continued, it would be negligent not to at least consider the possibility. "The dinosaurs had their chance, and nature selected them for elimination unfortunately," he said. Humans, on the other hand, had evolved into a space-faring species that could actually produce the technology necessary to ensure that didn't happen again. "Sometimes," Landis said, "I wonder if an intelligence test, of sorts, is being put in front of us, for us to figure out."

If it was a test, at least we were studying for it. There were a number of major projects soon coming online that would expand our NEO-finding capabilities, most notably the Vera C. Rubin Observatory in northern Chile (under construction at the time I write this but operational by the time you read this), which will be home to an 8.4-metre telescope outfitted with the largest digital camera ever built. There was also NASA's NEO Surveyor mission, a space-based infrared telescope "specifically designed" to hunt near hazardous objects, which Paul Chodas of CNEOS described to me as "the most important mission going forward" and MIT's Richard Binzel described as "one of the most consequential missions, and consequential endeavours, ever, in the history of humanity. Because if it identifies a threat that's a century, or centuries, away, identifying that threat, and allowing time for us to have a sensible approach to how to mitigate it, is huge. The dinosaurs could not do it, but we can."

It was an odd thing. Despite the apocalyptic nature of the threat, those I encountered in the planetary defence community were the most optimistic folks I met during my travels. They believed the world was worth saving. But more than that, they believed there would *still* be a world worth saving, at some indeterminate point in the future. That despite everything, we'd survive. It would have been easy to stick their heads in the sand, let some future scientist deal with the problem when it eventually arose. But it was comforting to know there was a group of people who weren't willing to give up on the world. Who had its back. Who felt it was worth fighting for, even if they wouldn't live to see the day we had to throw our best counterpunch at the universe.

One September evening, some ten months and 11 million kilometres after the launch, the DART spacecraft approached its target. I was home in Toronto, reading bedtime stories to my two-year-old son. Outside, a gentle rain fell as the sky slowly darkened.

Although it made me feel somewhat like a negligent father, my iPhone was propped up on a pillow, and as I read books I knew by heart, I kept an eye on the NASA broadcast of the (hopeful) collision. In the top right-hand corner of the screen, a timer counted down the minutes and seconds to impact. The mission had entered its "terminal phase," meaning the on-board autonomous navigation system (dubbed SMART Nav) was piloting the craft. Even though (fingers crossed) impact was more than an hour away, I could see Didymos, a prick of grey in the infinite blackness of space, beamed back to Earth. Viewers were informed that DRACO, the craft's on-board camera, had detected Dimorphos, though I couldn't yet see the target.

The timer counted down. At the hour mark Elena Adams appeared on screen, sitting at mission operations at the Johns Hopkins Applied Physics Lab in Laurel, Maryland, along with dozens of her colleagues, the team in matching blue polos. When they'd arrived that morning, they'd found fortune cookies under their seats, placed there by Adams. "Today you will make an impact," the fortunes promised.

One by one, her colleagues provided her with brief updates. Yes, things were going according to plan. "We're ready to go," Adams told the broadcast. Everyone seemed calm. I didn't learn until later that the mission had experienced a number of hiccups in recent days, including the fact that, a week earlier, it had been discovered that the spacecraft was seventy miles off-target. (There was a contingency plan in place that, if DART missed the target, they could use the NEXT-C engine to pilot the craft around the sun for another shot two years later.)

Fifty minutes. Forty. Didymos, slightly larger now. At the thirty-minute mark, the broadcast cut back to Adams for another update. "It is time for the last status poll," she told her team to applause. They were seven thousand miles away from impact. Things were looking good. "We're going to transition to precision lock at twenty minutes," she said. "That's our next milestone."

I continued to read my son stories about trucks and excavators and other construction vehicles. At the twenty-minute mark, an announcement: "We are precision locked and still tracking Dimorphos." The team broke out in cheers, and I looked from the book I was holding to my phone: There it was, barely perceptible but real: Dimorphos. "This was our last milestone," Adams said. "We're about 4,500 miles away from Didymos and Diphormos. So let's see what happens."

A beaming Lindley Johnson appeared on screen to discuss the mission. I wondered how he was feeling right now—after years and years of pushing for planetary defence to be taken seriously by NASA, the boulder was almost at the top of the hill. As head of the agency's Planetary Defense Coordination Office, he was asked to reassure viewers that neither Didymos nor Dimorphos posed a threat to the Earth. "This asteroid system is still almost 7 million miles away from the Earth," he said. "It's at its closest point in orbit right now to Earth, so from this point forward it's going to be moving away from Earth." There was no chance of a collision with our planet, but, as he'd been doing for more than thirty years, Johnson used the opportunity to advocate for continued vigilance "We've got to look for all the other unknown asteroids out there," he said.

Fifteen minutes until (maybe?) impact. Ten. Five. Three. Adams and her team were mostly standing at their monitors, watching the craft approaching its target at almost 14,000 miles per hour. Even now, two minutes out, Dimorphos was still a small dot on my screen, just above and to the right of its bigger sibling. But in the final minute it came into view, pixel by pixel, frame by stuttering frame. Didymos dropped off the screen. Thirty seconds. The spacecraft raced towards its fate. I could now make out rocks and boulders on the asteroid's surface. "It's amazing, guys. Oh my goodness look at that. Unbelievable." Adams and the team were seeing what I was seeing at the same time, for the first time. Closer. Ten, nine, eight. Cheers. Seven, six. Louder now. Closer, closer. Adams, jumping up and down. Five, four, three. And in the final seconds the camera captured exactly what Justin Atchinson told me, two years earlier, that he wanted to see: The surface of the asteroid taking up the entirety of the frame. And then a red screen. "And we have impact!" Adams cried, raising her arms in the air.

As I watched the celebration in the control room, hugs and handshakes and tears, I wondered: Centuries or millennia or millions of years from now, when a killer asteroid or troublesome comet had Earth in its sights, and humanity launched a mission to stop it—deflect it or blast it with a laser or bomb it out of the sky or something else entirely—would people talk about this moment, and this group of scientists and engineers and physicists who'd spent the better part of a decade on a mission to protect the future? Would any of their names be remembered? Would this mission be celebrated? Because the mission, as they later learned, was successful. It marked the first time humans had "purposely changed the motion of a celestial object." NASA had set out a "minimum successful orbit period change" of seventy-three seconds. The team shortened Dimorphos's orbit around Didymos by thirty-three minutes. They had literally smashed expectations.

"The successful impact of the DART spacecraft with Dimorphos and the resulting change in the orbit of Dimorphos demonstrates that kinetic impactor technology is a viable technique to potentially defend Earth if necessary," wrote many of the team members in a paper published in the journal *Nature*.

But I didn't know that, then. All I knew was that the spacecraft that I'd watched ascend into the sky had collided with an asteroid—all that work, years of it, ground into dust, now floating somewhere in space. A first step towards saving the future. I put my phone down as the party continued, and then put my son down in his crib, and turned off the lights and closed the door to his room, where I hoped he would sleep through the night.

NINE

ARTIFACTS

When I arrived at the Arizona State University Art Museum late on a Wednesday morning only to find it closed, I was annoyed but not overly concerned. After all, the exhibit that had brought me here technically didn't open for another 994 years, give or take the survival of the planet. What was more worrisome, when a couple of days later I returned to the Nelson Fine Arts Center, the labyrinthine complex on ASU's sprawling Tempe campus where the museum is housed, was that now I couldn't find what I'd travelled some three thousand kilometres to see in person.

It was apparently located on the third floor, on a terrace overlooking the centre's plaza, but I'd explored the small outdoor space for ten minutes to no avail. The museum was virtually empty on this afternoon; not only were there few visitors, but I didn't see a security guard or a docent who might point me in the right direction, and I wasn't particularly enthused about going all the way back down to the ticket counter in order to ask the young woman who'd taken my money several minutes earlier. Instead, I roamed from room to room, one of which contained a temporary exhibition on incarceration whose title, *Undoing Time*, was fitting considering the reason for my visit. Finally, realizing the museum was closing soon, and that it was my last day in town before flying home, I went back through two sets of double doors, out onto the South Sculpture Court, and down a gently sloping walkway, where only now did I spot a small cylinder, about two inches in diameter, bolted halfway up the metal trellis that enclosed the terrace. I'd been looking for something much bigger, and, well, camera-like. I crouched to read the small silver plaque that I'd inexplicably missed on my previous search:

> JONATHON KEATS (B. 1971) AMERICAN
> Untitled *(Tempe Skyline)*, 2015–3015
> PHOTOGRAPH ON COPPER
> At 12 p.m. on March 6, 2015, Jonathon Keats initiated a thousand-year-long-exposure of the Tempe skyline from these coordinates on the Arizona State University campus. Built into the ASU Art Museum's sculpture garden trellis, his cylindrical copper camera is engineered to take a single continuous picture through a pinhole aperture. The minuscule hole, pierced through a noncorrosive sheet of pure gold, focuses an image of the city onto a pigmented copper surface that gradually fades in natural light to produce a unique positive print. Recording alterations to the landscape, the photograph captures change through deep time.
> *Collection of the ASU Art Museum* 3015.001.000

These last digits represented a promise spanning centuries—an accession number. Although it would not be ready until the hard-to-fathom year 3015, the tiny image produced by the Millennium Camera, as it is colloquially known, will one day be entered into the museum's permanent collection of 13,000 objects, though I imagine that number will be slightly higher in the thirty-first century. An opening reception is already scheduled; drinks and appetizers will no doubt be served. Jonathon Keats, regretfully, is unlikely to make it.

"I don't have any intentions or any designs on being here in a thousand years, despite the fact that Arizona State University has signed the contract ensuring that the camera will be returned to me or my heirs," he said.

Keats was on my laptop screen, talking to me from Fontecchio, a medieval village in the Abruzzo region of central Italy. This was a couple of months before my trip to Arizona. Wearing what I later learned was his trademark uniform—natty suit, bow tie, and wire-rimmed glasses framed by nearly shoulder-length brown hair—he looked like a funeral director who wrote experimental poetry on the side.

He'd come to the small town for an artist residency, working on a project, he said to me with a straight face, in which he sought to "instil tolerance and overcome xenophobia by intentionally all becoming alien hybrids by ingesting asteroidal material." To do so, he'd buried a chondrite in the hills outside the village; the meteoritic minerals would seep into the groundwater and subsequently flow from the community's fourteenth-century public fountain—now christened a "fountain of tolerance." I said I could only guess at the myriad rules and regulations he must have navigated before being allowed to introduce alien material into the water supply. "Well, nobody knows, really, what the rules and regulations are, it turns out," he replied. Anyway, it was safe, he assured me, and said that he had provided the municipality a "meticulous analysis, down to parts per billion, of the contents of this meteorite," which had made its way to Earth from the asteroid belt between Mars and Jupiter, and which Keats had brought to Italy in his suitcase. (I was glad to finally be talking about a meteor that wouldn't destroy the planet.) The idea behind the project, an otherworldly solution to an earthly problem, was that everyone who drank from the fountain, he explained, "intentionally becomes 'other' together, and in our shared otherness we discover our similarities and our commonalities." My initial bewilderment turned to delight. It was classic Keats.

There were few living artists who shared the otherness that Jonathon Keats possessed, though calling him an artist—specifically a conceptual artist—was to tell only a part of his story. The term most commonly applied, by himself and others, was "experimental philosopher," though even this didn't quite encompass the scale or thought or dynamism of his work, which is both playful and probing, pensive and powerful, and which I have come to admire greatly. "His visions are not the standard concepts of conceptual art, but arcane, tangled trains and chains of proliferating, ever-ramifying speculation," wrote the acclaimed sci-fi author Bruce Sterling. "He generates theories and hypotheses in organic profusion. Jonathon Keats is so far outside the box that mankind will never invent any box in which he can be at ease [. . .] He wades through other people's disciplines as if they were tide pools."

Keats was born in 1971 in New York City but grew up outside San Francisco, where he still spent part of each year. His father was a stockbroker, and Keats was intrigued, and influenced, by his father's career—the mystifying magic of seemingly making something out of nothing. His first art project was to emulate his father. The often-told origin story finds a six-year-old Keats selling rocks outside the family's suburban home. Even though there were stones scattered around his rock stand that potential purchasers could simply take for free, the few customers he attracted all paid. "Looking back—and probably giving myself far too much credit—it seems to me that at the age of six I'd figured out the basic form of what I still do today," he once told an interviewer. (His father later became an art dealer, specializing in turn-of-the-century posters and woodblock prints. "He abandoned stock brokerage because, at some point, he just came to believe that it was meaningless," Keats said to me. "I don't think that I had any impact, as far as that decision was concerned, but I'll take credit for it anyway.")

In interviews, Keats often conjured a childhood on the margins, never quite fitting in with his peers, "a quiet, stubborn, and self-directed child," as he described himself, with "a tendency to go off on my own, following my interests, and therefore seeming to classmates and my parents like somewhat of an alien." In preschool, he did not speak for an entire year.

When he allowed himself to think of the future, he sometimes saw himself as a nuclear physicist, at other times a rabbi, perhaps. Ultimately, he saw himself as a tinkerer, a builder, a creator. Throughout his childhood he was "enamoured" with inventors and mad scientists, he said. He once designed and attempted to patent a perpetual motion machine, to no avail.

Instead of pursuing engineering, or maybe a degree in the sciences, Keats studied philosophy at Amherst College, on the other side of the country, in Massachusetts. It was a decision he made, he said, out of "a sense that I didn't really want to grow up. I wanted to be able to ask the same sorts of questions that I'd always been asking, and I wanted to be able to experiment, to try to discover whatever I could about the world in which we live." For his senior thesis he wrote a novel, one he described as "about its own creation in real time, which is to say the rate at which you were reading it was the rate at which that creative act was taking place." Alas, it went unpublished, as did a poetry collection he submitted to the avant-garde press New Directions while still an undergraduate; it comprised, for example, poems titled "Purple Poem Covered by a Giorgio Armani Ad" and "Red Poem Painted Red Painted Red," the latter of which was simply a red shape. The rejection to this collection read, in part: "Obviously you have a good imagination and an inventive streak but it simply doesn't work to dub something a collection of poems that just isn't one by any standard going." (Keats had since achieved some success in the literary world, publishing a short-story collection and two novels, although one was in Russian, a language he did not speak, in addition to several works of non-fiction, including a study of the American architect and futurist Buckminster Fuller.) After university Keats worked as a journalist and critic and magazine editor, before, as he told me, "finally just completely abandoning all semblance of responsibility and ending up where I am now." Which was presently in a small Italian village imagining ways to turn some poor nonna into an extraterrestrial.

Inspired by conceptual artists like Sol LeWitt, what Keats wanted to do—and what he continued to do, decades later—was "explore ideas in public with others," he said. His first public performance / artwork / installation / happening—there were many ways to describe what he did, none of them quite right—began at 8 p.m. on October 28, 2000, at an art gallery in San Francisco. Stemming from an idea he'd conceived while still at Amherst, *Twenty Four Hour Cogito* saw Keats sit in a wooden chair, à la Rodin's *The Thinker*, for a full day, "selling" his thoughts. The prices were determined by a formula derived from the number of minutes Keats had spent thinking that particular thought (which when completed was marked by the artist stamping a card on an old industrial time clock) and what the purchaser earned per minute at work. The substance of each thought was never revealed. There were nude models, and a bowl of fruit. There were no rocks involved, but it was only a stone's throw away from his childhood entrepreneurship. Something from nothing.

Later work included ballets choreographed for honeybees, pornographic movies for rhododendrons, and a restaurant for plants at which they were fed "gourmet sunlight." Keats sold "extradimensional properties" via his own real estate agency (approximately a hundred buyers on opening night) and outfitted fifty Leyland cypress trees with easels and instruments (pencils, for instance, or charcoal) so that they could produce art. He registered his brain as a sculpture with the U.S. Copyright Office and subsequently "orchestrated an IPO offering futures contracts" on his individual neurons. He once tried to genetically engineer God.

"The work is an absurd mirror world of the world in which we live. I want to take this parallel world and I want to live in it, and I want people to live in it with me. That act of living can be used to look on our own world," he told *BOMB* magazine in 2009. "Through what I do, and because my work is absurd, it becomes a way to draw people into the biggest question of all—the question of 'what do I do with my life.'"

Although time had always been one of the central preoccupations of Keats's work, his later projects began operating on increasingly long timelines—projects begun in the present day that would not be completed for centuries, if not millennia, long after he and we had departed both his mirror world and our own. In 2009 he published "the longest story ever told" on the cover of *Opium Magazine*, a now-defunct literary journal. The catch? The story's nine words were hidden behind layers of black ink, and would only slowly reveal themselves when exposed to sunlight, one word per century, over the next thousand years. What he called an "antidote to instant gratification" was clever to be sure, though he said the folks at the printing press believed him to be "insane." This, he told NPR, was "not an unusual response" to his work.

It was a project for another magazine, the following year, that set Keats on a path that led me to where I was now: crouched down on the museum terrace in the blistering Arizona heat. In 2010, he shared the blueprints for what he called "The Century Camera" in "The Slow Issue" of *GOOD* magazine. Readers could rip the design out from the magazine's spine, and after a quick "cut, prick, fold, glue," they'd have their own pinhole camera, ready for use; left to its own devices, it would produce a single faded image over the course of one hundred years. The editors of the publication promised to publish select prints in 2110.

Keats had long been interested in photography. When he was in high school he spent countless hours in darkrooms "always making a mess of things," as he put it to me. After college, lacking the space for a darkroom in his apartment, he studied the history of photography, looking for a technique that didn't require special equipment or numerous materials. It was then that he learned about cyanotype, a comparatively easy, and agonizingly slow, nineteenth-century photo process, invented around the same time as salt printing and the daguerreotype, whose necessary components he could mix in his own bathtub. "It's incredibly simple," he told me. "It's two chemicals, and you develop and fix it all at once in water. But the thing is that it's extraordinarily insensitive to light." He made his own paper, which he loaded into a 35mm camera, and left it in place for hours (or days) in order to get an image. In this way, he said, "I was not actually photographing space or a landscape, so much as time."

This idea was in the back of his mind, years later, when he was in Berlin. It was a city he visited often, and one he couldn't help but notice was gentrifying rapidly, the changes becoming more and more pronounced with every passing year. How could he capture these shifts over a long stretch of time? In partnership with a local gallery, Keats built one hundred pinhole cameras, more durable than those inserted into *GOOD* magazine, which he rented out for ten euros each to a hundred Berliners (the deposit would be returned in 2114). He invited participants to hide these small devices around the city, without divulging their whereabouts—a system of surveillance cameras monitoring the city as it evolved, although, said Keats, "it wasn't your neighbour or your government watching over you—it was those not yet born."

The project became a global news story almost immediately. "That suggested to me that there was something there," Keats said. He began to contemplate ways to adapt the cameras into an even larger project—something "more substantial" and "working over the longer term." Something that exceeded relatively short- or medium-term questions of urban development or gentrification, like in Berlin, to probe a topic that was epochal in nature—like the future of the planet. "For that it seemed that we really needed to get to a thousand years or more," he told me. He set about designing a prototype, sourcing materials from his local hardware store ("where they take me as the local mad scientist," he said) and eventually creating the first Millennium Camera.

Around this time he was in touch with Ed Finn, founding director of ASU's Center for Science and the Imagination, a hub devoted to "moonshot ideas" and "thoughtful optimism" that brings together the worlds of art, science, and technology. From there, Keats's proposal was passed along to the ASU Art Museum, where it was championed by the newly arrived curator Garth Johnson, who had known Keats for many years.

"The ethos of the place at the time," said Johnson, was that "you say yes to an idea and then figure out how to overcome the logistical hurdles."

"Once they realized that there wasn't going to be ongoing maintenance [. . .] they were really into it," Finn told me.

The first-ever Millennium Camera was installed on March 6, 2015; a second camera followed in June at Keats's alma mater, Amherst College, where it's located in Stearns Steeple, keeping a watch over the Mount Holyoke mountain range. When we spoke, the first of four had just been installed at Lake Tahoe, in Nevada, while another was eventually placed on a hiking trail in Tucson. There would be more. Keats envisioned a paparazzi's worth of cameras, set up around the world, photographing our changing planet. "It's a slow process," he said of the project, then caught himself. "That's appropriate, I guess."

Ultimately, he saw them as "philosophical instruments" that were "means to reckon with the un-reckonable," as he told a newspaper in 2018. But these cameras, he added, were "also meant to allow us to see the world, the future, and the greater context of human experience outside of the limited experience and the limited framework of our times." They pushed us out of our comfort zone. They made us imagine the world without us, which was going to happen whether we liked it or not.

Life, after all, was "a race against time," Keats told me. It was one of the reasons he'd been compelled to make time the foundation for so much of his art. "Time is ubiquitous and central to everything that we do, and yet is really not well defined, and not at all understood," he said. "Even at that earliest stage where I started to think about and to work with time as a material, it really was about this phenomenon that we're constantly operating within, with many assumptions—very few of which really have been explored." Artists have done everything they can with watercolours and ceramic; seconds and minutes and hours and days and years and centuries were still relatively untapped materials—and materials we don't fully understand.

And now I stood up from the small silver plaque and looked through the trellis in the direction the camera pointed, at Tempe's jagged skyline. I took in what it currently saw, the palm trees and construction cranes against a cloudless sky, and imagined what it might eventually see. Various possibilities opened up, like the alternate dimensions in which Keats once sold real estate. It could all be over in a few decades, the city immolated by fire or war or zombie apocalypse. Maybe the museum would be torn down, or new curators, several decades from now, might decide this wasn't a project worth preserving. Maybe it would survive, and produce something incredible, a record of all the years and all the people and all the things to have crossed its aperture. The camera represented all the possible futures, all at the same time. It was taking a photograph of everything that might happen, all at once. It was impossible to know the end result. This was the point.

"The state of unknowing, in general, is really a large part of what motivates me," Keats told me. "And trying to bring others into that state—not as a matter of causing discomfort, but as a matter of recognizing the fact that we don't know, and that it is actually a strength for us to be in that state of not knowing."

"It isn't resignation," he added, "but it is what, to me, seems to be the most vital aspect of being alive."

I rode the metro from downtown Oslo to its northern terminus, then exited the station and made my way down a hill towards a parking lot, mostly car-free at this early morning hour. I was, as usual, early; the ceremony wasn't scheduled to begin for another ninety minutes. It was cool and the sky was blanketed by ominous grey clouds, and I was glad to have worn a jacket. While I waited I took shelter from the wind on the steps of a restaurant not yet open for the day, and cursed myself for forgetting to bring a book. But I wasn't alone: On the far side of the parking lot, a few hundred feet away, volunteers were erecting a small canopy, and after a while I walked over to say hello. One of them handed me a cup of thick, black coffee. More people soon arrived, some coming by car but mainly from the direction of the station, descending the hill in a slow moving avalanche towards those of us waiting at the bottom. Eventually, hundreds of people were milling around the canopy, a low and constant murmur, and then the crowd began to move, slowly and steadily and all in the same direction, and I followed the procession out of the parking lot, men and women and children and babies and dogs, all heading deep into the forest.

Some time later, after following a one-and-a-half-kilometre dirt path that wound through the trees like a stream, the parade reached a small clearing. The ground rose gently, creating a natural amphitheatre, and those who'd arrived first staked out space near the front while others made their way up the slope to find a better view, careful to give a wide berth to the spruce saplings, the size of small kids, that sprouted from the ground here and there, the red bows wrapped around their limbs signalling their importance. I found a spot halfway up, put my knapsack down onto the soft earth, stood amidst a waist-high tangle of branches and shrubs, and waited for the ritual to begin.

Near the front of the clearing rested a couple of simple wooden benches, on which sat a number of people I recognized. There was the Norwegian writer Karl Ove Knausgaard, and the English novelist David Mitchell, the Zimbabwean author Tsitsi Dangarembga and Iceland's Sjón. Sitting between the latter pair, in an ankle-length purple floral dress and a tan turtleneck sweater vest, was Katie Paterson, the artist responsible for this morning's forest gathering.

I was one of the first people in the world to write about the Future Library, as Paterson's project was named, in the late summer of 2014, on my first day at the newspaper where I still work. That morning, as I was waiting in line for coffee, I learned an odd bit of news: Margaret Atwood, who I'd known for years through my job covering the book industry, was going to donate a manuscript—it could be a story or a poem, a play or a novel; anything—that would be stored in a special custom-built room in a then still under construction public library in downtown Oslo. It would remain unread by anyone for a hundred years, at which point most everyone presently alive, reading my story in the newspaper the following day, would be dead. Every year a different author would be invited to contribute a manuscript to the project, which I described in my article as "part Noah's Ark and part time capsule."

"It goes right back to that child part of us that used to bury things in the ravine, or in the backyard, and think, 'Maybe someone will come along and dig this up,'" Atwood told me when we spoke a few hours later on that day in 2014. It was also "a very hopeful project," she said. "It assumes, number one, that there are going to be people. Number two, that there's going to be an Oslo. Number three, that there's going to be a library. Number four, that people will still be reading. And number five, that they'll still be able to understand what you are writing now."

It should come as no surprise that the Future Library began with a book: a blank page in the journal Paterson carried with her everywhere, jotting down ideas that were "often on the brink of complete impossibility." She told me that she vividly remembered sitting on a train, doodling tree rings in her notebook, and being struck by the connection between the rings of a tree and the chapters in a book—each one marking the progression of a story. Her initial idea was "to grow a book," imagining a single author's unpublished manuscript printed on paper harvested from trees that had been purposefully planted for the occasion. "I saw a library as a forest and a forest as a library," she said.

Around this time Paterson was invited to a conference in Oslo, whose attendees were meant to discuss questions of art and time. Recalling the tree rings, Paterson asked the conference organizer, Anne Beate Hovind, if she could find her a cabin, ideally in the woods, so that she could contemplate and refine her initial idea; Hovind happily obliged. Paterson, who was living in Berlin at the time, soon found herself hours from Oslo, in a cabin without electricity or running water. It was the perfect setting. "I just needed to be amongst the trees," she told me.

Trees grow slowly; Paterson's idea emerged more quickly: one hundred authors, one hundred manuscripts, eventually printed on paper provided by trees planted at the project's outset, one hundred years earlier, "a forest of unread books growing for a century." Books to be read "by an unborn generation." A project that "connects us living with those yet to live."

"I'll be gone when people read the words," Paterson told me. "All of us will be gone."

Together, Paterson and Hovind secured a two-acre parcel of land in Nordmarka, a forest outside Oslo; Paterson wanted a location close enough to the city to remain accessible, but far enough removed that it still felt secluded. "When you're in there, it's just you and the trees and the rocks," Paterson told me before my visit. The existing trees were harvested, their wood used in the construction of the room in the library where the manuscripts would eventually be held, and a thousand spruce saplings were planted in their stead in the summer of 2014, a few months before Atwood was revealed as the project's first participant.

"Particularly at the beginning of the project, when we were proposing this idea, we really thought: Who on earth is going to take this on?" Paterson said. "It's full of risks. It's full of unpredictable elements. But yet: Here we are."

And now here I was, too, standing in the clearing, with the trees and the earth and the birds and the rocks—and a few hundred people. This year's handover, the sixth, had attracted its largest crowd ever, no doubt owing to the fact it was the first ceremony to be held in three years, no thanks to COVID. The pandemic was also to blame for the absence of the first American author chosen for the project, Ocean Vuong, who'd been forced to cancel his trip a few days prior after testing positive for the virus.

The ceremony itself, "a simple, grounded ritual," as Hovind put it in her welcoming remarks, lasted about an hour. After reading a short statement from Vuong, expressing his disappointment at not being able to attend, Hovind, who served as chair of the Future Library Trust, introduced the city forester, who pleaded with the crowd to be careful with the young trees but reported that, in the three years since the last gathering, they'd firmly established roots in the soil. Knausgaard and Dangarembga handed over their manuscripts and, after a brief musical interlude, announced the titles of their respective work, which was the only thing contributors were allowed to reveal about what they'd written: *Blinken Boken (The Blind Book)* and *Narini and Her Donkey*. ("In my country," said Dangarembga, "'Narini' means infinity.") Afterwards, Paterson rose from the bench and made her way to the microphone.

"We're standing in a forest," she began. "It's just an ordinary forest, but it's also a forest filled with promise. Imagine: This forest has just resonated with the words of Karl Ove Knausgaard and Tsitsi

Dangarembga, and over the coming century, the words of many others." To Knausgaard and Dangarembga, she said: "Today, your words have activated Future Library. They're now being stored inside the rings of these tiny, unfolding trees—well, they're not so tiny now—and these trees are like a bridge from here to the future. The core of Future Library is time and longevity but also hope and rituals. It's more important than ever that we expand our time horizons to envisage a longer now. There's a saying: We have not inherited the earth from our parents, we have borrowed it from our children. If my young son lives to read the book, his world is likely to change beyond recognition. Future generations may be invisible to our eyes, but we're connected through our actions. Future Library authors have described the project as a secular act of faith. A fairy tale. A humble bowing down. An act of optimism and a vote of confidence in the future. The project has been described as a century-long prayer. We have to believe in the world one hundred years from now. The past lives within the present, and our ancestors breathe through our children. We are the ancestors of the future, and your words breathe into that future and our children will bring this book to harvest."

Next came a presentation by Oslo's vice-mayor, who announced that a one-hundred-year agreement had been signed, one that guaranteed the city—meaning unknown politicians and administrators, most of whom were not yet born—would see the project through to its end: "I hereby pledge myself to the forest, the city, and the library," said the official. "On behalf of the city of Oslo, I present to you our guarantee—our guarantee that the Future Library will be protected by us." At this, Paterson put a hand to her throat; Dangarembga put an arm around her shoulder. "Here is the contract, a pact for one hundred years." The vice-mayor handed the leather-bound contract to Hovind, who held it aloft, like a championship trophy. There were cheers and whistling from the crowd—a moment of unbridled enthusiasm in an otherwise solemn ceremony. "We did it," Hovind cried, before falling into Paterson's embrace.

The ceremony ended with a chant from three Buddhist monks, and then the clearing fell quiet for a moment of silence. There was nothing but birdsong and the wind gently moving through the trees. I closed my eyes, and my mind raced forward through time. A century was both a lifetime and a split second. The saplings would become giants, blocking the sun. The children fidgeting at their parents' feet and the babies strapped to their parents' chests would become old men and women, if they were even still alive. I wondered if one of them might grow up to become an author who would one day attend the ceremony to hand over their own manuscript. Or perhaps one of their children, or even their grandchildren. A century was both a novel and a poem. I thought of my youngest son, back at home, a month away from his second birthday, and wondered if he would be here to receive this gift. There were so many years, so many decades, left to go, and the silence filling the forest stretched forward through the years and doubled back to this moment and connected us all.

An overcast afternoon in late June. The Docklands, east London. As soon as I stepped into the lighthouse at Trinity Buoy Wharf the music washed over me—both dream-like and eerie, like a ghost reaching out from another realm. From another time. Numbers scrawled in chalk on a broken sandwich board informed me that this particular arrangement had been playing non-stop for 23 years and 175 days.

I made my way up the winding staircase and emerged into a large space, with a gabled wooden ceiling, where I found a young woman sitting at a small desk, attending a meeting on Zoom. She put herself on mute and said I was free to look around. The person I was here to interview hadn't yet arrived—early again!—so I wandered up another flight of stairs, to the lighthouse's lantern room. The glass enclosure provided a nearly 360-degree view of the city. It was empty except for two simple white chairs and the sound of *Longplayer*, the music that had greeted me upon arrival, a centuries-long soundtrack that would still be playing long after I was gone.

The clouds looked threatening and a breeze rippled the Thames's silver-blue waters. I remained there for a few minutes and took in the sights, looking west across the river towards the O2 arena and beyond, imagining the city sprawled before me if I'd stood here 160 years ago, just after the lighthouse was built in 1864. I'd been listening to *Longplayer* on my phone over the past several days (there's an app for that), but in this environment, its environment, the music didn't sound like anything I'd heard before. It felt removed from time—the kind of music, I thought, that could have been playing in the woods during the Future Library ceremony. I felt in a trance, under a spell, and had to rouse myself back to the present moment, to the present place, and head back downstairs.

A handful of visitors had arrived while I'd been lost in thought in the lantern room, and I made small talk with a couple of them until I heard footsteps on the staircase below; a moment later Jem Finer emerged, looking rather amused, if slightly startled, at the group standing before him.

"Surprise!" I said, rather lamely.

I'd been in touch with Finer for a number of years, trying to find a date when we'd both be in London at the same time. Although he's probably best known as a founding member and songwriter for the riotous Celtic punk band the Pogues (I avoided telling him that "Fairytale of New York," which he co-wrote was, cliché of clichés, my favourite Christmas song), I was here to talk to him about his career as an artist, which, in a similar way to Keats's and Paterson's, made material use of time. And, like Keats and Paterson, he'd begun a work of art he'd never live to see—well, hear in this case—completed.

The first notes of *Longplayer* rang out in the nascent seconds of the year 2000 and had played without interruption ever since. The project's roots dated back even further. "Time was something that I'd always had a quite intense relationship with," said Finer, who was dressed in all black, with matching frames, topped with a shock of grey hair that gave him the look of an impish mad scientist. "And so I'd always wanted to somehow create a space for engaging in long flows of time."

His "time obsession," as he called it, was sharpened in the lead-up to the new millennium. What should have been an occasion to think collectively, as a society, about where we'd been and where we were going was turning into an excuse to throw a giant party and "waste loads of money that could be used for better things," he said. He'd enjoyed a wildly successful career composing and playing music of traditional lengths, but one day, while playing around with loops of music of varying durations, it struck Finer that, if he calculated things just so, he could compose a score that only repeated itself at a set time, be it a minute or an hour or a day. "So I thought, 'Hang on, I could very easily just work out how to make all these different length loops, so that the whole piece only repeats every thousand years.'"

He was commissioned by an organization called Artangel to bring his idea to life. How do you compose it? What is it played on? Where is it based? Who looks after it? How do you make it adaptable to changes in energy or technology? "I had to answer all those things in the composition," he said. As far as the question of where it should live, its original home was meant to be what was then called the Millennium Dome—the O2 arena I'd spotted from the lantern room. Instead, it remained at Trinity Buoy Wharf, where he'd been working on the project, and which for decades was the epicentre of Britain's lighthouse industry. (Michael Faraday once served as scientific advisor of Trinity House and conducted experiments here.) The project was given space for a year. "After a year," said Finer, "they said to us, 'Look, if you want to leave it here longer, you're very welcome to.' And we're still here." (Artangel later handed stewardship of the project over to a charitable trust, whose members include Ella Finer, Jem's daughter, herself an artist, and Edie Culshaw, the woman who'd greeted me when I arrived earlier). Finer kept an office just outside the lighthouse, in a converted shipping container. It was a very loose agreement, lacking even a formal lease. "We're not worrying about getting thrown out or anything," Finer assured me. Besides, even if that happened, it wouldn't affect the project, which was "independent of any location," he said. "*Longplayer* really doesn't have a home, and it shouldn't have a home. I mean in its original conception, it wasn't going to have any physical location at all. It was going to be a radio wave, a global radio transmission . . . but we couldn't raise the money for a global radio broadcast."

In any case, continued Finer, "in order for *Longplayer* to realistically stand a chance of playing for as long as possible, it has to be independent of any one technology."

A key technology was the instrument, and there were many facets to consider. The sonic source material had to be physical, to mitigate technological disruption; had to hold its tune throughout the centuries; and had to be (relatively) easy to play. It had to sound timeless, too, and eschew any cultural ties to its original time period. "If it had been started with sounds that were contemporary to the 1990s, it would already sound dated," Finer said. He settled on a form of standing bell called a Tibetan singing bowl, an "elemental" instrument that is played by striking it with a mallet or rubbing it like a wine glass, producing a sound that is "both physical and ethereal" and results in what he described as a "jarring dissonance."

"When you play a lot of singing bowls together, you don't necessarily hear a number of different singing bowls," he said. "I mean, how many singing bowls can you hear in that right now?" I listened again for a moment, and then offered that I could hear maybe three or four separate instruments, but that was a wild guess. "They combine symphonically, like voices in a synthesizer, to create a new voice. I mean, sometimes you hear 'bing bong bong,' and you can pick them out, but other times you just get these cloud-like textures of sound."

So how did it work? Finer walked over to the now-vacant desk and picked up a chart, a graphical representation of *Longplayer*'s score, showing six concentric circles, one nestled inside the other, like a map of some as-yet-undiscovered solar system. At its heart, *Longplayer* was a single piece of music, played by Finer on thirty-nine different bowls, lasting twenty minutes and twenty seconds, which includes moments of silence. "The silence is as much a part of the score as the sounds," he said. (On the waveform he was holding, this was represented by thirty-nine different dots, each one representing an instrument, with the score showing if the bowl was meant to be struck or rubbed around its rim to create a drone, along with the corresponding volume.) From that original composition, the "sonic seed from which everything else is created," Finer re-pitched it into five transpositions of various lengths—a higher pitch speeds up the score; a lower pitch slows it down—that were layered on top of the original. At any given time, a two-minute chunk of each piece was playing simultaneously. At the end of the two minutes, new chunks of each transposition began to play. Repeat for a thousand years. And then the loop would begin again.

"That unpredictability of what you're going to hear at any given point is a nice counterpoint to the fact that *Longplayer*'s got this really deterministic score, where you can calculate at any point in *Longplayer*'s duration what the sections will be, but you don't know until you hear them playing together what it's going to sound like," he said.

That was true, but you had a sense of what it was going to sound like—it was not a thousand-year composition that really changed. It's not like someone listening to the piece in 2074 would hear a section that someone in 2411 would miss; you weren't waiting around for a bitchin' guitar solo. Which might be the point—the music I heard on this day was almost indistinguishable to the music someone standing in the lighthouse centuries from now, or listening to it on their iPhone 257x, would hear, too. It was a bridge through time. Still, it had opened up the project to bad jokes, with people telling Finer they've already heard a particular part before. "Unless you skip a few thousand years in the future," he said, feigning exhaustion, "you have not heard it before." The layering of the six different transpositions meant that while there's no repetition, there is familiarity. He compared it to the weather. "You look at that sky out there today. It's not like, 'Wow, I've never seen anything quite like that.' You've seen that sky many times, but you've never seen that exact sky. The clouds are in different places, slightly different shades of colour."

In the middle of the room, on curving shelves that were vaguely lunar in shape, were stacked six rows of these bowls, with 39 on each tier, 234 in all. Our conversation was punctuated by chimes and gongs produced by these bowls—well, not *these* bowls, but bowls like this.

These bowls were not actually the ones on which Finer played the original score, nor were they doing much of anything at the moment, beyond publicizing donors of the project, who paid to have their names engraved on them. "Right now what we're hearing is performed by that iPad," said Finer, motioning to a solitary device at the far end of the room that glowed in the dark like a lighthouse beacon. The bowls had been used to perform *Longplayer*, however, on a number of occasions, beginning with a live performance starting on September 12, 2009—lasting a thousand minutes instead of a thousand hours, mind you—at the Roundhouse in London, which featured twenty-six musicians performing in shifts. You don't have to come to London to listen to it, however; there have been listening posts set up in cities like Sydney and San Francisco, and then there's the aforementioned app, which allowed one to listen to the project anywhere, at any time (I'm writing this sentence listening to it at this very moment).

There was a good chance the future will lack iPhones, or lack Trinity Buoy Wharf, which had slowly been transformed by development in the decades since Finer began working here. A question still being answered was how to ensure Longplayer continued to play for its entire duration. "I'll leave that to other people to figure out," said Finer. The subject of obsolescence—both concerning *Longplayer* and the world we inhabit—was at the heart of the project, and increasingly ate away at Finer.

"*Longplayer*, in essence, is a piece of music," he said. "But actually, at the same time, the music isn't the point of it at all. The point of it is its duration and what that duration can do as a catalyst for having some positive impact on the way people think about the future."

"Most thinking in the world we live in is very short-term thinking, and very destructive," Finer added.

To that end, he wanted *Longplayer* to be "a catalyst for thinking about [the] long term." Because of this, he was less concerned with ensuring *Longplayer* finished its performance, and more concerned with "how to keep the world going in a way that there will still be people around to listen to it." Said Finer: "I have no illusion that *Longplayer* can change anything, but it's the only power that I remotely have."

I opened my eyes. The silence in the clearing was broken by a final round of applause, and then the crowd began to disperse, heading back down the path, back through the forest, back to the metro station and their cars and home. I wandered down to the benches, where Paterson was still shaken from the ceremony.

"Oh my God! I can't believe that I didn't put on my waterproof eyeliner." She wiped her eyes. "Seriously, I was like: 'I'll be fine.' I was so emotional this time. Oh my God!" The announcement of the hundred-year contract, this moment of finality, was when she'd come undone. "That was the moment that broke me," she said. "It's real. Clearly it's real—the trees are growing, the authors are writing. But at that moment it secured its future." Oslo, she told me, had never agreed to such a long-term contract before. "It's just such an amazing commitment: to believe in the future. I think that's why I, suddenly, got so emotional. That was the bit that just went to the heart." Hovind, standing nearby, and just as stricken as Paterson, agreed. "You never know, when you start this kind of project, how it's going to work. If somebody is going to just kill it. So, for me, that they have embraced it is incredible." Hovind said it had taken a decade to reach an agreement, an undertaking that had begun before the first author had even been chosen. "It's a complicated thing to make things like this happen," she said. "But you have to be willing to take risks."

Paterson was standing next to one of the saplings, which had grown to shoulder height—far from the tiny trees of almost a decade prior. "I still think of them, somehow, as little saplings," she said. "They seemed so vulnerable." (In fact, she did step on one of the tiny saplings during the first ceremony, held in May 2015. "We were told it doesn't matter, because the forest reseeds itself.") Soon, I pointed out, the trees would take over the clearing, complicating the gathering. "I'm a bit nervous about what's going to happen when the trees get a bit bigger," she said.

Although the contract was signed, Paterson promised that for as long she was alive her commitment to the project would not waver. "I get to enjoy this for my whole living life," she said. "The other artworks that I do, they all think about time and the future, but nothing brings us all together like this one."

The previous morning I'd taken a bus to a small gallery about an hour outside the city to see some of these other artworks. It was her first solo exhibition in Norway. Paterson, who was born and raised in Glasgow (at the time of the ceremony, she lived outside the city with her husband and son), first came to prominence in 2007, when she was twenty-five, with a project entitled *Vatnajokull (the sound of)*. Paterson, inspired by a year in Iceland, submerged a waterproof microphone under the surface of an Icelandic lagoon on which floats the titular glacier, at the time the largest in Europe. The microphone connected to a nearby amp and phone; a telephone number (advertised at London's Slade Gallery, though anyone could call) allowed people around the world to dial in and listen to the sound of "a river of ice slowly disintegrating." Though Future Library is a work of anticipation—of something yet to be known—Paterson's art was often preoccupied by what had been, especially if what had been was now lost. For instance, the exhibition I'd come to see this day, *Evergreen*, was named after her textile work portraying every plant known to have gone extinct. I wondered what Richard Thorns would think of this.

I wandered through the gallery, contemplating both brand-new works and art I'd read about or seen online, plus twenty-six ideas for "artworks that may or may not come into being." On the ground floor, past a monitor playing a half-hour documentary about the Future Library on loop, I came face to face with 2009's "All the Dead Stars," a personal favourite, a map "documenting the locations of just under 27,000 dead stars—all that have been recorded and observed by humankind." Upstairs I found "–there lay the Days between–": a ticker board keeping track of how many mornings the sun has risen on the earth. Walking through one of the rooms I heard an eerie rendition of *Moonlight Sonata*—Paterson had translated the score into Morse code, then beamed it to the moon; once it bounced back it was "re-translated," the results of which were now playing, a haunting, halting piano wafting through the gallery. Even the curtains, blowing softly in the breeze, were part of the exhibition—a brand-new work called "First Light" in which pale blue silk curtains had been dyed the colour of the first stars, billions of years ago. Paterson's work was easy to grasp on the surface, yet contained unimaginable depth. It was both strangely alien and unquestionably human. Or, as the author David Mitchell said, it "asks questions more than it answers them." Paterson's art was "love letters [. . .] to what we have on earth. What's given us our life. What's given us our breath. From the trees in the Future Library, to a star exploding, billions of years ago." Her work, he said, "makes time visible."

A few hours after the handover ceremony, after taking the metro back to Oslo, I arrived at the Deichman library, a celebration of the book in building form, on the city's harbourfront. On the top floor, with views of the water and the city's opera house, a large crowd had gathered—many of the same people, no doubt, who'd been in the forest earlier that day—for the opening of the Silent Room, the vault-like room that would house the manuscripts for the next ten decades.

From the outside, its entrance looked like the mouth of a small cave. I'd been imagining it since the Future Library was first announced, years earlier, and in person it was much more modest than I'd expected. I stood next to a barefoot Karl Ove Knausgaard (shoes had to be removed before entering the room), who clutched his manuscript, much thicker than the others, like a father holding a baby he didn't want to give up for adoption. ("When I first heard about the project, the first book with Margaret Atwood, I thought 'I hope they will ask me,'" he'd told me earlier.) I wondered, if I ripped it from his clutches and fled the library, how much I could sell it for on eBay, and was immediately consumed by shame. (Paterson later confirmed to me the Silent Room is outfitted with an alarm system to prevent this kind of deranged thinking.) The mayor of Oslo, beaming, cut the ribbon, and the deposits began. Atwood had been unable to make it, so Paterson went in first, holding the pages of Atwood's manuscript, *Scribbler Moon*. It felt like she was gone for a long time, as if a worm hole had opened up and snatched her from 2022 and spit her out ninety-three years later. But, eventually, she emerged, *sans* manuscript, and then David Mitchell went inside, and then Sjón, and then members of the Future Library Trust deposited the manuscripts of Elif Shafak and Han Kang, and then Knausgaard and Dangarembga, and then all the manuscripts were inside, not to emerge for nearly a hundred years.

"I can't imagine a hundred years ahead," Knausgaard told me. "I won't be here. My children won't be here. No one I know will be here. It will be someone else. And it's very scary, very frightening and terrifying. But also: How can you say no to that? You can't."

Indeed, in the years since the project was announced it had become, I believed, one of the most important literary events of its time—being asked to participate in the Future Library, to my mind, was one of the highest honours a writer can receive, up there with the Nobel Prize, and perhaps even more prestigious, because while there are many laureates whose books are long out of print, and whose names are forgotten, every author in the Future Library was guaranteed a readership in a century's time.

Yet writers have a finite number of books in them; one would think they'd like all of them to see the light of day while they are still around. To be an author, and give a book you have written to an unknown audience—to plant it like a seed without seeing it sprout—is no small thing. There was no way I'd bury this book in the ground, unread for a hundred years, although some readers may wish I had.

After all the manuscripts had been safely stashed away, Knausgaard and Dangarembga took part in an on-stage discussion. As the event wrapped up, I snuck away to see the room myself. I removed my shoes and went inside, and, to my surprise, found Mitchell there, sitting on a bench, eyes closed. He must have heard me come in, because he opened his eyes and smiled. "I'm just thinking of all the people who will come sit here and think—I'm saying hello to them," he said.

The inside of the Silent Room was meant to conjure the inside of a tree (its one hundred layers, each with a drawer to contain the manuscripts, were built using the wood from the trees felled in clearing) but, to me, it could have been the inside of a bee hive, or the pods in *The Fly*, or a cave. It felt the closest I'll ever come to standing in a time machine. "I think of a cryogenic chamber, in one of those interstellar spaceships, that will cross the distance between the stars," said Mitchell. It was quiet and dark, the only light coming from the drawers that housed the manuscripts. Mitchell admitted he already had forgotten which one contained his pages; nor could he really remember the particulars of his submission. "Memories get foggy," he said. "I just hope it's as good as I remember thinking it was when I handed it in, because there's some kick-ass writers who've come between me and now, and that will only get more true as the years go by."

Now that the on-stage discussion had ended, a line was forming outside the room. Since the space could only accommodate a few people, I decided it was time to leave. I experienced a momentary sadness, realizing that this would be the last time I was near these works. As if thinking the same thing, Mitchell asked me to take a photograph. I took his phone and snapped a few shots of him sitting there, amongst the books—a time capsule of a time capsule.

"I see it as a hopeful project," Mitchell had said earlier. "Every work of art, every poem composed, or music composed, or every movement in dance, is a gesture of hope, because it's a gesture done against destruction, it's a gesture done against our deep-felt knowledge that one day we will not be here. It's a gesture acknowledging that we are living in a hard, horrible world, that one day none of us will be here. So it's a hopeful gesture. And a hopeful gesture does not have to be an optimistic gesture. It's a gesture against all of these things. Despite everything, you do this gesture. And the Future Library is a big gesture."

As I exited the vault back into the library, with its views of the water and opera house and sun and sky, there was a small part of me surprised to discover it was still 2022. Part of me was disappointed, too.

I wanted to be there, at the end, on the day the manuscripts emerged, when they'd finally accomplish their purpose in life and be read. Knowing that was an impossibility left me with a sudden, profound understanding of my own mortality. I'd of course talked to Paterson about this feeling before, when I'd asked her about not living to see the project through to its completion. Had she changed her mind, over the years, and come to regret starting something she would not herself finish? No, she said, it didn't bother her at all.

"The first instinct has stayed exactly the same for me: I have no qualms about not living to see the end point, as it were, because I'm so lucky to be part of it while it's alive and living right now."

I took a few photographs of the Millennium Camera, a rather meta undertaking, and then headed for the museum's exit. As I traced my route back towards the entrance, I wondered if one of my descendants would have the opportunity to return to Tempe for the image's unveiling. Yes, we were talking fifty generations from now, but maybe I'd make a demand, to be passed up through the branches of my family tree, that whoever was alive in the thirty-first century had to make a pilgrimage, like I had once done, to Arizona. They could maybe read one of the Future Library books on the flight.

Then again, although Keats was guaranteed a month-long exhibition in the spring of 3015, time sometimes leads us down unforeseen paths. Keats couldn't predict what the future held in store, though he seemed nonplussed about all the possible outcomes. "Happily I won't be here in a thousand years if it doesn't work out, so no one can really blame me directly," he once told an interviewer.

Even if it does work, what is art if the artist is not there to see the finished product? Is there even a finished product? "I guess that I'm not frustrated by, or concerned about, the fact that I won't be there at the termination because I don't really see a terminal point," he told me. "And I see any possibility of a terminal point being a failing rather than a success for the project. Irresolution is essential to me, and uncertainty is essential as a quality that I would like to instil in society."

On my way to the parking lot, I took a detour and headed to the corner of East Tenth Street and South Mill Avenue. I stood at the intersection, in what I thought was the field of vision of the camera, a couple hundred feet away. I stood there as traffic and students went by, and I wondered how many people walked by every day, oblivious to the camera. It was a rather unremarkable corner to photograph—there was a yoga studio, a sub shop, an e-cigarette store called Haus of Vapors. What would people in the future think of this world? What would they make of the decision to memorialize this particular place? Would they think this had been a sacred location?

I stood there, as the sun beat down, and hoped a small part of me might be captured, an echo of a negative, some essence of my soul, a piece of me to live to see the day.

Later that evening I sent several photos of the camera to Keats, who'd wanted to see how it was holding up, and I told him about standing there, "hoping a trace of me might end up in the photo." He replied fourteen minutes later: "We'll know in approximately 994 years whether you made the cut."

If you are reading this a thousand years from now, can you do me a favour? Go to Tempe, and if the gallery is not in ruins, find the image. Tell me if I'm standing there, a spectre, a shadow, a flicker in the seconds and minutes and hours and days and weeks and months and years and decades and centuries gone by, that have faded away like a photograph left out in the sun.

TEN

THE LAST KNIGHT

When Les Knight envisioned the future he knew he would not live to see, you were not in it. Neither was I, for that matter, nor his friends and family, or his ever-patient girlfriend, Heather. The young people in his life, like the students he encountered each day working as a substitute teacher in various Portland, Oregon, schools, were absent as well. Have you sometimes imagined your descendants—great-great-grandchildren, perhaps, or the future nieces and nephews of your future nieces and nephews—and the world they will inherit? Forget about them; they were missing, too. None of us were there; no one was there.

Instead, Les explained, he pictured something like the area around the Chernobyl Nuclear Power Plant, outside the ghost city of Pripyat, in northern Ukraine. The region has been almost entirely free of humans since the last days of April in 1986, when reactor No. 4 melted down, and residents were forced to evacuate from the town and the surrounding area—a number that grew to more than 350,000 people in subsequent years. In their place, wildlife returned, with the 1,100-square-mile Chernobyl Exclusion Zone becoming the third-largest nature reserve in Europe and a haven for animals—lynx, deer, bison, moose, foxes, wild boar, beavers, brown bears, wolves. It was a place overflowing with life, except that of our own species. This was the future Les Knight sought to bring into existence.

"That's what I envision," he said. "A world that flourishes the way it did before we flourished."

To be fair, Les warned me ahead of time that not everyone took kindly to the goal he had spent his life pursuing. Some people grew legitimately upset when he explained his mission. Accusations of racism, eugenics, eco-fascism, death-worship, and even genocide were regularly tossed his way, and he was called a "neo-Malthusian" on occasion, "like it's an evil thing to even mention that there are too many of us!" he said, slightly perplexed at the outrage. I figured he was being a touch hyperbolic. Surely, the folks attending the forty-first annual Public Interest Environmental Law Conference, on the campus of the University of Oregon, in the liberal college town of Eugene, would at the very least understand his point, if not appreciate his message. After all, he'd been coming to this event for years to spread the gospel of obsolescence.

"What is this? The euthanasia team?"

Les and I had been at the William W. Knight Law Center for a only few minutes when an older gentleman, sporting long grey hair and a fuzzy red sweater, walked by our table. (Most of the men attending the conference, I soon learned, either resembled Jerry Garcia or looked like they'd spent a summer following the Dead on tour.) The man slowed down and smirked, eying the large banner that hung behind us on the wall, before asking the question. As he continued down the hall, and before either of us had a chance to respond, he called out over his shoulder: "I'm almost there."

I turned to Les: "You weren't kidding."

The table at which we were sitting was covered by a dark green cloth adorned with the logo of Les Knight's organization, VHEMT. There were copies of their newsletter, *These Exit Times* ("Putting the mental in environmental since 1991"), as well as neat piles of rectangular stickers in various sizes and colours: "Vasectomy prevents Abortion"; "Thank you for not breeding"; "Thank you for thinking before breeding." A fishbowl containing white pins with the VHEMT logo, free for the taking, sat alongside a stack of dense two-page information sheets entitled "Why Breed?" that listed the reasons people say they want children, as well as suggested alternatives to having kids: "Rent children from talent agency on special occasions"; "Order custom-made, life-like doll." There was a framed award for "meritorious service to planet Earth and the human family," which Les encouraged male conference-goers to earn by getting a vasectomy. Affixed to a display straight out of a high school science fair were various charts and graphs listing, among other things, the amount of CO_2 emissions saved by not having a baby, and the date on which every country on earth would hit its "overshoot day" in 2023—meaning the date consumption surpassed resources. Sample fact boxes: "Each new US resident not created preserves 14 football fields of potential wildlife habitat for about 80 years"; "Planet Earth provides about 4.0 acres of biologically productive area per person"; "Average human's eco-footprint: 6.9 acres"; "Not creating one more of us saves 58.6 tons of CO_2-e per year." The aforementioned banner, which had caught the old hippy's attention, showed a smiling dinosaur and a grinning dodo bird; sandwiched between the two creatures was the silhouette of a human being, one arm around the dinosaur's shoulder, the other waving enthusiastically. "Visualize Voluntary Human Extinction," it read. Underneath the cartoon was the slogan of VHEMT, the Voluntary Human Extinction Movement: "May we live long and die out."

All right, I guess I could see why people sometimes reacted poorly to what Les Knight was proposing: the extinction of our species.

"So you want to eliminate the human race?" the broadcaster Tucker Carlson once asked Les. "How unhappy was your childhood?"

When Les was a child, his family moved from Portland to the small town of Madras, on the "dry" side of Oregon, east of the Cascades. It is the high desert, sagebrush and scrubland, and Les, born a couple of years after the end of the Second World War, and the middle of five children, spent much of his time outside, on his own. "I could just walk out of town in a very short time," he told me, "and be out where there weren't any people." He liked this, being alone. The empty world.

After high school he was drafted into a "terrorist organization," as he called the United States military, though he never served in Vietnam. After the war ended Les enrolled in college. He didn't have any plans, really, childhood dreams he was determined to pursue now that he was a free man. Life was a blank slate, the years and decades in front of him endless with possibility. He could do anything. He could be anything.

Around this time, he picked up a copy of *The Population Bomb* by the biologist Paul R. Ehrlich. The book, published in 1968, painted a dire portrait of the future, unless human procreation was reined in. "The birth rate must be brought into balance with the death rate or mankind will breed itself into oblivion," wrote Ehrlich. "We can no longer afford merely to treat the symptoms of the cancer of population growth; the cancer itself must be cut out."

The book crystallized what Les had long felt. He'd seen the devastation the timber industry was wreaking in the area around Madras where he'd hiked as a kid, the "great big clear-cuts" scarring the landscape—and this was only a small part of what we were doing to the planet. Things were growing dire. "Ever since we got fire about 500,000 years ago we've been adversely impacting the natural world," he said. "It's just that there weren't enough of us to make a difference. And the more and more of us there are, the bigger difference we make." If people were doing this, he thought, then perhaps there should be fewer people.

Les joined a national organization called Zero Population Growth, which Ehrlich had co-founded not long after the publication of his book, and which advocated for that very thing. It was understood that overpopulation had to be a central concern of the environmental movement, which was entering its golden age—the first Earth Day had been held in 1970, the same year the Environmental Protection Agency and Natural Resources Defense Council were formed in the United States, and an anti–nuclear weapons testing group called the Don't Make a Wave Committee was established in Vancouver; the following year they commandeered an old fishing boat and sailed towards an island off the coast of Alaska with the goal of stopping a U.S. nuclear weapons test. The boat was called the *Greenpeace*. In the United States, the National Environmental Policy Act, the Clean Water Act, the Clean Air Act, and the Toxic Substances Control Act were all signed into law or expanded during this decade, too. There was a realization that the planet was heading down the wrong path, and things needed to change. "It was an optimistic time, because it seemed like there was so much awareness that we [needed] to turn things around," Les recalled.

But things didn't turn around as quickly as Les hoped. If the seventies were a decade of promise, what followed was a decade marked by catastrophe—the *Amoco Cadiz* oil spill in 1978; Three Mile Island in 1979; the Union Carbide disaster in Bhopal in 1984; the discovery of a hole in the ozone above Antarctica in 1985, the same year as the bombing of Greenpeace's *Rainbow Warrior*; Chernobyl in 1986; the *Exxon Valdez* oil spill in 1989. There was also a growing understanding that the climate was changing because of our actions—in 1988, NASA scientist James Hansen warned a congressional hearing about the connection between greenhouse gas emissions and global warming.

Meanwhile, the Earth's population increased by almost a billion people between 1980 and 1990. Les remained a member of Zero Population Growth, but their goal was to stay under replacement-level fertility rate of 2.1 children per woman. (The group's rallying cry was "Stop at Two.") Les felt that this didn't go far enough. Instead of stopping at two, he thought we needed to stop at once.

Let's pause, here, for a moment. Les Knight was not dumb. He knew the idea of not only accepting human extinction but *embracing* human extinction—pursuing it, in fact—was completely irrational and went against our species' proclivity for self-preservation. There's an entire genre of blockbuster movie devoted to thwarting this very thing! I literally went to California for the launch of the world's first planetary defence mission! Not only do we not want our lives to end, and our species to be wiped out, we want to prolong it as long as possible. See: the Fountain of Youth, exercise, eating vegetables. Indeed, many of the men and women I'd met at the Interstellar Research Group's symposium in Tucson wanted to travel to the stars, in part, to ensure humanity's survival if the Earth one day became inhospitable. Humans might be the only species on the planet that understands death is a certainty—or the species that thinks about it the most, at any rate.

During a quiet moment when there was no one visiting the table, Les brought up the concept of terror management theory, which stemmed from the work of anthropologist Ernest Becker, author of the 1973 classic *The Denial of Death*. "He maintains that we are all motivated by a fear of death, and everything we do is related to that fear of death, subconsciously and sometimes consciously," Les explained. "So when we want to have something carry on our family name and genes and so on, it's to overcome a fear of death. But also to create art that will last, music, write stories that will be around after we're gone." Human extinction "negates" all of that, he continued, summing up the obvious. "If we're going extinct, nothing goes beyond our lives."

Far from a despairing proposition, to Les this was a selling point. When everything in our DNA is telling us to rage against dying, Les wanted us to walk into the light.

Later that afternoon, a young man approached the VHEMT table and picked up a copy of "Why Breed?"

"Oh, that's very provocative," he said, studying it closely, as if trying to figure out what, exactly, the organization was proposing. "So . . . overpopulation?"

"We're trying to figure out why people continue to procreate, despite all the evidence," Les said, and then explained the page the man was holding: "These are the reasons that they give for wanting to procreate. This is what they really mean when they say that. And these are alternatives so they don't have to."

"Okay. So what's your proposal?" asked the man. "Stay below the replacement rate?"

No, Les said, they were calling for "fewer and fewer of us" until, eventually, the planet was left without people.

The young man seemed confused. "So you're advocating that humans slowly go extinct? Wow."

"As long as there's one breeding couple, we'd be right back where we are in no time," said Les.

"Okay, so that's not extinction though. That's like drawing down the population."

"No, we want to go to the point of extinction," said Les.

It seemed the man still couldn't quite wrap his head around what Les meant. "So to the point of extinction but not all the way to extinction?"

"No, all the way to extinction." Les cleared his throat. "It was only 70,000 years ago there were about 10,000 of us. Now, look, there are 8 billion. We just can't stop."

"So why not find a solution to draw down to a sustainable level?" asked the man. "Why go all the way to extinction?"

"Considering the future," said Les, "the intentional creation of one more of us by anyone, anywhere, can't be justified."

"Wow," said the young man. "I'm just—it's pretty heavy stuff."

"I'm glad you think so," said Les, smiling.

"I mean, do you think that there's, like, an innate immorality to humans?"

"No, no," said Les. "We're not immoral at all. No, we're just incompatible with the biosphere. We don't really mean to be."

"But we evolved in the biosphere . . ."

"We did, yes."

". . . and we are part of nature in that sense, right?"

"Yes we are," said Les. "And every now and then a super-predator will come along throughout evolution, and they are so good at being predators that they eat all their prey and, of course, then they go extinct. We are super-predators who will eat just about anything." Les continued: "By the time we go extinct as super-predators, there's not going to be much left. Unless we all stop procreating. It's the alternative to involuntary human extinction."

"Involuntary," repeated the young man.

"That's messy," said Les.

"Yeah, a lot of pain and suffering," agreed the young man. "So it's better if we just kind of ease our way out?"

"Yeah," said Les. "A peaceful phase-out."

"So tell me about your organization."

"It's called the Voluntary Human Extinction Movement," said Les. "VHEMT. So they say, 'Are you serious?' 'No, we're vehement!'"

The Human Extinction Movement was formed in the 1980s while Les was living in Portland. He later added the word "voluntary" to the group's name, a signal he didn't actually want anyone to kill themselves, nor would he urge followers to commit murder, nor was he trying to impose mass sterility onto the world. "The number-one misunderstanding," he told me, is "that we want to increase death." He sighed. "No, we don't want to increase death. We just want to decrease births."

In the early years, news of the organization's existence mostly spread through word-of-mouth. Les published the first issue of *These Exit Times* in 1991; the website went live in 1996, introducing VHEMT to a global audience. (The website, which had been translated into more than thirty languages, from Belarussian to Turkish to Latin, looked like it hadn't been updated since 1996; it was a text-heavy collection of hyperlinks that mainly attempted to sway skeptics—Q: What good is a healthy biosphere if there are no humans around to enjoy it? A: The same good it was before we furless beach apes came along.) Offline, Les spread VHEMT's message at street fairs and conferences around Oregon, like the one we were presently attending, and by serving himself up to the media, who usually treated him as a harmless oddity. He'd recently appeared on Dr. Phil's daytime talk show, he told me proudly. "I've become well-known as the main spokesperson, but anybody can do it," Les said. "There's no hierarchy."

There was also no real way of knowing how many "followers" the movement had gained—or lost—over the years. Les just knew that the world's population kept growing, so he had to keep going, even if others didn't come along with him.

"It hasn't really caught on like we were hoping," I overheard Les tell one visitor to the table. "People continue to procreate like crazy."

Les wasn't on his own in Eugene, though. As usual, he was joined by his long-time partner, Heather, who produced all the charts and graphics for the organization, and also happened to be his next-door neighbour back in Portland. ("We used to live together," said Heather. "This is so much better.") They met through her brother, who Les had taught decades ago. "He introduced me to it and I liked the concept," she said, explaining it thusly: "It's really simple: We just stop making more of us. Live happy, healthy, long lives. Take care of the people that are already here. And just kind of phase out."

Also at the table was a member from Ashland, Oregon, a few hours to the south, whose name was Melissa, but who went by Rin, short for Setsurin, which she told me meant "snow forest." (It was a moniker she'd picked up during a decade living in a Buddhist community in California.) She'd become involved with VHEMT while employed in the urology department at the University of California, San Francisco's Center for Reproductive Health, where she worked for a doctor who was "adamant that having children was a human right," she told me. Feeling conflicted about the fact she was helping add to the population, she reached out to Les, offering to pass out the group's literature on the street. "I just wanted to set up a little table every now and then," she said. "Most of the time I would just sit there and smile." Appearing harmless was key. The name of the group, she acknowledged, made people think of a "suicide cult," making it important to soft-pedal their message. "We're VHEMT, but not obnoxiously vehement," she said.

This was true. I witnessed a distinct lack of aggression from the VHEMT trio during the weekend I spent in Eugene. They were enthusiastic about the idea of extinction, but they weren't pushy. Instead, they'd wait for people to come to them. (The dinosaur-and-dodo, drawn by the artist Nina Paley, served as a magnet; it was joined on Sunday by a giant poster of the same cartoon with the human's head cut out, encouraging Instagram-friendly photo-ops—extinction via influencer). If someone asked a question, they'd answer it thoroughly. If someone took issue with their mission, they'd listen respectfully. Yes, there were plenty of suicide jokes, but they didn't seem to take it personally.

Only once were voices anywhere close to raised, which happened when a woman from one of the other environmental organizations approached the table. Les remembered her: at a previous conference she'd allegedly stood in front of VHEMT's table holding her baby, trying to drive people away. She took issue with VHEMT's general objective—she wanted her kids to have kids, she said—and, specifically, a sticker they were handing out that read: "Thank you for not breeding."

"I'm a parent," she told Les. "I love my kids. I find that kind of offensive. If you said, 'Thank ME for not breeding,' and everyone who didn't breed had one, then that would be great. It wouldn't be, like, judgy and racist."

"Wouldn't it be virtue signalling to say, 'Thank me for not breeding'?" asked Les.

The woman departed in a huff, and Les turned to me: "When she said, 'I want my children to have more children,' I didn't say, 'Now, that's racist.' Because it is. It's the ultimate expression of racism, to want to have your own DNA" passed down.

"We need more white people," deadpanned Rin.

For the most part, however, VHEMT was received warmly, though with curiosity. There were just as many people who, upon learning about the organization's goals, took the opportunity to unburden themselves—to say that they, too, were unsure if our species deserved a place on this planet. Some folks, I noticed, treated Les almost like a therapist, someone with whom they could discuss their fears about the future, and what humans were doing to the Earth.

Perhaps people were comfortable sharing their innermost feelings with this total stranger because, as Rin put it to me, Les "presents as so non-judgmental."

"I think the reason that Les presents as being non-judgmental is because, as a person, he really is non-judgmental," added Heather.

"I'm very judgmental!" said Rin, who had just finished explaining her views on humanity to me: "It's not like I don't like people individually. I tend to like people individually. But as a species? My question is always, 'How can we be so awesome individually and so fucked up as a species?' I don't get how that works. But I sort of think it has something to do with groupthink."

"That's why there's so many of us," said Heather. "Because we're following the crowd."

Les called this "natalist conditioning," a term I heard him use several times over the weekend. To him, the decision to have kids wasn't up to us, necessarily. It was partly hard-wired in our genes, which made sense in the past, when if you didn't have as many people as the tribe next door you'd be taken over, or in the days when childhood mortality rates were higher. But it partly came from external pressure. "I don't know how much choice people have a lot of times," he told me. We were encouraged to see "every birth as a good thing," he said. "It's a leftover from a previous time, and people just can't shake it."

He was also battling against what he called "human supremacy," the idea that we should place our own existence above everything else with whom we share the planet. It was a form of narcissism, he said. Les felt that we couldn't have both—our survival would result in the continued destruction of the natural world, so if we didn't go extinct, the other species that call our planet home would, a sort of existential Catch-22. "Do we want to say goodbye to the mountain gorilla?" he asked me. That was the choice we were facing: us or them. Why should it be us?

"We think we're the greatest species on the planet, and that nature is there for us to exploit," he said. "And so it is a push against that mentality, and also knowing that the fewer of us there are, the more wildlife there can be." He described himself as "a deep ecologist," a person who thought of humans as just one of millions of species, all equal, and someone who believed that "nature has its own value, beyond what is good for us." It wasn't about creating a better planet for humans, it was about creating a better planet for everything. If that meant we had to go, so be it.

But think of what would be lost, you cry. One of the arguments Les heard most often was that he focused only on the bad things humans do and not the good. Why didn't he consider the monuments we've built, the music we've composed, the books we've written (ahem)? Humans have produced a lot of wonderful things, things that have unquestionably made the world a better, happier, more interesting place. Was that not worth something?

As Les saw it, it's not that those things lacked value—it's that they could not be compared to the wonders of the natural world. It wasn't a trade he wished to make.

"The greatest works of Shakespeare don't hold a candle to a tiger," he said.

Maybe I'm greedy, but I wanted both, and I felt it wasn't too late for a world in which both *Hamlet* and Debbie Martyr's beloved Sumatran tiger had a place. Walking around the conference that weekend, it was obvious I wasn't the only one who felt this way. Dozens of organizations had set up tables, from every corner of the environmental movement. There was a buzz, an energy, the momentum of people who all had a single goal in mind—saving the planet—even if they took different routes to get there. (VHEMT's road being one that took humans off a cliff.) It felt, to me, like what the 1970s must have felt like, but instead of Greenpeace and Earth Day we had the Sunrise Movement and Extinction Rebellion (ER).

Les scoffed when I asked him about parallels between the seventies and now. He was "disappointed" in the current state of the movement, which was "squandering" the moment. He thought that the issue of population growth was "absent" from the contemporary environmental discussion. Here we were, knowing that climate change was real, seeing it first-hand, coming at us like a train, and we were still pretending that . . . not that things could remain status quo, but that we could be a part of the solution. He'd even broken with Zero Population Growth, explaining that over the decades "they've scaled back their goals, because the idea of a population not growing was just a little too radical. So now they are Population Connection." He took umbrage with those who felt everything would work out in the end, that humans were too smart to destroy the planet, that carbon capture or nuclear fusion or some yet-undiscovered green technology would solve all our problems. These people, he said, were "hope-ium peddlers."

"That's what really gets me about the current environmental movement," agreed Rin. "They're trying to protect the environment so that we can continue business as usual."

Les took particular issue with Extinction Rebellion, the upstart civil disobedience network formed in 2018, which happened to have a table set up right next to VHEMT. The group, which had broken into the mainstream through a series of sit-ins and other actions in the United Kingdom that soon spread around the world, garnered the kinds of headlines that VHEMT could only dream of. I thought Les's wariness was partly born out of professional envy, but he maintained his suspicion was more about the fact that what ER stood for and what VHEMT stood for were at opposite ends of the environmental activism spectrum. "They're rebelling against extinction," he said. "We're rebelling *for* extinction."

As if he overheard our discussion, one of the volunteers from Extinction Rebellion wandered over to our table for a chat.

"A large bowl of free condoms would be more on message," the man told Les after learning about VHEMT's goal.

"We're not giving away the condoms this time because the Center for Biological Diversity is giving them away," said Les. "They're called 'Endangered Species Condoms.' On the package it says: 'Wrap with care, think of the polar bear,' and things like that." He pulled one out to show the man. "They've given a million away. So, that's potentially a million people prevented."

"So, is your basic tenet that if we just would ease off on the breeding we could maybe do less harm on the planet?" asked the Extinction Rebellion volunteer.

"If we were not here at all we'd do a whole lot less harm," Les said. "It's aspirational. I know I'll never see the day."

Les wasn't like the climate alarmists or doom-mongers I knew, the sort of person who made you seek out the nearest bridge, so bleak was the future they predicted. Yes, he made it clear he saw humans as a blight, a disease, an illness, sickening the Earth. That we inflict more pain than joy; that we do more harm than good. But he framed extinction as something almost noble, a goal that could unite the world in common cause, a gift we could leave the planet. He made extinction, if I can put it this way, seem like a hopeful thing.

Les got a vasectomy in 1973, when he was twenty-five years old. "I would have done it earlier but I didn't have the money," he said. He was still broke when he underwent the procedure, but fortunately had managed to find a medical school willing to perform "a discounted vasectomy in exchange for being a student doctor's first try at the procedure, which was successful."

His parents, upon learning about his plans, did not try to change his mind. "I assured them it wasn't because of an unhappy childhood that I wasn't producing offspring," he said. It's not as if they ended up without grandchildren; while Les and his two younger sisters are childless, his older brother and sister "procreated at replacement level."

I knew the answer before I asked the question, but I had to ask it anyway: Fifty years later, did he regret his decision not to have kids? Had he made a mistake? Did he ever doubt his mission?

"No, I never have," he said. "As a teacher, I get to be around kids all the time." (He made it clear that he did not talk to them about VHEMT.)

In any case, he did not want to make people who made a different decision feel bad, nor did he view them as the enemy. He understood the decision to have children was deeply personal, and often complex, and people had myriad reasons for doing so, even if Les felt those reasons could be proven foolish or faulty (see: "Why Breed?"). He was not trying to single out parents or prospective parents. Besides, not all VHEMT members were as steadfast in their pledge not to procreate as Les—some had fallen victim to the dreaded "baby rabies," as he called it. In fact, he told me, he was in possession of a VHEMT-themed licence plate given to him by a former member who helped set up the website back in the 1990s. This was someone who had seemingly been as serious in his commitment as Les, although "not serious enough to get a vasectomy." The man now had three kids. "We're still friends," said Les.

At that moment, a man interrupted our conversation. He told Les that he'd long been an admirer of VHEMT and the work they were doing. He had been a card-carrying member, in fact. Once, he said, he even harangued a woman on the streets of Boulder, Colorado, who had "in my view too many children for the Earth to support." He pulled his card out of his wallet and waved it at her while speechifying on the evils of overpopulation. "I'm sure I was far less sensitive than the quotes that I've read you make in the newspaper. I'm sure I was like a bull in the china shop. And she took quite offence."

This wasn't the sort of thing Les would do, but he was amused by the tale. Then the man made a confession.

"I have reproduced since then," he said. "You're now going to have to shoot me dead."

"But only one?" asked Les.

"Only one," the man replied. "Anyway, I appreciate the spirit of the whole thing. It's nice to see that you're still around and kicking."

"It's how many we don't have in the future," said Les. Then, with the same gravitas as a mall Santa asking a toddler if he'd been good this year, he asked: "And you're not having anymore?"

"Probably not," answered the man, though not with the greatest conviction. "I'm not demanding grandkids," he added. "I won't lie to you that I won't be sad, but that's my daughter's choice to make when the time comes."

It would be her choice—hopefully. Reproductive freedom was a core tenet of VHEMT's mission, a tenet that was under attack in the United States, thanks to the Supreme Court's overturning of *Roe v. Wade* the previous spring. The decision would inevitably result in more babies, which meant it was against everything VHEMT stood for. Les knew the numbers by heart: There were nearly 121 million unintended pregnancies around the world each year—half of the total number of pregnancies. Of these unintended pregnancies, over 60 percent ended in abortion. If access to birth control and abortion was curtailed, then VHEMT's goals would be even further away than they were right now.

"Reproductive freedom is really what our main cause is," Les said. "We're promoting voluntary human extinction, but the only way we're going to get there is everybody having reproductive freedom. So that's really the short-term goal. Which, again, we'll probably never see the day everybody on the planet has the wherewithal—the freedom and the wherewithal—to not procreate if they don't want to."

I noticed that, among the younger people who came by the table and vowed that they were not having kids, the majority were women. One woman unburdened herself to Rin and Heather, explaining how she was despondent over the fact that so many of her girlfriends were having children. She thought they'd been on the same page, that they understood, as she did, that the world was not a place into which we should bring in new life. It was a betrayal.

"Especially those who have been, like, climate activists and champions the whole time I've known them," she said. "And then all of a sudden, 'Oh, we're having a baby!' That's just inconsistent with everything else you say you stand for, but okay?"

There was a visibly pregnant woman with frizzy black hair whose face scrunched up into a sour expression every time she passed

VHEMT's table, which was often, since it was right next to the bathroom. Maybe I was projecting. Maybe she wasn't actually looking at us, had no idea who Les was or what VHEMT stood for. Still, I felt bad. I'm just a journalist, I wanted to tell her. I'm not with them! I love babies! Anytime a child walked by the table, or was pushed past in a stroller—and there were a surprising number of children, considering this was an environmental law conference—I felt a pang of guilt. I was thinking of my two kids at home, whom I missed, and whom I'd made a point of not mentioning the entire weekend.

I also felt guilty because, that very day, on the cover of the section I oversee at the newspaper where I work, we'd published an essay by my colleague John Ibbitson and the pollster Darrell Bricker, authors of *Empty Planet*, a book about the dangers of population decline. The book had come out in 2019, but now in 2023 they'd revisited their thesis: Not only were we unprepared for a lower global population, but the drop would come sooner and occur more sharply than we realized. This was not something to celebrate, they argued, but a crisis that would shape the decades to come. "We believe that population decline is a very bad thing, one that could define our future," they wrote.

I didn't mention the essay to Les, but we spent a fair amount of time discussing the idea that, as more and more countries fall under the replacement level of 2.1 children per woman, the world's population would naturally decrease—making the necessity of VHMET extinct, in a sense. I pointed out that China had lost population last year for the first time since the 1960s meaning we were clearly trending in the right direction. Look at Japan, look at South Korea, look at Italy! Wasn't this enough? Wasn't a gradual, organic population drop the best outcome for the world—and for us?

"The media, of course, is owned by people who want more people," Les had told me over breakfast when I raised the issue. "They're just always saying, 'Growth rate falling! Birth rate falling! Total fertility falling!'" Much of the fear-mongering about population decline was that it would harm the economy, he said. The more people there were, the higher the rent and the lower the wages. Fewer people meant fewer workers. "The ones who are higher up on the economic pyramid want lots more people down below," Les said. "It's always been that way under capitalism, and maybe even under the feudal system we replaced. The royalty always wanted lots of serfs out there working the fields."

And even if we were heading in the right direction, the urgency was such that the world couldn't wait for a gradual decline, a slow die-off. Besides, Les said, replacement-level fertility was "a virtually meaningless statistic, and yet it has been conflated with zero population growth." It's not as if parents drop dead the moment their second child is born to even things out. ("We aren't salmon; we don't spawn and die," Les once told a reporter.) Not to mention the fact that humans are living longer than ever, meaning multiple generations of a family are alive at the same time. If every woman had two children, and they had two children, and so on, the population would continue to rise. The United States, for instance, has had a rate at or below 2.1 since 1972, and yet the population has grown by 120 million people thanks to immigration, much of it from countries where the rate was much higher. Yes, the population will eventually hit a peak, but that's not expected to come for decades—during which time humans will continue to destroy the planet. The United Nations projects Earth's population to top out at 10.4 billion by 2080 and stay at that size until the turn of the century. This, Les felt, was unsustainable.

It was these people—the baby in the frizzy-haired woman's belly, the napping toddlers being pushed past VHEMT's table, my boys at home, those who would likely count among the planet's 10.4 billion people—that Les was most concerned about. That's one thing I didn't expect—I figured someone who'd dedicated his life to ending human life would put people second to the planet. But Les Knight loved people. He loved his friends and family and students. He knew he wouldn't be around to experience the worst of it—the fires and the droughts and whatever else nature throws our way. "It used to be that I was concerned about what a new person would do to the environment," he said. "Now I'm concerned about what the environment's going to do to that new person. It's not going to be pleasant." I heard it several times over the weekend—people coming up to the table and telling Les they weren't having kids not because they didn't want them, but for reasons that were either economic (impossible to afford kids; AI taking jobs) or climate-related (the planet will be inhospitable very soon). Why bring more humans into such a place? It was like inviting friends over to your house for dinner when the roof is on fire.

"People are not suffering in non-existence," said Les. "Do we have a right to bring them into existence, where they certainly will have some suffering, especially now with the way things are going? No, we don't have that right."

I had to give it to him: Les had a point. Even before I met him, I worried about the future; after spending the weekend with him, I *really* worried about the future, and the planet my sons will inherit. Was the human race a blight? It was hard to argue otherwise. The damage we were doing to the Earth was obvious. For several days, not that long after returning from Oregon, the smell of smoke greeted me whenever I left my home in Toronto, the result of forest fires raging hundreds, if not thousands, of miles away. At times that summer it felt like half the country was on fire. This was not normal.

So was Les right? Was the only (and ultimate) solution to all our troubles to pack our bags and skip town? As much as I liked Les, and agreed with many of the arguments he made, I didn't think so. And most people obviously didn't think so, either, otherwise VHEMT would have made itself (and us) extinct, like the pink-headed duck, years ago. So Les Knight, the most soft-spoken, big-hearted misanthrope I'd ever met, would keep trying.

"It's the Voluntary Human Extinction Movement!" said an older man to Les as he approached the table. "You're still coming back?!"

"Still hasn't caught on like I was hoping," said Les, laughing. "People are breeding like there's no day after tomorrow."

The man said he'd been coming to the conference for twenty years, and was surprised that Les was still here every single time. The perseverance was impressive; it was rare to be this committed to a cause. He told Les he'd been "a believer" in the overpopulation movement back in the 1970s.

"It hasn't worked out so well," said the man. "Maybe, sometime, society will wake up."

"That's what I'm hoping for," said Les. "Before it's too late."

EPILOGUE

CATHEDRALS

One summer morning, while driving towards the northern coast of Kent, a friend and I decided to stop in the town of Canterbury to visit its famed cathedral. It was an impromptu pilgrimage for me, an English major who'd spent countless late nights deciphering Chaucer, and completely unrelated to this book, or so I thought at the time.

My friend parked in a small lot near the Great Stour, and we meandered like the stream down the city's cobbled streets towards the centre of town. I bought tickets, we marched through Christ Church Gate, and there stood the cathedral, like it had been waiting for us to arrive. A moment later I was craning my neck to look up at the spine-like arches high above the nave, which took almost thirty years to build. It felt as if the room, blanketed by a heavy silence, was alive with all the years that had passed in the life of the cathedral. I sensed a slip in the fabric of time, one that reminded me of the Future Library ceremony in the woods outside Oslo.

We spent a couple of hours wandering through the cathedral, from the sheltered walkways of the Great Cloister to its medieval Chapter House, where the monks once gathered. I paused at the Martyrdom Chapel where, in 1170, knights of Henry II murdered a praying Archbishop Thomas Becket. Afterwards, we descended into the crypts—the western wing contained some of the earliest-surviving sections of the cathedral, dating back to the Norman conquest of England in the eleventh century, while the light-filled eastern section was the site of Becket's tomb until fire ravaged the cathedral in 1174. I saw St. Augustine's Chair and made my way through the quire to the Trinity Chapel, which housed Becket's shrine after the fire until it was destroyed on orders of Henry VIII in 1538. I hadn't set foot inside a church since visiting Bonnie Morton in Regina the previous year, although Canterbury's size and scope made Knox-Met feel like a one-bedroom condo by comparison. Everywhere I looked there were soaring pillars or elaborate stained-glass catching the sun. It was a monument to life, both physical and eternal.

And as I took everything in, the library's worth of history and stories this place contained, I thought back to my first interview with SETI researcher Seth Shostak. How he'd said his life's goal had been like building a cathedral. That he'd never live to see the work he'd started—to which he'd dedicated his days—complete. That he would not be around for the moment it was finished.

Heather Newton visited the cathedral long before she worked there. She was in her early twenties, in town visiting her mother, who'd recently moved to Kent, and decided to play tourist and check out Canterbury—I'd probably retraced her steps during my visit. When she went back home to Liverpool, the cathedral followed her. "I was absolutely captivated by it," she told me. "I couldn't stop thinking about it. It just stayed with me, the place stayed with me. But I never imagined that I would work there. That wasn't a thing that even crossed my mind."

Not long afterwards, her husband, a teacher who was looking for a career change, enrolled in a masonry course. He thought she'd like it—they'd met in art school—and so she eventually enrolled, too. In 1987, on a subsequent visit to Canterbury, she cold-called the cathedral, curious as to how a young stonemason might end up in its employ. They not only invited her to come by for an interview, but subsequently offered her a job. She'd worked at the cathedral ever since, in myriad roles, including head of conservation and head stonemason. Her job, and that of her colleagues, was to ensure the cathedral survived another thousand years.

The cathedral was very much a Ship of Theseus; while it had stood here since being founded by Augustine in the late sixth century, there had been several different buildings, across several different eras, on the site. Which meant, Newton said, that working here allowed her to "reach back centuries." She might, for instance, uncover fabric from the eleventh century, or stone crafted by another mason, hundreds of years earlier. When that occurred, "there's an immediate contact with that person," she said. "It's as though those years just don't exist, really."

For someone in conservation, the opportunity to work on one of the most historic buildings in the country—one "that so many hands have worked together to create," as Newton said—was a privilege, one whose importance she found hard to describe. "It's not a spiritual thing," she told me. "I think it would be for some people. Maybe it is. I don't know. It just sort of captures you, and you want to be part of it, part of that thing, that history, that craft. As a conservator, I'm looking at everything—it isn't just the stone, it's the timber, the textiles, the metals, all of those skills have come together [. . .] to make this amazing thing. I find it quite hard to put it into words, because it's just a feeling."

"It's an incredibly big sum of very, very complex parts," said her colleague Joel Hopkinson, the head of estates and fabric. "And yet, somehow, it manifests itself as being more than the sum of its parts. So, in several lifetimes, you couldn't know enough about the place." The cathedral, he continued, was "so layered, and so complicated, and so big. It's nicely impossible to fully penetrate, which is one of the charms of it."

It was also impossible to call it one thing. The cathedral meant different things to different people. It was a place of worship. It was a site of pilgrimage. It was an art object. It was a tourist attraction. It was an architectural wonder. It was a cultural centre. It was the soul of the town.

It was also a construction site. Strolling through the cathedral grounds, my eyes were drawn to scaffolding surrounding various towers and clinging to various walls, evidence of conservation efforts that were currently underway.

"It is a never-ending job," Newton told me. "We just can't do enough. There's so much that needs to be done. I walk around all the time, and everywhere I look there's something that could be done."

"We will never finish here," agreed Hopkinson. "We know we can't do it all, and there is a certain acceptance in that. What we can do is we can try and lay things in place for the future."

It was funny. For so long, as I researched and wrote this book, a place like this had only existed as an analogy. I'd lost track of the number of times that someone I interviewed said the work they were doing was like building a cathedral. But these people were only partially right. Yes, Canterbury Cathedral had been built, in various stops and starts, additions and subtractions, over the centuries. But, as Newton pointed out, "the building has never been finished, and it probably never will be." It was an ongoing project, one that would continue to link the future with the past. What Newton and her colleagues were doing was akin to piloting a world ship, as the folks in the interstellar community call them, one that had set out from Earth fifteen hundred years ago and had not yet reached its destination. They were the ones who had to ensure the engines kept firing, that the ship kept moving.

One day the job would fall to someone else; this she'd always known. You don't start a job like this thinking your work will ever be done. When I first spoke to Newton she was sixty-five; retirement was drawing near. She'd been at the cathedral for more than half her life. And not only had her career been about preserving the cathedral, it had been about preparing the next generation of masons and carpenters and conservators, those who would ensure pilgrims like me could walk through the cloisters in another century or ten.

"We are caretakers," she told me. "And it's really important that we understand that, and that we don't try and overstep our role, and get too much above ourselves, because we are just, in terms of the history of the building, the blink of an eye. One working lifetime in the life of a cathedral is very little. And what we do will, in the end, probably be replaced, superseded, by someone else's efforts. But that's okay. That's okay because we've done what we can do during our lifetimes to keep the place going, and hand the baton on to those coming behind us."

I conducted my first interview for what became the book you are reading at the start of 2019. I thought I'd be finished in two years. Life had other plans. A week or so after selling my book proposal that fall, my wife and I learned we were having a second child. The following March, my mother went into the hospital, her cancer having grown tired of remission; she died the following month, a few days after my thirty-ninth birthday. And then there was the pandemic.

As I was planning my first research trip, the world closed down. A week stretched into a month stretched into a year. Life stood still, yet continued at the same time. My wife and I helped our eldest son with school at the kitchen table and attempted to keep up with our day jobs, while bouncing a baby on our knees. For almost two years I conducted interviews from my basement and bedroom, over the phone and on Zoom, with folks around the world who suddenly had a lot of time to think about how they were spending their lives. (There's an entire other book out there I might have written. For instance, I was going to include a chapter about preppers—doomsayers preparing for an end of the world that I thought would never come. I spent hours talking to folks around North America, discussing the ins-and-outs of MREs and go-bags and which generators offered the best bang for your buck. When the pandemic struck, I found myself jealous of their foresight. It was a good reminder that we live to see some things come to pass.)

Then, just as life was returning to some semblance of normalcy, my publisher, who unfortunately happened to be my editor, left the industry. Next came the widespread availability of generative chatbots which felt like an existential threat to the very idea of writing, and which made me wonder if AI would soon be coming for my newspaper job—not to mention whether it would soon be writing the books I'd waited my whole life to write (not this one though!). Overlaid atop everything were the usual, terrible, machinations of world geopolitics, from war in Europe to devastation in the Middle East, to the creeping rise of authoritarianism in the country next to mine. How could I be expected to write a book at a time like this?

This is a book about perseverance, in part, but there were times when it was hard to find the will to work on it, let alone finish it. I admit, there were times I considered giving up. And even if I were to finish it, I thought, what would be the point? I despaired. Why was I doing this? I would lie in bed at night and think to myself: You, too, will never live to see the day.

And yet, almost every day, I would go down to the basement, or sit at my kitchen table, or go to a coffee shop, or the library, to work, even if it was just to conduct a single interview, or write a few notes, or read a chapter of a book. I did not know if this—finishing the book—would ever happen. (Frankly, as I write these words, I still don't know if it will happen.) But I began to better understand what the people I was writing about experienced, and why they continued to pursue their goals despite the fact there was no promise of success. Because I continued, too.

This book is also a record of lives I chose not to live. I wish I'd had the courage to spend my life looking for aliens, or creatures unknown to science, or hunt for lost treasure. This isn't quite regret, an admission that I'd give up my wife and kids and career to trade places with the likes of Jeremy Holden. But there was a point in my life, before I had any of those things, and was learning to exist in the world, when all these different paths were set out in front of me, and I chose one that seemed safe—a straight path, with plenty of sun and shade, and no dangerous animals hiding in the trees. I took the path I believed would lead to some kind of ending.

But there is courage in choosing an uncertain path. There is bravery in tossing the map away. There is something noble about pursuing a dream that might never be realized. If you are reading this, and still near the start of your life, imagine me reaching out from the page, grabbing you by the lapels, and shouting: *Don't think about the finish line. Just run.*

Because you don't run the race for a medal. You run the race to feel your heart strain against your chest; to feel the ground beneath your feet; to feel the wind in your hair. And if you never cross the finish line you hope there's someone waiting, in the distance, to take the baton from your hand.

Looking for gold in the scorching Arizona desert; listening to the stars for a faraway voice; paddling across a quiet volcano lake in search of a creature the world doesn't believe exists; writing a book—these are all acts of faith. They are all undertaken without promise, without guarantee. This is a good way to live.

One evening, after the conference in Eugene, we went to dinner—Les, Heather, Rin, and I—at a dive bar a few blocks away from campus. The food was bad and the conversation was good. I told them about some of the people I'd met during my travels, the things they'd been tirelessly pursuing, and how they'd changed my own thinking. The pregnant woman with the frizzy hair from the conference was sitting one table over, and I shrank into my chair when she passed us on the way out of the restaurant. We raised our glasses and toasted in celebration—to new friends, to the end of the human race.

The evening reminded me how much I liked people, and I thought to myself how, in the end, I didn't want Les to succeed. Yes, I understood his mission—he had goodness in his heart. But when I close my eyes and think about tomorrow, and next year, and next century, people are there. They deserve a chance to be born, to live, to try and fail like we have done. In the meantime, we need to hold the baton tightly, and not drop it for those following in our steps. We should live like the impossible is possible; that even if poverty doesn't end in our lifetime, it will happen one day. That when an asteroid comes hurtling out of the sky, we will be prepared.

When I imagine the future, I see a day when the Animal Protection Party has elected a member to Parliament. A day when the final note of a centuries-long soundtrack plays in a London lighthouse, and people are there to hear it. A day when the rainforest of Sumatra has been preserved and protected, not only for the animals that call it home, but just in case it hides an undiscovered ape. A day when an odd-looking duck emerges from the past. A day when those who are missing are never truly lost, and all the treasures being hunted have been found. A day when we finally make contact, and travel across the stars.

I know I won't live to see the day when these things happen. But maybe you have.

ACKNOWLEDGEMENTS

Tasleen Adatia. Tonia Addison. Jared Bland. Jenny Bradshaw. Kristin Cochrane. Shona Cook. Lloyd Davis. Natasha Hassan. Lisan Jutras. Ben Kaplan. James and Luke Medley. Steven Medley. Adam Park. Richard Poplak. Linda Pruessen. Nasim and Zainool Ramji. Maryam Siddiqi. Stephanie Sinclair. Martha Webb. Noelle Zitzer.

The Toronto Public Library and the Oshawa Public Library.

The Black Pony, Rooster Coffee, Red Rocket Coffee, and Tandem Coffee (2014–2023).

The Canada Council for the Arts.

This book is in memory of Maria Medley (1951–2020). I wish you were here to see this.

NOTES

Live to See the Day is the result of six years' work, including more than a dozen research trips and interviews with upwards of 260 people. I conducted my first interview on January 30, 2019; the last on June 13, 2024. Some of the individuals quoted in the book were interviewed several times, and in cases where travel took place, I often spent hours, if not days, with them. I thank them all for taking the time to talk with me, and for sometimes inviting a total stranger into their lives. I hope they see themselves, and their quests, reflected in these pages.

With only a handful of minor exceptions, words appearing in quotation marks signify a direct quotation, not from memory but from a recording I reviewed for accuracy. I have occasionally "cleaned" up these quotations, mostly to remove an "um" or similar verbal tics, or to delete a repeated word. All quotations come from interviews or events at which I was present (a lecture, for instance, or a press conference) unless otherwise noted. The titles mentioned under "Further Reading" are not necessarily books I read cover to cover; I might simply have flipped through them, or read a few different sections.

Some of these chapters take place years ago. Blame the pandemic, which delayed travel for the better part of two years; the fact I had a baby at home during much of the research stage; and my own procrastination. For example, the search for Lisa Maas occurred in the summer of 2021. However, these are meant to be snapshots of particular moments in time, and so I have not updated the lives of the people featured in this book beyond the conclusion of each chapter.

Is it an impossible task to write a book without any errors? Perhaps. Any mistakes are my own. Despite my best efforts, I imagine there are a few. If you spot something I've gotten wrong, or just want to say that you read the book, I can be reached at livetoseethedaybook@gmail.com.

PROLOGUE: THE FINISH LINE

My thanks to Liz White, who allowed me to accompany her on the campaign trail back in 2008, and graciously encouraged—or at least allowed—me to use her story as a jumping-off point for this book. I would also like to thank some of the folks in the animal rights and justice movement I spoke to: Stephen Best; Stephanie Brown; David Fraser; Leah Garces; Camille Labchuk; Rob Laidlaw; Barry MacKay; Jo-Anne McArthur; Erica Meier; Lesley Moffat; Sharon Núñez; Ron Orenstein; Dulce Ramirez; Marina von Keyserlingk; and Julie Woodyer. As well, thank you to the many "fringe" or perennial candidates I spoke with over the years, including Tiffany Bond; Ted Brown; Allen Buckley; Natalie Fleming; Evangeline Gordon; Howie Hawkins; Alyson Kennedy; Joe Schriner; Jerome Segal; and John Turmel. A special thanks to Kimball Cariou, who I spent a lovely afternoon with in Vancouver, but who doesn't appear in these pages; you're here in spirit.

1 "the riding in which she was campaigning": Liz White was running in Toronto–Danforth.

1 "would go to the incumbent Liberal—maybe the New Democratic candidate if things broke just the right way": The incumbent was Julie Dabrusin of the Liberal Party of Canada. While one could argue there were several progressive candidates, in this case I'm referring to Clare Hacksel of the New Democratic Party.

2 "The election was only a few days away": It was held on September 20, 2021.

3 "a Toronto-based national newspaper": *The National Post*.

3 "I pitched one of my editors": This was Maryam Siddiqi, who I worked with at both *The National Post* and then *The Globe and Mail*. I wanted to ensure I wasn't stealing credit for her idea, so emailed her to make sure. "I think you are remembering accurately!" she wrote back.

3 "I was also living in her riding": Toronto Centre.

4 "this was only her third time running for office": She ran in 2006 and 2008.

4 "volunteered for the campaign of a politician": The politician was Michael Copeland.

5 "Later that decade, she joined the protests against the Spadina Expressway": The protests proved successful (Jamie Bradburn, "Toronto Feature: Spadina Expressway," *The Canadian Encyclopedia*, last updated July 2, 2015, https://www.thecanadianencyclopedia.ca/en/article/toronto-feature-spadina-expressway).

5 "who'd recently moved to Toronto": Jacobs arrived in Toronto in 1968.

5 "at a tumultuous time in the organization's history": This is how Liz White characterized it, but if you want to learn more, Carolyn Morris explored the history of the Toronto Humane Society in a feature published by *Toronto Life*: https://torontolife.com/city/dogs-best-friend-the-story-behind-the-toronto-humane-societys-mutiny-raid-and-shut-down/.

6 "Liz ran in her first election six weeks later": The election took place on January 23, 2006.

6 "She received 72 votes, 30,802 fewer than the winner": Bill Graham of the Liberal Party, who received 30,874 votes. (Andrew Heard, "2006 Canadian Election Results," Simon Fraser University, n.d., https://www.sfu.ca/~aheard/elections/2006-ONT.html).

6 "My article was published a few days before the election": Mark Medley, "'Who Are You Calling Fringe?' Canadians will not wake up to an Animal Alliance Environment Voters government on Wednesday, and Liz White will most assuredly not be our prime minister. That's not stopping the Toronto-Centre candidate from giving this election everything she's got," *National Post*, October 11, 2008. The article appeared in the paper on October 11, 2008, while the election took place on October 14.

7 "215, 233, 159": She received 215 votes in the 2011 federal election; 233 votes in the 2015 federal election; and 159 in the 2019 federal election.

8 "hundreds of interviews": 263, to be exact.

8 "more than 100,000 kilometres of travel": I did the math; you'll have to trust me.

ONE: THE LISTENERS

Thanks to everyone in the SETI community I interviewed while researching this chapter, including Bill Diamond; Nathalie Cabrol; Wael Farah; Michael Garrett; John Gertz; Leonid Gurvits; Paul Horowitz; Manasvi Lingam; Avi Loeb; Alexander Pollak; Sara Seager; Sofia Sheikh; Seth Shostak; Andrew Siemion; Jill Tarter; Dan Werthimer; and Jason Wright. And a special thank you to Rebecca McDonald and Lindarae Polaha of the SETI Institute for helping facilitate my visit to Mountain View.

10 "one Monday in late January": January 22, 2024.

11 "shared the building with a robotics company": Matic Robots: https://maticrobots.com/

11 "the second-most famous in all of science": A statement like this is, of course, debatable, but the SETI Institute itself uses this descriptor ("Drake Equation," SETI Institute, https://www.seti.org/drake-equation-index).

12 "his father, who headed up the electronics branch of the Office of Naval Research": His father was Arnold Shostak, who died in 2007. You can find an interview with him in the National Radio Astronomy Observatory archives ("Interview with Arnold Shostak," National Radio Astronomy Observatory, June 20, 1976, https://www.nrao.edu/archives/items/show/15188).

12 "during the brief moments it wasn't in use . . . whom he'd first met in Holland": The details about Shostak's work prior to 1991, when he joined the SETI Institute, are taken from his book *Confessions of an Alien Hunter: A Scientist's Search for Extraterrestrial Intelligence* (National Geographic Books, 2009), pp. 163–72.

13 "Shostak joined the SETI Institute": He joined in 1991.

13 "His namesake paradox": For more, see "The Fermi Paradox," SETI Institute, n.d., https://www.seti.org/fermi-paradox-0.

14 "[T]he presence of interstellar signals is entirely consistent" and "a discriminating search for signals deserves a considerable effort": If you can't access the *Nature* article, you can find these passages in this *TIME* magazine article from November 1959: https://time.com/archive/6802699/science-anybody-out-there/.

14 "Morrison, who died in 2005, later recalled": David. W. Swift, *SETI Pioneers: Scientists Talk About Their Search for Extraterrestrial Intelligence* (University of Arizona Press, 1990), p. 24.

14 "Project Ozma": For more, see Seth Shostak, "Project Ozma," SETI Institute, last updated July 2021, https://www.seti.org/project-ozma.

14 "Beginning on April 8, 1960, . . . found nothing": Frank Drake and Dava Sobel, *Is Anyone Out There? The Scientific Search for Extraterrestrial Intelligence* (Delacorte Press, 1991), pp. 19-38.

14 "organized its first-ever SETI meeting . . . John C. Lilly, whose research involved": For more on the meeting and Lilly's work, see John Wenz, "The Order of the Dolphin," *Astronomy*, October 10, 2018, https://www.astronomy.com/science/the-order-of-the-dolphin-setis-secret-origin-story/; John Wenz, "The Secret Origins of the Search for Extraterrestrial Intelligence," *Discover*, last updated December 20, 2019, https://www.discovermagazine.com/the-sciences/the-secret-origins-of-the-search-for-extraterrestrial-intelligence; and Andrew C. Revkin, "John C. Lilly Dies at 86," *New York Times*, October 7, 2001, https://www.nytimes.com/2001/10/07/us/john-c-lilly-dies-at-86-led-study-of-communication-with-dolphins.html.

15 "mostly as 'a way of organising the meeting'": Swift, *SETI Pioneers*, 73.

15 "anywhere between 1,000 and 100,000,000 . . . later in life he settled on 10,000": Drake and Sobel, *Is Anyone Out There? The Scientific Search for Extraterrestrial Intelligence*, 62; and "Drake Equation," SETI Institute.

15 "Edward Purcell delivered a lecture": This was November 16, 1960. To read the entire lecture, see "Radioastronomy and Communication

Through Space: Brookhaven Lecture Series Number 1," (1960), https://doi.org/10.2172/4017898.

16 "a colleague handed Tarter a copy of *Project Cyclops*": Sarah Scoles, *Making Contact: Jill Tarter and the Search for Extraterrestrial Intelligence* (Pegasus Books, 2017), 66. You can find the *Project Cyclops* report at NTRS—NASA Technical Reports Server, https://ntrs.nasa.gov/citations/19730010095.

16 "Spearheaded by Barney Oliver, another Green Bank Dolphin . . . $6 billion to $10 billion": Swift, *SETI Pioneers*, 94; and *Project Cyclops*, 170–71.

18 "NASA began funding SETI in 1975": The information in this paragraph is taken from the following sources: Madeleine O'Keefe, "The Real Science Behind SETI's Hunt for Intelligent Aliens," *Ars Technica*, July 25, 2020, https://arstechnica.com/science/2020/07/the-real-science-behind-setis-hunt-for-intelligent-aliens/; Swift, *SETI Pioneers*, 359; Drake and Sobel, *Is Anyone Out There?* 197; Walter Sullivan, "Wide New Search for Life in Space Is Set to Begin," *New York Times*, December 21, 1982, https://www.nytimes.com/1982/12/21/science/wide-new-search-for-life-in-space-is-set-to-begin.html; and Scoles, *Making Contact*, 152–53.

18 "eliminated all SETI funding . . . '[M]illions have been spent'": "This Number Has Been Disconnected," *New York Times*, November 14, 1993, https://www.nytimes.com/1993/11/14/magazine/sunday-november-14-1993-this-number-has-been-disconnected.html; and Marina Koren, "Congress Is Quietly Nudging NASA to Search for Aliens," *The Atlantic*, May 9, 2018, https://www.theatlantic.com/science/archive/2018/05/seti-technosignatures-nasa-jill-tarter/558512/.

19 "employed 138 staff . . . annual operating budget of $28 million": From my interview with Bill Diamond, though you can read the independent auditor's report here: https://www.calameo.com/read/004812363a7e369ff0856.

19 "in 2015 announced a $100 million initiative called Breakthrough Listen": The information on Breakthrough Listen in this paragraph is

taken from the following sources: Ian Sample, "Stephen Hawking Launches $100m Search for Alien Life Beyond Solar System," *The Guardian*, July 21, 2015, https://www.theguardian.com/science/2015/jul/20/breakthrough-listen-massive-radio-wave-project-scan-far-regions-for-alien-life; "Longtime SETI Champion Franklin Antonio Dies," SETI Institute, May 16, 2022; and "$200m Gift Propels Scientific Research in the Search for Life Beyond Earth," SETI Institute, November 8, 2023, https://www.seti.org/press-release/200m-gift-propels-scientific-research-search-life-beyond-earth.

20 "only the *R* variable had been known": The information in this paragraph is taken from the following sources: "Drake Equation," SETI Institute; "Kepler/K2," NASA, https://science.nasa.gov/mission/kepler/; and Phil Plait, "The Sky Is Full of Stars—and Exoplanets, Too," *Scientific American*, October 6, 2023, https://www.scientificamerican.com/article/the-sky-is-full-of-stars-and-exoplanets-too/.

21 "his childhood in Depression-era Chicago": Drake and Sobel, *Is Anyone Out There?*, 2.

21 "once been featured in an article": Tom Dalzell, "How Quirky Is Berkeley? Elephants!" *Berkeleyside*, March 11, 2019, https://www.berkeleyside.org/2019/03/11/how-quirky-is-berkeley-elephants.

22 "Werthimer was a member of a group that called itself the Homebrew Computer Club": Space Sciences Laboratory at the University of California, Berkeley, https://www.ssl.berkeley.edu/full-directory/name/dan-werthimer/.

22 "he'd co-founded and served as principal investigator for SETI@Home": The information in this paragraph about the SETI@Home project is taken from the following sources: "Dan Werthimer and Paul Horowitz to Share 2021 Drake Award," SETI Institute, https://www.seti.org/press-release/dan-werthimer-and-paul-horowitz-share-2021-drake-award.

22 "harvested by the Arecibo Observatory": SETI@home, https://setiathome.berkeley.edu/anniversary_info.php.

22 "came to an end": Daniel Oberhaus, "SETI@home Is Over. But the Search for Alien Life Continues," *Wired*, March 3, 2020, https://www

.wired.com/story/setihome-is-over-but-the-search-for-alien-life-continues/.

22 "collapsed in 2020": Eric Hand, "Arecibo Telescope Collapses, Ending 57-year Run," *Science*, December 1, 2020, https://www.science.org/content/article/arecibo-telescope-collapses-ending-57-year-run.

23 "an array whose 350 telescopes": Robert Sanders, "Were Galaxies Much Different in the Early Universe?" *UC Berkeley News*, January 24, 2023, https://news.berkeley.edu/2023/01/24/were-galaxies-much-different-in-the-early-universe/.

24 "PANOSETI": Robert Sanders, "New Telescope to Look for Laser Pulses from Life Around Other Planets," *UC Berkeley News*, March 2, 2020, https://news.berkeley.edu/2020/03/02/new-telescope-to-look-for-laser-pulses-from-life-around-other-planets/.

25 "founded The Penn State Extraterrestrial Intelligence Center": "About Us," Penn State Extraterrestrial Center, https://www.pseti.psu.edu/about/.

25 "Shelley Wright (no relation to Jason Wright) at UC San Diego": Alan Boyle, "Scientists Look for New Ways to Track the Technosignatures of Alien Civilizations," *GeekWire*, January 10, 2019, https://www.geekwire.com/2019/scientists-look-new-ways-track-technosignatures-alien-civilizations/#:~:text=Shelley%20Wright%2C%20an%20astrophysicist%20at,field%20in%20the%20last%20decade.%E2%80%9D.

25 "the first interstellar object known to have visited our solar system, which had been identified in 2017": "'Oumuamua," NASA, https://science.nasa.gov/solar-system/comets/oumuamua/.

30 "it was suggested we dig enormous ditches": The information in this paragraph about early suggestions for alerting the universe to our presence discussed in Victoria Laskow, "Victorians Wanted to Contact Aliens Using Giant Mirrors," *Slate*, May 17, 2016, https://slate.com/human-interest/2016/05/victorians-wanted-to-contact-aliens-using-giant-mirrors.html.

30 "at the insistence of Carl Sagan": "Pioneer Plaque," NASA, https://science.nasa.gov/resource/pioneer-plaque (though it should be said they were co-designed by Frank Drake). Information on Pioneer 10

and II and Voyager 1 and 2—including what the missions carried into space, can be found on the NASA website.

31 "In 1974, Drake harnessed": He was part of a team that included contributions from Sagan (Bill Steele, "It's the 25th Anniversary of Earth's First Attempt to Phone E.T.," *Cornell Chronicle*, November 12, 1999, https://news.cornell.edu/stories/1999/11/25th-anniversary-first-attempt-phone-et-0).

31 "300,000 stars": The Great Cluster in Hercules, Messier 13: Ibid.

31 "He felt we were notifying the universe of our existence and they were going to come and eat us": Swift, *SETI Pioneers*, 76.

31 "a 2015 *New York Times* op-ed": Seth Shostak, "Should We Keep a Low Profile in Space?" *New York Times*, March 2, 2015, https://www.nytimes.com/2015/03/28/opinion/sunday/messaging-the-stars.html.

32 "dated back to the late 1950s": The information in this paragraph is taken from the following sources: Robert Sanders, "UC Berkeley Passes Management of Allen Telescope Array to SRI," *UC Berkeley News*, April 13, 2012, https://news.berkeley.edu/2012/04/13/uc-berkeley-passes-management-of-allen-telescope-array-to-sri/; "Trouble at Hat Creek," *Centauri Dreams*, April 27, 2011, https://www.centauri-dreams.org/2011/04/27/trouble-at-hat-creek/; and "Donors Help Re-open Mothballed Telescopes Searching for ET," BBC News, August 16, 2011, https://www.bbc.com/news/science-environment-14544953.

32 "twenty-six of the forty-two six-metre antennas had been upgraded, twenty of which were used at any given time": From my interview with Alexander Pollak, January 25, 2024.

33 "The original feeds had been replaced": The information in this paragraph is taken from my interview with Alexander Pollak.

36 "two-thirds of North Americans": Steven Simpson, "The Truth Is Out There," Ipsos, July 19, 2021, https://www.ipsos.com/en-ca/news-polls/Truth-Out-There-Two-Three-Canadians-Believe-Alien-Life and Courtney Kennedy and Arnold Lau, "Most Americans Believe in Intelligent Life Beyond Earth; Few See UFOs as a Major National Security Threat," Pew Research Center, June 30, 2021, https://www.pewresearch.org/short-reads/2021/06/30/most-americans-believe

-in-intelligent-life-beyond-earth-few-see-ufos-as-a-major-national-security-threat/.

FURTHER READING

Al-Khalili, Jim ed. *Aliens: The World's Leading Scientists on the Search for Extraterrestrial Life*. Picador, 2016.

Green, Jaime. *The Possibility of Life: Science, Imagination, and Our Quest for Kinship in the Cosmos*. Hanover Square Press, 2023.

Gunn, James E. *The Listeners*. Charles Scribner's Sons, 1972.

Lem, Stanislaw. *His Master's Voice*. Translated by Michael Kandel. MIT Press, 2020 (originally published in 1967).

Loeb, Avi. *Extraterrestrial: The First Sign of Intelligent Life Beyond the Earth*. Houghton Mifflin Harcourt, 2021.

Sagan, Carl. *Contact*. Simon & Schuster, 1985.

Squeri, Lawrence. *Waiting for Contact: The Search for Extraterrestrial Intelligence*. University Press of Florida, 2016.

TWO: THE PATH

Jeremy Holden invited me to spend a week with him in Sumatra, despite the fact we'd only spoken on the phone a few times, and despite the fact he currently lives in Cambodia. I will never forget my time in the rainforest, even if I didn't spot orang-pendek myself. Thanks to our guides Doni Effendi and Sonny for rescuing us. Murray Collins, Catherine Foyle, Debbie Martyr, and Kelly Whitlock all shared their memories about Jeremy and insight into what makes him tick. And thanks to Jonathan Fong for his hospitality in Singapore before I left for Indonesia. I also spoke to a lot of people in the cryptozoology community, who have been searching and hunting for their own versions of orang-pendek. Thank you to Cliff Barackman; Matt Bille; Thom Cantrell; Loren Coleman; Adam Davies; Jonathan Downes; Steve

Feltham; Richard Freeman; Ken Gerhard; John Kirk; Ronny LeBlanc; Scott Mardis; Carl Marshall; Jeff Meldrum; Gary Opit; Dick Raynor; Adrian Shine; Lori Simmons; Bill Steciuk; Thomas Steenburg; and Roland Watson.

40 "had collapsed": "Hundreds More Feared Dead in Sumatra Quake," *The Guardian*, October 3, 2009, https://www.theguardian.com/world/2009/oct/03/indonesia-quake-levelled-villages-rescue-aid.

40 "Sumatran earthquake of 2009": "7.6 Magnitude Earthquake off Sumatra," NASA Earth Observatory, September 30, 2009, https://earthobservatory.nasa.gov/images/40537/76-magnitude-earthquake-off-sumatra.

40 "more than eleven hundred people": "Earthquakes Cause over 1700 Deaths in 2009," ReliefWeb, January 8, 2010, https://reliefweb.int/report/indonesia/earthquakes-cause-over-1700-deaths-2009.

40 "It was my forty-second birthday": April 24, in case you want to mark it in your calendar.

41 "which measured 7.3 on the Richter scale": Aidil Ichlas, "Indonesians Told to Stay Alert after Magnitude 7.3 Earthquake," Reuters, April 24, 2023, https://www.reuters.com/world/asia-pacific/indonesians-told-stay-alert-after-magnitude-73-earthquake-2023-04-25/.

44 "The animals found in its borders could fill a zoo": Sumatra Bird and Mammal List, *Wild Sumatra*, https://www.wildsumatra.com/wildlife-in-sumatra/.

44 "We had 2,000 metres to climb": *Wild Sumatra*, https://www.wildsumatra.com/itineraries/mt-tujuh/.

44 "the highest caldera lake": Ibid.

47 "Marco Polo referred to them": Bernard Heuvelmans, *On the Track of Unknown Animals*, rev. 3rd ed., trans. Richard Garnett (Kegan Paul International, 1995; originally published in French in 1955), 121.

47 Ibid., 127.

47 Ibid., 133.

50 "Debbie recounted the moment": The October Archive, "The X Creatures E01—Yeti, Myths, and Men," YouTube, 28:54, https://www

.youtube.com/watch?v=6FtTbgEjlw8. Debbie Martyr's description comes at about the nineteen-minute mark.

58 "published books about the frogs of Cambodia": *Amphibians of Cambodia: A Field Guide* (Editions Chimaira, 2008; updated in 2023).

64 "returned to Sumatra in 1995": Oona Riley, "Expedition to Sumatra Aims to Prove Existence of Ape Dubbed 'Short Man,'" *The Guardian*, March 6, 1995, http://www.bigfootencounters.com/articles/martyr94.htm.

64 "from Fauna and Flora International": Since rebranded as Fauna & Flora.

65 "Jeremy also secured $10,000 from the BBC": Jeremy Holden provided this figure, but an article from *The Sunday Times* confirms the BBC's involvement (Nicholas Hellen and Jonathan Leake, "The Orange Ape That Walks Like a Man," *Sunday Times*, October 12, 1997, http://www.bigfootencounters.com/articles/orangeape.htm).

66 "less than six hundred in the wild": "Sumatran Tiger," Fauna & Flora, https://www.fauna-flora.org/species/sumatran-tiger/.

66 "were listed as 'Critically Endangered'": Ibid.

66 "In 2000, she founded": "Kerinci Seblat Sumatran Tiger Project," Wildcats Conservation Alliance, https://conservewildcats.org/portfolio/kerinci-seblat-sumatran-tiger-protection-project/.

66 "In 2015, she was named a Member of the Order of the British Empire": https://x.com/FaunaFloraInt/status/614418275129249792; "New Year Honours 2015: The Full List," *The Guardian*, December 30, 2014, https://www.theguardian.com/uk-news/2014/dec/30/-sp-new-years-honours-2015-full-list; Tim Knight and Mark Rose, *With Honourable Intent: A Natural History of Fauna & Flora International* (William Collins, 2017), https://www.fauna-flora.org/wp-content/uploads/2017/11/With-Honourable-Intent-sample-pages.pdf.

66 "had been discovered a couple of years earlier"; "'Hobbits' on Flores, Indonesia," Smithsonian National Museum of Natural History, https://humanorigins.si.edu/research/asian-research-projects/hobbits-flores-indonesia.

66 "just 50,000 years ago": *Homo floresiensis*, Smithsonian National Museum of Natural History, https://humanorigins.si.edu/evidence/human-fossils/species/homo-floresiensis.

67 "reality-TV shows with names like *MonsterQuest*": Documentary TV FULL HD, "The Search for the Real Hobbit: Monster Quest," YouTube, 2:22:56, https://www.youtube.com/watch?v=JU7sMhR_Tt8.

69 "But the sniffling went on for quite a while": To be clear, when I fact-checked this with Jeremy Holden, he denied it was him I heard: "[I]t wasn't me you heard snivelling in my tent. Beauty can easily make me cry, but I don't think I have ever shed a tear motivated by self-pity."

69 "a 2019 estimate": Dyna Rochmyaningsih, "Saving Sumatran Elephants Starts with Counting Them. Indonesia Won't Say How Many Are Left," *Mongabay*, August 8, 2022, https://news.mongabay.com/2022/08/saving-sumatran-elephants-starts-with-counting-them-indonesia-wont-say-how-many-are-left/. The exact numbers were 924 and 1,359.

69 "farms": Teguh Suprayitno, "In Sumatra, Potato Appetite Bites into a UNESCO-Listed Tiger Haven," Mongabay, May 8, 2023, https://news.mongabay.com/2023/05/in-sumatra-potato-appetite-bites-into-a-unesco-listed-tiger-haven/.

69 "and tea plantations": "Kerinci: Tea, Tigers, and Southeast Asia's Highest Volcano," Remote Lands, March 16, 2018, https://www.remotelands.com/travelogues/kerinci-tea-tigers-southeast-asias-highest-volcano/.

69 "illegal logging camps": Jeremy Hance, "Smallholders and Loggers Push Deeper into Sumatra's Largest Park," *Mongabay*, November 29, 2023, https://news.mongabay.com/2023/11/smallholders-and-loggers-push-deeper-into-sumatras-largest-park/.

69 "palm oil operations": "Illegal Plantations Threaten Sumatran Tiger with Extinction," Earthsight, July 12, 2017, https://www.earthsight.org.uk/news/idm/illegal-plantations-threaten-suamtran-tiger-extinction.

69 "poachers were active": Loren Bell, "Sting Operation Nets Tiger Poachers," *Mongabay*, February 24, 2015, https://news.mongabay.com/2015/02/sting-operation-nets-tiger-poachers/.

69 "on a list": "Tropical Rainforest Heritage of Sumatra," UNESCO World Heritage Centre, https://whc.unesco.org/en/list/1167/.

69 "cut the poverty rate in half": "The World Bank in Indonesia," World Bank Group, https://www.worldbank.org/en/country/indonesia/overview.

71 "The serow": Ian Morse, "In Sumatra, a Vulnerable, 'Mythical' Wild Goat Lives an Unknown Life," *Mongabay*, March 31, 2021, https://news.mongabay.com/2021/03/in-sumatra-a-vulnerable-mythical-wild-goat-lives-an-unknown-life/.

FURTHER READING

Bader, Christopher D., Joseph D. Baker, and F. Carson Mencken. *Paranormal America: Ghost Encounters, UFO Sightings, Bigfoot Hunts, and Other Curiosities in Religion and Culture*. New York University Press, 2017.

Davies, Adam. *Extreme Expeditions 2: Manbeasts—A Personal Investigation*. Self-published, 2020.

Dickey, Colin. *The Unidentified: Mythical Monsters, Alien Encounters, and Our Obsession with the Unexplained*. Viking, 2020.

Freeman, Richard. *In Search of Real Monsters: Adventures in Cryptozoology*, Vol. 2. Mango Publishing, 2022.

Nugent, Rory. *Drums Along the Congo: On the Trail of Mokele-Mbembe, the Last Living Dinosaur*. Houghton Mifflin, 1993.

Pisani, Elizabeth. *Indonesia, Etc: Exploring the Improbable Nation*. W.W. Norton, 2014.

Regal, Brian. *Searching for Sasquatch: Crackpots, Eggheads and Cryptozoology*. Palgrave MacMillan, 2011.

Zada, John. *In the Valley of the Noble Beyond: In Search of the Sasquatch*. Greystone Books, 2019.

THREE: MIDDLE CHILDREN

My attendance at the IRG symposium was facilitated by Stephen Fleming of the University of Arizona. I would also again like to thank Philip Lubin for inviting me to Santa Barbara over Thanksgiving, during a pandemic, no less. Speaking of which, many of my initial interviews for this chapter coincided with the height of COVID; my conversations with the following people allowed me to leave my house and roam the stars: Robert Baker; H. Fearn; Matthew Gorban; Jeff Greason; George Hathaway; Andrew Higgins; Gerald Jackson; Les Johnson; Geoffrey Landis; Mathias Larrouturou; Kelvin Long; Douglas Loss; Greg Matloff; Philip Mauskopf; Ralph McNutt; Greg Meholic; Marc Millis; Gonzalo Munevar; Paul Murad; Kenneth Roy; Nicholas Rupert; Mark Shelhamer; Prashant Srinivasan; Martin Tajmar; Colin Warn; Harold "Sonny" White; Lance Williams; Jim Woodward; and Pete Worden. Also, Paul Gilster has been chronicling space exploration on his website *Centauri Dreams* (https://www.centauri-dreams.org) for years; it's the best resource in the world if you want to learn more about what it will take for humankind to reach the stars.

76 "1 billion kilometres per hour . . . triple star system": Jenny Winder, "Light Years Explained," *Sky at Night Magazine*, February 17, 2024, https://www.skyatnightmagazine.com/space-science/lightyear; and "Alpha Centauri: A Triple Star System about 4 Light Years from Earth," NASA, June 6, 2018, https://www.nasa.gov/image-article/alpha-centauri-triple-star-system-about-4-light-years-from-earth/.

76 "about 75,000 years" The time varies depending on the source, with some suggesting over 73,000 years and others more than 77,000 years ("The Nearest Neighbor Star," Imagine the Universe, NASA, https://imagine.gsfc.nasa.gov/features/cosmic/nearest_star_info.html; and Tom Jones, "How Long Would it Take to Reach the Nearest Star?" Tom Jones, May 17, 2024, https://astronauttomjones.com/2024/05/17/how-long-would-it-take-to-reach-the-nearest-star/).

76 "discovered in 1915": Deborah Byrd, "Proxima Centauri Discovered 109 Years Ago," *EarthSky*, October 11, 2024, https://earthsky.org/space/this-date-in-science-discovery-of-proxima-centauri/.

77 "spaceship convention": I'm stealing this description from journalist Nick Stockton, author of a 2016 *Wired* feature on what was then still called the Tennessee Valley Interstellar Workshop. See Nick Stockton, "The Far-Out Summit Where Geniuses Learn to Build Starships," *Wired*, April 12, 2016, https://www.wired.com/2016/04/far-meeting-rocket-scientists-learn-space/.

77 "their pioneering textbook on the subject": Eugene Mallove and Gregory Matloff, *The Starflight Handbook: A Pioneer's Guide to Interstellar Travel* (John Wiley & Sons, 1989).

78 "the list of presentations": "IRG 2021 Abstracts," Interstellar Research Group, https://irg.space/irg-2021-abstracts/.

78 "The symposium grew out of": From my interview with Kenneth Roy, September 24, 2021.

79 "Its ultimate goal": "Statement of Purpose," Interstellar Research Group, https://irg.space/statement-of-purpose/.

79 "president of the IRG": Douglas Loss was president at the time of the symposium, but stepped down in 2025.

79 "quoting the writer Randall Munroe": "The universe is probably littered with the one-planet graves of cultures which made the sensible economic decision that there's no good reason to go into space—each discovered, studied, and remembered by the ones who made the irrational decision."

82 "was the fastest craft ever launched": John Uri, "15 Years Ago: New Horizons Launched to Pluto and Beyond," NASA, January 20, 2021, https://www.nasa.gov/history/15-years-ago-new-horizons-launched-to-pluto-and-beyond/.

82 "Whereas the Apollo missions took three days to get to the moon, New Horizons did it in eight hours": Daisy Dobrijevic, "How Long Does It Take to Get to the Moon?" Space.com, August 9, 2023, https://www.space.com/how-long-does-it-take-to-get-to-the-moon.

82 "Ever since Lucian went to the Moon": Lucian, translated from the Greek by Paul Turner, *True History and Lucius or The Ass* (Indiana University Press, 1974).

82 "Francis Godwin": Domingo Gonsales, *The Man in the Moone: Or, a Discourse of a Voyage Thither* (1638).

82 "in a chariot pulled by a flock of geese": "Flying Chariots and Exotic Birds," Max-Planck-Gesellschaft, July 17, 2019, https://www.mpg.de/13725319/flying-chariots-and-exotic-birds.

82 "some sixty years later": *The Consolidator: Or, Memoirs of Sundry Transactions from the World in the Moon* (1705).

82 "Cyrano de Bergerac": *A Voyage to the Moon* (published posthumously in 1656), https://www.gutenberg.org/files/46547/46547-h/46547-h.htm.

83 "using an enormous gun": In *From the Earth to the Moon* (1865).

83 "in a gigantic balloon": "The Unparalleled Adventure of One Hans Pfaall" (1835).

83 "H.G. Wells invented": *The First Men in the Moon* (1901).

84 "in his 1861 essay": Anne Craig, "Former Queen's Principal Explained Space Travel in 1861," *Queen's Gazette*, October 5, 2015, https://www.queensu.ca/gazette/stories/former-queen-s-principal-explained-space-travel-1861.

84 "hitching a ride on a comet": "Let us follow the course of some comet in its wanderings across our system" and "The great advantage of the comet, as a convenient vehicle for an excursion, is, that it gives near, as well as extensive views of the system."

84 "wrote its author": David Lasser, *The Conquest of Space* (Apogee Books, 2002), 26.

84 "a leading physicist in the interstellar community": For more on Jim Woodward, I recommend Daniel Oberhaus's profile in *Wired*: "Gravity, Gizmos, and a Grand Theory of Interstellar Travel," September 2020, https://www.wired.com/story/mach-effect-thrusters-interstellar-travel/.

84 "a series of nuclear bombs": "Propulsion Test Vehicle, Project Orion," National Air and Space Museum, https://airandspace.si.edu/collection-objects/propulsion-test-vehicle-project-orion/nasm_A19721008000.

84 "Saturn V rocket": "The History of the Saturn V Rocket," *Sky at Night Magazine*, March 11, 2020, https://www.skyatnightmagazine.com/space-missions/saturn-v-rocket-history-facts.

85 "Limited Nuclear Test Ban Treaty": "The Limited Nuclear Test Ban Treaty," Office of the Historian, https://history.state.gov/milestones/1961-1968/limited-ban.

85 "wrote the physicist Gregory Matloff": Gregory Matloff, in Les Johnson and Jack McDevitt, eds., *Going Interstellar: Build Starships Now!* (Baen Books, 2021), 150–51.

85 "he said in 1960": This was in the same lecture I reference in chapter 1: "Radioastronomy and Communication Through Space: Brookhaven Lecture Series Number 1," (1960), https://doi.org/10.2172/4017898.

85 "barring a catastrophe": From his article "Interstellar Transport," published in the October 1968 issue of *Physics Today*, 45, https://galileo.phys.virginia.edu/classes/109.jvn.spring00/nuc_rocket/Dyson.pdf.

85 "At the end of 1972": Alan Taylor, "The Last Time Humans Walked on the Moon," *The Atlantic*, November 30, 2022, https://www.theatlantic.com/photo/2022/11/photos-apollo-17-50th-anniversary/672297/.

85 "Project Daedalus": Kelvin Long, "Icarus: Revisiting the Daedelus Starship," *Centauri Dreams*, March 19, 2009, https://www.centauri-dreams.org/2009/03/19/icarus-revisiting-the-daedalus-starship/.

85 "a nuclear fusion-based propulsion system": https://www.bis-space.com/technical-projects/ and https://www.daviddarling.info/encyclopedia/D/Daedalus.html.

85 "Project Icarus": Long, "Icarus."

85 "In 1975, he stood": Paul Gilster, "Interstellar Flight in Congressional Report," *Centauri Dreams*, May 26, 2016, https://www.centauri-dreams.org/2016/05/26/interstellar-flight-in-congressional-report/ and "by the year 2000, with human-manned missions to begin twenty-five years later": Gilster, "Interstellar Flight in Congressional Report."

85 "he conceded in the pages": Robert L. Forward, "A Program for Interstellar Exploration," *Journal of the British Interplanetary Society* 29 (1976): 611–32, https://path-2.narod.ru/design/base_e/IEP.pdf.

86 "1962 speech at Rice University": "Address at Rice University on the Nation's Space Effort," John F. Kennedy Presidential Library and Museum, https://www.jfklibrary.org/learn/about-jfk/historic-speeches/address-at-rice-university-on-the-nations-space-effort.

87 "a tiny percentage": Paul M. Sutter, "How NASA's NIAC Program Creates Futuristic Space Technology," *Popular Mechanics*, December 8, 2023, https://www.popularmechanics.com/space/a45892623/nasa-niac-futuristic-space-technology/.

92 "now ran his own shop": "Jeff Greason," Electric Sky, http://www.el-sky.com/bio/jeff-greason/.

95 "The occasion": You can watch the presentations here: Limitless Space Institute, "LSI Interstellar Initiative Grants Kickoff Meeting," YouTube, 5:47:35, https://www.youtube.com/watch?v=XITIuZIe6F8&t=3088s.

96 "been awarded between US$100,000 and US$250,000": "Limitless Space Institute Announces Inaugural Interstellar Initiative Grants Awards," Limitless Space Institute, https://www.limitlessspace.org/press-release-i2-2020/.

96 "One leading figure in the field": This was Kelvin Long, co-founder of the aforementioned Project Icarus and founder of the Interstellar Research Centre.

99 "Philip Lubin wanted to be an astronaut": What follows is mostly taken from multiple, hours-long interviews I conducted with Philip Lubin between November 24, 2020, and November 26, 2021. For more, Kate Greene's 2019 profile in the *MIT Technology Review* is a good primer ("Inside Starshot," *MIT Technology Review*, June 26, 2019, https://www.technologyreview.com/2019/06/26/134468/starshot-alpha-centauri-laser/).

99 "a spherical escape pod measuring a claustrophobia-inducing thirty-six inches in diameter": "The Personal Rescue Enclosure: NASA's Unusual Plan to Save Shuttle Astronauts," New Space Economy, https://newspaceeconomy.ca/2024/05/06/the-personal-rescue-enclosure-nasas-unusual-plan-to-save-shuttle-astronauts/.

101 "who were first to theorize": More on this in the chapter 8 notes.

102 "wrote to Galileo": Barbara Becker, "Exploring the Cosmos: Week 4, Galileo," Department of History, University of California, Irvine, http://faculty.humanities.uci.edu/bjbecker/ExploringtheCosmos/week4e.html.

102 "a tiny, lightweight craft": Nicola Davis, "Breakthrough Starshot Successfully Launch World's Smallest Spacecraft," *The Guardian*, July 28, 2017, https://www.theguardian.com/science/2017/jul/28/breakthrough-starshot-successfully-launch-worlds-smallest-spacecraft.

102 "Relativistic speed": In a nutshell, some significant fraction of the speed of light.

102 "In a talk": The aforementioned TED Talk.

102 "about 25 percent the speed of light": Charles Q. Choi, "Lasers Could Send a Wafer-Thin Spaceship to a Star," *Popular Science*, February 23, 2016, https://www.popsci.com/lasers-could-send-spaceship-to-star/.

103 "issued a press release": Shelly Leachman, "California Scientists Propose System to Vaporize Asteroids That Threaten Earth," *The Current*, UC Santa Barbara, February 14, 2013, https://news.ucsb.edu/201/013465/california-scientists-propose-system-vaporize-asteroids-threaten-earth.

103 "sent Worden a paper": Philip Lubin, "A Roadmap to Insterstellar Flight," April 2015, https://www.nasa.gov/wp-content/uploads/2015/05/roadmap_to_interstellar_flight_tagged.pdf.

103 "here called DEEP-IN": Philip Lubin, "DEEP-IN Directed Energy Propulsion for Interstellar Exploration," NASA, May 7, 2015, https://www.nasa.gov/general/deep-in-directed-energy-propulsion-for-interstellar-exploration/.

104 "in January 2016": Paul Gilster, "DE-STAR and Breakthrough Starshot: A Short History," *Centauri Dreams*, October 5, 2018, https://www.centauri-dreams.org/2018/10/05/de-star-and-breakthrough-starshot-a-short-history/.

104 "Lubin recalled Milner telling him": I tried, several times, to interview Yuri Milner but was unsuccessful.

104 "became the first human in space": April 12, 1961.

104 "the press conference": Watch it here: "Full Breakthrough Starshot Announcement and Press Conference Interstellar Travel," YouTube, 1:15:51, https://www.youtube.com/watch?v=nwVPrEWdIfI.

104 "a fleet of laser-propelled nanocrafts": Jake Parks, "Breakthrough Starshot: A Voyage to the Stars Within Our Lifetimes," *Astronomy*, June 17, 2021, https://www.astronomy.com/science/breakthrough-starshot-a-voyage-to-the-stars-within-our-lifetimes/.

106 "all potential challenges": "Challenges," Breakthrough Starshot, https://breakthroughinitiatives.org/challenges/3.

FURTHER READING

Clegg, Brian. *Final Frontier: The Pioneering Science and Technology of Exploring the Universe*. St. Martin's Press, 2014.

Hampson, Robert E. and Sandra L. Mellock, ed. *The Founder Effect*. Baen Books, 2020.

Johnson, Les. *A Traveler's Guide to the Stars*. Princeton University Press, 2022.

MacDonald, Alex. *The Long Space Age: The Economic Origins of Space Exploration from Colonial America to the Cold War*. Yale University Press, 2017.

Stine, G. Harry. *Halfway to Anywhere: Achieving America's Destiny in Space*. M. Evans and Company, 1996.

Taylor, Travis S. and Les Johnson. *Saving Proxima*. Baen Books, 2021.

Wall, Michael. *Out There: A Scientific Guide to Alien Life, Antimatter, and Humane Space Travel (For the Cosmically Curious)*. Grand Central Publishing, 2018.

Weil, Elizabeth. *They All Laughed at Christopher Columbus: An Incurable Dreamer Builds the First Civilian Spaceship*. Bantam Books, 2002.

FOUR: WITHOUT A TRACE

I accompanied Matthew Nopper and Nick Oldrieve on two different searches, in the summers of 2020 and 2021. Thanks to everyone I spoke to at these searches, including Dave Burr; Cindy Follis; Kelly Greenley; Melanie Lambert; Joan Monk; Shelley Pearce; Beth Purkis; Marg Thomas; Michelle Weis; and Renee Willmon. Other sources of insights were Todd Matthew of The Doe Network and Lana Prosper of the RCMP's Centre for Missing and Exploited Children.

108 "If you follow Highway 26": This description would have been accurate in the fall of 2021; not sure how significantly this stretch of road has changed.

109 "a young woman named Lisa Maas": "Lisa Maas," Please Bring Me Home, https://pleasebringmehome.com/canada/lisa-maas/.

109 "a former reporter with the local paper": Bayshore News Team, "Search Ramps Up in Lisa Maas Cold Case," Bayshore Broadcasting, August 31, 2018, https://www.bayshorebroadcasting.ca/2018/08/31/search-ramps-up-in-lisa-maas-cold-case/.

111 "oldest drinking establishment in town": "The Pub Restaurant Owen Sound," River District Owen Sound, https://owensoundriverdistrict.ca/en/about-the-river-district/business-directory/show/the-pub-restaurant-owen-sound.

111 "Lisa left the party with the man": "Lisa Maas," Please Bring Me Home.

111 "green 1976 Plymouth Fury": "Still Searching for Lisa Maas After 29 Years," *Owen Sound Hub*, July 20, 2017, https://owensoundhub.org/news/3507-still-searching-for-lisa-maas-after-29-years.html.

111 "Her car was found . . . five months pregnant": "Lisa Maas," Please Bring Me Home.

111 "one of her friends told *The Globe and Mail*": Timothy Appleby, "Without a Trace: Anguish of Knowing 2 Missing Women's Fate Bedevils Friends, Relatives," *The Globe and Mail*, August 23, 1988.

111 "no one was charged with a crime": Claire McCormack, "Search Held for Lisa Maas on 35th Anniversary of Her Disappearance," Bayshore Broadcasting, July 19, 2023, https://www.bayshorebroadcasting.ca/2023/07/19/bones-to-be-analyzed-in-search-for-lisa-maas-who-went-missing-in-1988/.

112 "Lois Hanna had vanished in nearby Kincardine": She went missing after a dance in Lucknow, but lived in Kincardine (Peter Edwards, "She Left the Dance Alone. Why Lois Hanna's Family Is Still Fighting Visions of 'Watching Her Walk Away,'" *Toronto Star*, July 18, 2021, https://www.thestar.com/news/gta/she-left-the-dance-alone-why-lois-hanna-s-family-is-still-fighting-visions-of/article_c881c510-af3e-5d6b-bcac-482ecde3cb30.html; and "South Bruce OPP Continue to

Investigate Disappearance of Lois Hanna," *Kincardine Record*, July 3, 2024, https://www.kincardinerecord.com/story.php?id=16706.

112 "In 2008, an Owen Sound *Sun Times* reporter": Rick Vanderlinde, "Ontario Cold Case: Amateur Sleuths Search for Lisa Maas 30 Years Later," Stayner–Wasaga Beach *Sun*, November 16, 2018, https://www.simcoe.com/news/crime/ontario-cold-case-amateur-sleuths-search-for-lisa-maas-3-years-later/article_da263b25-2ba8-5ad1-a04a-491b598149b7.html.

112 "the list was whittled down to a single name": Vanderlinde, "Ontario Cold Case"; and Rob Gowan, "Resources Brought in for Maas Search," Owen Sound *Sun Times*, May 9, 2018, https://www.owensoundsuntimes.com/2018/05/09/resources-brought-in-for-maas-search; Peter Edwards, "'As Long as You've Got Breath in Your Body': Lisa Maas's Father Is Still Searching for His Daughter—and Her Killer," *Toronto Star*, August 29, 2021, https://www.thestar.com/news/gta/as-long-as-you-ve-got-a-breath-in-your-body-lisa-maas-s-father/article_7a1101d1-585c-55d9-8c48-bd08eb35edb1.html.

112 "on another search in another town for another lost girl": This was a search, conducted in Clarington, Ontario, on July 27, 2020, for Noreen Greenley, who went missing on the night of September 14, 1963. See: "Noreen Greenley," Please Bring Me Home, https://pleasebringmehome.com/canada/noreen-greenley/.

117 "nickname was Mouse": She had a mouse tattoo on her shoulder. She was also wearing a Mickey Mouse sweatshirt the day she went missing ("Lisa Maas," Please Bring Me Home).

118 "discovered Lisa's car": Greg Cowan, "Volunteers Search Seven Sites of Interest on 35th Anniversary of Lisa Maas's Disappearance," *Owen Sound Sun Times*, July 16, 2023, https://www.owensoundsuntimes.com/news/local-news/volunteers-search-seven-sites-of-interest-on-35th-anniversary-of-lisa-maas-disappearance.

118 "brothers of Lois Hanna": Scott Miller, "Hundreds Expected for Search in 31-Year-Old Cold Case," CTV News, September 17. 2019, https://www.ctvnews.ca/london/article/hundreds-expected-for-search-in-31-year-old-cold-case/.

120 "Nick Oldrieve is in the newspaper": "Man Thinks He Knows Where Lisa Maas's Remains Are," *Barrie Examiner*, July 21, 2016, https://www.simcoe.com/news/man-thinks-he-knows-where-lisa-maass-remains-are/article_5c59b4ee-13ea-5a14-9359-01e695f85979.html.

123 "Although he was raised near Owen Sound": "Man Thinks He Knows," *Barrie Examiner*.

125 "an article that had just been published": Peter Edwards, "As Long as You've Got a Breath in Your Body," *Toronto Star*, August 29, 2021, https://www.thestar.com/news/gta/as-long-as-you-ve-got-a-breath-in-your-body-lisa-maas-s-father/article_7a1101d1-585c-55d9-8c48-bd08eb35edb1.html.

FURTHER READING

Halber, Deborah. *The Skeleton Crew: How Amateur Sleuths Are Solving America's Coldest Cases*. Simon & Schuster, 2014.

FIVE: ACTS OF BEAUTY

The bulk of this chapter is based on interviews with Bonnie Morton, whom I spent three days with in Regina back in 2022. I also want to thank her friends and colleagues, including Nicole Desormeaux; Peter Gilmer; Debby McGraw; Harriett McLachlan; Thelma O'Watch; Bruce Porter; Joseph Reynolds; Barry Rieder; and Carol Schick. And thanks to all the other anti-poverty activists and housing advocates I spoke to over the years, including: Sheila Baxter; Gary Bloch; John Clarke; Cathy Crowe; Dan Johnstone; George Lessard; Philip Mangano; Karen O'Shannacery; John Rook; Jean Swanson; and Sam Tsemberis.

133 "students would no longer be provided with free bus passes": Ashley Martin, "Driving Poverty Out of Business," *Regina Leader-Post*, December 24, 2014, https://www.pressreader.com/canada/regina-leader-post/20141224/282286728622604?srsltid=AfmBOop7-WAp9bUUutXJ1KtO8gfUa-85fjD8-_SEXpvgXlo_vBeitVLQ.

135 "A small riot ensued": This is just my way of honouring one of my favourite pieces of journalism ever: "Secrets of the Magus" by Mark Singer, *The New Yorker*, April 5, 1993: https://www.newyorker.com/magazine/1993/04/05/ricky-jay-magician-secrets-profile.

135 "Knox-Metropolitan United Church": For more about the history, see https://web.archive.org/web/20120313235221/http://www.knoxmet.org/about.html.

135 "dates back to 1912": "Knox-Metropolitan United Church (Regina)," Saskatchewan Council for Archives & Archivists, https://memorysask.ca/knox-metropolitan-church-regina and "when part of the current building was rebuilt after being levelled by the Regina Cyclone": John E. Stewardson, "Regina's Day of Wrath: The Killer Cyclone of 1912," *Canada's History*, April 10, 2016, https://www.canadashistory.ca/explore/environment/regina-s-day-of-wrath-the-killer-cyclone-of-1912 and "the deadliest tornado in Canadian history": Taylor C. Noakes, "Regina Cyclone, 1912," *Canadian Encylopedia*, August 25, 2022, https://www.thecanadianencyclopedia.ca/en/article/regina-cyclone.

135 "stretch back to 1882": "Knox Metropolitan United Church (Regina)," Saskatchewan Council for Archives & Archivists, https://memorysask.ca/knox-presbyterian-church-regina.

137 "based out of Knox-Met since 1971": Regina Anti-Poverty Ministry, https://antipovertyministry.ca/rapm-archives/.

140 "streaming the service on YouTube": Sunday Morning Worship, Knox-Metropolitan United Church, April 3, 2022, YouTube, 1:05:32, https://www.youtube.com/watch?v=fMh-W4KdI_o&t=971s.

141 "Regina families opening their homes to people fleeing the war in Ukraine": Pratyush Dayal, "With Ukrainian Citizens on Their Way, Sask. Resettlement Organizations Say They Need More Support," CBC News, March 12, 2022, https://www.cbc.ca/news/ukrainians-on-way-resettlement-organizations-more-support-1.6381806.

147 "she'd spoken at the United Nations": In 2006, as part of a Canadian delegation presenting before the International Committee on Social Economic and Cultural Rights.

SIX: GOLD IN THEM HILLS

This chapter wouldn't have been possible without the hospitality of Ron and Jayne Feldman, who let me hang around Apache Junction with them for a few days. Thanks also to their sons, Jesse and Josh Feldman, as well as all the other treasure hunters I spoke to over the years, including Bob Schoosc and Wayne Tuttle.

149 "The sun seemed to rise": Ron Feldman, *Deep Fault* (self-published, 2005), 19.

150 "A devastating wildfire": Jim Walsh, "How Fire Heroes Saved Lost Dutchman Park," East Valley.com, October 25, 2020, https://www.eastvalleytribune.com/news/how-fire-heroes-saved-lost-dutchman-park/article_4531af08-1566-11eb-934a-97bb72259a88.html.

152 "he told Gary": Ron Feldman, *Lost Dutchman Gold Mine: Evolution of a Treasure Hunter* (self-published, 1968), 21.

153 "one long-time Dutch hunter warned me": This was Wayne Tuttle.

153 "According to a legendary Dutch hunter named Adolph Ruth": Curt Gentry, *The Killer Mountains: The Great Story of the Last Search for the Lost Dutchman Mine* (New American Library, 1968), 103.

153 "his bullet-shattered skull was found in these mountains in 1931": Tom Kollenborn, "Legacy of Adolph Ruth," Apache Junction Public Library, 2001, https://www.ajpl.org/legacy-of-adolph-ruth/.

154 "averages more than a hundred degrees": Climate and Average Weather Year-Round in Apache Junction, Weatherspark.com, https://weatherspark.com/y/2622/Average-Weather-in-Apache-Junction-Arizona-United-States-Year-Round.

154 "The men disappeared": "Three Men Missing in Arizona Treasure Hunt," ABC News, July 14, 2010, https://abcnews.go.com/US/arizona-gold-treasure-hunt-men-missing/story?id=11162084.

154 "stumbled across their remains": Ron Dungan, "Lure of Gold in Ariz. Mountains Leads Hikers Astray," *USA Today*, February 22, 2013, https://www.usatoday.com/story/news/nation/2013/02/22/hikers-dutchmans-gold-rescue-teams/1938193/.

155 "I discovered the legend of Oak Island": It was through Randall Sullivan's article in *Rolling Stone*, which years later he expanded into a book.

155 "what might be found": "12 Treasure That Could Be Under Oak Island," History, https://www.history.co.uk/shows/the-curse-of-oak-island/articles/12-treasures-that-could-be-under-oak-island.

158 "The story, or at least one of them, went like this": What follows is drawn from multiple sources. Even then, you will find conflicting information in these sources. There truly is no single story when it comes to the legend, which is why it's a legend.

158 "established several mines in Arizona": W.C. Jameson, *The Silver Madonna and Other Tales of America's Greatest Lost Treasures* (Taylor Trade, 2013), 39.

158 "unfathomable riches had long been shared": Jameson, *The Silver Madonna and Other Tales*, 38. Also: Clay Worst as told to Geoffrey Gray, "The Cactus with 12 Arms," *Alta*, December 21, 2022, https://www.altaonline.com/dispatches/a42101918/lost-dutchman-mine-arizona-clay-worst-geoffrey-gray/.

158 "conflict with the local Apache tribes . . . extracted": Gentry, *The Killer Mountains: The Great Story of the Last Search for the Lost Dutchman Mine* (New American Library, 1968), pp. 7, 51, and 52.

158 "one version claims the Peralta family patriarch, Don Miguel": Robert Blair, *Tales of the Superstitions: The Origins of the Lost Dutchman Legend* (Arizona Historical Foundation, 1975), 87. Another version of this is mentioned here: Bob Willis, "Has the Lost Dutchman Mine Been Found?" *True West*, April 1, 2005, https://truewestmagazine.com/article/has-the-lost-dutchman-mine-been-found/.

159 "a mysterious map": "Arizona: Search for Last Dutchman's," *Time*, June 22, 1959, https://time.com/archive/6870860/arizona-search-for-last-dutchmans/.

159 "who arrived in Arizona around 1864": Jesse Feldman, *The Dutchman's Trail: The Legend of the Superstition Mountains* (self-published, 2022), 92.

159 "as the writer Robert Blair put it": Blair, *Tales of the Superstitions*, 53.

159 "Waltz saved a man in a bar fight who turned out to be a Peralta": Jameson, *The Silver Madonna and Other Tales*, 41.

159 "'eighteen-inch wide quartz vein'": Feldman, *The Dutchman's Trail*, 53.

159 "the author would stop": Blair, *Tales of the Superstitions*, 32: "A recent author, Robert Allen, credits Waltz with having taken an Apache teenager named Ken-tee as his bride— a claim utterly lacking in credibility or authority, save perhaps in Mr. Allen's mind."

160 "an old stagecoach route": Danielle Tumminio, "Riding Arizona's Apache Trail," CNN, September 27, 2012, https://www.cnn.com/travel/article/arizona-apache-trail.

162 "We were a long way from Buffalo": All the biographical details come from my interviews with Ron Feldman, and his memoir, *Lost Dutchman Gold Mine*.

164 "His name was Orvus Lee Howk!": David Howard, "Treasure Hunters May Have Found Jesse James's Lost Gold," *Popular Mechanics*, April 18, 2023, https://www.popularmechanics.com/adventure/outdoors/a42953312/jesse-jamess-lost-gold/.

164 "Robert Jacobs . . . died in 1994": Ron Feldman, *Lost Dutchman Gold Mine*, 51, 52, and 106.

165 "The Treasure Hunter of the Year Awards have been presented annually since 1993": Here's the 2025 ceremony, which was the 33rd annual: Legend of the Superstition Mountains, "Chasing Legends 373," YouTube, 31:13, https://www.youtube.com/watch?v=akKtUTM8owU.

166 "When Schoose first came to Apache Junction, in 1965": Bob Schoose told me his first visit was in 1965, though other reports suggest 1966: Tom Kollenborn, "Building a Dream: Goldfield Ghost Town," Apache Junction Public Library, https://www.ajpl.org/building-a-dream-goldfield-ghost-town/.

166 "the Dutch Hunter Rendezvous": https://www.facebook.com/profile.php?id=100064510247547# and Tom Kollenborn, "The Dutch Hunters' Rendezvous," *Tom Kollenborn Chronicles*, October 3, 2011, https://superstitionmountaintomkollenborn.blogspot.com/2011/10/dutch-hunters-rendezvous.html.

167 "'friendly, open, kind, smart and beautiful, all in one package'": Feldman, *Lost Dutchman Gold Mine*, 158.

169 "a mine called the Silver Chief": For more: Mysteries of the Superstition Mountains, "Scientific Proof: Is the Lost Dutchman Mine Hidden in the Superstition Mountains?" YouTube, 16:45, https://www.youtube.com/watch?v=oc3fIHLykVo.

169 "fashioned into a matchbox": Dan Gleason, "The Legend of the Lost Dutchman Mine," *Cowboys & Indians*, January 1, 2018, https://www.cowboysindians.com/2018/01/the-legend-of-the-lost-dutchman-mine/.

170 "Another problem when it came to proving Ron's theory": "Superstition Wilderness," U.S. Department of Agriculture, Forest Service, https://www.fs.usda.gov/r03/tonto/wilderness.

170 "Jesse Capen, whose body was discovered in 2012": Kirk Mitchell, "Lost Dutchman Seeker's Remains Confirmed to be Jesse Capen's," *Denver Post*, April 20, 2016, https://www.denverpost.com/2013/01/23/lost-dutchman-seekers-remains-confirmed-to-be-jesse-capens/.

170 "'beyond obsessed'": "Colorado Man Disappears in Search for Gold Mine," *Denver Post*, January 17, 2010, https://www.denverpost.com/2010/01/17/colorado-man-disappears-in-search-for-gold-mine/.

170 "more than a hundred books and maps": Martin Cizmar, "Jesse Capen Went Searching for the Lost Dutchman Gold. Now They're Searching for Him," *Westword*, June 3, 2010, https://www.westword.com/news/jesse-capen-went-searching-for-the-lost-dutchman-gold-now-theyre-searching-for-him-5108429.

172 "controlled nineteen mining claims of varying profitability": "Ron Feldman Mining Claims," TheDiggings.com, https://thediggings.com/owners/23325.

172 "discovered in 1893 . . . purchased it in 2003": "Mammoth No. 3," TheDiggings.com, https://thediggings.com/mines/amc50451.

172 "Mother Hubbard, Tom Thumb and the Black Queen": "Ron Feldman Mining Claims," TheDiggings.com, https://thediggings.com/owners/23325.

FURTHER READING

Falkner, John Meade. *Moonfleet*. Puffin Classics, 2025.

Feldman, Ron. *Crooked Mountain*. World Publishing, 2000.

———. *Double Cross*. Self-published, 2010.

Sullivan, Randall. *The Curse of Oak Island: The Story of the World's Longest Treasure Hunt*. Atlantic Monthly Press, 2018.

SEVEN: ONCE WAS LOST

Thanks to Richard Thorns for all the conversations over the years, as well as hosting me in Crowborough. Thank you to Christina Biggs, Anna-Marie Buss, James Donaldson, the late Sam Mackenzie, and David Thorns for sharing their thoughts on Richard and his quest, and to Robin Moore for first mentioning the pink-headed duck to me. At one point, this chapter was going to also focus on the search for the thylacine in Australia, and the myriad attempts to bring it back through science. While this section no longer appears, I do want to thank everyone I spoke to, including Michael Archer; Col Bailey; Nick Mooney; Andrew Pask; and Chris Rehberg.

174 "He worked as a clerk in a small department store": The majority of this chapter is based on interviews with Richard Thorns.

174 "a volume called *Vanishing Birds*": Tim Halliday, *Vanishing Birds: Their Natural History and Conservation* (Sidgwick & Jackson), 1978.

176 "In 2014, he published a book called *In Search of Lost Frogs*": Robin Moore, *In Search of Lost Frogs: The Quest to Find the World's Rarest Amphibians* (Firefly Books, 2014).

176 "the Search for Lost Species": You can view the current list here: "Most Wanted Lost Species," Re:wild, https://www.rewild.org/lost-species/top-25-most-wanted-lost-species.

176 "Launched in 2017": Richard Conniff, "Scientists Launch Worldwide Search for Lost Species," *Scientific American*, https://www.scientificamerican.com/article/scientists-launch-worldwide-search-for-lost-species-slide-show/.

177 "first noted by biologists in 1790" P.G.P. Ericson, Y. Qu, M.P.K. Blom, et al., "A Genomic Perspective of the Pink-Headed Duck *Rhodonessa Caryophyllacea* Suggests a Long History of Low Effective Population Size," *Scientific Reports* 7, 16853 (2017), doi.org/10.1038/s41598-017-16975-1.

177 "still listed as critically endangered": "Pink-headed Duck," International Union for Conservation of Nature's Red List, https://www.iucnredlist.org/species/22680344/125558688.

177 "the last confirmed sighting in the wild was made in June 1935": Julian P. Hume, "A High Price to Pay: New Light on the Extinction of the Pink-headed Duck *Rhodonessa caryophyllacea*," *Forktail* 33 (2018): 56–63, https://www.researchgate.net/profile/Julian-Hume/publication/326982084_A_high_price_to_pay_new_light_on_the_extinction_of_the_Pink-headed_Duck_Rhodonessa_caryophyllacea/links/5b6fe844a6fdcc87df72cd24/A-high-price-to-pay-new-light-on-the-extinction-of-the-Pink-headed-Duck-Rhodonessa-caryophyllacea.pdf.

177 "This date has been disputed": Re:wild, for instance, lists the date as 1949: "Pink-headed Duck," Re:wild, https://www.rewild.org/lost-species/pink-headed-duck.

177 "an essential paper" Hume, "A High Price to Pay."

177 "a devastating loss of habitat, and over-hunting": Andrew W. Tordoff et al.,"The Historical and Current Status of Pink-headed Duck *Rhodonessa caryophyllacea* in Myanmar," *Bird Conservation International* 18 (2018): 38–52, doi: 10.1017/S0959270908000063.

177 "wrote Salim Ali": Salim Ali, *The Wildfowl Trust Eleventh Annual Report*, https://wildfowl.wwt.org.uk/index.php/wildfowl/issue/view/11.

177 "By the time local governments attempted to save the species, in the mid-1950s": Wrote Salim Ali: "As a precautionary measure the capture or killing of the Pinkheaded Duck, and the taking of its eggs has, since 1956, been totally prohibited by law, but it is clear that unfortunately protection has come too late," Ali, *The Wildflower Trust Eleventh Annual Report*.

178 "according to the French ornithologist Jean Théodore Delacour": Hume, "A High Price to Pay."

178 "There exist a number of striking black-and-white photographs": Several of the images can be found here, among other places:

"Pink-headed Duck," Harteman Wildfowl Aviaries, https://harteman.nl/Pinkheadedduck/.

178 "All were dead by 1938": A letter to Alfred Ezra dated September 1, 1938, from S. Dillon Ripley of the Smithsonian: "I am sorry indeed that your last pink headed duck is dead, and hope that you will be successful in getting others without too much delay. I still remember very vividly seeing your bird when I was with you at the end of May" (quoted in Hume, "A High Price to Pay").

178 "Ezra obtained his ducks from his brother, David": All details from this paragraph come from Hume, "A High Price to Pay."

178 "the dodo, which has been gone for centuries": The last confirmed sighting occurred in 1662: "The Oxford Dodo," Museum of Natural History, https://oumnh.ox.ac.uk/learn-the-oxford-dodo.

178 "the British explorer, who went missing searching for the mythical city of Z": For more, read David Grann's 2009 book *The Lost City of Z: A Tale of Deadly Obsession in the Amazon*.

179 "the military junta running Myanmar": For background: Lindsay Maizland, "Myanmar's Troubled History: Coups, Military Rule, and Ethnic Conflict," Council on Foreign Relations, January 31, 2022, https://www.cfr.org/backgrounder/myanmar-history-coup-military-rule-ethnic-conflict-rohingya.

179 "still called Burma": The country has been known as Myanmar since 1989.

179 "a coup in February 2021": Hannah Beech, "Myanmar Coup Puts the Seal on Autocracy's Rise in Southeast Asia," *New York Times*, April 12, 2021, https://www.nytimes.com/2021/04/12/world/asia/myanmar-coup-autocracy-democracy.html.

180 "now called Hoopers": "Hoopers Tunbridge Wells," Hoopers Department Stores, https://hoopersstores.com/pages/hoopers-tunbridge-wells.

181 "Richard had brought along a map, as well": This detail comes from the October 31, 2022, episode of the BBC Radio 4 series *The Untold: "Quest for the Pink-Headed Duck."*

182 "There was something like six ghosts": When I fact-checked this with Richard, he wanted to be clear that "the hospital had six ghosts."

184 "when Robert Ballard found the wreck of the *Titanic* in 1985": "1985 Discovery of RMS *Titanic*," Woods Hole Oceanographic Institution, https://www.whoi.edu/know-your-ocean/ocean-topics/ocean-human-lives/underwater-archaeology/rms-titanic/1985-discovery-of-rms-titanic/.

184 "images of the doomed ship on the ocean floor": Lily Rothman, "See Photos of the Wreck of the *Titanic* When It Was First Discovered," *Time*, September 1, 2015, https://time.com/4008791/titanic-wreck-photos/.

186 "though he left Asia convinced it was still out there, just difficult to find": Rory Nugent, *The Search for the Pink-Headed Duck: A Journey into the Himalayas and Down the Brahmaputra* (Houghton Mifflin, 1991), 222.

186 "The Bombay Natural History Society organized a major search in the 1950s": Ali, *The Wildfowl Trust Eleventh Annual Report*.

186 "A 'handful' of historical records": Tordoff et al.,"The Historical and Current Status of Pink-headed Duck *Rhodonessa caryophyllacea* in Myanmar."

186 "where there had not been a confirmed sighting since 1910": "Pink-headed duck," Re:wild.

186 "when a dead duck, currently in the collections of the American Museum of Natural History, was found at a bazaar in Mandalay": Tordoff et al.,"The Historical and Current Status of Pink-headed Duck *Rhodonessa caryophyllacea* in Myanmar."

186 "Richard wasn't the first researcher to reach this conclusion": All details from this paragraph come from Tordoff et al.,"The Historical and Current Status of Pink-headed Duck *Rhodonessa caryophyllacea* in Myanmar."

187 "a 2008 report" Tordoff et al.,"The Historical and Current Status of Pink-headed Duck *Rhodonessa caryophyllacea* in Myanmar."

189 "which encompasses 17,000 square kilometres": Jeremy Hance, "Myanmar Creates World's Largest Tiger Reserve, Aiding Many Endangered Southeast Asian Species," *Mongabay*, August 4, 2010, https://news.mongabay.com/2010/08/myanmar-creates-worlds-largest-tiger-reserve-aiding-many-endangered-southeast-asian-species/.

190 "the leopard barbel fish had been rediscovered": Lindsay Renick Mayer and Milo Putnam, "Rediscovery of Lost Leopard-spotted Fish in Türkiye Spurs Hope in the Midst of Global Freshwater Fish Decline," Re:wild, January 8, 2024, https://www.rewild.org/press/rediscovery-of-lost-leopard-spotted-fish-in-tuerkiye-spurs-hope.

190 "the previous month a trapdoor spider": Devin Murphy and Lindsay Renick Mayer, "Lost Tap-dancing Spider Rediscovered Barricaded in a Burrow in a Small Portuguese Town After 92 Years," Re:wild, December 14, 2023, https://www.rewild.org/press/lost-tap-dancing-spider-rediscovered-barricaded-in-a-burrow.

190 "a blind mole thought lost since 1936": Devin Murphy, "FOUND: Iridescent Blind Mole with Super-hearing Powers Rediscovered 'Swimming' Through Sand Dunes of South Africa," Re:wild, https://www.rewild.org/press/found-iridescent-blind-mole-with-super-hearing-powers-rediscovered-swimming.

190 "a dozen lost species had been found since Robin Moore launched his search in 2017": "Rediscoveries of Re:wild's Most Wanted Lost Species," Re:wild, https://www.rewild.org/lost-species/lost-species-found.

192 "it's one of my favourite novels": Just to be clear: We're talking about *Great Expectations* by Charles Dickens, published in 1861. And if you haven't read it, put down this book and get that one.

192 "in 2012 he was struck by a speeding motorcycle": We talked about the incident, but for more details, read Sarah Laskow's wonderful article about Richard: Sarah Laskow, "In Search of the Elusive Pink-Headed Duck," *Atlas Obscura*, June 1, 2017, https://www.atlasobscura.com/articles/pink-headed-duck-search-lost-species-extinct.

193 "I followed the updates about rebels gaining ground in the north": James Griffiths, "Myanmar's Civil War Nears a 'Tipping Point' as Democratic Rebels Prepare for Victory," *Globe and Mail*, November 29, 2023, https://www.theglobeandmail.com/world/article-myanmars-democratic-rebels-preparing-for-victory-with-civil-war-near-a/.

193 "Sam Mackenzie had died": November 22, 2023.

FURTHER READING

Mezrich, Ben. *Woolly: The True Story of the Quest to Revive One of History's Most Iconic Extinct Creatures*. Atria Books, 2017.

O'Connor, M.R., *Resurrection Science: Conservation, De-Extinction and the Precarious Future of Wild Things*. St. Martin's Press, 2015.

Pilcher, Helen. *Bring Back the King: The New Science of De-Extinction*. Bloomsbury Sigma, 2016.

Shakespeare, Nicholas. *In Tasmania*. Overlook Press, 2006.

Shapiro, Beth. *How to Clone a Mammoth: The Science of De-Extinction*. Princeton University Press, 2015.

Wray, Britt. *Rise of the Necrofauna: The Science, Ethics, and Risks of De-Extinction*. Greystone Books, 2017.

EIGHT: SENTINELS

Thanks to Eric Christensen for facilitating my visit to the Catalina Sky Survey, and to Kacper Wierzchos for letting me job-shadow him for an evening, even if the weather didn't cooperate. From the DART and HERA missions I'd like to thank Elana Adams; Justin Atchinson; Ian Carnelli, Nancy Chabot; Andy Cheng; Michael Kueppers; Cheryl Reed; and Andy Rivkin. And from the wider planetary defence community, thanks to Richard Binzel; Clark Chapman; Paul Chodas; David Dearborn; Jessie Dotson; Kelly Fast; Alan Harris; Lindley Johnson; Rob Landis; Ed Lu; Franck Marchis; Matthew Payne; Irwin Shapiro; Megan Bruck Syal; and Donald Yeomans. These interviews were coordinated, in part, by Corinne Becksinger (Edmiston) in the Office of Communications at NASA's Ames Research Center; Joshua Handal, Public Affairs Officer at NASA Headquarters; Nolan O'Brien, Public Information Officer at the Lawrence Livermore National Library; and Justyna Surowiec and Nicole Choi from the Johns Hopkins University Applied Physics Laboratory. Lisa Singleton from

NASA's Outreach and Guest Operations Office helped ensure I made it to the DART launch, while Faith Tusynski arranged my visit to Meteor Crater.

196 "The sign said watch for falling rocks": Since it was dark, and I was driving, I asked Kacper Wierzchos to take a photo of the sign the next time he drove by. The sign read "Watch for rocks," but they were definitely the falling kind.

196 "it was once home to the highest-elevated golf course in the world": David Leighton, "Street Smarts: The Story Behind Barnum Hill—and Golf—in Tucson's Reid Park," *Arizona Daily News*, February 1, 2021, updated July 2, 2024, https://tucson.com/news/local/street-smarts-the-story-behind-barnum-hill-and-golf-in-tucsons-reid-park/article_8ef31493-9302-5630-9d09-d4161618fb06.html.

197 "originally part of a radar station operated by the Air Force between 1956 and 1969": "1956 to 1959: Fighting the Cold War, Mt. Lemmon Skycentre," https://skycenter.arizona.edu/content/history; and Rick Wiley, "Photos: Mt. Lemmon Air Force Station Watched for Soviet Bombers," Tuscon.com, July 7, 2023, https://tucson.com/news/retrotucson/photos-mt-lemmon-air-force-station-watched-for-soviet-bombers/collection_171d19fa-023b-5f8b-b350-664eac8fbe08.html#6.

198 "a senior research specialist": His title changed since my visit, to senior survey operations specialist: "Kacper Wierzchos," Lunar & Planetary Laboratory, University of Arizona, https://catalina.lpl.arizona.edu/person/kacper-wierzchos.

198 "the Catalina Sky Survey": "Catalina Sky Survey: About CSS," Lunar & Planetary Laboratory, University of Arizona, https://catalina.lpl.arizona.edu/about.

199 "Hale-Bopp, discovered in 1995": C/1995 O1 (Hale-Bopp), NASA, https://science.nasa.gov/solar-system/comets/c-1995-o1-hale-bopp/.

199 "founded in 1998": "Catalina Sky Survey: History," Lunar & Planetary Laboratory, University of Arizona, https://catalina.lpl.arizona.edu/about/history.

199 "discovered in March 1993 by Eugene and Carolyn Shoemaker and David Levy": "Comet Shoemaker-Levy 9," NASA, https://science.nasa.gov/solar-system/comets/p-shoemaker-levy-9/.

200 "CSS was started by the American astronomer Steve Larson": "Catalina Sky Survey: About CSS."

200 "the team first took over an old telescope on nearby Mount Bigelow": S. Larson, ed. R. Seaman, "History of the Catalina Sky Survey," Planetary Science Institute, January 12, 2022, https://sbnarchive.psi.edu/pds4/surveys/gbo.ast.catalina.survey/document/CSS_history_v6.pdf.

200 "the CSS consisted of": "Catalina Sky Survey: Facilities," Lunar & Planetary Laboratory, University of Arizona, https://catalina.lpl.arizona.edu/about/facilities.

201 "CSS observers don't work on the days around a full moon": "Catalina Sky Survey: Operations," Lunar & Planetary Laboratory, University of Arizona, https://catalina.lpl.arizona.edu/about/operations.

201 "each one 10,560 pixels by 10,560 pixels": "Catalina Sky Survey: Facilities."

202 "receives hundreds of thousands of observations each night": Michael Rudenko, "Minor Planet Center: Data Processing Challenges": Lunar & Planetary Laboratory, University of Arizona, 2016, https://www.cambridge.org/core/services/aop-cambridge-core/content/view/8D781431D681F342D43B099BF0D76D3C/S174392131500839Xa.pdf/minor-planet-center-data-processing-challenges.pdf.

202 "the NEO confirmation page": "The NEO Confirmation Page," International Astronomical Union Minor Planets Center, https://minorplanetcenter.net/iau/NEO/toconfirm_tabular.html.

203 "more NEOs than any other survey in the world": Since my visit, it has been eclipsed by Pan-STARRS in Hawaii: Pan-STARRS, Institute for Astronomy, University of Hawaii, 2018, https://www2.ifa.hawaii.edu/research/Pan-STARRS.shtml.

203 "It was responsible for": "Discovery Statistics," Center for Near Earth Object Studies, https://cneos.jpl.nasa.gov/stats/site_all.html.

205 "named after the asteroid": "Ever Wonder Where the Name B612 Came From?" B612 Foundation, May 19, 1999, https://b612foundation.org/ever-wondered-where-the-name-b612-came-from/.

206 "In the June 6, 1980, issue": Luis W. Alvarez, Walter Alvarez, Frank Asaro, and Helen V. Michel, "Extraterrestrial Cause for the Cretaceous-Tertiary Extinction," *Science* 288, no. 4448 (June 6, 1980): 1095–108, https://www.science.org/doi/10.1126/science.208.4448.1095.

207 "discovered under the Yucatan Peninsula in the 1970s": Valerie Jablow, "A Tale of Two Rocks," *Smithsonian Magazine*, April 1998, https://www.smithsonianmag.com/science-nature/a-tale-of-two-rocks-151643588/.

207 "not identified until 1991": Alan R. Hildebrand, Glen T. Penfield, David A. Kring, Mark Pilkington, Antonio Camargo Z., Stein B. Jacobsen, William V. Boynton, "Chicxulub Crater: A Possible Cretaceous/Tertiary Boundary Impact Crater on the Yucatán Peninsula, Mexico," *Geology* 19, no. 9 (1991): 867–71, https://pubs.geoscienceworld.org/gsa/geology/article-abstract/19/9/867/205322/Chicxulub-Crater-A-possible-Cretaceous-Tertiary.

207 "And while there were still those who disagreed with the asteroid theory": Bianca Bosker, "The Nastiest Feud in Science," *The Atlantic*, September 2018, https://www.theatlantic.com/magazine/archive/2018/09/dinosaur-extinction-debate/565769/.

207 "in 2010 an international panel of scientists": Peter Schulte et al., "The Chicxulub Asteroid Impact and Mass Extinction at the Cretaceous-Paleogene Boundary," *Science* 327, no. 5970 (2010): 1214–18, https://www.science.org/doi/10.1126/science.1177265.

207 "albeit one that was fifteen kilometres wide": "Chicxulub: The Asteroid That Killed the Dinosaurs," *New Scientist*, https://www.newscientist.com/definition/chicxulub/.

207 "more than a billion times stronger than the atomic bomb": Jareen Imam, "Scientists to Drill at Site of Dinosaur-Killing Asteroid Crater," CNN, March 4, 2016, https://edition.cnn.com/2016/03/04/world/scientists-drill-impact-crater-irpt. Later research claimed it was as much as 10 billion times more powerful (Rory Sullivan, "Asteroid as Powerful as 10 billion WWII Atomic Bombs May Have Wiped Out the Dinosaurs," CNN, September 10, 2019, https://www.cnn.com/2019/09/10/world/dinosaur-extinction-discovery-intl-scli-scn).

207 "said Joanna Morgan": Imperial College London, "Asteroid Killed off the Dinosaurs, Says International Scientific Panel," *Science Daily*, https://www.sciencedaily.com/releases/2010/03/100304142242.htm.

207 "Most strikes go by unnoticed": Monica Cull, "Thousands of Meteorites Hit Earth Each Year—Here's What They Bring," *Discover*, December 20, 2023, https://www.discovermagazine.com/thousands-of-meteorites-hit-earth-each-year-heres-what-they-bring-44566.

207 "the Tunguska River": John Uri, "115 Years Ago: The Tunguska Asteroid Impact Event," NASA, June 30, 2023, https://www.nasa.gov/history/115-years-ago-the-tunguska-asteroid-impact-event/.

207 "the 10-to-15-megaton": "Tunguska Devastation," European Space Agency, July 6, 2023, https://www.esa.int/ESA_Multimedia/Images/2018/06/Tunguska_devastation.

207 "an estimated 80 million trees": Uri, "115 Years Ago."

207 "goes one particularly memorable description": Larry Niven and Jerry Pournelle, *Lucifer's Hammer* (Playboy Press, 1977), 291.

208 "In 1971, he edited and published": You can find it here: T. Gehrels, *Physical Studies of Minor Planets*, NASA, 1971, https://ia601305.us.archive.org/2/items/physicalstudiesooogehr/physicalstudiesooogehr.pdf.

208 "the Spacewatch program": For more information, see: Spacewatch, University of Arizona, https://spacewatch.lpl.arizona.edu/.

208 "Torino Scale": "Torino Impact Hazard Scale," Center for Near Earth Object Studies, https://cneos.jpl.nasa.gov/sentry/torino_scale.html.

209 "An asteroid is a round or irregularly shaped rocky body": Tricia Talbert, "What's the Difference Between Asteroids, Comets and Meteors? We Asked a NASA Scientist," NASA, December 13, 2021, https://www.nasa.gov/directorates/smd/whats-the-difference-between-asteroids-comets-and-meteors-we-asked-a-nasa-scientist-episode-16/.

209 "mostly found in the main belt between Mars and Jupiter": "Asteroid Facts," NASA, https://science.nasa.gov/solar-system/asteroids/facts/#h-asteroid-classifications.

209 "a meteoroid can be a small asteroid": Talbert, "What's the Difference Between the Asteroids, Comets and Meteors?"

209 "a meteor is a meteoroid that has entered Earth's atmosphere": Ibid.

209 "a meteorite is what's left to find": "Meteors and Meteorites," NASA, https://science.nasa.gov/solar-system/meteors-meteorites/.

209 "the first meeting on impact hazards in Snowmass, Colorado, . . . nuclear weapon": Clark R. Chapman, "History of the Asteroid/Comet Impact Hazard," Southwest Research Institute, Boulder Office, Solar System Science and Exploration Division, last updated August 20, 1999, https://www.boulder.swri.edu/clark/ncarhist.html.

209 "Don Yeomans, the former director": Jeffrey Kluger, "The Man Who Guards the Planet," *Time*, May 29, 2014, https://time.com/135476/the-man-who-guards-the-planet/.

210 "a story appeared on the front page of *The New York Times*": Warren E. Leary, "Big Asteroid Passes Near Earth in a Rare Close Call," *New York Times*, April 20, 1989, https://www.nytimes.com/1989/04/20/us/big-asteroid-passes-near-earth-unseen-in-a-rare-close-call.html.

210 "diameter was the size of a football field": "Asclepius," Spacereference.org, https://www.spacereference.org/asteroid/4581-asclepius-1989-fc.

210 "the astronomer Clark R. Chapman": Although I never got a hold of David Morrison, I did manage to track down Clark R. Chapman, more than thirty years after his book hit shelves. I wanted to ask him why, before almost anyone else, he'd been so insistent on raising the spectre of asteroid annihilation. "I guess I've always had the view that while, for damn sure, the prominent causes of death are cancer and automobile accidents and things like that, you shouldn't ignore entirely the rare things, 'cause rare things happen." (Interview, February 24, 2020.)

210 "might strike the Earth, though not until August 14, 2126": William J. Broad, "Big Comet May Strike Earth in August 2126," *New York Times*, October 27, 1992, https://www.nytimes.com/1992/10/27/science/big-comet-may-strike-earth-in-august-2126.html.

210 "which was called": Ethan Siegel, "The Most Dangerous Object Known to Humanity," *Forbes*, August 11, 2016, https://www.forbes.com/sites/startswithabang/2016/08/11/the-most-dangerous-object-known-to-humanity/?sh=6b2ee9a15cf0.

210 "a lengthy write-up in *Newsweek*": "The Science of Doom," *Newsweek*, November 22, 1992, last updated March 13, 2010, https://www.newsweek.com/science-doom-196978.

210 "Chapman and Morrison published an article in *Nature*": C. Chapman and D. Morrison, "Impacts on the Earth by Asteroids and Comets: Assessing the Hazard," *Nature* 367 (1994): 33–40, https://www.nature.com/articles/367033a0.

211 "could strike the planet in 2028": "Asteroid Headed for Earth," *Science*, March 11, 1998, https://www.science.org/content/article/asteroid-headed-earth.

211 "The same year that the Near-Earth Object Program Office—which later became CNEOS—was founded": "JPL Selected for Near Earth Object Program Office," Jet Propulsion Laboratory, California Institute of Technology, July 14, 1998, https://www.jpl.nasa.gov/news/jpl-selected-for-near-earth-object-program-office/.

211 "the U.S. Congress tasked NASA": "Twenty Years of Tracking Near Earth Objects," Jet Propulsion Laboratory, California Institute of Technology, July 23, 2018, https://www.jpl.nasa.gov/news/twenty-years-of-tracking-near-earth-objects/.

211 "They had until the end of the following decade to complete this mission": "JPL Selected for Near Earth Object Program Office."

211 "said Roger Ebert in his one-star review": Roger Ebert, "Armageddon," RogerEbert.com, https://www.rogerebert.com/reviews/armageddon-1998.

211 "the number of newly discovered asteroids larger than a kilometre": "Discovery Statistics," Center for Near Earth Object Studies.

212 "In 2004, the discovery": "Apophis," NASA, https://science.nasa.gov/solar-system/asteroids/apophis/.

212 "the 340-metre-wide Apophis": "Earth Is Safe from Asteroid Apophis for 100-Plus Years," NASA, https://www.nasa.gov/solar-system/nasa-analysis-earth-is-safe-from-asteroid-apophis-for-100-plus-years/.

212 "a 2.7 percent chance of striking the planet": "Asteroid Apophis: Will It Hit Earth? Your Questions Answered," Planetary Society, https://www.planetary.org/articles/will-apophis-hit-earth.

212 "on April 13, 2029" –https://science.nasa.gov/solar-system/asteroids/apophis/.

212 "soon downgraded to zero": "Earth Is Safe from Asteroid Apophis for 100-Plus Years."

212 "in 2005 the U.S. Congress introduced": "US Congress HR1022: George E. Brown, Jr., Near-Earth Object Survey Act," https://trackbill.com/bill/us-congress-house-bill-1022-george-c-brown-jr-near-earth-object-survey-act/307863/.

212 "the goal had been to find 90 percent of these objects by 2020": "NEO Survey and Deflection Analysis and Alternatives," Center for Near Earth Object Planetary Studies, March 2007, https://cneos.jpl.nasa.gov/doc/neo_report2007.html.

212 "In a 2024 update": Lindley Johnson and Kelly Fast, "NASA Planetary Defense and NEO Observations Program," NASA, January 30, 2024, https://www.hou.usra.edu/meetings/sbagjan2024/presentations/Tuesday/1015_Johnson.pdf.

214 "His postings included the North American Aerospace Defense Command (NORAD) and the Space and Missile Systems Center": Elizabeth Howell, "Defenders of the Planet," *Smithsonian Magazine*, December 2017, https://www.smithsonianmag.com/air-space-magazine/fight-against-killer-asteroids-180967109/.

215 "a study called Spacecast 2020": "Spacecast 2020, Vol. 1," Air University, Maxwell Air Force Base, June 1994, https://apps.dtic.mil/sti/pdfs/ADA295142.pdf.

216 "which found more than half of the one-kilometre-or-larger NEOs discovered between 1998 and 2005": According to my math, 278 out of 458, "Discovery Statistics," Center for Near Earth Object Studies.

216 "On the morning of February 15, 2013, an asteroid roughly twenty metres in diameter": Kate Howells, "What Was the Chelyabinsk Meteor Event," Planetary Society, February 15, 2023, https://www.planetary.org/articles/what-was-the-chelyabinsk-meteor-event.

216 "brighter than the sun": Ian Sample, "Scientists Reveal the Full Power of the Chelyabinsk Meteor Explosion," *The Guardian*, November 6, 2013,

https://www.theguardian.com/science/2013/nov/06/chelyabinsk-meteor-russia.

217 "represented less than one percent of NASA's overall budget": Casey Dreier, "How NASA's Planetary Defense Budget Grew by More Than 4000% in Ten Years," Planetary Society, September 26, 2019, https://www.planetary.org/articles/nasas-planetary-defense-budget-growth.

217 "within 8 million kilometres of Earth's orbit": Tricia Talbert, "What Is a Near-Earth Object?," NASA, February 12, 2019, https://www.nasa.gov/solar-system/did-you-know/.

217 "at two seconds past 10:21 p.m.": Stephen Clark, "Falcon 9 Launch Timeline with DART," *Spaceflight Now*, June 12, 2025, https://spaceflightnow.com/2021/11/23/falcon-9-launch-timeline-with-dart/.

218 "exercising in the basement": Andy Cheng, "What Could Be More Exciting Than Crashing a Spacecraft into an Asteroid?" DART, November 19, 2018, https://dart.jhuapl.edu/News-and-Resources/article.php?id=20181119.

218 "the first time we spoke": On February 12, 2020.

219 "a 2010 study": National Research Council, "Defending Planet Earth: Near-Earth-Object Surveys and Hazard Mitigation Strategies" (Washington, DC: National Academies Press, 2010), https://nap.nationalacademies.org/download/12842.

220 "the Double Asteroid Redirection Test—DART": For more information, see: "Double Asteroid Redirection Test (DART)," NASA, https://science.nasa.gov/mission/dart/.

220 "identified an asteroid named Didymos": "Didymos & Dimorphos," NASA, https://science.nasa.gov/solar-system/asteroids/didymos/.

220 "Measuring about 780 metres in diameter": Ibid.

220 "10 million kilometres away": "Target Asteroid," European Space Agency, https://www.esa.int/Space_Safety/Hera/Target_asteroid2.

220 "This 160-metre satellite": "Didymos & Dimorphos."

221 "failed to obtain the necessary funding": "The Story So Far," European Space Agency, https://www.esa.int/Space_Safety/Hera/The_story_so_far.

221 "secured in late 2019": "Hera Frequently Asked Questions," https://www.esa.int/Space_Safety/Hera/Hera_Frequently_Asked_Questions.

221 "it would launch three years after DART": "Hera," https://www.esa.int/Space_Safety/Hera.

223 "The craft itself was a box . . . weighed 610 kilograms": "Impactor Spacecraft," DART, "DART Impactor," DART, https://dart.jhuapl.edu/Mission/Impactor-Spacecraft.php.

223 "New navigation system": The "Small-body Maneuvering Autonomous Real Time Navigation (SMART Nav) system," which meant the DART spacecraft could "guide itself without operator assistance." DART press kit, p. 8: https://dart.jhuapl.edu/News-and-Resources/files/DART-press-kit-web-FINAL.pdf.

223 "a solar-powered ion propulsion system": Ibid.

223 "the craft's 'eye'": "SMART Nav: Giving Spacecraft the Power to Guide Themselves," Johns Hopkins Applied Physics Laboratory, https://www.jhuapl.edu/interactive/navigating-double-asteroid-redirection-test-on-its-own.

223 "lone instrument": Kevin Wilcox, "DART Takes Aim at Asteroid Moonlet," NASA, September 29, 2021, https://appel.nasa.gov/2021/09/29/dart-takes-aim-at-asteroid-moonlet/.

223 "would be witnessed by the Light Italian CubeSet for Imagining of Asteroids": Tricia Talbert, "DART Gets Its CubeSat Companion, Its Last Major Piece," NASA, October 1, 2021, https://www.nasa.gov/science-research/planetary-science/dart-gets-its-cubesat-companion-its-last-major-piece/.

223 "deployed a couple weeks before impact": "Bullseye! NASA's DART Mission Impacts Asteroid Target in World First," NASA, September 26, 2022, https://dart.jhuapl.edu/News-and-Resources/article.php?id=20220926.

223 "The spacecraft would hit the asteroid going almost 23,000 kilometres per hour.": Lewis Dartnell, "DART Impact Mission Shows We Could Deflect Earth-bound Asteroid," *Sky at Night Magazine*, April 18, 2023,

https://www.skyatnightmagazine.com/space-science/dart-impact-mission-could-deflect-earth-bound-asteroid.

223 "a $250 million dollar spacecraft": The mission's total cost was approximately $330 million: Steve Gorman, "NASA Launches Test Mission of Asteroid-Deflecting Spacecraft," Reuters, November 24, 2021, https://www.reuters.com/lifestyle/science/nasa-launch-test-mission-asteroid-deflecting-spacecraft-2021-11-23/.

224 "The team had been running simulations": "Smart Nav: Giving Spacecraft the Power to Guide Themselves," Johns Hopkins Applied Physics Laboratory.

226 "Our guide was a twenty-something woman named Penny": Penny is not her real name.

226 "the 638-kilogram Holsinger meteorite": William Ascarza, "Mine Tales: Unraveling the Mystery, the Marvels of Meteor Crater," *Arizona Daily Star*, June 19, 2016, updated July 15, 2016, https://tucson.com/news/local/mine-tales-unraveling-the-mystery-marvels-of-meteor-crater/article_7e58014e-d245-54ee-9cb7-05e1f0d7808e.html.

226 "measuring forty-six metres in diameter . . . per hour": Ascarza, "Mine Tales"; and Meteor Crater, Jet Propulsion Laboratory California Institute of Technology, March 12, 2002, https://www.jpl.nasa.gov/images/pia03490-meteor-crater-az/.

226 "travelling 12 kilometres per second . . . Hiroshima": H. Melosh, G. Collins, "Meteor Crater Formed by Low-Velocity Impact," *Nature* 434, no. 157 (2005): https://www.nature.com/articles/434157a; and Dean Smith, *The Meteor Crater Story*, 2nd ed., revisions by Neal Davis (Meteor Crater Enterprises, 2018), 1–2.

226 "The leading theory holds that it hailed from the asteroid belt between Mars and Jupiter": Smith, *The Meteor Crater Story*, 6.

226 "it was first recorded by one of General Custer's scouts in 1871": Brandon Barringer, "Daniel Moreau Barringer (1860–1929) and His Crater (The Beginning of the Crater Branch of Meteoritics)," *Meteoritics* 2 (1964): 183–200, https://articles.adsabs.harvard.edu/cgi-bin/nph-iarticle_query?bibcode=1964Metic...2..183B&db_key=AST&page_ind=7&data_type=GIF&type=SCREEN_VIEW&classic=YES.

226 "In 1902, a lawyer and mining engineer from Philadelphia, Daniel Moreau Barringer, learned of the crater from an employee": Ibid.

227 "would be worth upwards of half a billion dollars . . . opened to the public": Smith, *The Meteor Crater Story*, pp. 18, 19, and 32–33.

227 "2 million people could sit on the crater's slopes": "Meteor Crater," *Discover Flagstaff*, https://www.flagstaffarizona.org/directory/meteor-crater/.

227 "It was 550 feet deep": "Meteor Crater, Arizona, USA," NASA, January 25, 2019, https://science.nasa.gov/resource/meteor-crater-arizona-usa/.

227 "didn't stop a madman who, in 2013": "Truck Driver Who Leapt into Mine Shaft at the Bottom of Arizona's Meteor Crater to 'Appease Gods' Is Rescued," *Daily Mail*, January 12, 2013, https://www.dailymail.co.uk/news/article-2261337/Truck-driver-leapt-shaft-Arizonas-meteor-crater-appease-gods-rescued.html.

228 "from 1963 until 1971 the crater served as a training site for astronauts": William C. Phinney, "Science Training History of the Apollo Astronauts," NASA, https://ntrs.nasa.gov/api/citations/20190026783/downloads/20190026783.pdf.

228 "proven Barringer's theory irrefutably correct": Tony Reichhardt, "Crater Face," *Smithsonian Magazine*, May 2004, https://www.smithsonianmag.com/air-space-magazine/crater-face-6074025/.

228 "up to twenty-four kilometres away": Smith, *The Meteor Crater Story*, p. 3.

228 "October 3, a piece of meteorite crashed through the roof of a house in the small town of Golden, B.C.": Claire Palmer, "Meteor Gives Golden Woman Late Night Shock," *Golden* (B.C.) *Star*, October 8, 2021, https://thegoldenstar.net/news/meteor-gives-golden-woman-late-night-shock/.

228 "a retired woman named Ruth Hamilton": Ibid.

228 "'the size of a large man's fist . . . the size of a melon'": John Yoon and Vjosa Isai, "Meteorite Crashes Through Ceiling and Lands on Woman's Bed," *New York Times*, October 14, 2021, https://www.nytimes.com/2021/10/14/world/canada/meteorite-bed.html; and Angela McInnes, "Western Scientists Study Meteorite Made Famous After Crashing Into B.C. Woman's Bedroom," CBC News, January 16,

2022, https://www.cbc.ca/news/canada/london/western-scientists-study-meteorite-made-famous-after-crashing-into-b-c-woman-s-bedroom-1.6316212.

228 "she told a reporter": "Woman Rocked Awake by Meteorite Chunk Crashing Into Her Bedroom," CBC News, October 12, 2021, https://www.cbc.ca/news/canada/british-columbia/meteorite-crashes-into-womans-bedroom-golden-bc-1.6207904.

229 "then international . . . keep it for herself": Brieanna Charlebois, "Scientists Study Trajectory of Meteorite That Landed on a B.C. Woman's Pillow in October," *Globe and Mail*, January 17, 2022, https://www.theglobeandmail.com/canada/article-scientists-study-trajectory-of-meteorite-that-landed-in-bc-in-october/; and Ruth Hamilton, "Experience: A Meteor Crashed On to My Bed," *The Guardian*, February 18, 2022, https://www.theguardian.com/lifeandstyle/2022/feb/18/experience-a-meteorite-crashed-on-to-my-bed.

230 "was called 'The DART Song'": "The DART Song," by Andy Rivkin and His Gedankenband, Bandcamp, https://andyrivkin.bandcamp.com/track/the-dart-song

230 "headline in *The Guardian*": Associated Press, "Skyscraper-Sized Asteroid to Pass Within 1.7m Miles of Earth," *The Guardian*, February 1, 2024, https://www.theguardian.com/science/2024/feb/01/asteroid-near-earth-nasa.

230 "announced *USA Today*": Eric Lagatta, "NASA Tracks 5 'Potentially Hazardous' Asteroids That Will Fly by Earth Within Days," *USA Today*, September 6, 2023, https://www.usatoday.com/story/news/nation/2023/09/06/asteroids-fly-near-earth/70774634007/.

230 "the *Jerusalem Post* told readers": Aaron Reich, "747-sized Asteroid Skimmed by Earth, and Scientists Didn't See It Coming," *Jerusalem Post*, September 23, 2021, https://www.jpost.com/science/747-sized-asteroid-skimmed-by-earth-and-scientists-didnt-see-it-coming-680052.

230 "a trailer": NASA (@NASA), "NASA's DART Mission to an Asteroid (Official Mission Trailer)," Facebook, September 26, 2022, https://www.facebook.com/watch/?v=846771886704068.

231 "delivered a brief videotaped message": NASA, "'Don't Look Up' Director Adam McKay Previews NASA's DART Asteroid Mission," November 16, 2021, 48 sec., https://www.youtube.com/watch?v=quBrcCaJvro.

231 "the first time I'd attended a rocket launch": You can watch the whole thing here: NASA, "Watch NASA's DART Mission Launch," YouTube, 2:06:44, https://www.youtube.com/watch?v=EoOUvEh3HWk&list=PL2aBZuCeDwlRsa9T49dlm6vlZLfn1fSZ7&index=3.

233 "outfitted with the largest digital camera ever built": "What Is Rubin Observatory?" Vera C. Rubin Observatory, https://rubinobservatory.org/about.

234 "One September evening": September 26, 2022.

234 "and 11 million kilometers": "Mission Overview," DART, https://dart.jhuapl.edu/Mission/index.php.

234 "the NASA broadcast": You can watch the feed here: NASA, "Watch a Live Feed from NASA's DART Spacecraft on Approach to Asteroid Dimorphous," YouTube, 1:49:50, https://www.youtube.com/watch?v=6Z1EomW2ag&list=PL2aBZuCeDwlRsa9T49dlm6vlZLfn1fSZ7&index=1.

234 "was piloting the craft": R.T. Daly, C.M. Ernst, and O.S. Barnouin, et al., "Successful Kinetic Impact into an Asteroid for Planetary Defence," *Nature* 616 (2023): 443–47, https://doi.org/10.1038/s41586-023-05810-5.

235 "When they'd arrived that morning": The fortune cookie detail comes from David W. Brown's article in *The New Yorker*: David W. Brown, "How NASA Launched Its Asteroid Killer," *New Yorker*, October 6, 2022, https://www.newyorker.com/tech/annals-of-technology/how-nasa-launched-its-asteroid-killer.

235 "seventy miles off-target . . . another shot two years later": Ibid.

236 "at almost 14,000 miles per hour": Jonathan Amos, "Dimorphos: Nasa Flies Spacecraft into Asteroid in Direct Hit," BBC, https://www.bbc.com/news/science-environment-63039191.

236 "'purposely changed the motion of a celestial object'": "Didymos and Dimorphos," NASA, https://science.nasa.gov/solar-system/asteroids/didymos/.

236 "NASA had set out a 'minimum successful orbit period change' of seventy-three seconds": Justyna Surowiec, "NASA Confirms DART Mission Impact Changed Asteroid's Motion in Space," DART, October 11, 2022, https://dart.jhuapl.edu/News-and-Resources/article.php?id=20221011.

236 "orbit around Didymos by thirty-three minutes": "NASA Study: Asteroid's Orbit, Shape Changed After DART Impact," Jet Propulsion Laboratory, California Institute of Technology, March 19, 2024, https://www.jpl.nasa.gov/news/nasa-study-asteroids-orbit-shape-changed-after-dart-impact/

237 "a paper published": Daly, et al. "Successful Kinetic Impact."

FURTHER READING

Binzel, Richard P. and Tom Gehrels and Mildred Shapley Mathews. *Asteroids II*. The University of Arizona Press, 1989.

Chapman, Clark R. and David Morrison. *Cosmic Catastrophes*. Plenum Press, 1989.

Dillow, Gordon. *Fire in the Sky: Cosmic Collisions, Killer Asteroids, and the Race to Defend the Earth*. Scribner, 2019.

Gehrels, Tom, ed. *Asteroids*. The University of Arizona Press, 1979.

———. Physical Studies of Minor Planets. NASA, 1971.

Norman, David. *When Dinoasuars Ruled the Earth*. Marshall Cavendish Books Limited, 1985.

Nugent, Carrie. *Asteroid Hunters*. Simon & Schuster, 2017.

Ord, Toby. *The Precipice: Existential Risk and the Future of Humanity*. Hachette Books, 2020.

Walsh, Bryan. *End Times: A Brief Guide to the End of the World—Asteroids, Supervolcanoes, Rogue Robots, and More*. Hachette Books, 2019.

NINE: ARTIFACTS

Thanks to Margaret Atwood; Tsitsi Dangarembga; Jem Finer; Ed Finn; Anne Beate Hovind; Garth Johnson; Jonathon Keats; Karl Ove Knausgaard; Gordon Knox; David Mitchell; Katie Paterson; and Sjón. And thanks to Siobhan Maguire for helping facilitate my interviews with Katie.

239 "about two inches in diameter": Daniel Oberhaus, "This Camera Will Take a 1000-Year Photo to Document Climate Change, *Vice*, October 23, 2018, https://www.vice.com/en/article/this-camera-will-take-a-1000-year-photo-to-document-climate-change/.

240 "buried a chondrite": Greg Nichols, "Experimental Artist Adds Meteorite to Italian Groundwater," ZDNet, August 25, 2021, https://www.zdnet.com/article/experimental-artist-adds-meteorite-to-italian-groundwater/.

240 "from the asteroid belt between Mars and Jupiter . . . brought to Italy in his suitcase": Mike Wall, "Art Project Creates 'Human-Alien Hybrids' with Meteorite-Infused Water," Space.com, September 24, 2021, https://www.space.com/keats-fountains-of-tolerance-alien-hybrid-art-project; and Greg Nichols, "Experimental Artist Adds Meteorite to Italian Groundwater," ZDNet, August 25, 2021, https://www.zdnet.com/article/experimental-artist-adds-meteorite-to-italian-groundwater/.

241 "wrote the acclaimed sci-fi author Bruce Sterling": Julie Decker and Alla Efimova, eds., *Thought Experiments: The Art of Jonathon Keats* (Hirmer Verlag and Anchorage Museum, 2021), 9.

241 "The often-told origin story": "Jonathon Keats [interview]," *The Public Life of the Mind*, https://www.thepubliclifeofthemind.co.uk/jonathon-keats.

241 "he once told an interviewer": Ashley P. Taylor, "Straight Talk with Jonathon Keats," *SciArt Initiative*, February 2014, https://www.sciartmagazine.com/straight-talk-jonathon-keats.html.

241 "specializing in turn-of-the-century posters and woodblock prints": From my interview with Keats.

241 "as he described himself . . . did not speak for an entire year": Decker and Efimova, *Thought Experiments*, 342.

242 "He once designed and attempted to patent a perpetual motion": Decker and Efimova, *Thought Experiments*, 343–44.

242 "The rejection to this collection read": Decker and Efimova, *Thought Experiments*, 33–34.

242 "although one was in Russian": Jonathon Keats, "This Library Exhibits Some of the Greatest Books That Don't Exist," *Forbes*, December 30, 2024, https://www.forbes.com/sites/jonathonkeats/2024/12/30/this-library-is-exhibiting-some-of-the-greatest-books-that-dont-exist/.

243 "*Twenty Four Hour Cogito*": Jesse Hamil, "The Thinking Man's Art / For 24 hours Straight, a Conceptual Artist Clocks Whatever Comes Into His Head," SFGate, October 31, 2000, https://www.sfgate.com/entertainment/article/The-Thinking-Man-s-Art-For-24-hours-straight-a-3236681.php.

243 "ballets choreographed for honeybees": "Communicating Across Species: Jonathon Keats' Honeybee Ballet," *BigThink*, August 15, 2013, https://bigthink.com/surprising-science/communicating-across-species-jonathons-keatss-honeybee-ballet/.

243 "pornographic movies for rhododendrons": Adam Gopnik, "Plant TV," *New Yorker*, March 7, 2010, https://www.newyorker.com/magazine/2010/03/15/plant-tv.

243 "a restaurant for plants": Nicola Twilley, "A Gourmet Restaurant for Plants, Not People," *The Atlantic*, April 19, 2011, https://www.theatlantic.com/health/archive/2011/04/a-gourmet-restaurant-for-plants-not-people/237536/.

243 "registered his brain as a sculpture": Maggie Shiels, "The Man Who Sold His Brain," BBC, October 27, 2003, http://news.bbc.co.uk/2/hi/uk_news/magazine/3217423.stm?ref=longnow.org.

243 "orchestrated an IPO": Jonathon Keats and William L. Fox, "Enlarging the Question," October 30, 2024, https://longnow.org/ideas/centuries-bristlecone-keats-interview/.

243 "He once tried to genetically engineer God": Jeanne Carstensen, "Project Aims at Genetically Engineered God / SF Artist Tries to Find

Almighty on Tree of Life Beside Bacteria, Slime Mold," SFGate.com, October 20, 2004, https://www.sfgate.com/entertainment/article/project-aims-at-genetically-engineered-god-sf-3237252.php.

243 "he told *BOMB* magazine": "Making Good: Jonathon Keats," *BOMB*, September 4, 2009, https://bombmagazine.org/articles/2009/09/04/making-good-jonathon-keats/.

244 "over the next thousand years": Scott Thill, "Story That Takes 1,000 Years to Read Is Antidote to Media Whirlwind," *Wired*, June 17, 2009, https://www.wired.com/2009/06/story-that-takes-1000-years-to-read-is-antidote-to-media-whirlwind/.

244 "antidote to instant gratification": "Literary Magazine Prints Story with 1,000-Year Reading Time," Rhizome, May 19, 2009, https://rhizome.org/community/15472/.

244 "This, he told NPR": Scott Simon, "Fade From Black: A Magazine's Long Story," NPR, June 27, 2009, https://www.npr.org/2009/06/27/106007588/fade-from-black-a-magazines-long-story.

244 "In 2010, he shared the blueprints": Jonathon Keats, "The Century Camera," GOOD, January 23, 2010, https://www.good.is/articles/the-century-camera.

244 "he learned about cyanotype": Austin Rogers, "Artist Jonathon Keats' Century Camera Project," *Fstoppers*, May 27, 2014, https://fstoppers.com/film/exclusive-interview-artist-jonathon-keats-century-camera-project-9284.

245 "In partnership with a local gallery": Jonathon Keats, "Millennium Camera," *The Common*, November 1, 2015, https://www.thecommononline.org/millenium-camera/.

245 "rented out for ten euros": Joey Esrich, "Take a Picture. It'll Last Longer," *Slate*, March 5, 2015, https://slate.com/technology/2015/03/experimental-philosopher-jonathon-keats-millennium-camera-experiment.html.

246 "keeping a watch over the Mount Holyoke mountain range": "Ready for the Year 3015? World's Slowest Photograph Will Chart a Millennium's Evolution," Amherst College, April 2015, https://www.amherst.edu/news/news_releases/2015/04-2015/node/604805.

246 "the first of four had just been installed at Lake Tahoe": Oberhaus, "This Camera Will Take a 1,000-Year Photo."

246 "on a hiking trail in Tucson": Julia Binswanger, "This Camera Is Taking a 1,000-Year-Long Exposure Photo of Tucson's Desert Landscape," *Smithsonian Magazine*, February 1, 2024, https://www.smithsonianmag.com/smart-news/camera-taking-1000-year-long-exposure-photo-tucson-desert-landscape-180983706/.

246 "he told a newspaper in 2018": Eoin O'Carroll, "Forget New Year's Resolutions. This Art Prompts Thinking in 'Deep Time,'" *Christian Science Monitor*, December 31, 2018, https://www.csmonitor.com/Science/2018/1231/Forget-New-Year-s-resolutions.-This-art-prompts-thinking-in-deep-time.

247 "to its northern terminus": Frognerseteren.

248 "to write about the Future Library": Mark Medley, "Margaret Atwood's Next Project Is Due in the 22nd Century," *Globe and Mail*, September 5, 2014, https://www.theglobeandmail.com/arts/books-and-media/margaret-atwoods-next-project-is-due-in-the-22nd-century/article20380962/.

249 "living in Berlin at the time": "Katie Paterson—Future Library," *Instrment*, March 16, 2016, https://www.instrmnt.co.uk/content/2016/3/16/katie-paterson-.

249 "a two-acre parcel of land in Nordmarka": Medley, "Margaret Atwood's Next Project."

250 "The existing trees were harvested, their wood used": Billie Miro Breskin, "The Future Library: An Untold Anthology Growing Up in Oslo," *Vogue Scandinavia*, May 22, 2024, https://www.voguescandinavia.com/articles/the-future-library-an-untold-anthology-growing-in-oslo.

250 "a thousand spruce saplings": Aaron Netsky, "Forest of the Future Library," *Atlas Obscura*, https://www.atlasobscura.com/places/forest-of-the-future-library.

250 "planted in their stead in the summer of 2014": Catherine Borgeson, "Growing a Book for One Hundred Years," Long Now Foundation, October 28, 2014, https://longnow.org/ideas/growing-a-book-for-one-hundred-years/.

250 "introduced the city forester": Jon Karl Christiansen.

251 "a one-hundred-year agreement had been signed": Richard Fisher, "The Norwegian Library with Unreadable Books," BBC, June 30, 2022, https://www.bbc.com/future/article/20220630-the-norwegian-library-with-unreadable-books.

253 "a founding member and songwriter": Colm McAuliffe, "Jem Finer of the Pogues: A Millennium in Music," *New Statesman*, October 22, 2015, https://www.newstatesman.com/culture/2015/10/jem-finer-pogues-millennium-music.

254 "commissioned by an organization called Artangel": "Overview of Longplayer," Longplayer.org, https://longplayer.org/about/overview/.

254 "Michael Faraday once served as scientific advisor": "The Faraday Effect," Trinity Buoy Wharf, https://www.trinitybuoywharf.com/whats-on/the-faraday-effect.

254 "a charitable trust": "Overview of Longplayer."

255 "on thirty-nine different bowls": Allison Meier, "A Song That Will Outlive Us All," *Hyperallergic*, June 25, 2015, https://hyperallergic.com/217035/a-song-that-will-outlive-us-all/.

255 "lasting twenty minutes and twenty seconds": "Longplayer," *Atlas Obscura*, February 23, 2010, https://www.atlasobscura.com/places/longplayer.

255 "six rows of these bowls": "Where to Find Longplayer," Longplayer.org, https://longplayer.org/visit/.

257 "beginning with a live performance starting on September 12, 2009": "Overview of Longplayer."

257 "twenty-six musicians": "Longplayer Live," Longplayer.org, https://longplayer.org/events/longplayer-live/.

259 "a small gallery": Galleri F15.

259 "her first solo exhibition": "Katie Paterson—Evergreen," Galleri F15, https://gallerif15.no/exhibitions_f15/katie-paterson/?lang=en.

259 "born and raised in Glasgow": "Katie Paterson," Ingleby Gallery, https://www.inglebygallery.com/artists/55-katie-paterson/overview/.

263 "he once told an interviewer'": Nathan Broderick, "Thousand Year Photo (Director's Cut)," YouTube, 2015, 4:29, https://www.youtube.com/watch?v=fPnbZZQkFXc&feature=emb_title.

TEN: THE LAST KNIGHT

Les Knight and the VHEMT team proved to be wonderful company over my weekend in Eugene, Oregon. And although I had no idea it would prove so fortuitous when he pitched me the idea, thanks to John Ibbitson (along with his co-author Darrell Bricker) for the essay on population decrease that ran the same weekend as the conference.

265 "working as a substitute teacher": Les Knight, "I Campaign for the Extinction of the Human Race," *The Guardian*, January 10, 2020, https://www.theguardian.com/lifeandstyle/2020/jan/10/i-campaign-for-the-extinction-of-the-human-race-les-knight.

265 "the ghost city of Pripyat": "Abandoned City of Pripyat," *Atlas Obscura*, https://www.atlasobscura.com/places/abandoned-city-of-pripyat.

265 "the last days of April in 1986": The initial explosion occurred on April 26.

266 "more than 350,000 people": "Chernobyl Accident 1986," World Nuclear Association, February 1, 2025, https://world-nuclear.org/information-library/safety-and-security/safety-of-plants/chernobyl-accident.

266 "the 1,100-square-mile Chernobyl Exclusion Zone becoming the third-largest nature reserve in Europe and a haven for animals": "How Chernobyl Has Become an Unexpected Haven for Wildlife," UN Environment Programme, September 16, 2020, https://www.unep.org/news-and-stories/story/how-chernobyl-has-become-unexpected-haven-wildlife.

266 "regularly tossed his way": Cara Buckley, "Earth Now Has 8 Billion Humans. This Man Wishes There Were None," *New York Times*, November 23, 2022, https://www.nytimes.com/2022/11/23/climate/voluntary-human-extinction.html.

266 "the forty-first annual Public Interest Environmental Law Conference": Public Interest Environmental Law Conference, https://pielc.org/.

268 "the broadcaster Tucker Carlson once asked Les": mr1001nights, "Tucker Carlson vs. Les Knight," YouTube, 4:44, https://www.youtube.com/watch?v=Rm1QojjwGdo.

268 "published in 1968": Charles C. Mann, "The Book That Incited a Worldwide Fear of Overpopulation," *Smithsonian Magazine*, January 2018, https://www.smithsonianmag.com/innovation/book-incited-worldwide-fear-overpopulation-180967499/.

268 "'we got fire about 500,000 years ago'": It was likely far earlier than that: Sara Novak, "The Dawn of Fire: When Did Early Humans First Discover Fire?" *Discover*, September 21, 2023, https://www.discovermagazine.com/planet-earth/when-did-early-hominins-first-discover-fire.

268 "Zero Population Growth, which Ehrlich had co-founded not long after the publication of his book": "Our Mission and Goals," Population Connection, https://populationconnection.org/about-us/.

269 "the first Earth Day had been held in 1970": "Our History," Earthday.org, https://www.earthday.org/history/.

269 "the Environmental Protection Agency": "EPA History," Environmental Protection Agency, https://www.epa.gov/history.

269 "Natural Resources Defense Council": "About NRDC," NRDC, https://www.nrdc.org/about.

269 "Don't Make a Wave Committee was established in Vancouver": "Our Founders," Greenpeace, https://www.greenpeace.org/international/explore/about/founders/.

269 "The boat was called the *Greenpeace*": Barbara Stowe, "I Am the Daughter of Greenpeace's Founders. As the Organization Turns 50, I Wish the World Didn't Need it Any More," *Globe and Mail*, October 2, 2021, https://www.theglobeandmail.com/opinion/article-i-am-the-daughter-of-greenpeaces-founders-as-the-organization-turns-50/?login=true.

269 "in 1988, NASA scientist James Hansen": Oliver Milman, "Ex-NASA Scientist: 30 Years On, World Is Failing 'Miserably' to Address Climate Change," *The Guardian*, June 19, 2018, https://www.theguardian.com/environment/2018/jun/19/james-hansen-nasa-scientist-climate-change-warning.

269 "by almost a billion people between 1980 and 1990": "World Population by Year," Worldometer, https://www.worldometers.info/world-population/world-population-by-year/.

269 "he thought we needed to stop at once": Les Knight, "I Campaign for the Extinction of the Human Race."

270 "Humans might be the only species on the planet that understands death is a certainty": Brandon Keim, "How Animals Understand Death," *Nautilus*, April 28, 2025, https://nautil.us/how-animals-understand-death-1204412/.

270 "anthropologist Ernest Becker": Keith Helmuth, "Ernest Becker: A Memoir and an Appreciation," Ernest Becker Foundation, March 5, 2019, https://www.ernestbecker.org/helmuth-on-becker.

270 "the 1973 classic *The Denial of Death*": Glenn Hughes, "The Denial of Death and the Practice of Dying," Ernest Becker Foundation, https://www.ernestbecker.org/lecture-texts/practice-of-dying.

272 "was formed in the 1980s": Knight, "I Campaign for the Extinction of the Human Race."

272 "Les published the first issue of *These Exit Times* in 1991": "*These Exit Times*, no. 1," Environment and Society Portal, https://www.environmentandsociety.org/mml/these-exit-times-no-1.

272 "the website went live in 1996": Les Knight, "I Campaign for the Extinction of the Human Race."

272 "translated into more than thirty languages": Voluntary Human Extinction Movement, https://www.vhemt.org/.

272 "Q: What good is a healthy biosphere": "Q: What good is a healthy biosphere if there are no humans around to enjoy it?" Voluntary Human Extinction Movement, https://www.vhemt.org/philrel.htm#worldview.

272 "recently appeared on Dr. Phil's daytime talk show": https://www.foxnews.com/media/extinction-activist-wants-humans-voluntarily-die-feed-em-breed-em.

274 "drawn by the artist Nina Paley": "VHMET-related cartoons," Voluntary Human Extinction Movement, https://www.vhemt.org/paleyart.htm.

277 "Extinction Rebellion, the upstart civil disobedience network formed in 2018": "About Us," Extinction Rebellion, https://rebellion.global/about-us/.

277 "a series of sit-ins and other actions in the UK that soon spread around the world": "Extinction Rebellion 2019, A Year to Remember," Extinction Rebellion, https://rebellion.global/press/2019/12/30/xr-2019/.

278 "Les got a vasectomy in 1973, when he was twenty-five years old": Cara Buckley, "Earth Now Has 8 Billion Humans"; Knight, "I Campaign for the Extinction of the Human Race."

278 "a discounted vasectomy": Knight, "I Campaign for the Extinction of the Human Race."

280 "overturning of *Roe v. Wade* the previous spring": Nina Totenberg and Sarah McCammon, "Supreme Court Overturns Roe v. Wade, Ending Right to Abortion Upheld for Decades," NPR, June 24, 2022, https://www.npr.org/2022/06/24/1102305878/supreme-court-abortion-roe-v-wade-decision-overturn.

280 "There were nearly 121 million unintended pregnancies": "Nearly Half of All Pregnancies Are Unintended—A Global Crisis, Says New UNFPA Report," United Nations Population Fund, March 30, 2022, https://www.unfpa.org/press/nearly-half-all-pregnancies-are-unintended—-global-crisis-says-new-unfpa-report.

280 "over 60 percent ended in abortion": Edith M. Lederer, "U.N. Report: Nearly Half of All Pregnancies Are Unintended," AP News, March 30, 2022, https://apnews.com/article/abortion-health-united-nations-sexual-and-reproductive-health-c04bec37899bdb8126146389baf21327.

281 "we'd published an essay": John Ibbitson and Darrell Bricker, "Population Decrease Is Irreversible. How Will We Manage the Decline of Humanity?" *Globe and Mail*, March 3, 2023, https://www.theglobeandmail.com/opinion/article-population-decrease-is-irreversible-how-will-we-manage-the-decline-of/.

281 "China had lost population last year": Evelyn Cheng, "China's Population Drops for the First Time in Decades," January 17, 2023, https://www.cnbc.com/2023/01/17/chinas-population-drops-for-the-first-time-in-decades.html.

282 "has had a rate at or below 2.1 since 1972 and yet the population has grown by 120 million": "Fertility Rate, Total (Births per Woman)—US," World Bank Group, https://data.worldbank.org/indicator/SP.DYN.TFRT.IN?locations=US.

282 "The United Nations projects Earth's population to top out at 10.4 billion by 2080": "World Population to Reach 8 Billion This Year, as Growth Rate Slows," UN News, July 11, 2022, https://news.un.org/en/story/2022/07/1122272. (This was later amended to 10.3: "UN Projects World Population to Peak Within This Century," https://www.un.org/en/UN-projects-world-population-to-peak-within-this-century).

283 "the smell of smoke greeted me whenever I left my home in Toronto": "Wildfire Smoke Has Led to 'High Levels of Air Pollution' in Toronto, Environment Canada Says," CBC News, https://www.cbc.ca/news/canada/toronto/special-air-quality-statement-toronto-forest-fire-smoke-1.6866738.

FURTHER READING

Bricker, Darrell, and John Ibbitson. *Empty Planet: The Shock of Global Population Decline*. Signal, 2019.

Erlich, Paul R. *The Population Bomb*, rev. ed. Ballantine Books, 1988.

Weisman, Alan. *The World Without Us*. HarperCollins, 2007.

EPILOGUE: CATHEDRALS

It was my friend Adam Park who suggested we drop by Canterbury Cathedral; he inadvertently gave this book an ending. Thanks of course to Joel Hopkinson and Heather Newton for telling me about their work at the cathedral, as well as John David of York Minster, which I'd have loved to visit.

285 "which took almost thirty years to build": "AD 1000—Canterbury Cathedral," *Current Archaeology*, May 24, 2007, https://archaeology.co.uk/articles/specials/timeline/canterbury-cathedral.htm.

286 "in 1170, knights of Henry II murdered a praying Archbishop Thomas Becket": Lloyd de Beer and Naomi Speakman, "Thomas Becket: The Murder That Shook the Middle Ages," British Museum, December 28, 2019, https://www.britishmuseum.org/blog/thomas-becket-murder-shook-middle-ages.

286 "was the site of Becket's tomb": John Jenkins, "Why Did They Move Thomas Becket's Bones?," British Museum, July 7, 2021, https://www.britishmuseum.org/blog/why-did-they-move-thomas-beckets-bones.

286 "which housed Becket's shrine after the fire until it was destroyed on orders of Henry VIII in 1538": Alec Ryrie, "How to Erase a Saint: Thomas Becket and Henry VIII," British Museum, July 5, 2021, https://www.britishmuseum.org/blog/how-erase-saint-thomas-becket-and-henry-viii.

287 "including head of conservation and head stonemason": "Heather Newton," City and Guilds of London Art School, https://www.cityandguildsartschool.ac.uk/heather-newton/.

FURTHER READING

Follett, Ken. *The Pillars of the Earth*. William Morrow, 1989.